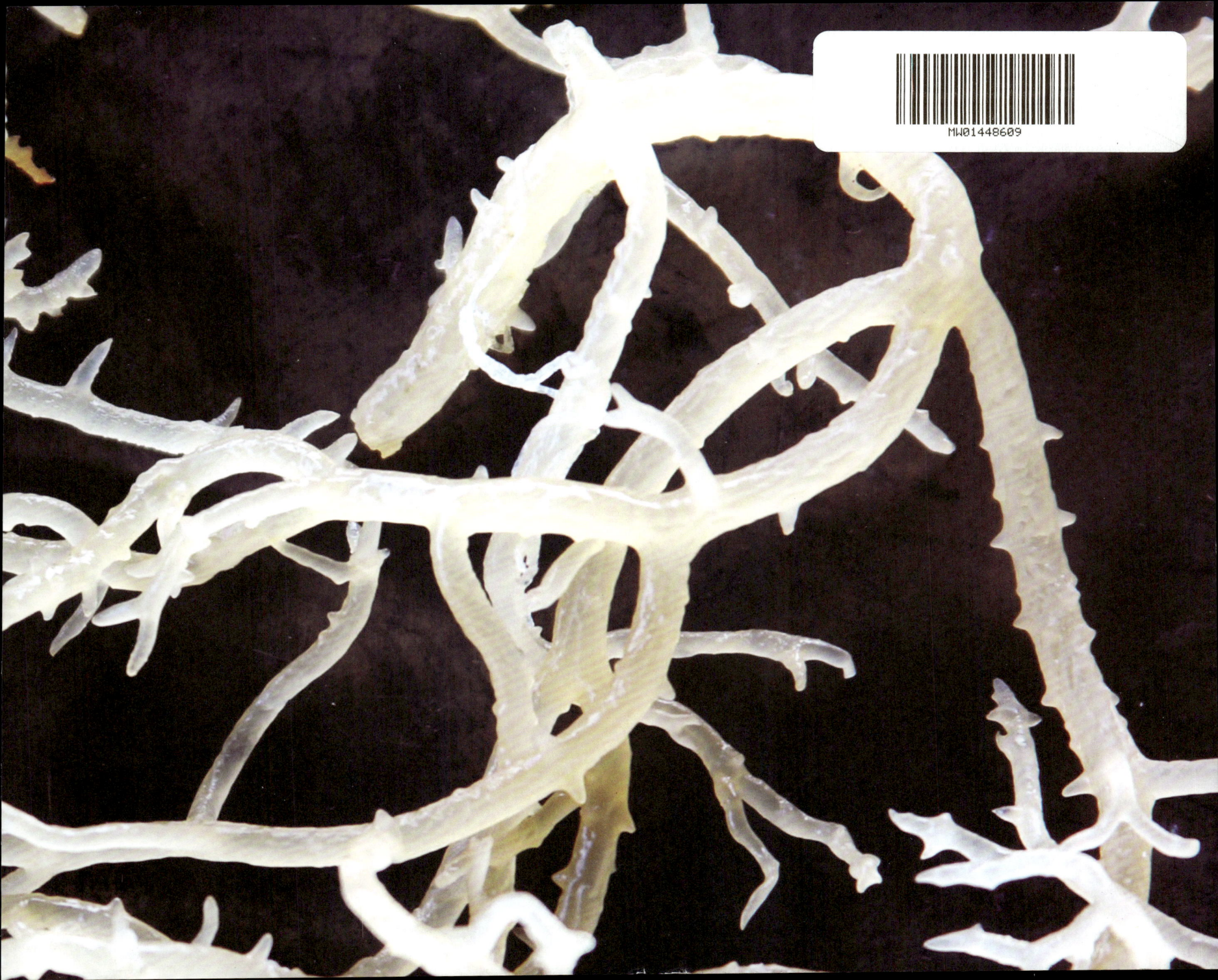

WILD PLATE

modern · living · cuisine

LAUREL ANDERSON

PHOTOGRAPHED BY LAUREL ANDERSON

DESIGNED BY LAUREL ANDERSON

DISCLAIMER

The author of this book is not a certified nutritionist or health care professional. This book is intended to share food preparation material, and information to educate the reader. The author declares to the best of their knowledge, that all material in this book at the time of printing is accurate; although new studies come out, and information is constantly changing. The recipes and information in this book are provided for educational purposes only. Everyone needs are different, and these recipes are merely an alternative method for preparing food in the kitchen. This book is not intended to provide medical advice, or take the place of medical treatment from qualified health care professionals. Always consult a physician before making any changes to your current eating habits. Consuming raw or undercooked food may increase your risk of food borne illness. The author takes no liability, or responsibility, to any persons or things with respect to any illness, loss or damage, alleged to be caused directly or indirectly by the information in this book, or any possible consequences from reading, following or consuming the recipes and information provided throughout this book.

First Edition December 2013
ISBN 978-0-9912374-01

Text © 2013 Laurel Anderson
Photographs © 2013 Laurel Anderson

Published by
Laurel Anderson
Olympia, WA 98502

All rights reserved® No portion of this book may be reproduced, distributed, or transmitted in any form or stored in a database without written consent from the publisher.

Designed by Laurel Anderson
Printed and bound in China

Anderson, Laurel.
  Wild Plate / Laurel Anderson; photographs by Laurel Anderson. 1st ed.
p.cm.
ISBN-978-0-9912374-01
1. Vegan, cooking 2. Vegetarian, cooking. 3. Raw foods 4. Cookbooks. 5. Dietary I. Title
TX000.A000 2013

To my family and close friends who have given me unconditional support, encouragement, guidance, and love. Without all of you, this book would still be just an idea. Thank you for planting the seed and helping it grow.

C O N T

INTRODUCTION

INTRODUCTION	2
WHAT IS RAW FOOD?	3
FOODS THAT MAY BE UNFAMILIAR	5
HOW TO USE SYMBOLS	10
TOOLS + EQUIPMENT	11
SHOPPING FOR YOUR PRODUCE	15
SOAKING	17
DEHYDRATION	19
LOWDOWN ON SWEETENERS	21
THE BUZZ ON HONEY	23
TO ALL THE CHOCOHOLICS	25
HOW TO CRACK A YOUNG THAI COCONUT	27
NUT FLOURS	29

E N T S

RECIPES

CHAPTER ONE + JUICES...31
CHAPTER TWO + INFUSED H2O..47
CHAPTER THREE + SMOOTHIES..61
CHAPTER FOUR + MILKS AND CREAM.....................................71
CHAPTER FIVE + MILKSHAKES..81
CHAPTER SIX + CONDIMENTS...91
CHAPTER SEVEN + SALADS..107
CHAPTER EIGHT + APPETIZERS..131
CHAPTER NINE + ENTREES..159
CHAPTER TEN + DESSERTS..203
CHAPTER ELEVEN + BREAKFASTS.......................................247
ACKNOWLEDGMENTS...267
INDEX...271

WILD:
GROWING
LIVING IN A NATURAL STATE
cultivated . enthusiastic
RAW
untamed

INTRODUCTION

I am not a professionally trained chef or nutritionist. I am simply an artist with an intense passion for good food, health, design, and sustainability. *Wild Plate* is the result of hours of experimentation and trial and error that pushed me to my limits, tapping into my creativity and allowing new forms of artistic expression into my life. Before starting this book, I had never even thought about doing food photography. Once I picked up the camera and got behind the lens, the food began to take on a new meaning for me. Veinlike patterns flowing through the skins of soaked almonds or fractal-like explosions of magenta and snow-white rings of a chiggora beet, began to morph into what I saw not just as food, but edible living art. The food was telling a story of its own, and I was the interpreter.

Before my raw food journey began, I was telling different stories—stories told through dance. I was a professional dancer for over ten years and know firsthand how important it is to take care of our bodies. Being on stage six nights a week demanded a high level of physical endurance. Good nutrition became an important component in my being able to maintain the physical stamina necessary to deliver an optimal performance every night. It was during that time in my life that I truly learned if we respect and nurture our bodies by fueling them with nutrient-dense foods, in time we will reap the rewards of more energy, better health, and vitality.

Whether you're a seasoned raw foodie, vegan, vegetarian, omnivore, carnivore, or just looking for some inspiration in the kitchen, my hope is to get readers like you to try one of these scrumptious recipes once a day, week, or even once a month. Consider it a fun challenge along with a fresh and interesting outlook on food. Remember, its doesn't have to be all or nothing. Allow your taste buds and senses to experience something new by dowsing them with a culinary burst of flavors and textures. There's no right or wrong way to use this book. Allow yourself to make mistakes and have fun with these recipes. I encourage you to use your senses and taste everything as you go. This is a golden rule in my kitchen. Depending on the season, quality, freshness, and origin of the ingredients you've selected, the recipe will vary slightly each time you make it.

Wild Plate was written to accommodate a variety of diets, so sink your teeth into savory *truffle-infused pesto raviolis* or remedy a tough day by sipping your blues away on a *chocolate banana salted caramel milkshake.* There's something for everyone to make and enjoy.

There's a revolution happening in the raw-food world, as more people are discovering this path to health and well-being. I invite you to experience one of nature's finest gifts, living cuisine. Are you ready to get **WILD?**

LIVING CUISINE/RAW FOOD

A raw-food diet is predominately vegan and prepared without cooking, grilling, or steaming and is never heated above a temperature of 118 degrees. This allows the nutrients and enzymes in the food to stay intact. Raw foods are still essentially living when you eat them. If you were to put them into soil in their whole form, they would sprout and grow into something beautiful. It is said that eating food closest to its natural state allows the digestive system to cleanse itself, giving your body the nutrition it needs to heal. Eating a raw-food diet has been linked to improving conditions such as heart disease, obesity, skin disorders, fatigue, autoimmune diseases, diabetes, headaches, and more.

I am often asked how one can get enough protein with a raw-food diet. Surprisingly vegetables of all kinds including dark, leafy greens such as spinach, kale, lettuce varieties, and collards have an abundance of protein. Seeds, nuts, and sea vegetables are staples in a raw-food diet and are another important source of protein. You'd be surprised how fulfilling and satisfying a diet rich in raw foods can be. You may even find that you are less hungry the more you eat healthy, whole, nutritious foods. Weight loss is quite often a result. Most people overeat when their bodies and brains are undernourished. This can occur when food is deficient in nutrients or enzymes. There is a switch in the brain that is triggered when it has reached the amount of nutrition it needs. A signal is then sent to the rest of your body, giving you those feelings of fullness, even though your stomach might not have reached its full capacity. Because of this people oftentimes end up eating smaller portions.

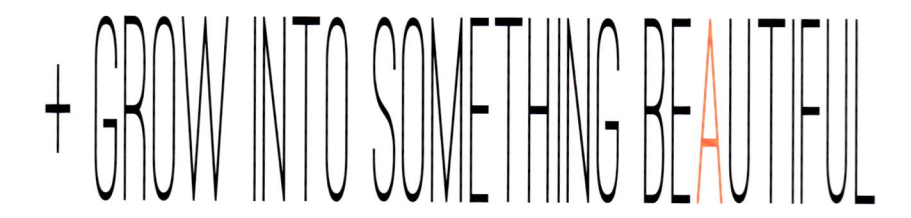

+ GROW INTO SOMETHING BEAUTIFUL

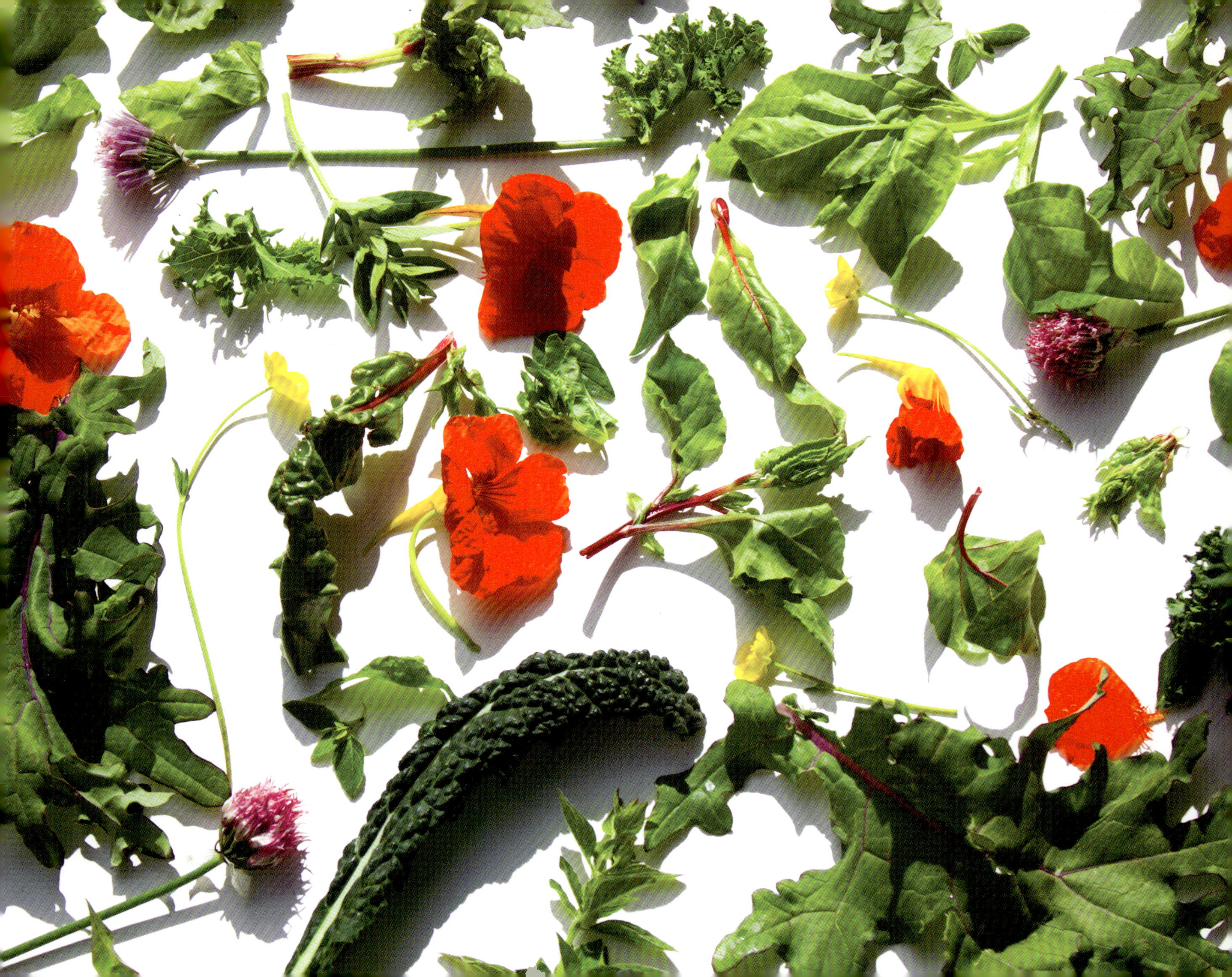

FOODS THAT MAY BE UNFAMILIAR

ACAI One of the world's greatest superfoods, acai berries come from a specific type of palm tree native to South America. They are blackish purple and about the size of a blueberry. Acai comes in various forms, including powder, dried, frozen, and juice. It tastes like a combination of blackberries, raspberries, and dark chocolate. It's slightly bitter and not as sweet as other berries. It's most widely known for its high amounts of antioxidants. My favorite brand of acai is *Sambazon*. Not only are their products organic, but they also use fair-trade practices.

ASIAN PEAR Available year-round, Asian pears resemble a golden yellow apple with tiny brown spots. The interior is creamy white, crisp, juicy, and very sweet. They are rich in Vitamin C and fiber and incredibly refreshing.

BLACK MISSION FIGS One of the high-quality figs, black mission figs grow on trees and have a beautiful dark purple skin with hints of light green closer to the stem. The flesh is pale pink with crunchy seeds. The black mission fig has a luscious, florally sweet taste and when dried turns chewy, sweeter, and black in color, hence the name black mission figs. When fresh the figs are typically in season June through September, and dried figs are available year-round.

BLOOD ORANGES A smaller variety of citrus orange, with a darker orange rind that sometimes has small patches of dark pink, the flesh of a blood orange is true to its name. It can vary in color from dark bloodred to crimson to bright pink or a combination of all three. They are a great winter citrus, usually available December through April. The blood orange tastes like a regular orange but is typically much sweeter when picked at its peak. They are great for eating on their own, in salads, and to complement both desserts and cocktails.

CAROB POWDER Made from the pods of the tropical carob tree, carob is commonly used as a chocolate substitute but has quite a different flavor than chocolate. It's sweeter, less bitter and has a slight roasted-coffee taste. The color resembles cocoa powder, and carob has a high amount of calcium along with many other health benefits.

CELTIC SEA SALT Harvested from the Celtic Sea, this is a coarse sea-salt that gets its grayish color from the clay lining of the salt beds where it is harvested. It is rich in trace minerals and usually sun-dried to retain its moisture and nutritional elements.

CHIA SEEDS A member of the sage family, these tiny little black-and-white seeds have more protein than any other seeds and have been labeled a superfood. When added to liquid, they become gelatinous and make a great pudding or porridge. I also love adding them to my smoothies for extra thickness.

CACAO BUTTER Made from pressing the fat out of cacao beans at low temperatures cacao butter is white and smooth and stable at room temperature, making it essential for making chocolates.

CACAO PASTE Made from raw cacao beans ground down at low temperatures into a smooth unsweetened paste it's a perfect base for making raw chocolates, truffles, and sauces.

COCONUT BUTTER Made from both the oil and fibrous flesh of the coconut, coconut butter when liquefied is smooth, creamy, and very fragrant. This is not the same thing as coconut oil, so read labels carefully.

DRIED LAVENDER Dried purple lavender flowers have a sweet floral essence and are a wonderful complement to desserts and beverages.

EDIBLE FLOWERS These have beautiful, vibrant colors with delicate petals that range in taste from slightly sweet to peppery to bitter to sour to tart. There are many different kinds, and I suggest doing your research before foraging for your own. I like to buy my edible flowers from my local farmers market. Some grocery stores and co-ops carry them prepackaged in the herb section. A few of my favorites include pansies, roses, nasturtiums, snapdragons, orchids, jasmine, hibiscus, lavender, fuschia, bee balm, chrysanthemums, and marigolds. Edible flowers are great for garnishing or using in salads.

GALANGAL ROOT Resembling ginger root, with a lighter skin and flesh, galangal root has a strong peppery ginger flavor mixed with a hint of pine. Galangal can be found in whole-root form, crushed, or ground. I prefer getting it in whole root form, as it's more flavorful. It keeps well in the freezer too. If galangal root is unavailable, look for fingerroot or fresh ginger root. The fingerroot is similar in flavor but not as strong and, if using ginger root, use double the amount called for in the recipe to give it the right amount of flavor.

GOJI BERRIES Also known as the *wolfberry,* goji berries when dried look like bright reddish-orange raisins with a chewy texture and sweet-sour taste. They are loaded with antioxidants, placing them in the superfood category, and loaded with other healthful benefits.

HIBISCUS FLOWERS These large, bright, colorful flowers come from the hibiscus tree native to tropical and subtropical regions. When steeped, dried hibiscus flowers have a similar taste to pomegranate and cranberries, tart yet slightly sweet. Hibiscus has many medicinal properties and is excellent used to make teas and other beverages or as a colorful garnish on desserts. The red flowers can also act as a natural pink coloring.

IRISH MOSS A seaweed that grows off the Atlantic coastline, fresh irish moss is a deep purple that turns to a light tan when dried. It is the perfect thickening agent and creates a jellylike texture when soaked and blended. When processed irish moss is known as carrageen and used as a thickener in ice creams, salad dressing, and a variety of other products. It has a long list of nutritional benefits and a slightly salty, neutral taste. It's perfect as a gelatin replacement for desserts, smoothies, and more.

JICAMA Native to Central America, jicama is a tuberous root that resembles a turnip. It has a rough, light brown skin and white, starchy flesh that is slightly sweet with nice crunch.

KAFFIR LIME LEAVES The shiny, dark green oval or heart-shaped leaves of the Kaffir lime tree add a clean, floral, citrus flavor to recipes that is unique. If you can't find kaffir lime leaves, use double the amount of lime zest, although the flavor won't be as aromatic.

KELP NOODLES A raw noodle made from the inner portion of the sea kelp plant, kelp noodles are clear, crunchy, and very neutral in taste. They will soak up flavors and become soft when marinated in a salty sauce for a few hours.

KONA COFFEE Grown on the Kona slopes on the west side of the Big Island of Hawaii. The climate and volcanic soils create a rich, strong, robust coffee that is unique in flavor and quality. If you don't have Kona coffee, a regular premium coffee will work too.

LECITHIN Acting as an emulsifier and thickener for foods, organic non-GMO soy lecithin has many health benefits. Lecithin naturally occurs in our brains; therefore, adding lecithin as a supplement can help with overall brain function. Buttery yellow in color, lecithin typically comes in powder or granule form. If you have a soy allergy, try sunflower lecithin granules.

LEMONGRASS A tropical, lemon-flavored, tall grass with a woody base the core of lemongrass is tender and can be chopped up just like a green onion. Lemongrass is used mostly in savory dishes but is great in some dessert recipes as well.

MACA POWDER From the high Andes, maca is a tuber that resembles a turnip. It is dried at low temperatures and ground into a light tan powder. It has a sour note and earthy, malty flavor and is considered a superfood. Used extensively throughout history in South America, maca has a long list of health benefits, including supporting the endocrine system and libido, and giving a great boost in energy. It's full of proteins and various vitamins and minerals.

MACHE Also know as *lambs lettuce,* mache is a dark green lettuce that grows in clumps, is very durable, and is found abundantly growing in the wild. It has a light, nutty flavor and is very easy to grow.

NUTRITIONAL YEAST An inactive yeast that is pale yellow in color and has a tangy cheese flavor. Nutritional yeast usually comes in flakes or powder and is packed with vitamin B12 and other nutrients.

PASSION FRUIT Originally from South America, passion fruits grow on vines in tropical climates and have many different varieties. The fruits skin ranges in color from deep purple to bright orange and yellow. When ripe the skin wrinkles, making it appear old, but it actually is a sign the fruit is ripe and perfect for eating. The inside is filled with small brownish-black seeds encased in a yellow-orange or gray jellylike coating. This is the part that's eaten or used for juice. Passion fruits have an exotic taste that's sweet-sour with hints of pineapple, guava, and citrus. They have multiple health benefits, including relieving stress and calming the nerves. Passion fruits are typically in season May through August.

PROBIOTIC POWDER A mix of nondairy live bacterial strains that are made by fermentation, probiotics are essential to human health and support the gastrointestinal tract and are commonly used to culture miso and yogurt. My probiotic of choice is *New Chapter All Flora Probiotic Capsules.* It's made from apples and jerusalem artichoke inulin and easily absorbable.

PSYLLIUM HUSK Soluble fiber from the husk of the psyllium plant's seeds, psyllium husk is regulary used as a dietary supplements and is great for the digestive system. Psyllium husk swells when liquid is added to it, creating a gelatinous texture that is perfect for raising raw breads without yeast and acting as a binding agent.

QUINOA An ancient seed native to South America, quinoa has a high protein content and all nine essential amino acids. It's excellent sprouted and has a light, nutty flavor. There are different varieties and colors of quinoa, the most common being an ivory-colored seed.

SEA SALT Salt that comes from the sea from an evaporation process of sea water. Trace minerals are left in the salt, making it easier for our bodies to process. My favorite is Himalayan sea salt. It is considered to be the most pure form of salt on the planet and can date back to 250 million years from a primordial ocean that is now dried deep in the Himalayas.

SMOKED PAPRIKA Made from dried, smoked sweet red peppers ground into powder, smoked paprika has a vibrant red-orange color and great smoky undertones and flavor.

SPIRULINA POWDER A bluish dark-green powder made from algae, spirulina has been used as a dietary supplement for thousands of years. Spirulina is rich in plant proteins and a wide variety of other vitamins and minerals. It contains all nine essential amino acids, allowing your body to assimilate it quickly to give you a quick boost of energy.

TANGELOS A citrus hybrid fruit that's part tangerine and part grapefruit, tangelos have a red-orange thick rind and pronounced neck with sweet-sour juicy interior segments that are deep orange in color.

TURMERIC POWDER Like ginger, turmeric is a root usually grown in tropical climates. The skin is tan and when peeled reveals a light yellow flesh. When ground, turmeric powder is bright yellow and can be used as a natural food coloring and is one of the main ingredients in yellow curry. Turmeric also has many medicinal properties, including being a great anti-inflammatory.

WAKAME A deep green, stringy seaweed that when dried turns almost black, wakame has a salty-sea taste and is packed full of nutrition.

WATERMELON RADISH Part of the daikon radish family, the watermelon radish has a white and green exterior and when sliced displays a beautiful explosion of magenta pink and white rays, hence its name. It has a mild peppery, sweet taste and is very crisp and refreshing. They taste just as delicious as they look. Watermelon radishes are in season fall through winter.

WHEAT-FREE TAMARI   A fermented soy sauce that has much more depth and flavor than regular soy sauce.   It is slightly thicker and much smoother in texture. My favorite tamari is *San-J* brand. It's available in organic non-GMO, which is really important when using any soy products. If you have a soy allergy, substitute wheat-free tamari for coconut aminos, which have a similar taste but are lighter in flavor.

YOUNG THAI COCONUTS   Imported from Thailand, these coconuts usually come with the brown husk removed and are white on the exterior. The interior of the coconut has a delicate, white, jellylike textured meat and a natural, sweet water that is delicious! If the water and jelly have a purplish tint, then the coconut has gone bad. See instructions on page 27, for how to crack a young Thai coconut.

IRISH MOSS

HOW TO USE SYMBOLS

Throughout this book you will see symbols on the top left and right corners of each recipe. These symbols are designed to identify the equipment necessary as well as the level of difficulty with a quick browse of each page. For example, if you'd like to make something fast and simple, you can refer to a one-star recipe or maybe you're up for a challenge and would like to try a four-star. The equipment and soaking symbols can really help if you have a time constraint and access to only certain pieces of equipment. For example, if a recipe calls for a dehydrator, and you don't have one, you'll be able to know immediately without having to go through each recipe's instructions. These symbols can save you a lot of time in the kitchen and help tremendously with time management, especially when a recipe calls for soaking.

- ● SOAKING
- ♥ JUICER
- ◉ HIGH-SPEED BLENDER
- ⊙ FOOD PROCESSOR
- ⏰ DEHYDRATOR

- + SIMPLE
- + + INTERMEDIATE
- + + + CHALLENGING
- + + + + ADVANCED

TOOLS AND EQUIPMENT

DEHYDRATOR
An electrical unit that dehydrates food at very low temperatures. A dehydrator is great for raw food preparation, because most dehydrators have an adjustable temperature setting, which allows the food to stay below that magic number of 118 degrees, allowing the enzymes and nutrients to stay intact. My preferred dehydrator is an Excalibur nine-tray. I have tried many, and so far the Excalibur has provided the best heat distribution and doesn't make too much noise when in use. Excaliburs also have the option of automatic shut-off timers and come in a variety of colors for the kitchen. I like using my dehydrator for breads, crackers, chips, cookies, cakes, crepes, wraps, dried herbs, fruits, veggies, and more.

TEFLEX DEHYDRATOR SHEETS
Flexible nonstick sheets that fit into the trays of your dehydrator. Teflex sheets are reusable and easy to clean with soap and water. If you don't have and don't want to purchase teflex sheets, you can also use unbleached parchment paper; however, you may get more creases in things such as wraps or crepes. Teflex sheets are essential when dehydrating liquid-based recipes.

HIGH-SPEED BLENDER
A high-speed blender also means a high-power blender. There are a lot of options on the market for high-speed blenders, and it can be overwhelming deciding which one to purchase. Look for one that has between two and three horsepower and a good warranty. I prefer using a Vitamix brand 5200 blender for all my creations in the kitchen. It has variable speeds and comes with a black tamper for incorporating harder-to-blend foods and thicker sauces. Another feature I love on the Vitamix is its automatic shut-off switch when the motor starts to overheat. This ensures the motor will not burn out like most household blenders can. I personally burned out four household blenders before committing to buying a Vitamix and so glad I did. If the motor does shut off on you—and it's happened to me a few times from overuse—no need to worry! Let it rest and cool down for about thirty minutes, and it will be up and running again like new. Vitamix also has a great warranty and very durable carafes that can last you a lifetime. In this book a high-speed blender will allow you to blend, chop, puree, churn, grind, and cream everything necessary to create beautiful raw-food dishes. I feel it is the most important and versatile electrical kitchen tool for preparing living cuisine. Do your research, and figure out which high-speed blender will meet your needs and budget. I highly recommend the investment.

FOOD PROCESSOR
An electrical kitchen appliance to help with the preparation of food by using interchangeable blades and discs that

can shred, slice, grind, chop, or puree, creating a variety of textures. A food processor really comes in handy and reduces prep time significantly. I prefer an eleven-cup Cuisinart for my kitchen. It's durable, powerful, has a large feed tube, and a reputation of lasting a very long time. In fact, my grandfather just gave me his Cuisinart from the early 70s. It's a little heavy but still works beautifully. Again I encourage you to do your research and purchase what works best for you and your individual needs.

NUT-MILK BAG
A very fine mesh filtration bag that allows liquid such as nut milks to flow through and solids to remain in the bag. A nut-milk bag is reusable and an essential for the raw-food kitchen. I always have two of these in my tool box in case one gets a tear or for making multiple recipes. Nut-milk bags are great for milks, cream, and creating nut cheeses and flours.

ZESTER
A kitchen utensil used for achieving fine shreds or curls from the skin of citrus fruits.

RUBBER SPATULA
Typically a long wood handle topped with a flat, flexible rubber blade. Used for mixing, stirring, spreading, and lifting foods.

SPRINGFORM PAN
Two-piece round pan that has a removable bottom and held in place by an interlocking band and outer clamp. This allows easy removal of cheesecakes, savory cheeses, and more. By your releasing the clamp, the sides of the pan spring away in a clean manner.

PIE PLATE
Used to set pies, pie plates are commonly nine inches in diameter and one to three inches deep. A pie plate has sloped sides and can be made of glass, ceramic, metal, or tin.

8-INCH X 8-INCH BAKING DISH
A square, deep dish usually made of glass, ceramic or metal this baking dish can be used to hold and set various foods or used as a serving dish.

STRAINER/COLANDER
Allows liquids to drain through a perforated base or bowl, leaving the solid food inside.

CERAMIC KNIFE
Made of a hard ceramic blades, these knifes rarely need sharpening and are perfect for using on fresh fruits and vegetables. Ceramic knives don't corrode and will not oxidize foods as fast as metal knives do therefore, retaining their color and freshness longer. Do not use these on glass surfaces, for they will chip and if dropped the blade can easily break so handle with care.

CHEF'S KNIFE
Made of metal and typically with an eight–inch steel blade, there are various shapes of a chef's knife, depending on if it's German, French, or Japanese. They all have slightly different qualities, but a good knife will be very sharp, durable, strong, and feel good in your hand. A chef's knife can be used for many different kitchen tasks, including chopping, mincing, slicing, and cracking coconuts.

JUICER
Electrical kitchen appliance that extracts juice from fruits, vegetables, grasses, and in some cases makes ice creams and nut butters. There are so many different juicers on the market for all needs and budgets. Typically there are three different kinds of juicers to choice from.

Centrifugal— grinds fruits and vegetables then pushes them into a filter that spins the juice out. These juicers are the least expensive but can heat up during the process, causing the enzymes in the juice to be compromised and usually have a juicier leftover pulp.

Masticating— crushes the fruit and vegetables and then squeezes out the juice at a slower rate than a centrifugal juicer so it doesn't heat up as fast, keeping more of the enzymes intact. The pulp is also much dryer, and it produces about 20 percent more juice that a centrifugal juicer. A masticating juicer will usually come with attachments to make nut butters, ice cream, sorbet, and more, making it the most versatile.

Pressed juicer— extracts juice through pressure. The fruits and vegetables are not exposed to any heat, keeping almost all the enzymes intact and allowing maximum nutrition, creating richer, more full-bodied flavors with a fresh, crisp taste that rivals no other. It produces the most amount of juice and also has the highest price tag. However, if you really want the ultimate juicer that will last a lifetime, this is the one to buy. Personally I have tried all three types and chosen to have a masticating juicer in my kitchen. I enjoy being able to use it for so many things and it has a bonus: it's really easy to clean. Plus it's small and can easily fit on my countertop or in a kitchen cupboard. I encourage you to talk to friends who have juicers themselves or jump online to read reviews and then determine which juicer will work best for your needs.

MANDOLINE SLICER
A kitchen utensil that has an adjustable razor sharp blade, allowing fruits and vegetables to be sliced extremely thin or thick. I like the OXO mandoline slicer. It's reasonably priced and easy to clean and it has a safety guard. Mandoline slicers are extremely sharp, so please be extra careful when using one. There are a lot of chefs who wear mesh metal gloves while using a mandoline to prevent casualties.

CHEESECLOTH
A gauzelike, lightweight cotton cloth used for removing the liquid or whey of cheeses, a cheesecloth helps hold the structure of the cheese together while it's fermenting. Cheesecloth usually comes in bleached white or natural unbleached. I prefer the unbleached cheesecloth, but either one will do.

ICE CREAM SCOOP
A kitchen utensil mainly used to serve ice cream, but is great for serving savory items and thick substances as well. An ice cream scoop has a sturdy handle with an oversized hemispherical metal spoon on the end, which scoops out beautiful round portions. I like using the old-fashioned spring-handle scoops. They have character and never fail to create a picture-perfect scoop.

CANDY THERMOMETER
A large glass thermometer commonly used to test candies and chocolates while heating and tempering. This is essential for making the tempered chocolate recipe in this book. Candy thermometers are inexpensive and can be found at most kitchen supply stores, craft stores, and larger supermarkets.

PYRAMID MOLDS
Pyramid-shaped mold used to shape sweet or savory dishes. Usually made of stainless steel, it comes in various sizes. These are fun to use and can really jazz up food presentation from great to incredible!

MIXING BOWLS
A kitchen essential, mixing bowls come in various materials, including glass, metal, ceramic, and plastic. They come in multiple sizes ranging from small to extra large. I prefer glass bowls and like to have all sizes for multitasking in the kitchen for recipes both small and large.

MEASURING CUPS
Another kitchen essential, measuring cups are usually available in glass, metal, ceramic, or plastic. They typically have measurements starting with 1/4 cup up to 1 cup but are also available in larger measurements. I have both glass and metal measuring cups in my kitchen, and both are used equally.

MEASURING SPOONS
These essential measuring spoons are usually available in glass, metal, ceramic, and plastic. They measure small amounts: typically between 1/8 teaspoon and 1 tablespoon. I prefer using metal measuring spoons for easy cleaning and durability.

PLASTIC SQUEEZE BOTTLE
Although plastic is not my top choice for anything in the kitchen, plastic squeeze bottles with a pointed tip can really come in handy for garnishing items and creating unique sauce patterns. I reuse these over and over and always have a few in my kitchen for making beautiful food presentations with drizzles and swirls.

WHISK
Another essential—the whisk—I'll be referring to in this book is a wire whisk, also known as a balloon whisk, made of metal with wires that are formed in the shape of a teardrop and meet at the top, with a handle. A whisk is used to incorporate ingredients and whip air into the mixture. They really come in handy for dressings and sauces.

SHOPPING FOR YOUR PRODUCE

My favorite place to shop for fresh produce is a farmers market. Not only is it supporting local farmers, but you'll be purchasing the freshest, most vibrant foods that have been harvested at their prime, meaning they will be more nutritionally dense instead of being harvested weeks before, packed, and shipped across the country or sometimes across the world. That being said, this option is not always available. My next choice would be a local food co-op or health-food store. There is also the option of purchasing hard to locate items on the Internet through various websites.

The taste and scent of a vegetable or fruit in its prime can be much different than when it's underripe or overripe, which in the end can dramatically change the taste of your recipe. Don't be afraid to pick up your produce and put it right under your nose, feel its weight in your hands, and give it a good look with your eyes. Use all your senses. Like all things in life, it can be trial and error. Try not to get discouraged if you don't pick that perfect, buttery avocado the first or second time. It can take some practice.

VEGETABLES
When choosing what vegetables to buy, keep an eye out for deep, rich colors. They should look fresh and alive, not wilted or faded in color. The stocks should be sturdy and firm to the touch, without soft spots or bruises. If a vegetable looks like it's been sitting there awhile it probably has.

FRUITS
Color can be a good indicator but not always a reliable one. Usually apples, bananas, berries, cherries, and tomatoes will have vibrant and saturated colors when ripe. Other fruits, however, cannot be totally judged for ripeness by color but more by their aroma, texture, and weight. As fruits get riper, they become soft. The gentle squeeze test works well for all stone fruits but not necessarily for fruits with a rind. The weight of a fruit can be a good indicator. If it's heavy, it's a good sign the fruit has reached maturity and is densely packed with juicy flavor and nutrition.

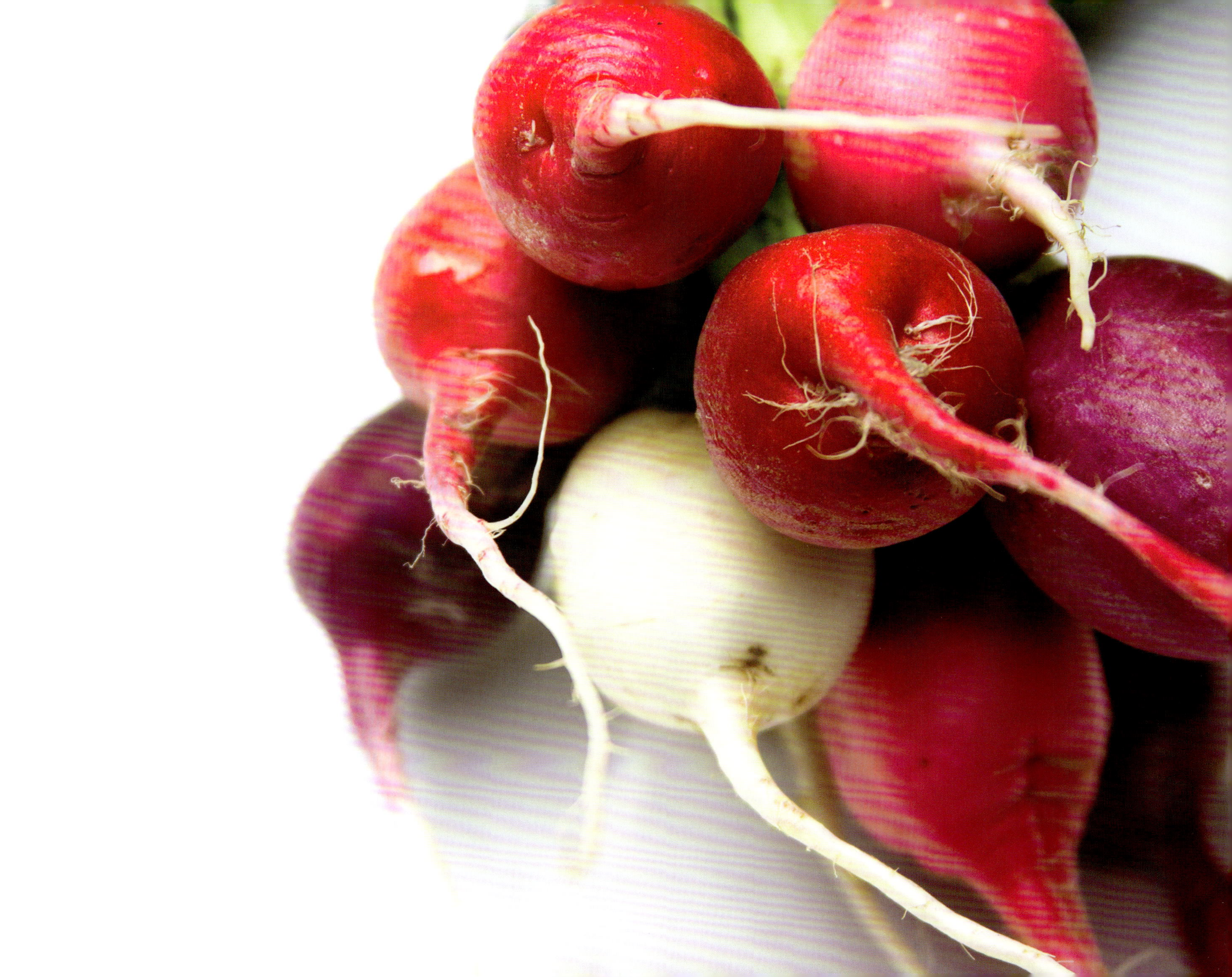

SOAKING

Soaking seeds and nuts is an important part of a living foods kitchen. The point of soaking is so enzyme inhibitors located in various seeds and nuts get released, allowing them to be more digestible. Soaking can also remove the bitterness that can accompany some varieties. You can use the chart below as a reference point when soaking seeds and nuts for this book or when creating your own recipes. I have included sprouting times for all items if you're feeling ambitious and want to go the extra mile. For the recipes in this book sprouting is not necessary with the exception to quinoa.

INGREDIENT	DRY AMONUT	SOAK TIME	SPROUT TIME	YIELD
QUINOA	1 CUP	3 HOURS	1-2 DAYS	3 CUPS
CASHEWS	1 CUP	4-6 HOURS	NOT SPROUTABLE	2 CUPS
PECANS	1 CUP	4-6 HOURS	NOT SPROUTABLE	2 CUPS
WALNUTS	1 CUP	4-6 HOURS	NOT SPROUTABLE	2 CUPS
PUMPKIN SEEDS	1 CUP	6-8 HOURS	1 DAY	2 CUPS
SUNFLOWER SEEDS	1 CUP	6-10 HOURS	1 DAY	2 CUPS
ALMONDS	1 CUP	8-10 HOURS	1-2 DAYS	2 CUPS
MACADAMIA NUTS	1 CUP	NO SOAKING REQUIRED	NOT SPROUTABLE	1 CUP
PISTACHIOS	1 CUP	NO SOAKING REQUIRED	NOT SPROUTABLE	1 CUP
HEMPSEEDS	1 CUP	NO SOAKING REEQUIRED	NOT SPROUTABLE	1 CUP
CHIA SEEDS	1/4 CUP	20 MINUTES- 24 HOURS	1-5 DAYS	2 CUPS

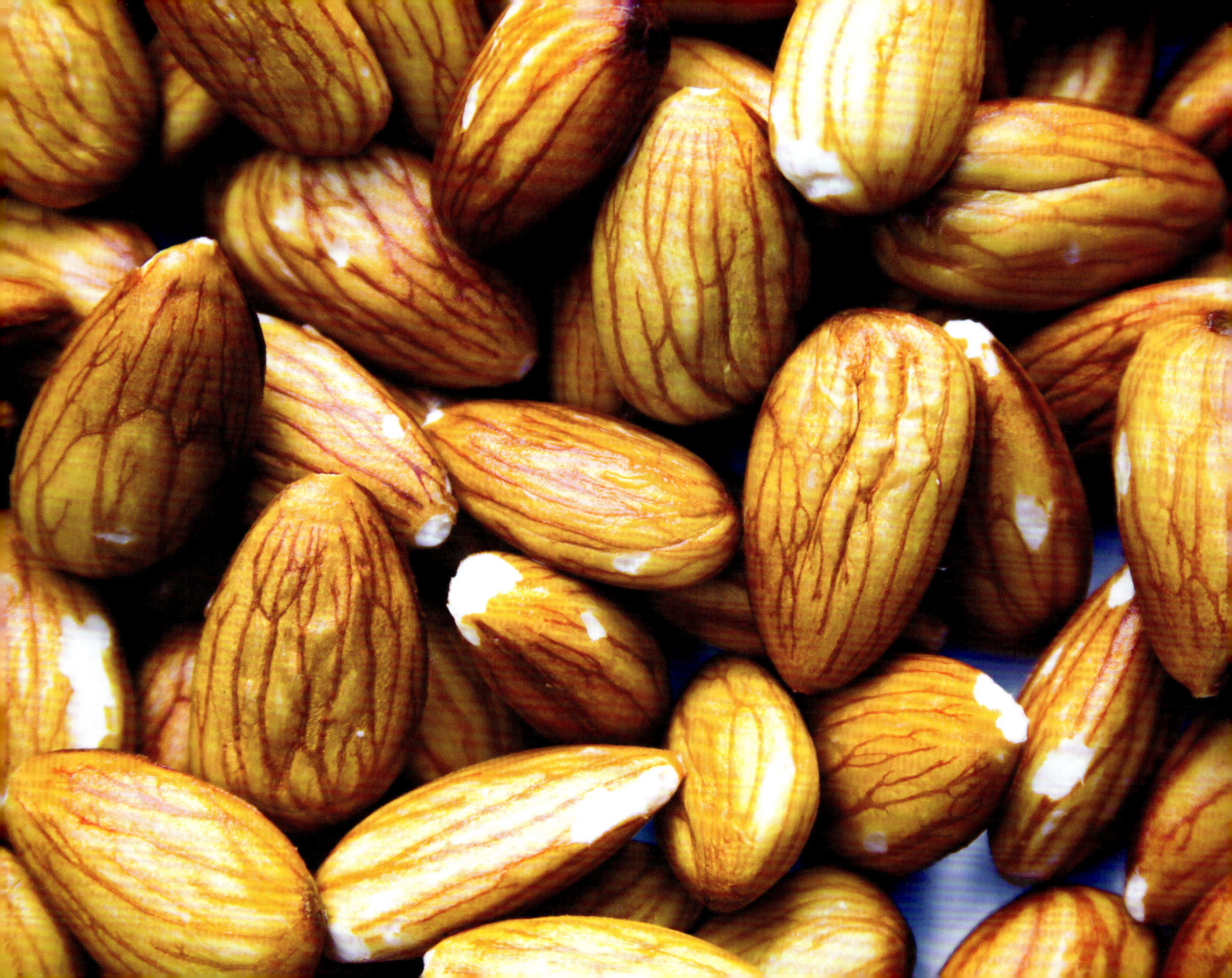

DEHYDRATION

It is not necessary to have a dehydrator: however, there are some incredibly fun and enticing recipes in this book that require one. The possibilities and potential are endless with these reasonable priced units.

In order to keep food raw truly "living," you don't want to heat it above 118 degrees. Once the food exceeds this temperature, the vitamins, minerals, and enzymes begin to evaporate into the air, and the foods start to lose their full nutritional value.

Dehydrators allow us to create and enjoy cookies, crackers, breads, chips, dried fruits, candied nuts, granolas and to indulge in raw recipes with soft cooked-like textures that are mouthwateringly good. In my opinion it's well worth the investment. You can purchase them new or used, and one dehydrator can be used to make several recipes all at once.

I know the drying times with dehydrators can seem daunting, but it's all about planning ahead. Just whip up your recipes, dehydrate and continue going about your day. In a few hours (or sometimes days) you'll have some tasty "living" treats that are guaranteed to be well worth the wait.

My dehydrator of choice is the nine-tray Excalibur plus nine teflex sheets. It covers all my needs and the teflex sheets make it easy to spread out liquid-based items and keep granolas and seeds from slipping through the cracks. The sheets are reusable, meaning less waste and a lower carbon footprint.

Throughout this book I dehydrate different recipes at a temperature ranging between 105–115 degrees. I personally have found that these are the best temperatures to ensure that the food is evenly dehydrated and doesn't go above 118 degrees. The last thing you want is to put all the time, energy and money into creating a beautiful dehydrated raw recipe only to have it get overheated, and lose all that extra nutrition.

Although my pick is Excalibur, I encourage you to do your research and decide what works best for you.

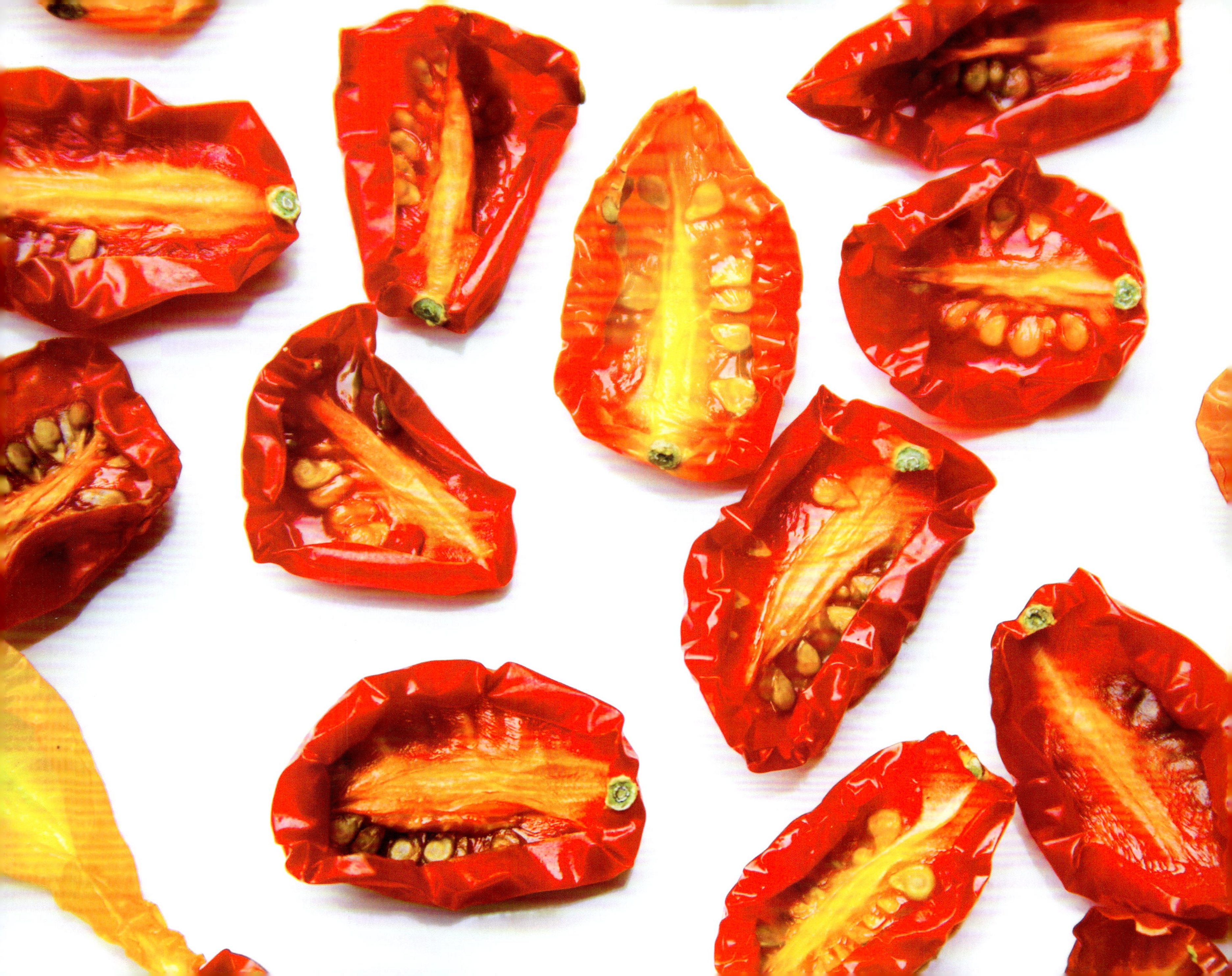

THE LOWDOWN ON SWEETENERS

There are many options for natural sweeteners on the market, allowing a variety of choices for virtually everyone. The ones I've listed are low glycemic, meaning they don't cause a severe spike in blood-sugar levels. However, some have a higher glycemic index number than others. Consult a glycemic index chart for more details on the number associated with a particular sweetener.

STEVIA

Native to South America, stevia is known as the sweet leaf plant or *Stevia rebaudiana*, and is part of the sunflower family. The plant has little green leaves that are extremely sweet. In its concentrated form, stevia has up to three hundred times the sweetness of sugar. The leaves are usually dried and ground into a powder or made into a liquid concentrate which is my favorite way to use the plant. Stevia is available in most markets throughout the United States and comes in a variety of flavors.

It is gaining popularity for many reasons, the major one being it has zero calories and doesn't effect blood-sugar levels, making it a perfect natural substitute for diabetics and people following low-carb, low-sugar lifestyles. The good benefits don't stop there. The plant leaves contain photochemical compounds that have been known to lower cholesterol, blood pressure, indigestion and heartburn. It can assist with absorption of calcium; therefore, helping with osteoporosis, tooth decay, gingivitis, mouth sores and chronic fatigue –so many amazing benefits from such a tiny plant!

I find the taste very mild and delightful; however, the flavor can vary quite dramatically, depending on the form of stevia you've chosen. The green powder has more of a licorice undertone, and lower-quality versions will have a slightly bitter aftertaste. The white powder is pretty good, but depending on the quality, it can be difficult to mix into liquids and can have a bit of an aftertaste. My personal favorite is the liquid-based stevia without alcohol. Stevia is great to use in beverages and desserts of all kinds.

COCONUT SUGAR AND SYRUPS

Coconut syrup is made from the sap of the coconut palm blossoms and is extracted by a tapping process and then collected and evaporated at very low temperatures, which turn it into a thicker syrup. For coconut sugar, the syrup is evaporated even longer, until it transforms into coconut sugar crystals. There are also nutritional benefits in these products, including seventeen amino acids, vitamin C and B vitamins. I would describe the taste and texture of the syrup as a thick yet mild caramel-flavored molasses. The sugar crystals are like a crumbly, unrefined light brown sugar. I encourage you to experiment with this natural sweetener.

MAPLE SYRUP

Although it's not "raw," maple syrup is accepted and widely used in raw food recipes. It is made by "tapping" the maple tree and collecting the sap. The sap is then heated to evaporate the water, so you have a sweet, thick, concentrated maple syrup. Maple syrup contains zinc and manganese which can be great for the immune system and heart health. It's sweeter than sugar and lower in calories. There are typically two grades of maple syrup to choose from. They are determined by the translucency and density of the syrup. Grade A is very mild in flavor, light in color, and is usually referred to as amber. Grade B is very thick and earthy in flavor with a rich dark brown color. I like using Grade B when making anything with chocolate.

YACON SYRUP

Another amazing plant from South America is the yacon root. It is very low on the glycemic index which means it won't cause a spike in your blood sugar. It also contains magnesium, iron, calcium, potassium, antioxidants, and aids in building the immune system. The sweet taste and thick, gooey texture remind me a lot of molasses. I use this throughout the book as a caramel base and it works perfect! If you can't find yacon syrup use coconut syrup.

AGAVE NECTAR

In recent years there has been much debate about this praised natural sweetener as to what constitutes raw agave. After researching and gathering information on my own, it seems that truly raw agave nectar is clear, sweeter, and much thinner in consistency than its dark or amber counterparts. Personally I love using raw agave in desserts, because it has a neutral taste and adds the perfect amount of sweetness and consistency. If you're on the fence about agave, perhaps do some research for yourself and decide if it's right for your diet.

DATES

Dates are the dark fruits harvested from the date palm and thought to be one of the earliest known fruits. They originate from Morocco but are now grown throughout the world. Dates are a rich source of dietary fiber and have an array of vitamins and minerals. They are perfect when you want to thicken something up and make it sweet at the same time. They also act as a binding agent in raw foods. I like using dates for piecrusts, cake bases, and smoothies. They are great stuffed with a little almond butter as a snack. As a kid my parents use to give me dates instead of sugary candy and referred to them as nature's candy. My dates of choice are Medjool dates, also known as the king of dates, as they are luxuriously sweet and when fresh melt in your mouth.

To make date paste:
Place 1 cup dates and 2 tablespoons water in food processor with "S" blade attachment. Pulse for about 2 minutes, until dates are broken down and paste is almost smooth. Store in airtight container in refrigerator up to three weeks.

THE BUZZ ON HONEY

Honey is another one of those ingredients that is controversial in the vegan raw world. If you chose not to use honey, no worries—just substitute it for raw agave. It will still taste delicious! In order to get the most nutritional benefits from your honey, use raw, wild-crafted honey that hasn't been heated or processed. Most honey that comes in those cute little bears is, unfortunately, processed. When honey is truly raw, it will be thicker, to where you will need a spoon to scoop it out, and a bit creamy as opposed to the more-clear, liquefied, and processed version.

This liquid gold has been found in tombs of the ancient Egyptians and been praised for thousands of years as a cure for various diseases and aliments. Surprisingly honey never spoils. It contains a long list of vitamins, minerals, and live enzymes, including B-complex; vitamins A, C, D, E and K; sulfur; magnesium; iron; calcium; phosphorus; chlorine; potassium; iodine; copper; manganese; iodine; antioxidants; and sodium. It can also help relieve pain with its anti-inflammatory compounds, balance out the liver, stabilize blood pressure, help with digestion, soothe ulcers, reduce fevers, remove toxin buildup, soothe a sore throat, help with diarrhea, and is an excellent source of energy.

Manuka honey is especially amazing. It is usually produced in New Zealand from bees that collect pollen and nectar from the tea tree bush. When manuka honey comes in contact with bodily fluid, an enzyme in the honey slowly releases natural hydrogen peroxide and kills off bacteria, healing wounds at a rapid rate. After decades of research, scientists have now given the antimicrobial, antiviral, antibacterial, antiseptic, antifungal, and anti-inflammatory properties an abbreviation called UMF (unique manuka factor). Although all manuka honey is great, not all kinds are equal. When purchasing manuka honey make sure it has either UMF or MGO on the label. MGO (methylglyoxal) is the key to the antibacterial activation in the honey. It is found in all honey; however, manuka honey has the highest concentration, with levels of100–1000mg, as opposed to levels from1–10mg in regular honey. Always look for a brand that has numbers after it as well that are no less than active 16+ or MGO 250+. If you see a number lower than this, the honey may not contain the really strong antiviral, antibacterial, and antiseptic qualities. A jar of manuka honey is not cheap but well worth the price. Consider it natures tasty medicine.

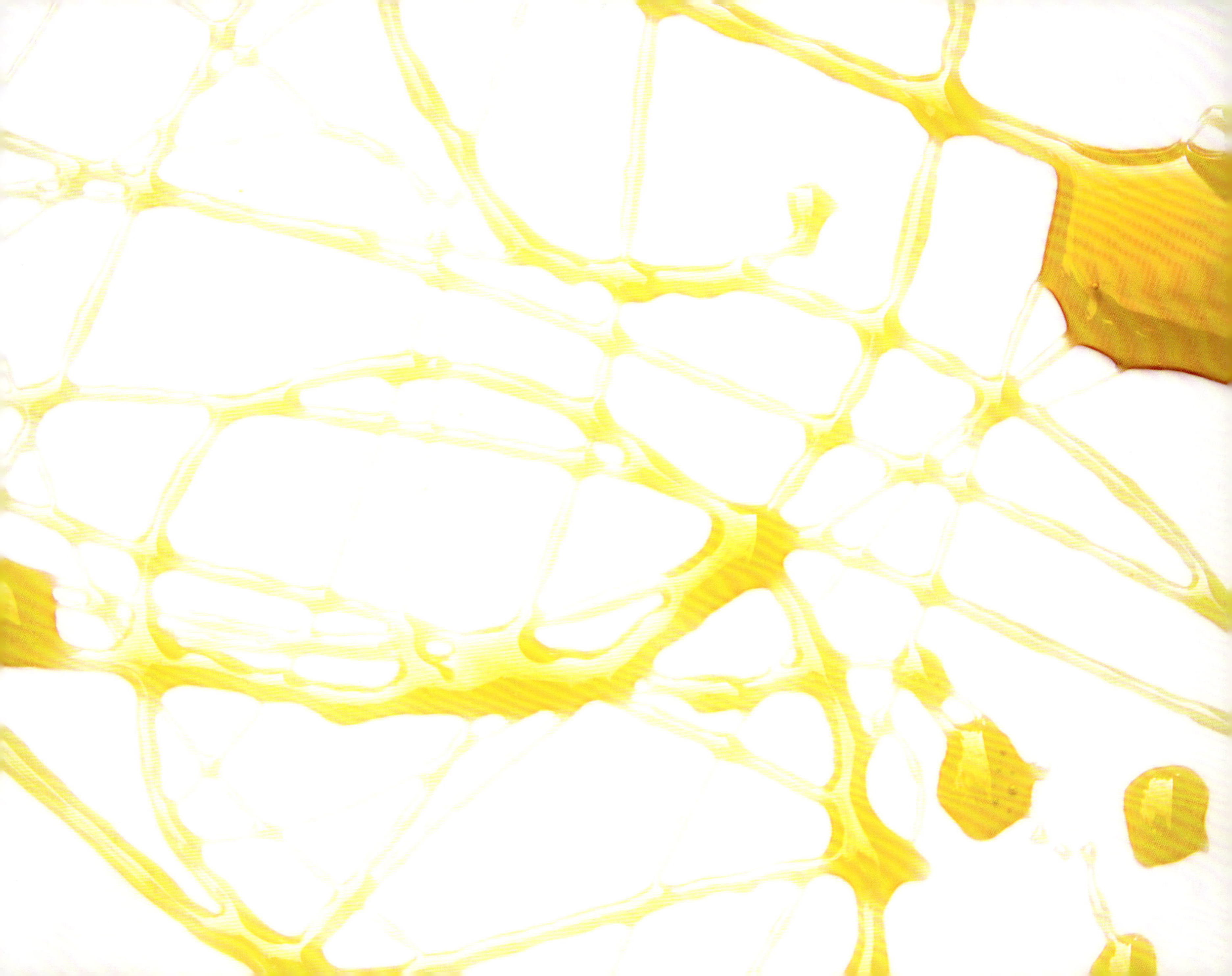

TO ALL THE CHOCOHOLICS

Admitting I am a chocolate addict would be an understatement. I LOVE CHOCOLATE! Raw chocolate is one of my favorite ingredients to use and is hands down my dessert of choice. Whether you're using it for sweet or savory recipes, it can take flavors to insane levels of complexity that will send your body and mind into a state of bliss—literally. Raw cacao contains a plethora of natural mood enhancers.

Phenylethylamine, also called the love chemical, is a neurotransmitter that gives us that incredible feeling of being in love. Anandamide, also called the bliss chemical, is very similar to THC, in that it relaxes you and can alleviate pain. It can also dilate your blood vessels and bronchial tubes, thus creating the sensational "runner's high" that you hear people talking about. Tryptophan is an amino acid that is vital to the production of melatonin and serotonin which can elevate your mood, rid anxiety and stress, and help some people sleep better. Finally, theobromine, which is related to caffeine. When theobromine is unheated, it is very mild and doesn't give your body the same side effects as caffeine—just a mild energy boost. However, when theobromine in cacao is heated above 118 degrees, these beneficial nutrients are destroyed and are chemically transformed into caffeine which can cause the well-known "jitters" or restlessness that people can sometimes experience.

Raw chocolate contains the highest levels of antioxidants and magnesium—more than any other food on this planet that we currently know of. Magnesium is important, because it supports the heart and cardiovascular system and helps the body to absorb nutrients. Antioxidants are essential for preventing oxidation, hence their name. Oxidation speeds up the aging process and creates free radicals that float through our bodies, eventually creating chain reactions that link up like small armies trying to become stronger and ultimately destroying our healthy cells. Antioxidants are like the superheroes to these damaged cells and come swooping in knocking out the bad guys (free radicals). All of us have free radicals in our bodies. Our everyday environments have a multitude of contributing factors; they form through exposure to toxins, chemicals, pollutants, smoke, and sunburns, and the process of breaking down the foods we ingest on a daily basis. That's why it's so important to eat foods containing high antioxidants, and raw chocolate is at the top of that list.

The cacao tree produces large alien-like shiny pods of fruit that when ripe turn brilliant shades of green, yellow, orange, or red, depending on the variety. The inside of this hard-shelled fruit has a creamy white or yellowish pith that encases the precious cacao bean. The beans are removed from this pith then dried and sold in various forms, such as powder, butter, oil, paste, nibs and whole beans. So go ahead and grab some mouthwatering raw chocolate, and enjoy to your heart's content.

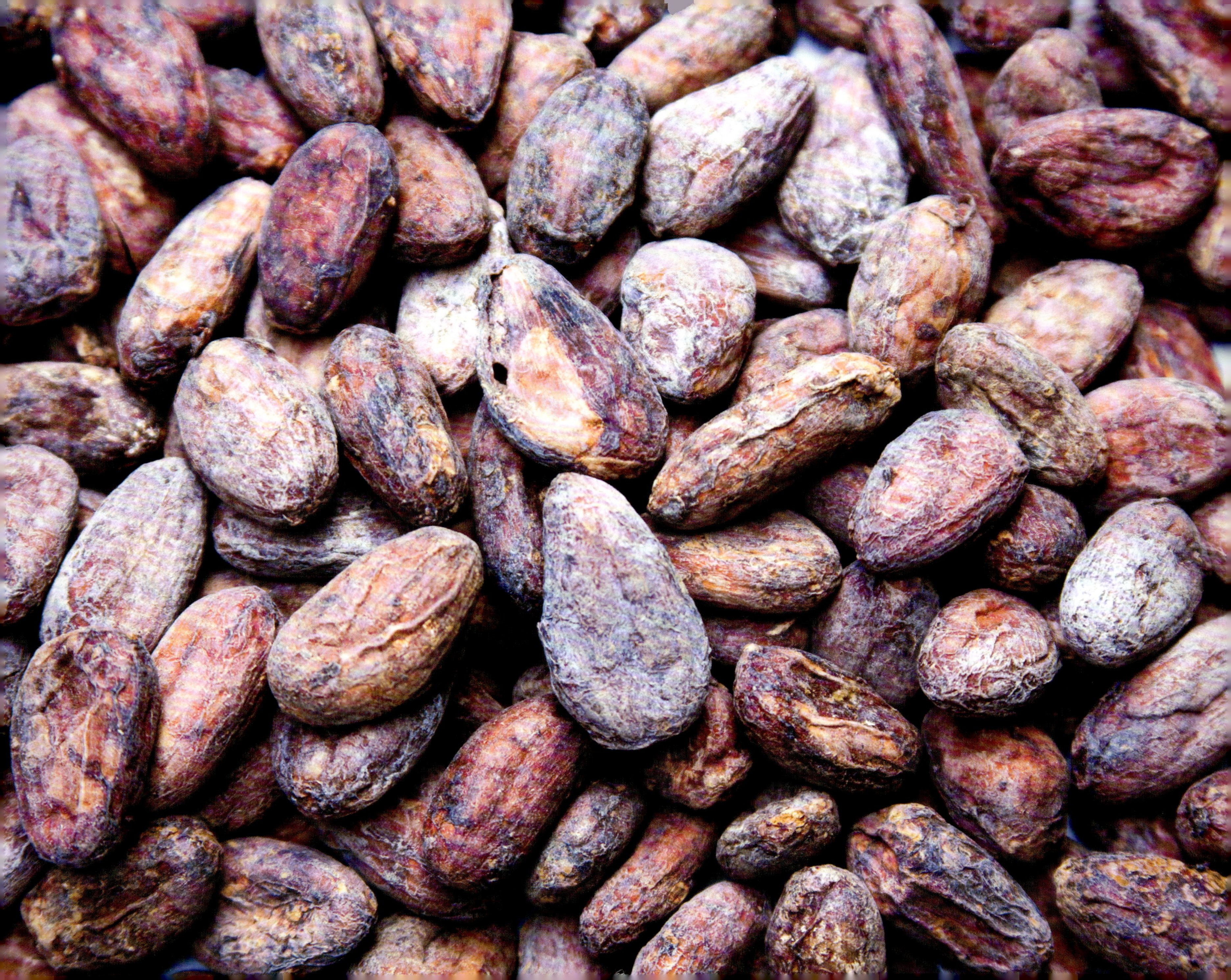

HOW TO CRACK A YOUNG THAI COCONUT

TOOLS YOU'LL NEED
1. Sharp, heavy-duty, very sturdy chef's knife
2. Cutting board
3. Metal spoon

INSTRUCTIONS
1. With the edge of the chef's knife, score the top of the coconut all the way around, until you've scored a full circle on the coconut. You want to mark an opening wide enough so it will be easy to scrape the meat out with a spoon.
2. Holding the knife in one hand and coconut in the other, tap the edge of the knife into the marked line all the way around the coconut, until a full circle has been cut through the shell.
3. Using your fingers pop the pointed top off the coconut.
4. The coconut will be filled with a clear water. Pour water into desired container and set aside to drink, use in a recipe, or store in airtight container for later use.
5. Using a metal eating spoon, scrape the meat out of the coconut. If the meat is a little tough, turn the spoon around, using it backward to get under the meat, and scrape away, lifting the meat from the hard brown shell.
6. Remove all the shell fragments by placing the coconut meat in a strainer and rinsing under cold water. Using your fingers, pull off shell fragments and brown pieces. Rinse one more time, until all your coconut meat is clean.
7. Discard the shell and either use the coconut meat and water immediately or keep in airtight containers for up to 3 days. You can also freeze coconut meat in airtight containers for 2–4 months.

NOTE:
One large young Thai coconut usually produces about 1/2–3/4 cup meat and 12–14 ounces of water. If the inside of the coconut has a darker brown or purplish tint to it, it has gone bad and will not be very tasty. Discard it, and try opening a new one. Typically if I buy a case of nine coconuts, one of the nine will be bad. If you need a specific amount of meat or water, its always good to buy one or two extra coconuts just in case. It's better to have too much than not enough for a recipe.

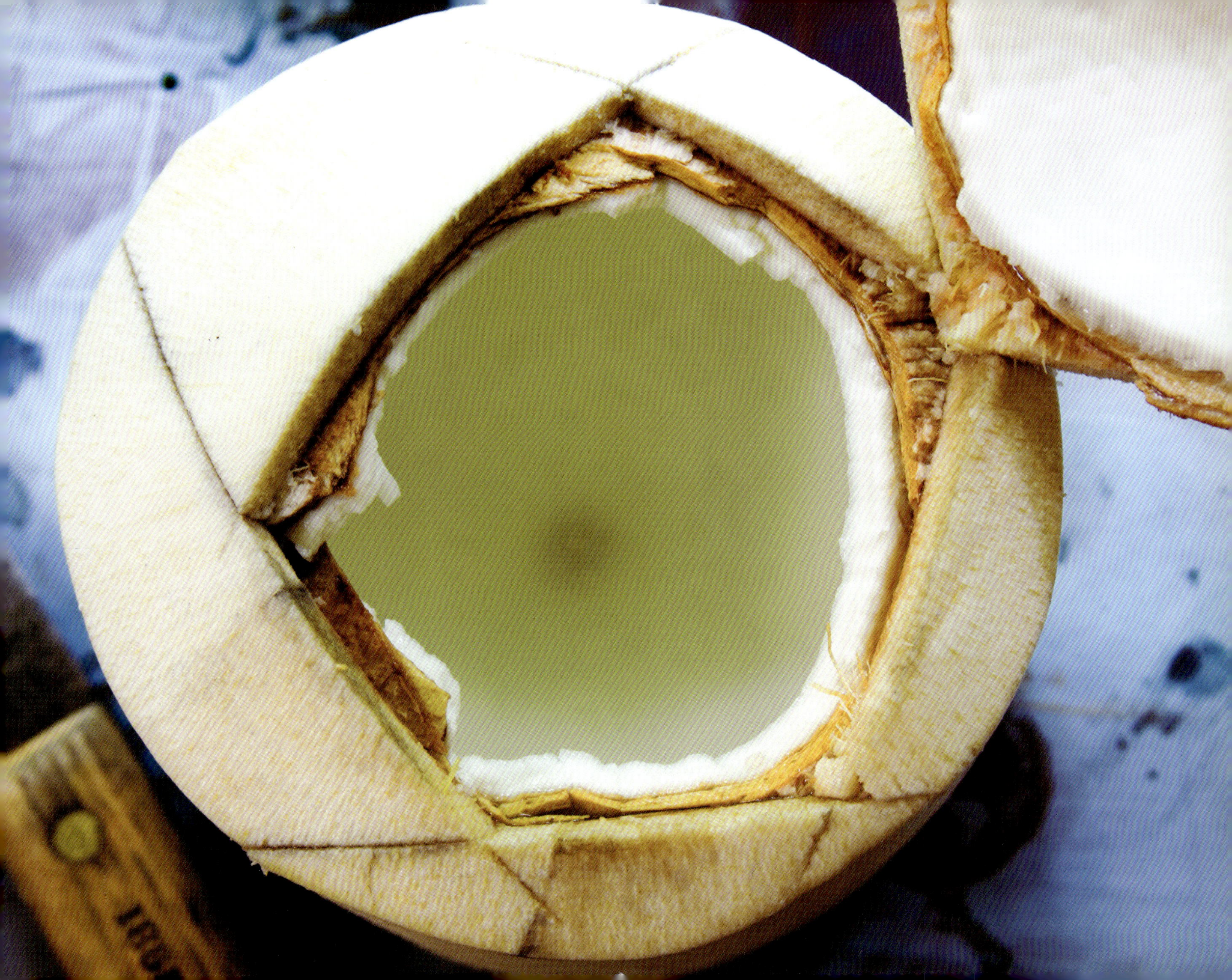

NUT FLOURS

Nut flours are a great alternative to grain flour for both raw food recipes and cooked. They are high in protein and low in carbohydrates and sugar. They are incredibly easy to make and add wonderful rich flavor and cakey texture to desserts, breads, crackers and more. When making almond milk, you not only get the milk but also, if you keep the leftover pulp in the nut-milk bag, you now have fresh almond flour which can be used in a variety of recipes in this book.

ALMOND FLOUR
1 cup raw almonds

PECAN FLOUR
1 cup raw pecans

CASHEW FLOUR
1 cup raw cashews

INSTRUCTIONS THREE WAYS

1. In a high-speed blender, add 1 cup nuts of choice. Start out blending on low, gradually working your way up to high for about 20 seconds. You want the flour to be fine, without big chunks. Avoid over-blending which will release too many oils, creating nut butter instead of flour.

2. In a coffee grinder, add 1/4 cup nuts of choice. Pulse until nuts are broken down into a fine flour. Over-grinding can also result in releasing too many oils, creating nut butter —which is great, but not what we're looking for in this recipe. Continue until 1 cup is ground into flour.

3. This technique won't work with cashews, as they are a soft nut and will blend into a creamy nut milk on their own. This is my favorite way to make nut flours, and it works great for almonds and pecans. In a high-speed blender, make nut milk by adding 1 cup soaked nuts and 3 cups water. Blend on high for about 2 minutes, until almonds or pecans are broken down into a coarse, sandy like consistency. Line bowl or pitcher with nut-milk bag and strain milk. Squeeze out as much water as possible. For a wet flour, simply put almond pulp in container and store in refrigerator or freezer. For dry nut flour, spread out leftover pulp on a dehydrator tray lined with a teflex sheets. Dehydrate at 115 degrees until moisture is removed and flour is dry.

NOTE: Store all nut flours refrigerated in airtight containers 3–4 days or in freezer up to 2 months.

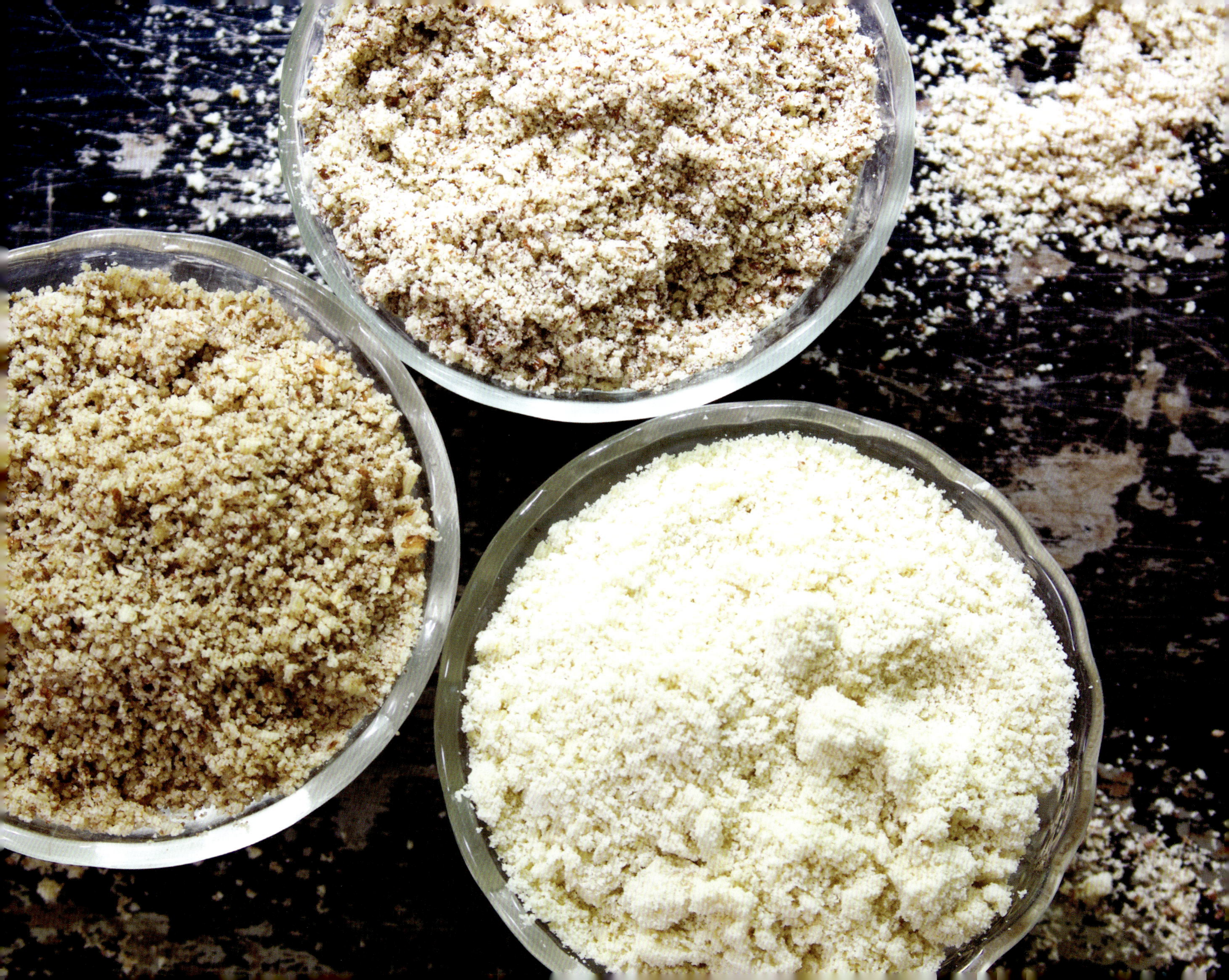

J U I

C　　　　　　　E　　　　　　　S

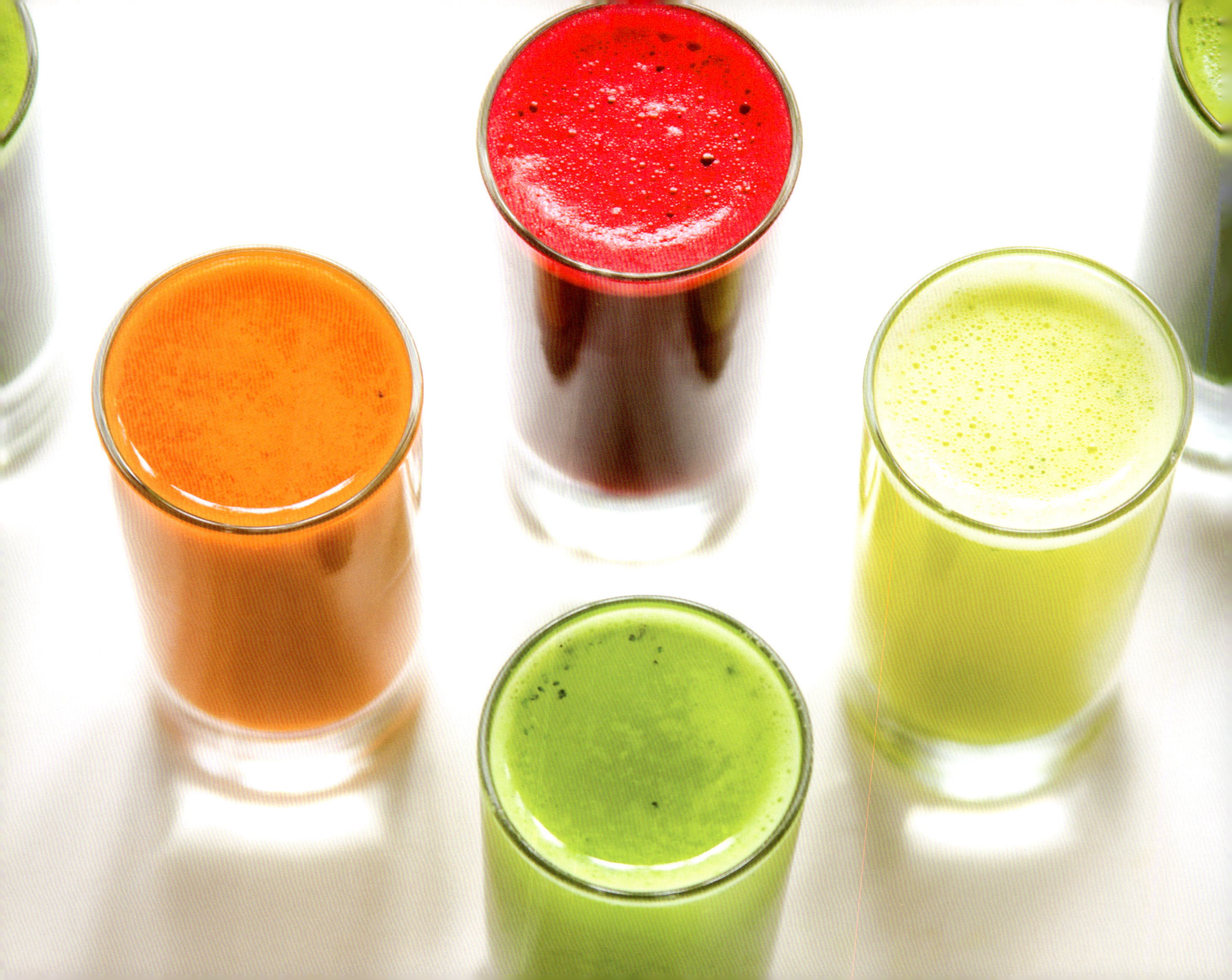

GREEN KALE, CUCUMBER, AND APPLE JUICE

MAKES 32 OUNCES (SERVES 4-6)

JUICE
3 medium apples, peeled and quartered
2 medium cucumbers, unpeeled and quartered
1 whole head green kale, washed thoroughly

Straight up—I love green juice! I try to have one every day, and when I don't get my fix, I can feel the effects. It's like having all your vitamins in a glass with a sweet, earthy, mild taste. Juicing allows our digestive systems to rest, so our bodies can disperse the juice's healing energy to other areas that really need it. Green juice provides living enzymes, pure oxygen, vitamins, minerals and high levels of chlorophyll and phytonutrients. It is very alkaline, helping to restore the body to a balanced pH level, which is important for maintaining optimal health.

Make the juice
1. The trick for not getting your juicer clogged up is alternating ingredients, so the more fibrous vegetables go through easily.
2. Start with apple, kale, cucumber, kale, and repeat until all ingredients are juiced. Pour into pitcher, stir, and serve immediately.

Note: Recommend drinking immediately for ultimate enzymatic benefits, but can be stored up to 3 days in refrigerator in airtight container. Will lose a small amount of enzymes each day it's kept in refrigerator.

GINGER ROOT, PINEAPPLE, AND **BEET** JUICE

MAKES 32 OUNCES (SERVES 4-6)

JUICE

3 medium fresh beets, green tops removed
1 medium ripe pineapple, quartered
1-inch piece fresh ginger root

Make juice
1. In preferred electrical juicer, juice beets, pineapple and ginger root. Stir and pour into glasses. Serve immediately.

Note: Recommend drinking immediately for ultimate enzymatic benefits, but can be stored up to 3 days in refrigerator in airtight container. Will lose a small amount of enzymes each day it's kept in refrigerator.

APPLE, **CARROT**, AND KIWI JUICE

MAKES 32 OUNCES (SERVES 4-6)

JUICE

12 medium carrots, unpeeled
3 medium apples, quartered
4 ripe kiwis, peeled

Make juice
1. In preferred electrical juicer, juice carrots, apples and kiwis. Stir and pour into glasses. Serve immediately.

Note: Recommend drinking immediately for ultimate enzymatic benefits, but can be stored up to 3 days in refrigerator in airtight container. Will lose a small amount of enzymes each day it's kept in refrigerator.

PINEAPPLE, CUCUMBER, BROCCOLI, AND SPINACH JUICE

MAKES 32 OUNCES (SERVES 4-6)

JUICE
4 cups broccoli, chopped
4 cups fresh spinach, washed thoroughly
1 medium ripe pineapple, rind removed and quartered
1 medium cucumber, unpeeled and quartered

Make juice
1. In preferred electrical juicer, juice broccoli, spinach, pineapple, and cucumber. Stir and pour into glasses. Serve immediately.

Note: Recommend drinking immediately for ultimate enzymatic benefits, but can be stored up to 3 days in refrigerator in airtight container. Will lose a small amount of enzymes each day it's kept in refrigerator.

PARSLEY, KALE, CELERY, APPLE, GINGER, AND LEMON JUICE

MAKES 32 OUNCES (SERVES 4-6)

JUICE
1 head green kale, washed thoroughly
1 cup fresh parsley, tightly packed
1 medium cucumber, unpeeled and quartered
3 medium apples
4 ribs fresh celery
1 fresh lemon, peeled
4 medium cloves garlic, peeled
1½-inch piece fresh ginger root

Make juice
1. In preferred electrical juicer, juice kale, parsley, cucumber, apples, celery, lemon, garlic and ginger. Stir and pour into glasses. Serve immediately.

Note: Recommend drinking immediately for ultimate enzymatic benefits, but can be stored up to 3 days in refrigerator in airtight container. Will lose a small amount of enzymes each day it's kept in refrigerator.

GREEN APPLE, CUCUMBER, AND PINEAPPLE, MINT JUICE

MAKES 32 OUNCES (SERVES 4-6)

JUICE
2 medium green apples, unpeeled
1 medium ripe pineapple, rind removed and quartered
1 medium cucumber, unpeeled and quarterd
1/2 cup fresh mint leaves, tightly packed

Make the juice
1. In preferred electrical juicer, juice green apples, pineapple, cucumber and mint. Stir and pour into glasses. Serve immediately.

Note: Recommend drinking immediately for ultimate enzymatic benefits, but can be stored up to 3 days in refrigerator in airtight container. Will lose a small amount of enzymes each day it's kept in refrigerator.

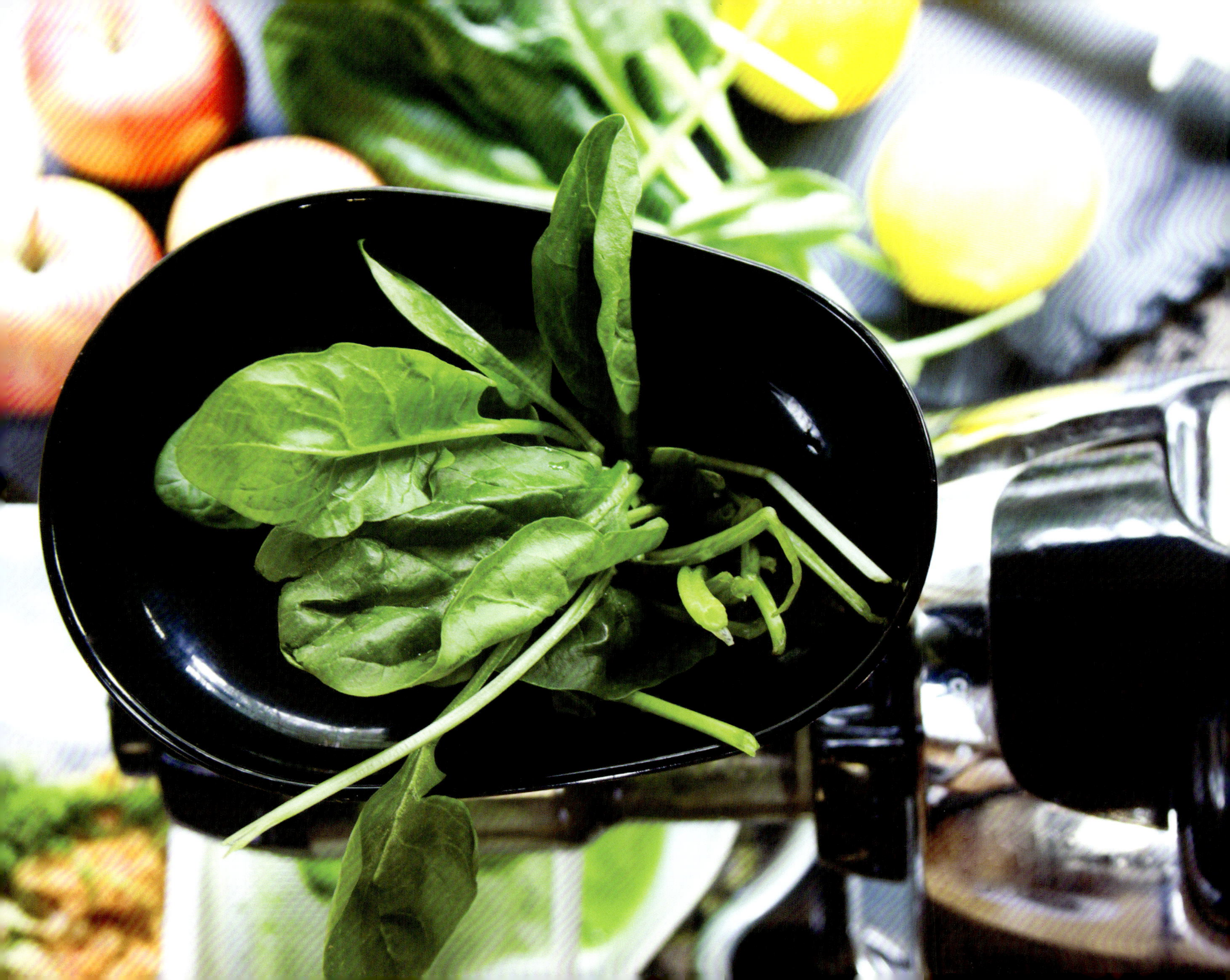

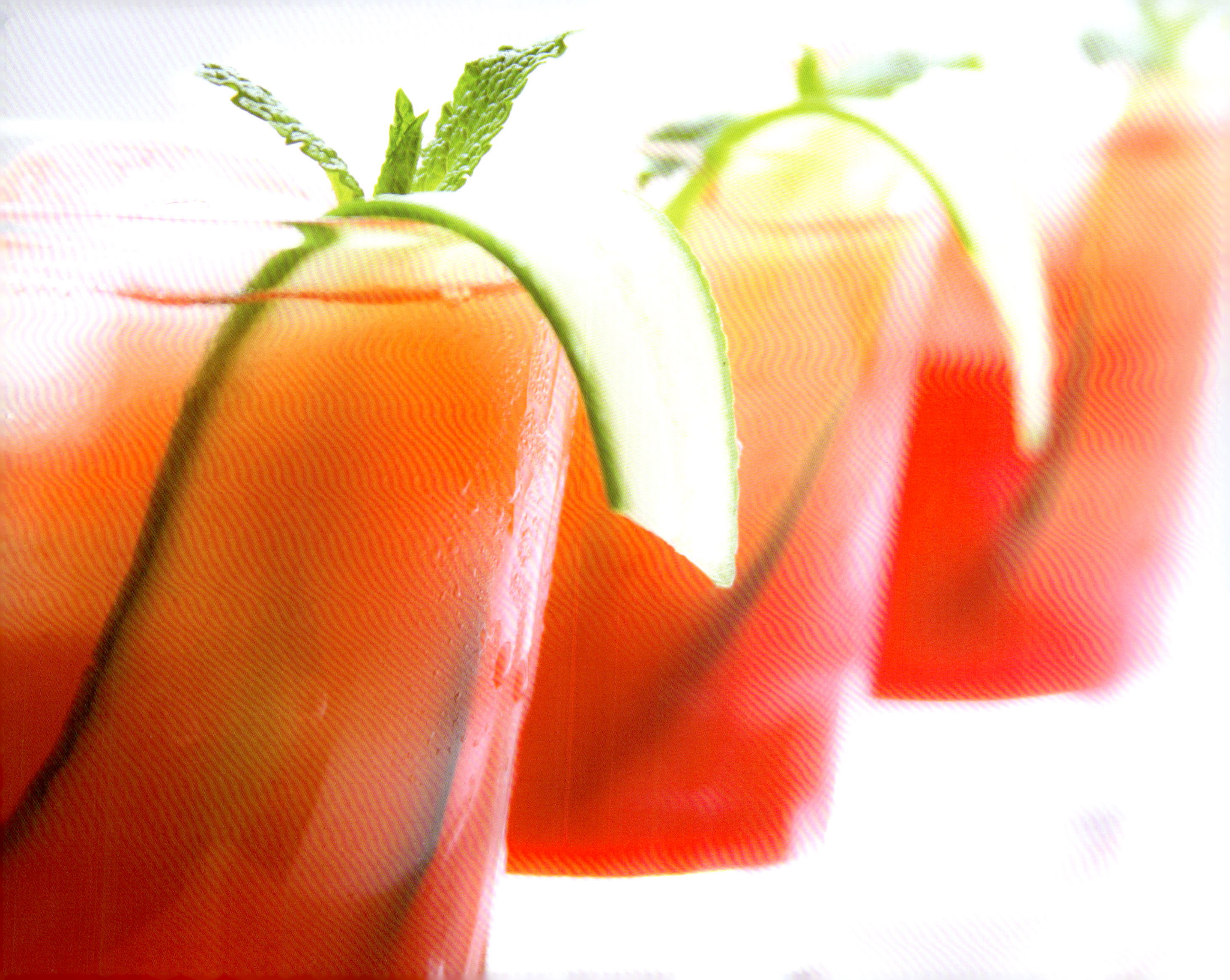

FRESH-PRESSED WATERMELON JUICE, MINT, AND SLICED CUCUMBER

MAKES 32 OUNCES (SERVES 4-6)

JUICE
6 cups watermelon, rind removed, cubed
1 medium cucumber, unpeeled and thinly sliced
4 fresh mint sprigs
ice cubes

This naturally sweet juice needs no added sugar and is incredibly hydrating. Perfect on a hot summer day served poolside over ice with a sprig of mint and fresh cucumber.

Make the juice
1. In preferred electrical juicer, juice watermelon.
2. Fill glasses with ice, pour juice and garnish with fresh mint sprigs and sliced cucumber. Serve immediately.

Note: Recommend drinking immediately for ultimate enzymatic benefits, but can be stored up to 3 days in refrigerator in airtight container. Will lose a small amount of enzymes each day it's kept in refrigerator.

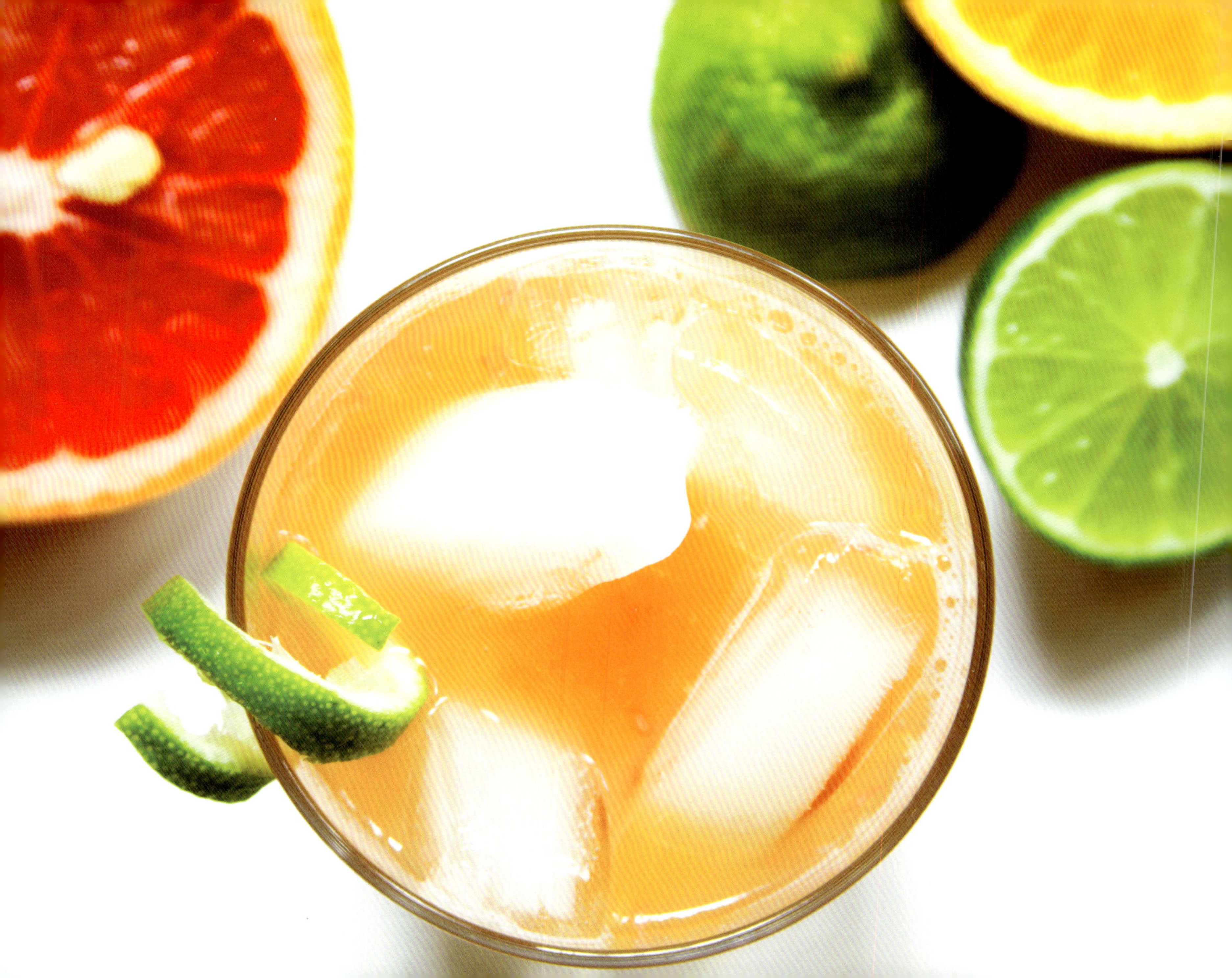

RUBY RED **GRAPEFRUIT**, ORANGE, AND REFRESHING LIME JUICE

MAKES 32 OUNCES (SERVES 4-6)

JUICE
4 large ruby red grapefruits, peeled
6 oranges, peeled
1 lime, peeled

Tart ruby red grapefruit, sweet orange, and refreshing lime, blend together to create a beautiful, thirst-quenching beverage that is loaded with vitamin C, creating a super charged, immune boosting, winter citrus juice.

Make the juice
1. In preferred juicer, juice grapefruits, oranges and lime. Serve over ice immediately. Sometimes when juicing whole citrus in an electrical juicer the pith can make it bitter the next day. If you're planning on drinking it for a few days, cut fruits in half and juice in citrus juicer.

Note: Recommend drinking immediately for ultimate enzymatic benefits, but can be stored up to 3 days in refrigerator in airtight container. Will lose a small amount of enzymes each day it's kept in refrigerator.

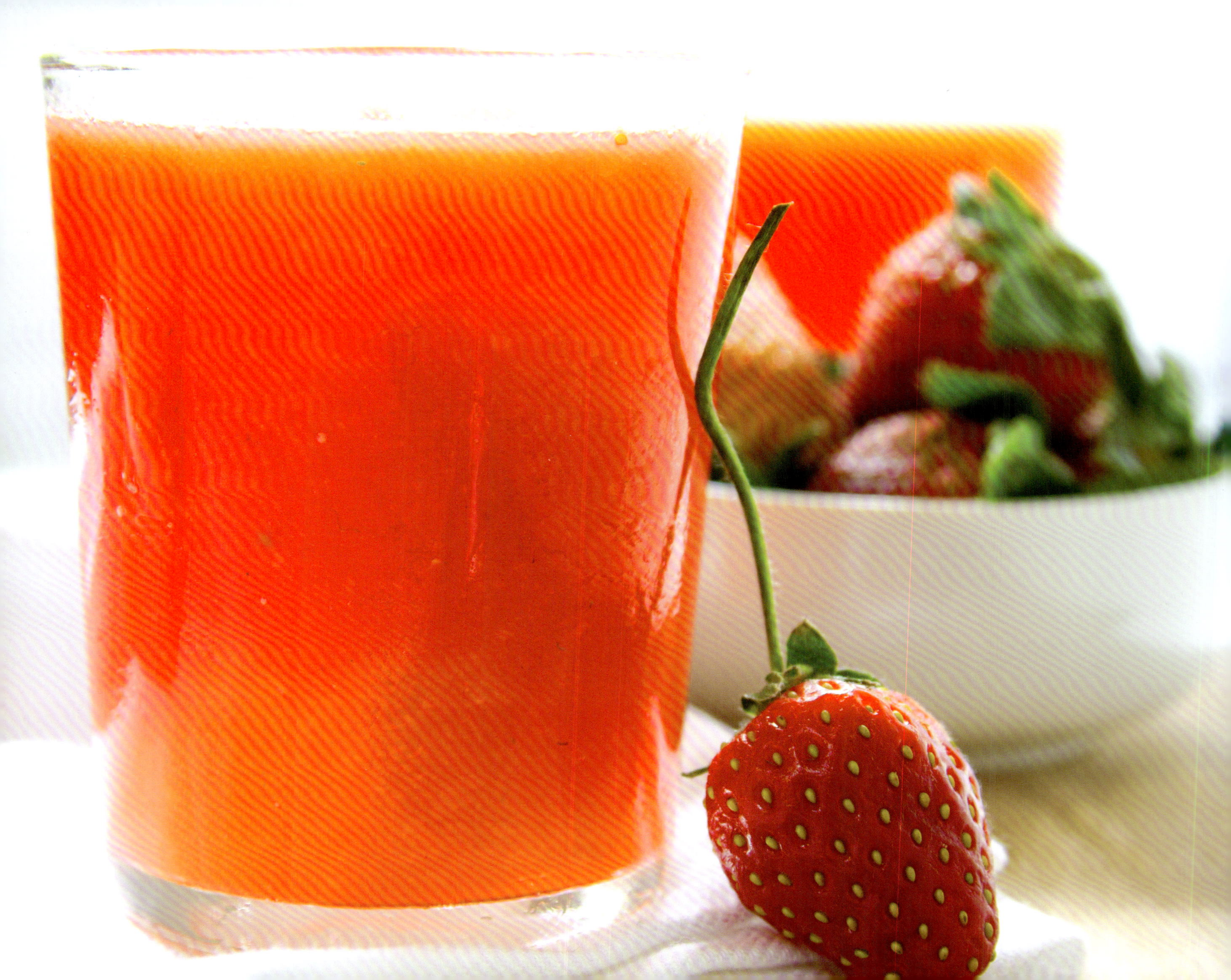

ORANGE, HAWAIIAN PAPAYA, AND STRAWBERRY JUICE

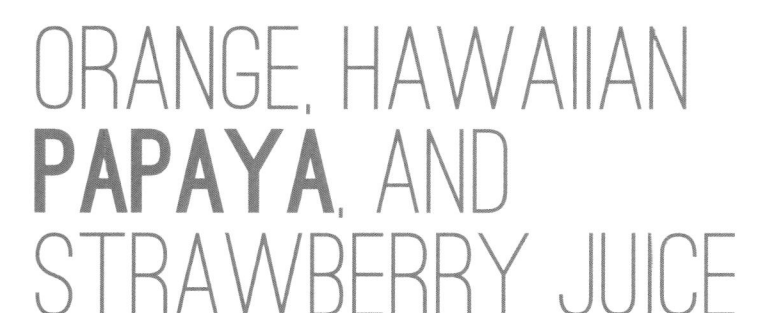

MAKES 32 OUNCES (SERVES 4-6)

JUICE

7 oranges, peeled
2 cups ripe strawberries, tops removed
1 medium ripe Hawaiian papaya, peeled, with seeds removed

While planning for a trip to Hawaii, my friend Molly and I decided to do a five-day juice feast. I packed my juicer in my carry-on along with my swimsuit and flip-flops and off we went. The abundance of fresh produce on the islands made it easy to make the most beautiful juices. Every few days we would wake up at the crack of dawn and walk to the local farmers market for the best selection of fresh fruits and vegetables of the day. This was one of our favorite fruit juices. The papaya adds a thick, smoothie-like texture, creating a very satisfying and filling juice.

Make the juice
1. In preferred electrical juicer, juice oranges, strawberries and papaya. This juice will have a beautiful marbled effect. Do not stir.
2. Pour into glasses and serve immediately.

Note: Recommend drinking immediately for ultimate enzymatic benefits, but can be stored up to 3 days in refrigerator in airtight container. Will lose a small amount of enzymes each day it's kept in refrigerator.

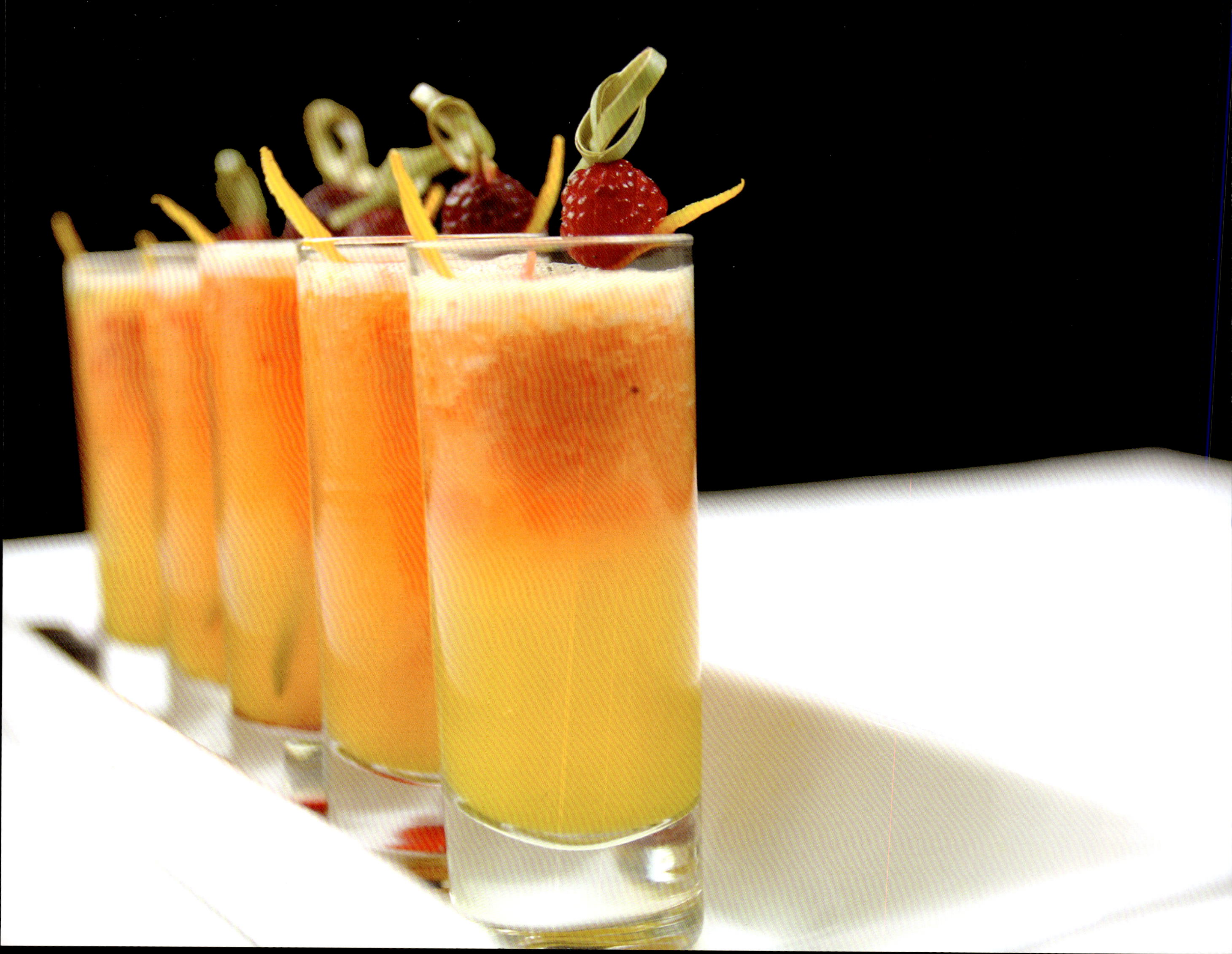

PINEAPPLE, AND SUMMER RASPBERRY JUICE

MAKES 32 OUNCES (SERVES 4-6)

JUICE
2 ripe pineapples, rind removed and quartered
3 cups fresh raspberries

This vibrant juice has an array of colors that resembles a dazzling Hawaiian sunset.

Make the juice
1. In preferred electrical juicer, juice pineapple and raspberries. To keep the beautiful stacked colors, do not stir.
2. Slowly pour into glasses and serve immediately.

Note: Recommend drinking immediately for ultimate enzymatic benefits but can be stored up to 3 days in refrigerator in airtight container. Will lose a small amount of enzymes each day it's kept in refrigerator.

I N F U S

E D H 2 0

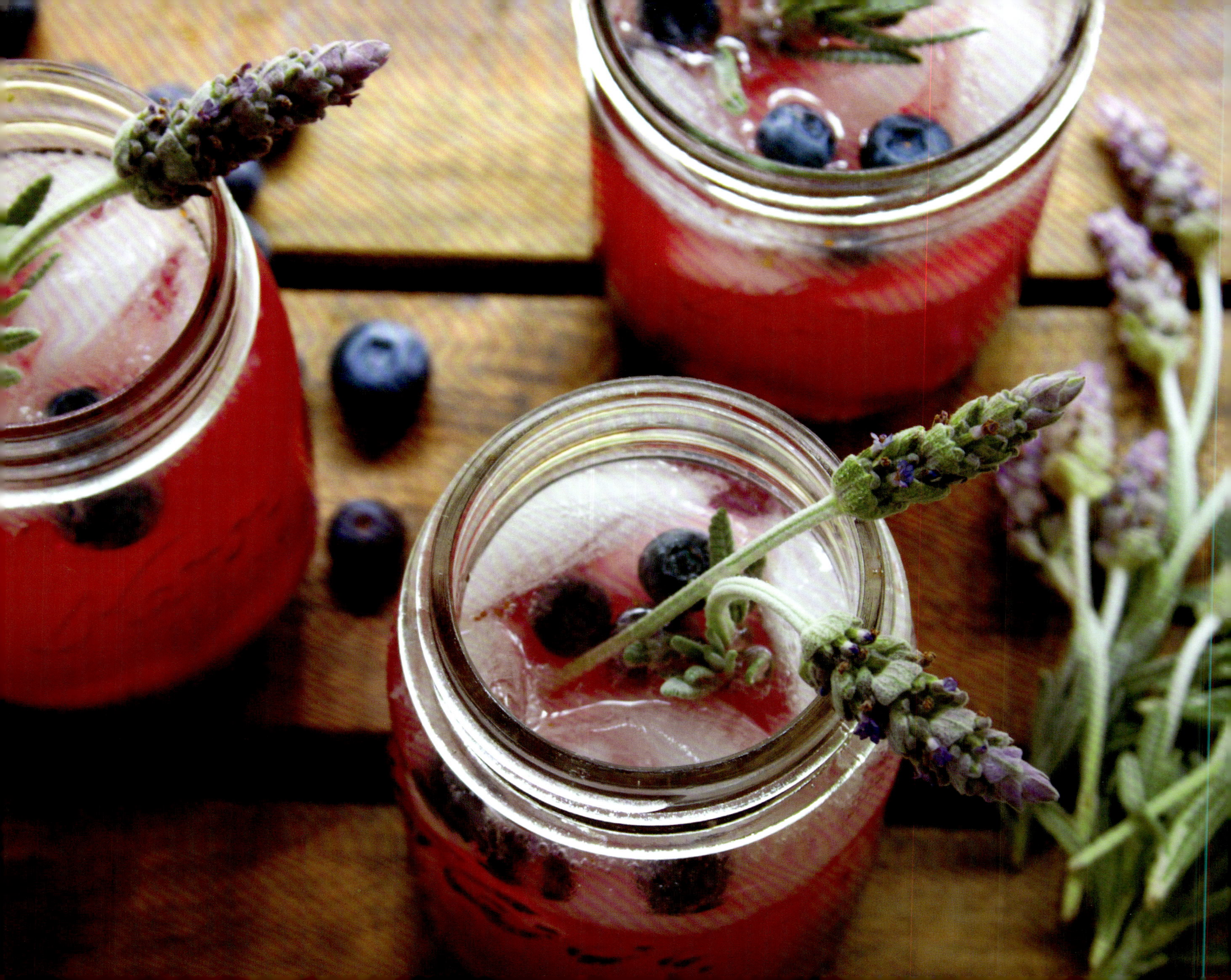

FRAGRANT LAVENDER, AND BLUEBERRY LEMONADE

MAKES 32 OUNCES (SERVES 4-6)

LEMONADE
2 cups boiling water
1 cup cold water
3/4 cup light raw agave
1/2 cup lemon juice, fresh-squeezed
1/2 cup fresh blueberries
2 tablespoons edible dried lavender

The aromatic floral essence of lavender combined with sweet, ripe blueberries creates a refreshing cocktail perfect for sipping on a hot summer day.

Make the lemonade
1. Steep dried lavender in boiling water for 30 minutes.
2. While the lavender is steeping, juice lemons.
3. In a large pitcher, place blueberries and agave then lightly mash with fork. Add lemon juice and fresh water, stir with wooden spoon.
4. When lavender is done steeping, discard buds and pour lavender water over blueberries. Stir with wooden spoon and place in refrigerator for 1–2 hours to chill. Serve over ice with a few fresh whole blueberries and lavender sprigs.

Note: Keeps in refrigerator up to 3 days in airtight container.

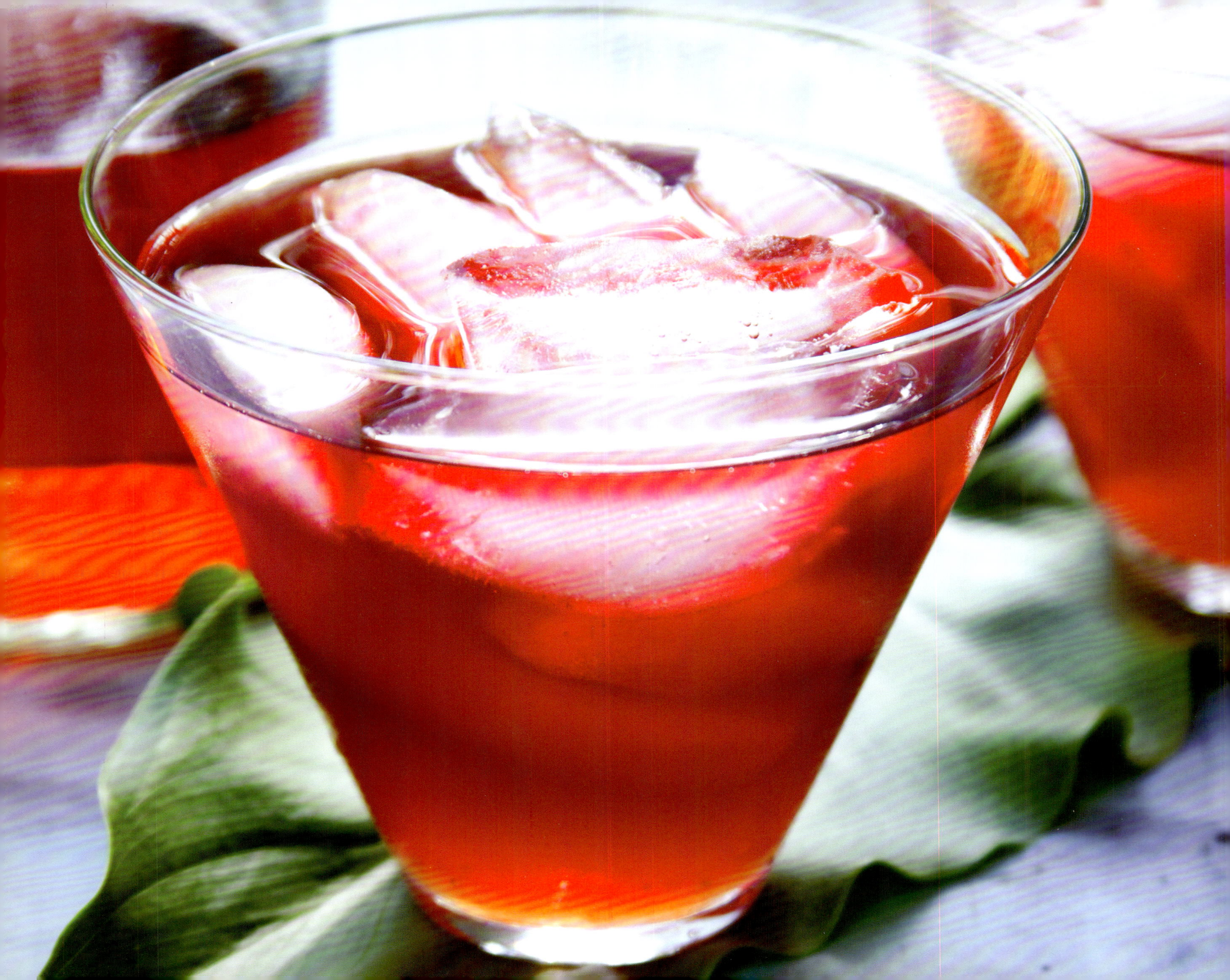

FRESH-SQUEEZED LEMON, AGAVE, AND HIBISCUS FLOWERS

MAKES 32 OUNCES (SERVES 4-6)

LEMONADE

3 cups water
1/2 cup lemon juice, fresh-squeezed
1/4 cup dried hibiscus flowers
1/4 cups raw light agave

When I was on Vieqes Island off Puerto Rico, I took a kayaking trip to an incredible bioluminescent bay. While I was paddling through lush jungle-lined canals, beautiful hibiscus flowers in red, pink, orange, and yellow were falling like snowflakes from the trees, leaving a picturesque scene on the rippling water. Our guide began to tell us about all the healing benefits of the hibiscus flower. I was immediately intrigued. After paddling in the hot sun all day, I developed an uncontrollable thirst for a refreshing lemonade. The only problem was we were in the middle of the jungle. I started daydreaming about all the different kinds of lemonade I could create, and the first one that came to mind was a gorgeous hot-pink hibiscus lemonade to quench my thirst.

Make the lemonade
1. Pour water and dried hibiscus flowers in a large pitcher or jar. Let stand for 1-2 hours to steep.
2. Strain hibiscus water through nut-milk bag or mesh strainer.
3. Add lemon juice and agave to pitcher and stir with spoon until well combined. Serve over ice immediately.

Note: Keeps in refrigerator up to 3 days in airtight container.

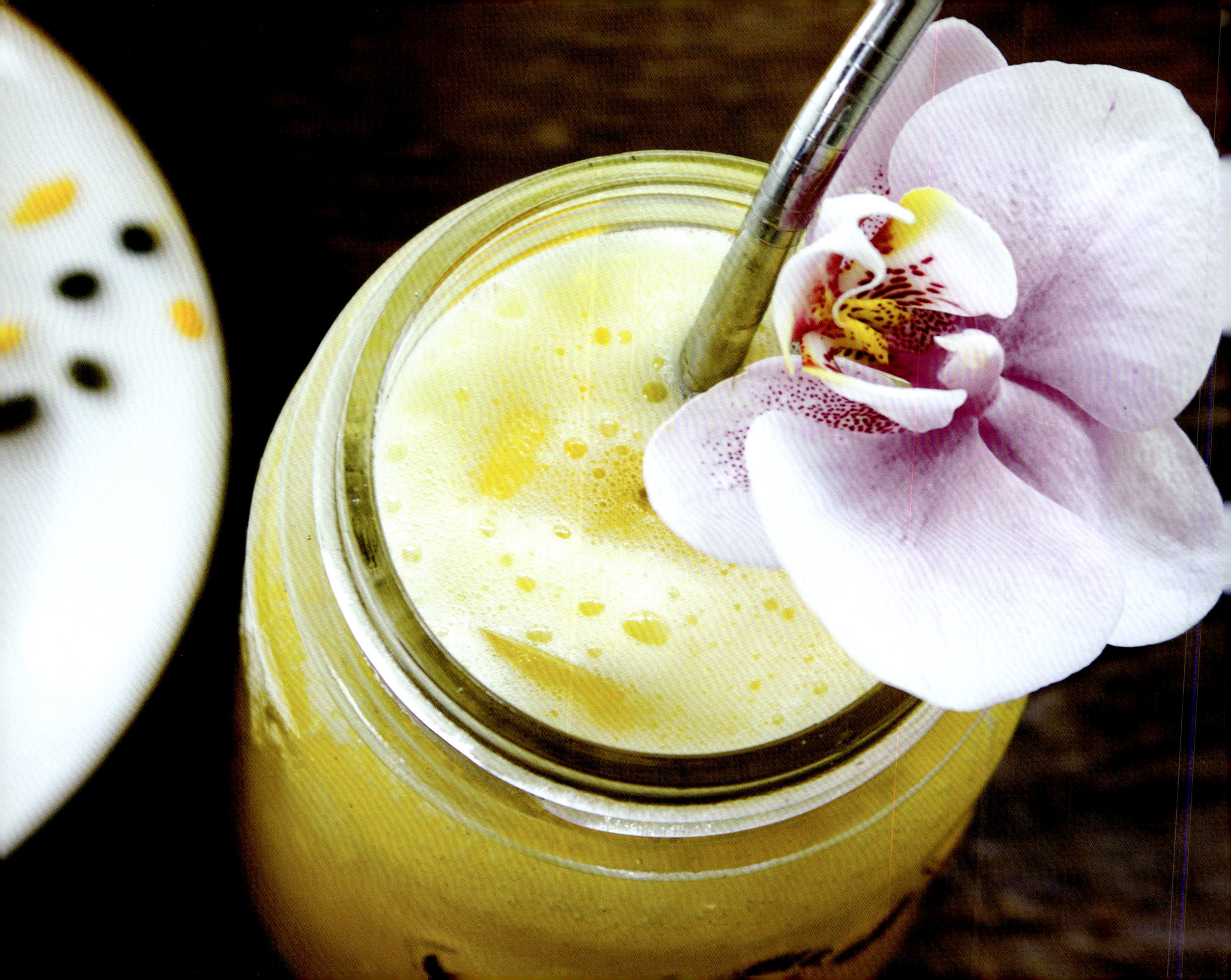

PASSION FRUIT LEMONADE SWEETENED WITH MANUKA HONEY

MAKES 32 OUNCES (SERVES 4-6)

LEMONADE
8 cups water
1 fresh passion fruit, skin removed, juiced
or 1/2 cup unsweetened passion fruit puree
2 cups lemon juice, fresh-squeezed
1/4 cup manuka honey or light raw agave

Passion fruits contain a natural antianxiety compound that helps with relieving stress. If you've had a long day and need to unwind, this is the perfect fruity beverage to help calm the nerves.

Make the lemonade
1. In preferred juicer, juice lemons and passion fruit.
2. Place all ingredients in large pitcher and stir with spoon until well combined. Serve over ice and garnish with edible orchid flowers.

Note: Keeps in refrigerator up to 3 days in airtight container.

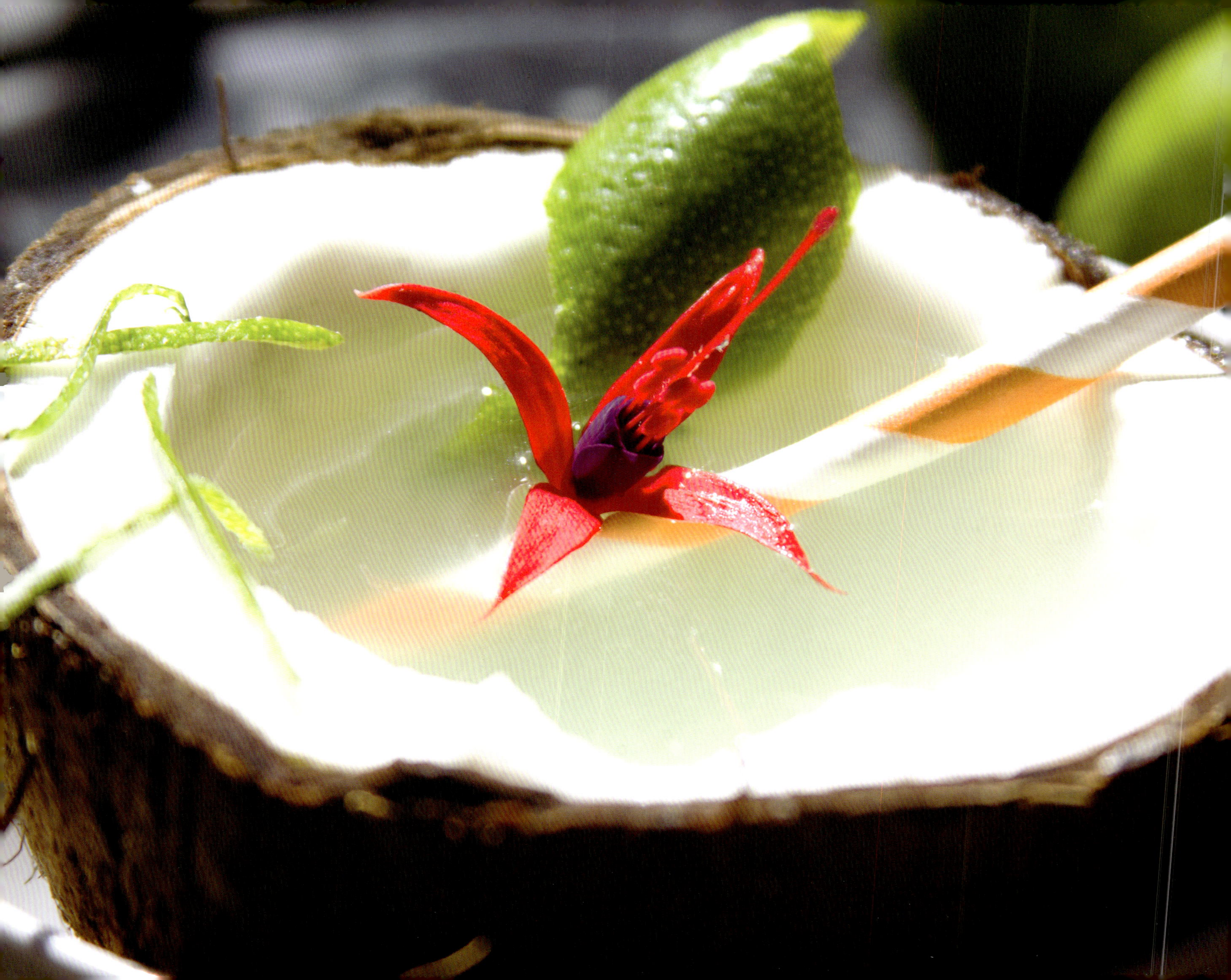

COCONUT-INFUSED FRESH-SQUEEZED LIMEADE

MAKES 32 OUNCES (SERVES 4-6)

LIMEADE
3 cups water
1/2 cup lime juice, fresh-squeezed
1/3 cup raw light agave
1/2 teaspoon coconut extract

This refreshing sweet-tart limeade has an essence of coconut that will transport you to a tropical paradise.

Make the limeade
1. In preferred juicer, juice limes.
2. In large pitcher add lime juice, water, agave, and coconut extract. Stir with spoon and pour over ice. Serve immediately.

Note: Keeps in refrigerator up to 3 days in airtight container.

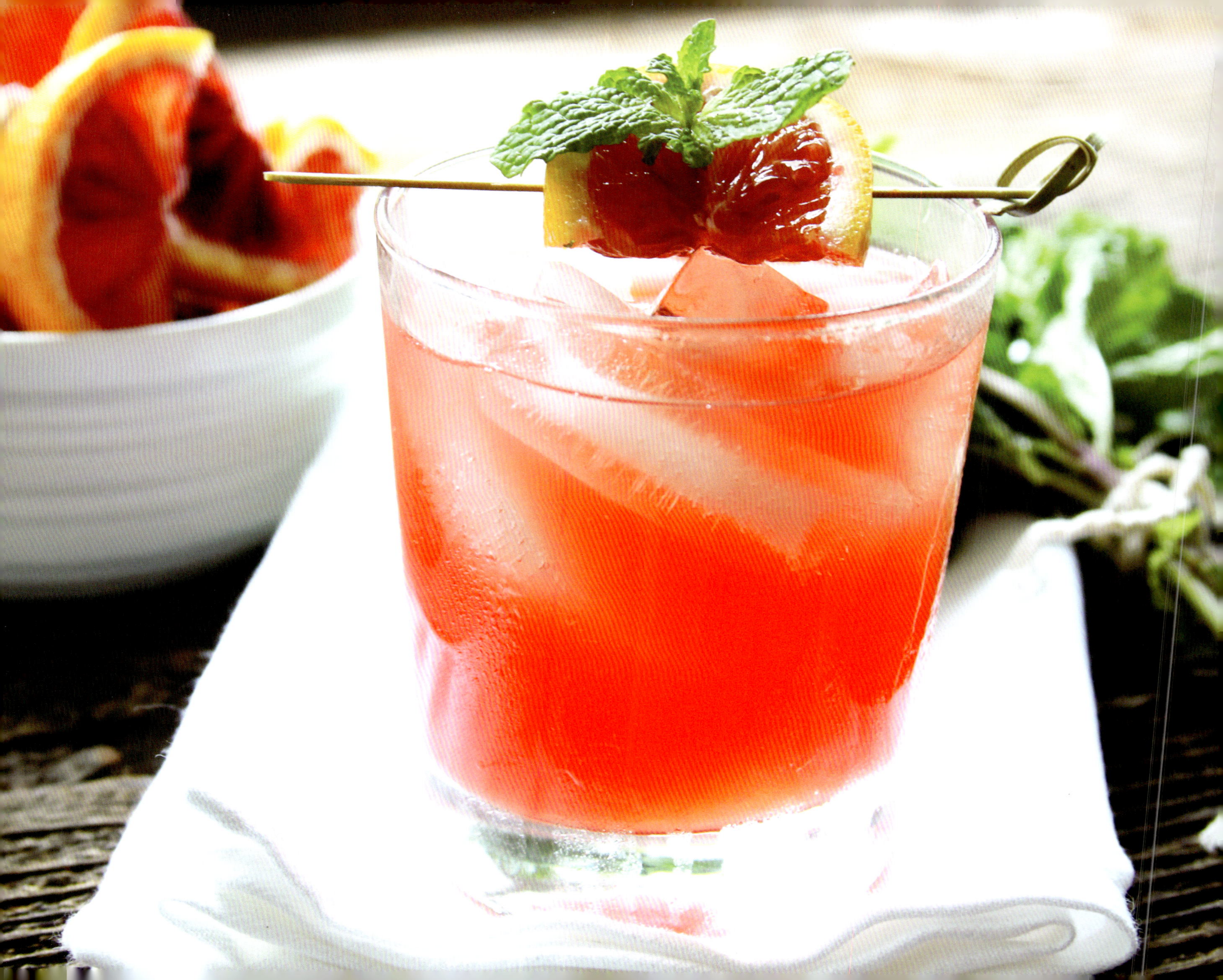

SPARKLING WATER, LIME, **BLOOD ORANGE**, AND FRESH MINT

MAKES 32 OUNCES (SERVES 4-6)

COCKTAIL
2 cups blood orange juice, fresh-squeezed
2 cups sparkling water
2 cups crushed ice
1/4 cup lime juice, fresh-squeezed
1/4 cups tightly packed, fresh mint leaves
3 tablespoons light raw agave

The exploding fiery colors of a blood orange are equally visually stunning as they are delicious. In this cocktail, sweet crimson-colored juice mixed with tart lime and minty sparkling water make it the perfect nonalcoholic drink.

Make the cocktail
1. In preferred juicer, juice blood oranges and limes separately.
2. In large pitcher add, fresh mint, agave and crushed ice. Muddle until just combined.
3. Add blood orange juice, sparkling water and lime juice. Stir with spoon and pour into glasses. Serve immediately.

Note: Blood-orange and lime juice keep in refrigerator up to 2 days in airtight container.

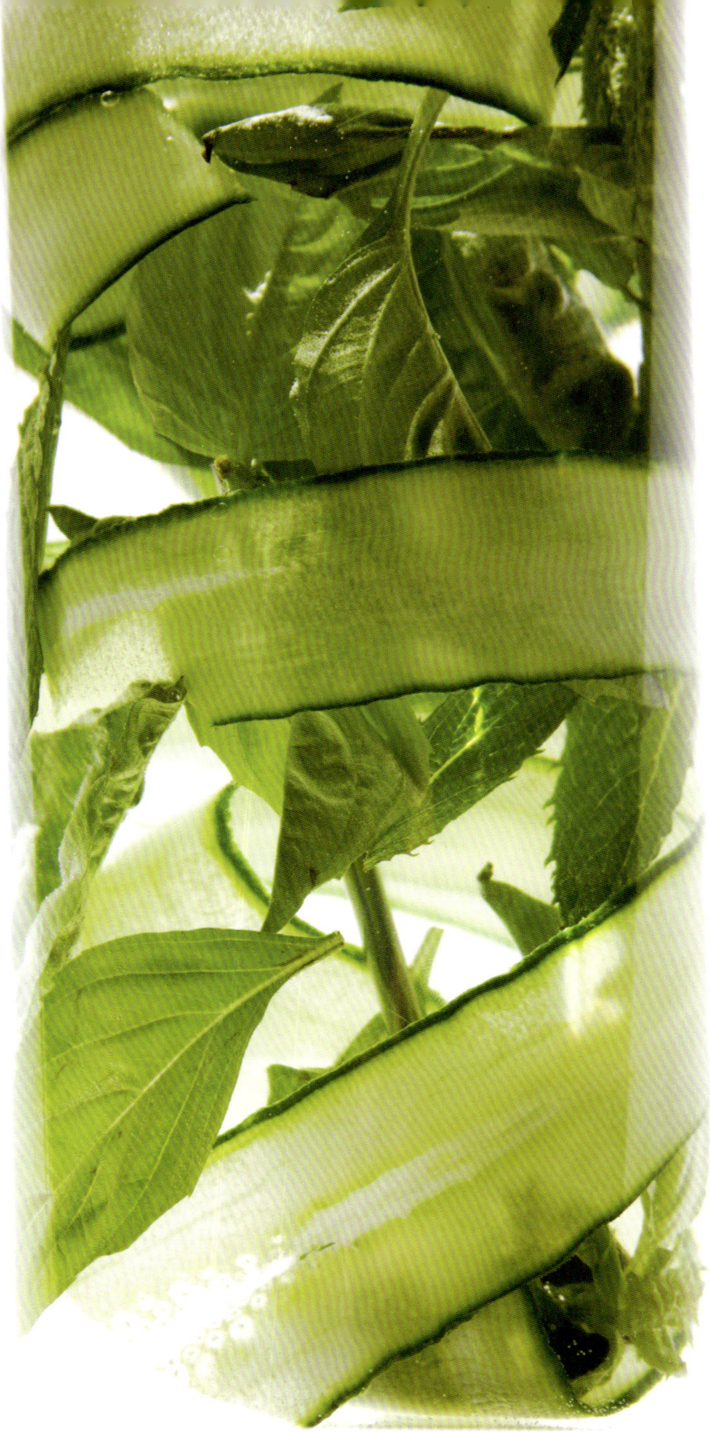

WATER, **BASIL**, HYDRATING CUCUMBER, AND MINT

MAKES 32 OUNCES (SERVES 4-6)

WATER
4 cups fresh water
1/2 cup fresh mint leaves, loosely packed
1/2 cup English cucumber, unpeeled and sliced thin lengthwise
1/2 cup fresh basil leaves, stems removed and tightly packed

Here's a fun and tasty way to liven up your daily dose of water with added hydration and nutrition. Keep a pitcher of this in your fridge at all times. I suggest doubling the recipe!

Make the water
1. Pour water into large pitcher. Add mint, cucumber and basil.
2. Cover and store in refrigerator 2-3 hours to let the flavors infuse.

Note: Keeps in refrigerator up to 4 days in covered pitcher just keep adding fresh water to the pitcher with mint, basil and cucumber.

S M O O

T H I E S

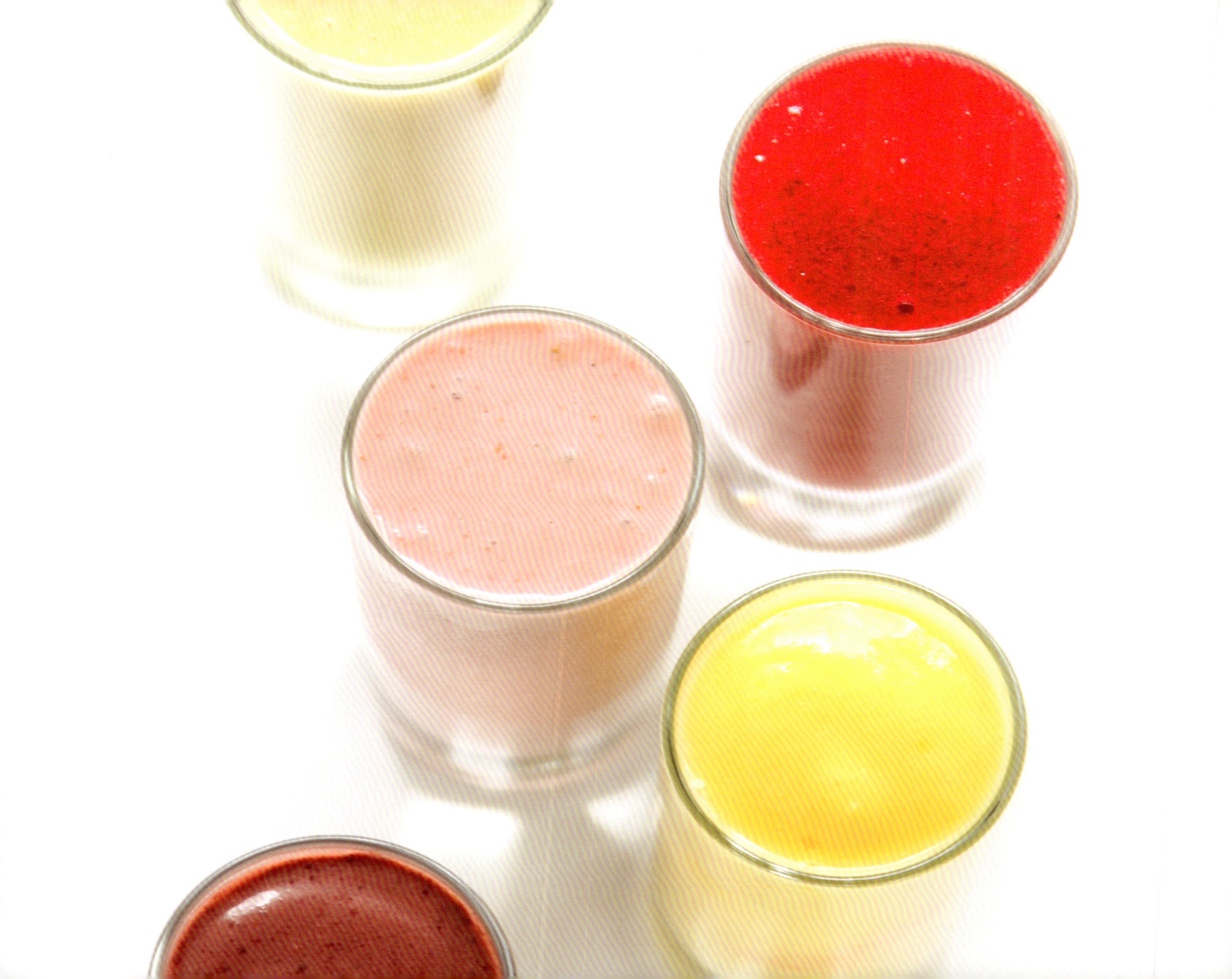

GOJI BERRY, GOLDEN PEACH, AND PURE ACAI

MAKES 32 OUNCES (SERVES 4-6)

SMOOTHIE

1 ½ cups vanilla almond milk (see page 76)
1 ½ cups frozen unsweetened berries
1 (3 ½ ounce) packet organic unsweetened pure acai
2 medium fresh peaches, pitted and unpeeled
2 tablespoons dried goji berries
1 ½ tablespoons light raw agave
2 teaspoons golden flax seeds, ground

Make the smoothie
1. In high-speed blender place almond milk, frozen berries, acai, peaches, goji berries, agave and ground flax. Blend on high about 1 minute, until goji berries are broken down and consistency is thick, smooth, and creamy. Serve immediately.

Note: Keeps in refrigerator up to 2 days in airtight container.

SWEET MANGO AND COCONUT CREAM WITH PINEAPPLE AND PAPAYA

MAKES 32 OUNCES (SERVES 4-6)

SMOOTHIE

1 ½ cups coconut cream (see page 74)
1 medium papaya, flesh only, seeds removed
1 cup frozen pineapple
1 cup frozen mango
1 tablespoon raw honey or light raw agave

Make the smoothie
1. In high-speed blender place coconut cream, papaya, pineapple, mango and honey. Blend on high for about 1 minute, until smooth and creamy. Serve immediately.

Note: Keeps in refrigerator up to 2 days in airtight container.

SWEET CREAM, VANILLA, AND STRAWBERRIES

MAKES 32 OUNCES (SERVES 4-6)

SMOOTHIE

2 cups frozen strawberries
1 ½ cups coconut cream (see page 74)
2 tablespoons light raw agave nectar
2 tablespoons golden flaxseed, ground
1 teaspoon vanilla extract

Make the smoothie
1. In high-speed blender place strawberries, coconut cream, agave, ground flax seeds and vanilla. Blend on high for about 1 minute, until consistency is smooth and creamy. Serve immediately.

Note: Keeps in refrigerator up to 2 days in airtight container.

TANGY ORANGE, BANANA, AND HOT PINK BEET

MAKES 32 OUNCES (SERVES 4-6)

SMOOTHIE

5 oranges, peeled
2 frozen bananas
1 cup crushed ice
1/4 cup beet juice, freshly juiced

Make the smoothie
1. In high-speed blender place oranges, frozen bananas, beet juice and ice. Blend on high for about 1 minute, until smooth and creamy. Serve immediately.

Note: Keeps in refrigerator up to 2 days in airtight container.

RAW PISTACHIOS, CANTALOUPE, HONEYDEW, AND WILD HONEY

MAKES 32 OUNCES (SERVES 4-6)

SMOOTHIE

1 ½ cups frozen cantaloupe
1 cup frozen honeydew melon
1/2 cup orange juice, fresh-squeezed
1/4 cup raw pistachios, shelled, meat only
1 tablespoon wild honey or raw light agave

Make the smoothie

1. In high-speed blender place frozen cantaloupe, frozen honeydew, orange juice, pistachios and honey. Blend on high for about 1 minute, until smooth and creamy. Pour into glasses and garnish with pistachios and a drizzle of honey.

Note: Keeps in refrigerator up to 2 days in airtight container.

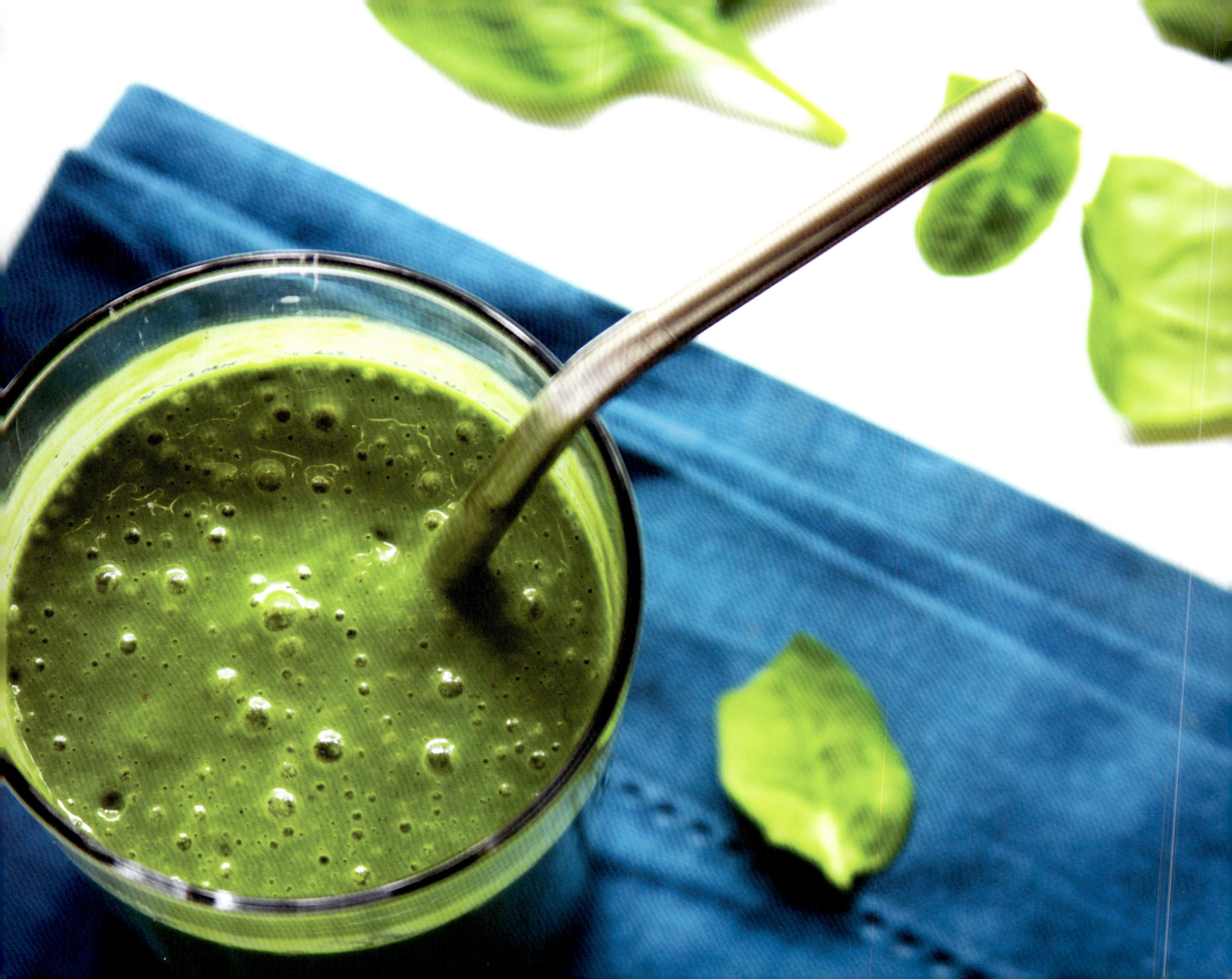

FRESH SPINACH, BANANA, MANGO, PINEAPPLE, AND SPIRULINA

MAKES 32 OUNCES (SERVES 4-6)

SMOOTHIE
1 ½ cups vanilla almond milk (see page 76)
1 cup fresh spinach, tightly packed
1 cup frozen pineapple
1 medium frozen banana
1/2 cup frozen mango
1 tablespoon raw light agave
1 teaspoon spirulina powder

Almost every morning I like to start my day with an icy green smoothie. It allows the digestive system to wake up while giving a blast of energy to the bodies cells. There are hundreds of green smoothie variations to create; however, this is one of my favorites.

Make the smoothie

1. In high-speed blender place almond milk, spinach, frozen pineapple, banana, mango, agave, and spirulina. Blend on high for about 1 minute, until spinach is broken down and smoothie is thick and creamy. Pour into glasses and serve immediately.

Note: Keeps in refrigerator up to 2 days in airtight container.

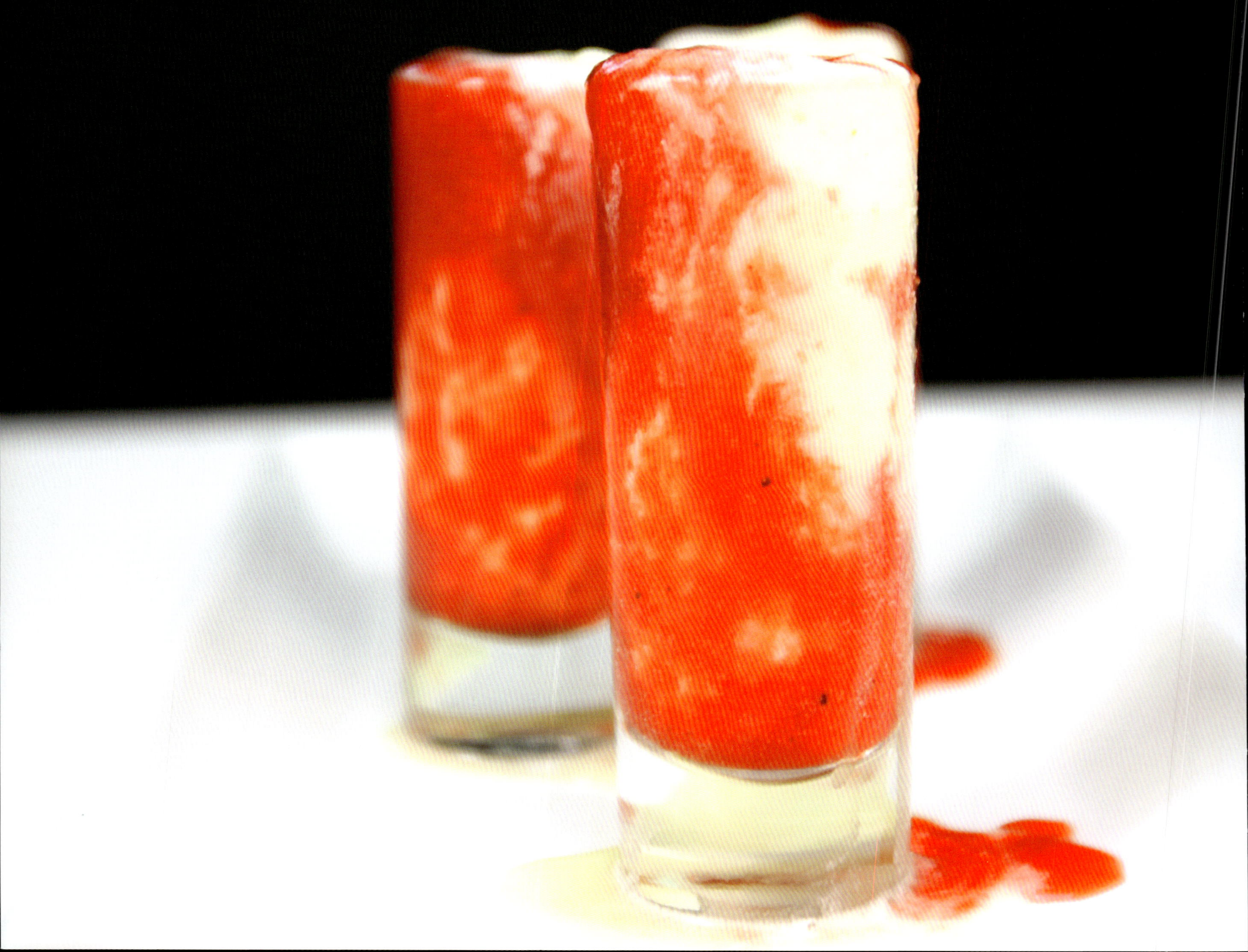

CREAMY COCONUT, PINEAPPLE, AND STRAWBERRY PUREE

MAKES 32 OUNCES (SERVES 4-6)

LAVA

1 cup fresh strawberries, tops removed and quartered
1 tablespoon light raw agave
1/2 teaspoon vanilla extract

COLADA

1 ½ cups frozen pineapple
1 cup coconut cream (see page 74)
3 tablespoons light raw agave
1 cup crushed ice

With a bright red strawberry puree flowing down into a creamy frozen pineapple-coconut smoothie this tropical drink is perfect served poolside with a cute cocktail umbrella and pineapple wedge.

Make the lava
1. In high-speed blender place strawberries, agave and vanilla. Blend on high for about 30 seconds, until strawberries are broken down and smooth. Pour into glasses of choice and rinse out blender carafe for the colada.

Make the colada
1. In high-speed blender place frozen pineapple, coconut cream, agave, and ice. Blend on high for about 1 minute, until smooth and creamy. Pour into glasses on top of red lava.

Note: Keeps in refrigerator up to 2 days in airtight container.

MILKS

C R E A M

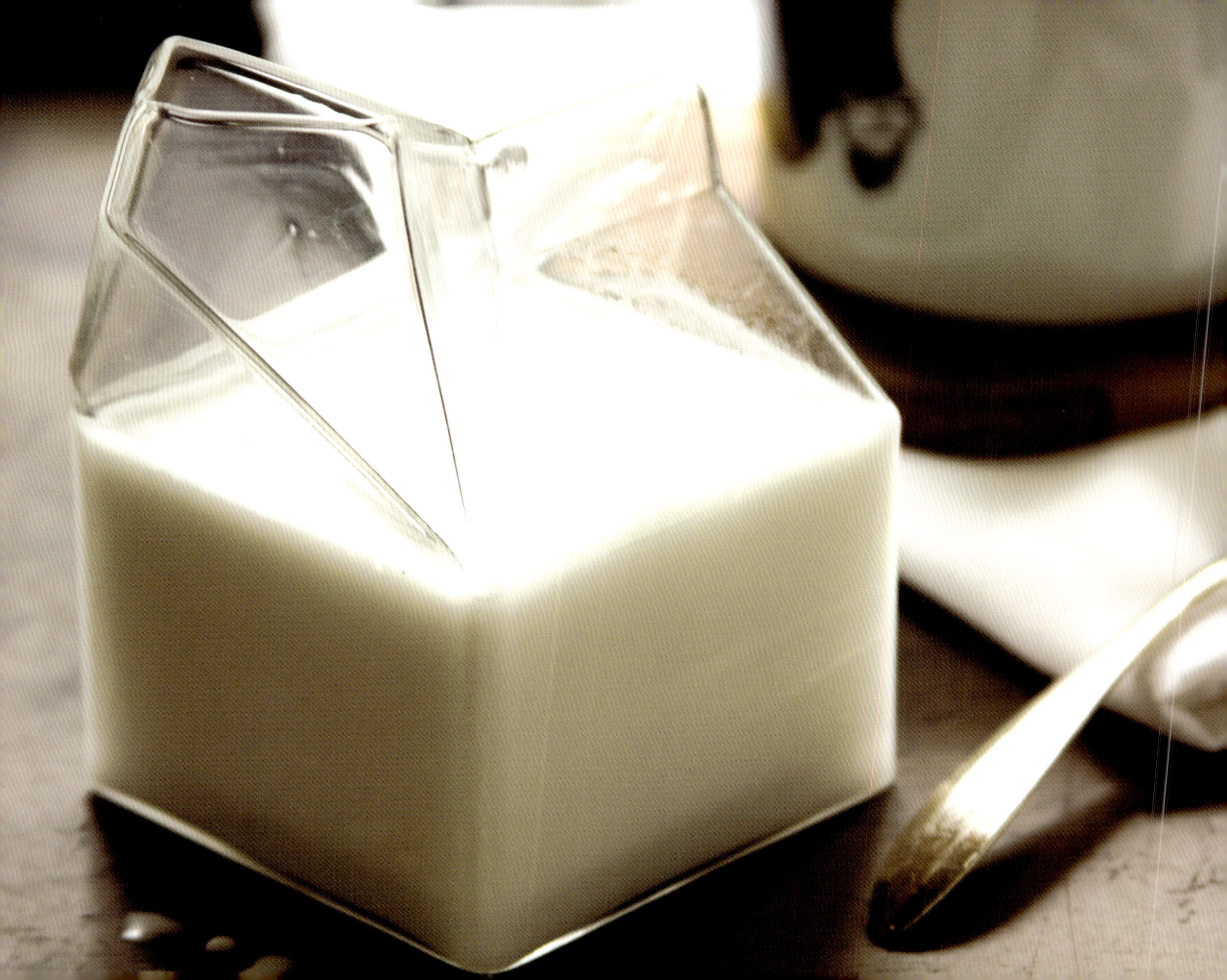

FRESH COCONUT CREAM

MAKES 48 OUNCES

CREAM
5 cups unsweetened raw coconut, shredded, soaked 1 hour
4 cups water

I am obsessed with anything coconut, so naturally I had to put this dairy-free alternative in this book. It's perfect as a base for soups, ice cream, poured over granola, or stirred into coffee or tea.

Make the cream
1. Soak shredded coconut in 4 cups water for 1 hour, so it breaks down easier in the blender.
2. In high-speed blender place shredded coconut, and soaking water. Blend on high for about 2 minutes, until thick and creamy. The coconut pulp won't fully break down, so don't get discouraged.
3. Over a bowl strain cream through nut-milk bag and squeeze from top to bottom until most of the liquid is removed and coconut pulp is slightly dry. Reserve pulp for coconut flour in other recipes.

Note: Keeps in refrigerator up to 4 days in airtight container.

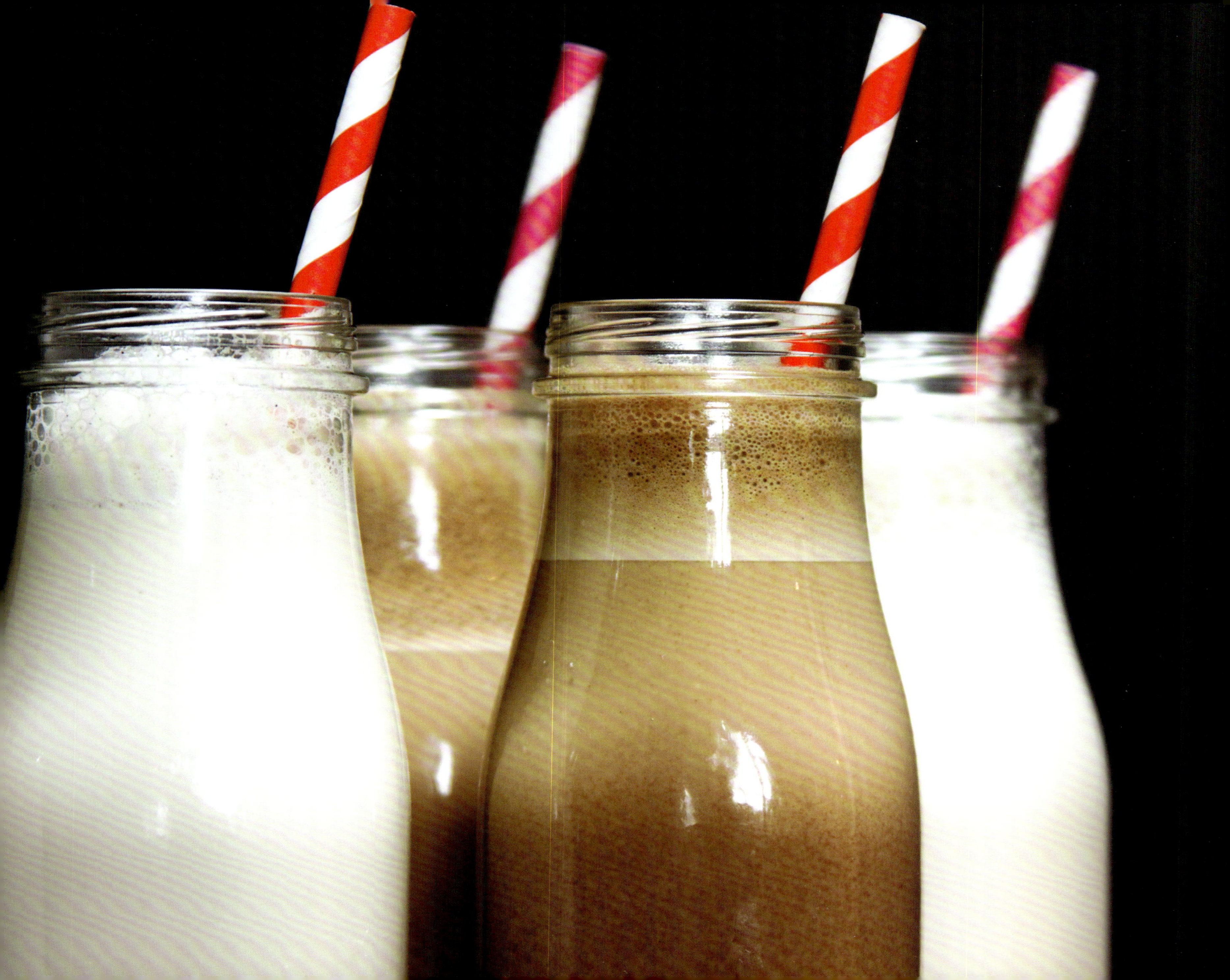

CREAMY VANILLA ALMOND MILK

MAKES 44 OUNCES (SERVES 4-6)

MILK
4 cups water
2 cups raw almonds, soaked 8–10 hours, drained and rinsed
2 ½ tablespoons raw light agave
1 tablespoon raw coconut oil
1 teaspoon vanilla extract
1 teaspoon lecithin granules (optional for extra creaminess)
1/2 vanilla bean, scraped, seeds only
1/4 teaspoon sea salt

This almond milk does a body good! Although it may not give you that famous white milk mustache, it will give you loads of calcium, vitamins, and minerals.

Make the milk
1. In high-speed blender place almonds and water. Blend on high for about 2 minutes, until almonds are broken down to a sand-like consistency.
2. Place nut-milk bag over pitcher. Pour almond milk through bag and squeeze until most the liquid is removed and pulp in bag is slightly dry. Save almond pulp to use in cakes, breads, or cookies.
3. Rinse carafe and pour milk back into blender. Add agave, coconut oil, vanilla extract, lecithin, vanilla bean and sea salt. Blend on high about 1 minute, until smooth and creamy.

Note: Keeps in refrigerator up to 3 days in airtight container.

DARK CHOCOLATE ALMOND MILK

MAKES 44 OUNCES (SERVES 4-6)

MILK
4 cups water
2 cups raw almonds, soaked 8–10 hours, drained and rinsed
1/2 cup raw cacao powder
1/2 cup raw light agave
1/4 cup raw coconut oil
1 tablespoon vanilla extract
2 teaspoons lecithin granules (optional for extra creaminess)
1/4 teaspoon sea salt

As a kid I never liked plain milk but chocolate milk was another story. Occasionally I would come home from school, climb up on a stool and search the cupboards for my dads secret stash of chocolate syrup to make a tall glass of chocolate milk. This velvety smooth almond milk is a take on the classic that will satisfy any sweet tooth minus the sugar and dairy.

Make the milk
1. In high-speed blender place almonds and water. Blend on high for about 2 minutes, until almonds are broken down to sand-like consistency.
2. Place nut-milk bag over pitcher or bowl. Pour almond milk through bag and squeeze from top to bottom until most of the liquid is removed and pulp in bag is slightly dry. Set almond pulp aside to use in cakes, breads, or cookies.
3. Rinse carafe and pour milk back into blender. Add cacao, agave, coconut oil, vanilla extract, lecithin and sea salt. Blend on high for about 1 minute, until smooth and creamy.

Note: Keeps in refrigerator up to 3 days in airtight container.

SWEET AND **SPICY CHAI** COCONUT MILK

MAKES 32 OUNCES (SERVES 4-6)

MILK

6 organic chai tea bags (my favorite is organic TAZO black tea)
5 cups water
1 ½ cups unsweetened raw coconut, shredded, soaked 1 hour
1/3 cup raw light agave
3 tablespoons raw coconut oil
1 vanilla bean, scraped, seeds only
1 teaspoon vanilla extract
1/8 teaspoon sea salt

There's something really comforting about a cup of chai tea. It warms the soul with with it's rich, earthy spices, and when paired with sweetened coconut milk, and exotic vanilla, tastes like drinking a cup of love. With it's array of herbs and spices, chai has many nutritional benefits. This raw version is great for improving digestion, calming the mind, and enhancing the immune system. Chai can be very mild, or extremely spicy. I prefer a mild black tea blend, but choose which chai you like the best.

Make the milk
1. Soak shredded coconut in 5 cups water for 1 hour, so it breaks down easier in the blender.
2. In high-speed blender place shredded coconut, and soaking water. Blend on high for about 2 minutes, until thick and creamy. The coconut pulp won't fully break down, so don't get discouraged.
3. Over a bowl strain milk through nut-milk bag and squeeze from top to bottom until most of the liquid is removed and coconut pulp is slightly dry. Reserve pulp for coconut flour in other recipes.
4. Rinse carafe and pour coconut milk back into blender. Add agave, tea and spice blend from chai tea bags, coconut oil, vanilla bean, vanilla extract, and sea salt. Blend on high for about 2 minute, until warm, smooth and creamy.
5. Over a bowl or pitcher, strain milk through nut-milk bag one more time, to remove grainy spices from tea bags. Serve warm straight from the blender, or chill in refrigerator.

Note: Keeps in refrigerator up to 3 days in airtight container.

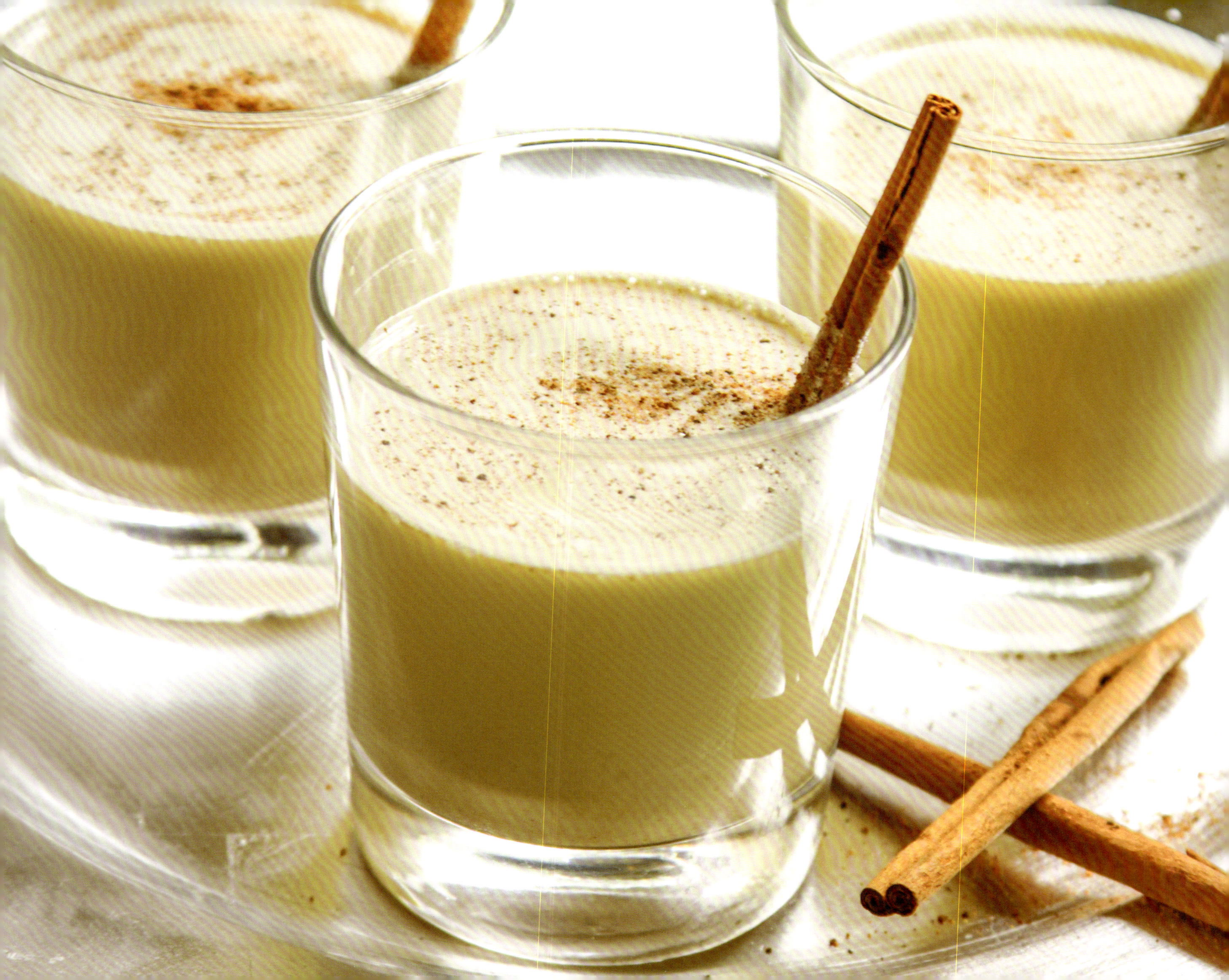

GRATED NUTMEG, CINNAMON, GINGER, AND ALMOND MILK

MAKES 32 OUNCES (SERVES 4-6)

MILK
4 cups vanilla almond milk (see page 76)
1/2 cup light raw agave nectar
2 tablespoons raw coconut butter
1 teaspoon grated nutmeg
1/2 teaspoon ground ginger
1/2 teaspoon ground cinnamon
1/2 teaspoon turmeric powder
1/4 teaspoon sea salt

As a kid, one of the things I really looked forward to when the holidays rolled around was a thick, cold glass of eggnog. When I decided to cut all dairy out of my diet, the thought of never having eggnog was a bit devastating. This is a quick and tasty alternative that is great served in a punch bowl at a holiday party or sipping by the fire.

Make the milk
1. In high-speed blender place almond milk, agave, coconut butter, nutmeg, ginger, cinnamon, turmeric and sea salt. Blend on high for about 2 minutes, until smooth and creamy.
2. Pour into glasses and garnish with cinnamon sticks and ground nutmeg.

Note: Keeps in refrigerator up to 3 days in airtight container.

MILKS

H A K E S

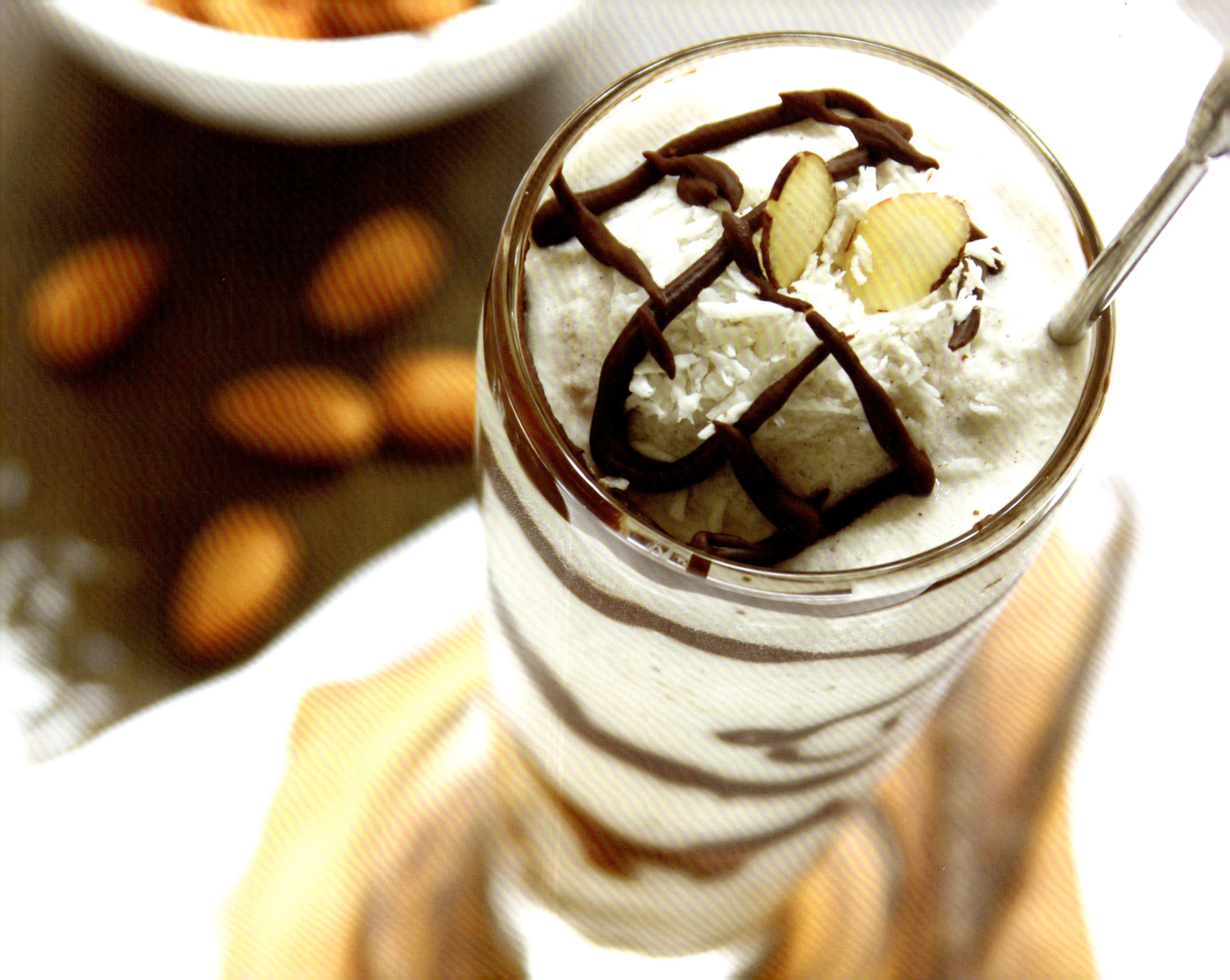

SWEET ALMOND, COCONUT, AND DARK CHOCOLATE MILKSHAKE

MAKES 32 OUNCES (SERVES 4-6)

MILKSHAKE
2 cups crushed ice
1 cup vanilla almond milk (see page 76)
1 cup young Thai coconut meat
1/4 cup raw light agave
2 tablespoons virgin raw coconut oil
2 teaspoons raw maca powder
1 teaspoon coconut extract
1 teaspoon almond extract
1 vanilla bean scraped, seeds only
1/4 teaspoon sea salt

GARNISH (OPTIONAL)
1/4 cup unsweetened raw coconut, shredded
1/4 cup chocolate sauce (see page 240)
1 tablespoon slivered almonds

This silky-smooth milkshake is great for the endocrine system, which helps regulate hormones; the shake has high amounts of B vitamins and medium-chain fatty acids which are known to support the metabolism. Drink up!

Make the milkshake
1. In high-speed blender place almond milk, coconut meat, agave, maca powder, coconut extract, almond extract, sea salt and vanilla bean. Blend on high for about 2 minutes, until consistency is thick and smooth.
2. Add coconut oil and blend until combined and there is no frothy oil film on top of the shake. This is from the coconut oil not being broken down completely. So keep blending for about 1 minute, until it's smooth.
3. Add ice and blend another 15–20 seconds, until it's a soft ice-cream texture. Pour into glasses, drizzle with chocolate sauce, and sprinkle on the shredded coconut and a few slivered almonds. Serve immediately.

Note: Keeps in refrigerator up to 3 days in airtight container.

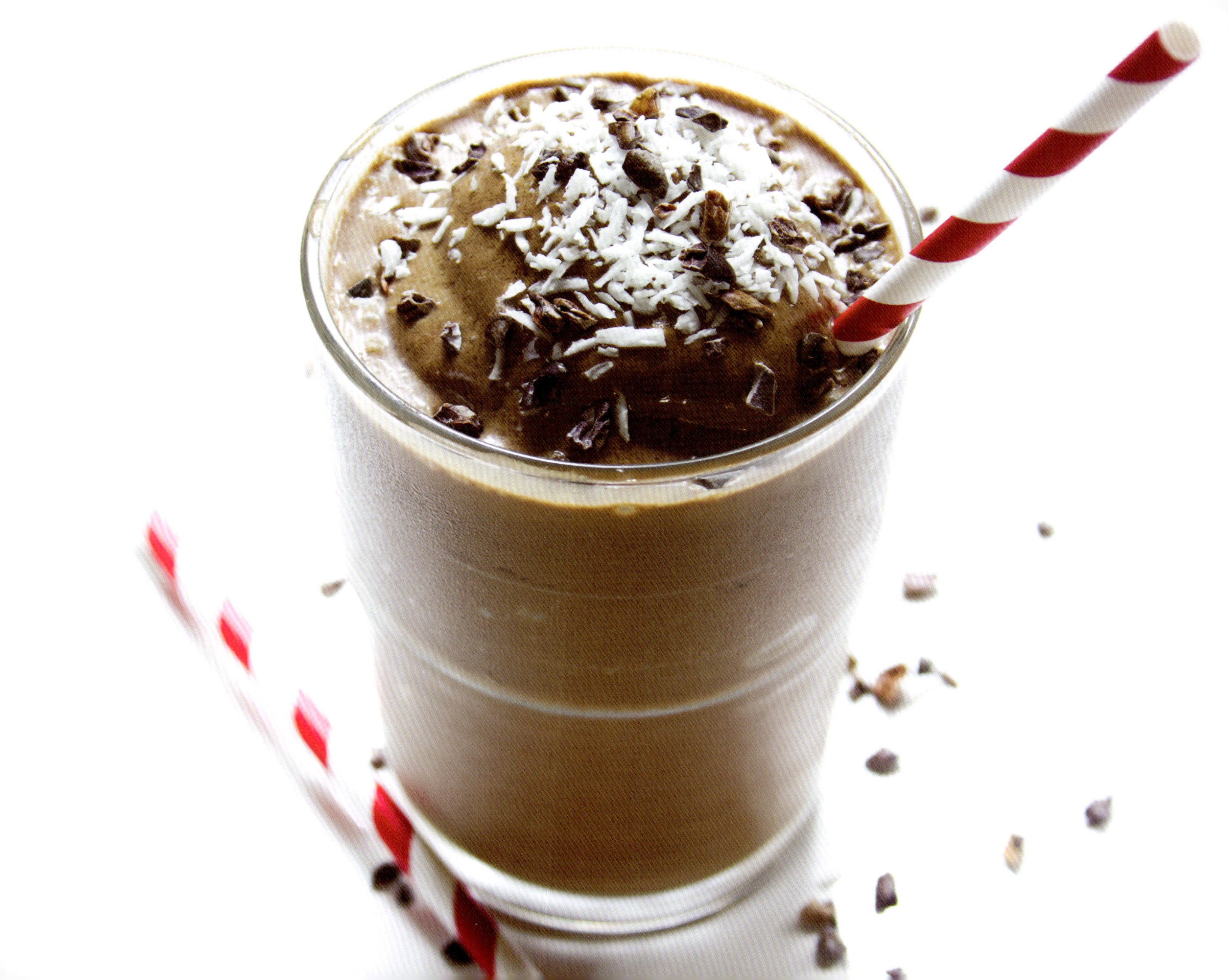

CLASSIC **CHOCOLATE** MILKSHAKE

MAKES 32 OUNCES (SERVES 4-6)

MILKSHAKE
2 cups crushed ice
1 cup purified water
1/3 cup raw cacao powder
1/4 cup young Thai coconut meat
1/4 cup raw macadamia nuts
3 tablespoons maple syrup
2 tablespoons raw light agave
2 tablespoons dried goji berries
1 ½ tablespoons virgin raw coconut oil
1 tablespoon vanilla extract
1/4 teaspoon sea salt

GARNISH (OPTIONAL)
1 tablespoon unsweetened raw coconut, shredded
1 tablespoon raw cacao nibs

When I was the head chef at a restaurant in Hollywood, California, I had five days to develop a tasty menu before doors opened for business. A chocolate milkshake was one of the many items I was determined to make so amazing people would be shocked it was healthy. This ended up being one of my favorite items on the menu. It supercharged me for a full day in the kitchen.

Make the milkshake
1. In high-speed blender place macadamia nuts, water, sea salt, and vanilla. Blend on high for about 1 minute, until macadamia nuts are broken down and smooth.
2. Add cacao powder, coconut meat, maple syrup, agave and goji berries, and blend about 30 seconds, until creamy.
3. Add coconut oil and blend on high about 1 minute, until well combined. The coconut oil should be totally broken down with no chunky or grainy textures. This is now your base for the milkshake.
4. Add 2 cups ice to blender carafe and blend on high, until it's the texture of soft ice cream. Pour into glasses of choice and garnish with shredded coconut, and cacao nibs. Serve immediately.

Note: Keeps in refrigerator up to 3 days in airtight container.

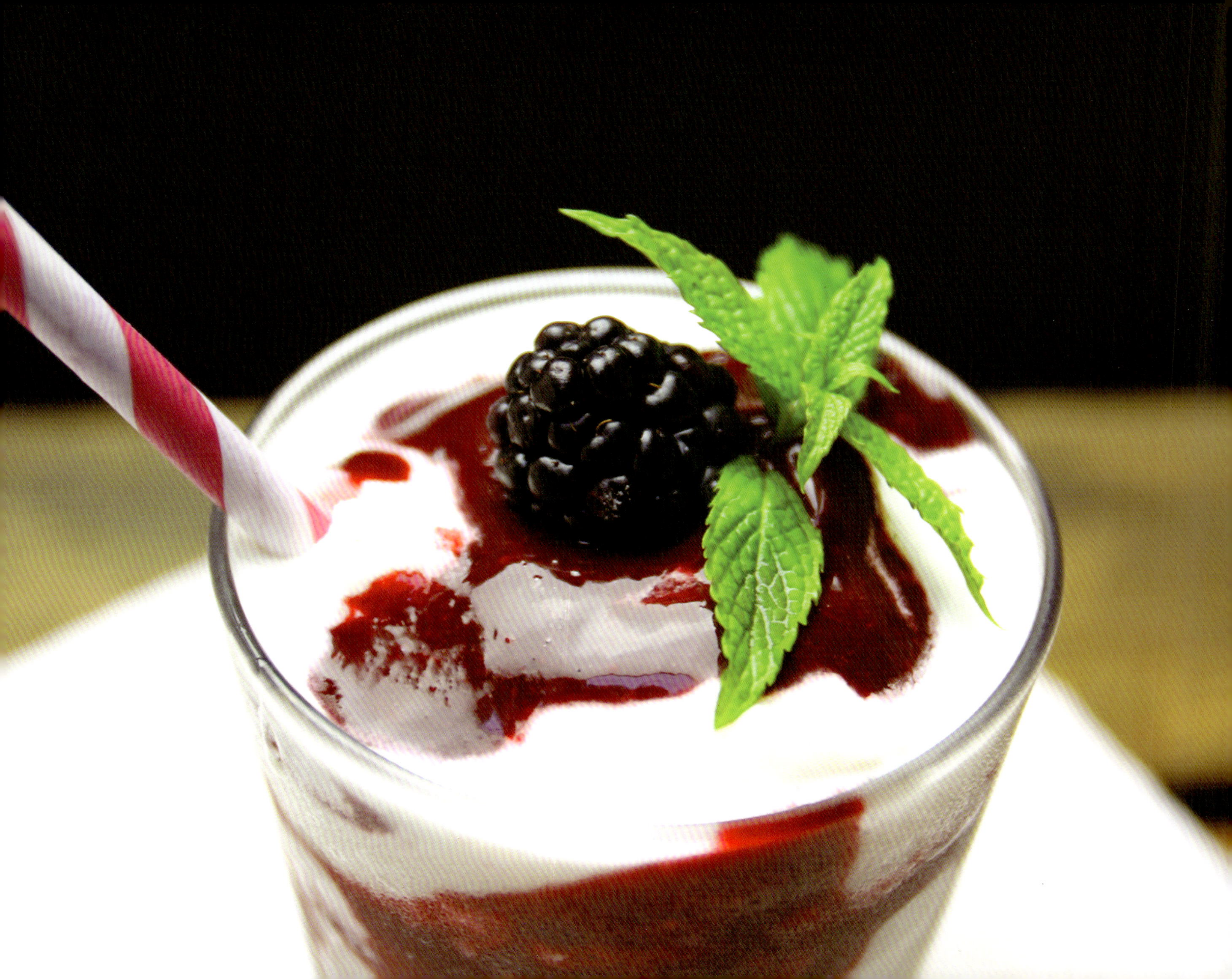

VANILLA MALT MILKSHAKE WITH **BLACKBERRY** SWIRL

MAKES 32 OUNCES (SERVES 4-6)

MILKSHAKE

2 ½ cups crushed ice
1 ½ cups coconut cream (see page 74)
1/4 cup raw light agave
2 tablespoons virgin raw coconut oil
2 teaspoons raw maca powder
1 teaspoon vanilla extract
1/2 vanilla bean, scraped, seeds only

BLACKBERRY SWIRL

2 cups fresh blackberries
1/4 cup raw light agave
2 teaspoons lemon juice, fresh-squeezed

GARNISH (OPTIONAL)

1/4 cups fresh blackberries
4 sprigs of mint

A frosty malted vanilla bean milkshake swirled with sweet-tart blackberry sauce this milkshake is both healthy and refreshing.

Make the blackberry swirl
1. In high-speed blender place blackberries, agave and lemon juice. Blend on low for about 20 seconds, until just combined and a thick, syrup-like consistency is achieved. Pour into glasses of choice. Wash blender carafe and make shake.

Make the milkshake
1. In high-speed blender place coconut cream, agave, coconut oil, maca powder, vanilla extract, and vanilla bean. Blend on high about 2 minutes, until coconut oil is broken down and there is no chunky and oily froth on top layer. Keep blending on high if there is, until smooth.
2. Add ice and blend another 20 seconds, until ice is broken down and milkshake is the consistency of melted ice cream. Pour into glasses over blackberry sauce and give it one or two swirls to incorporate the blackberry sauce.
3. Garnish each glass with a few blackberries and a fresh mint sprig. Serve immediately.

Note: Keeps in refrigerator up to 3 days in airtight container.

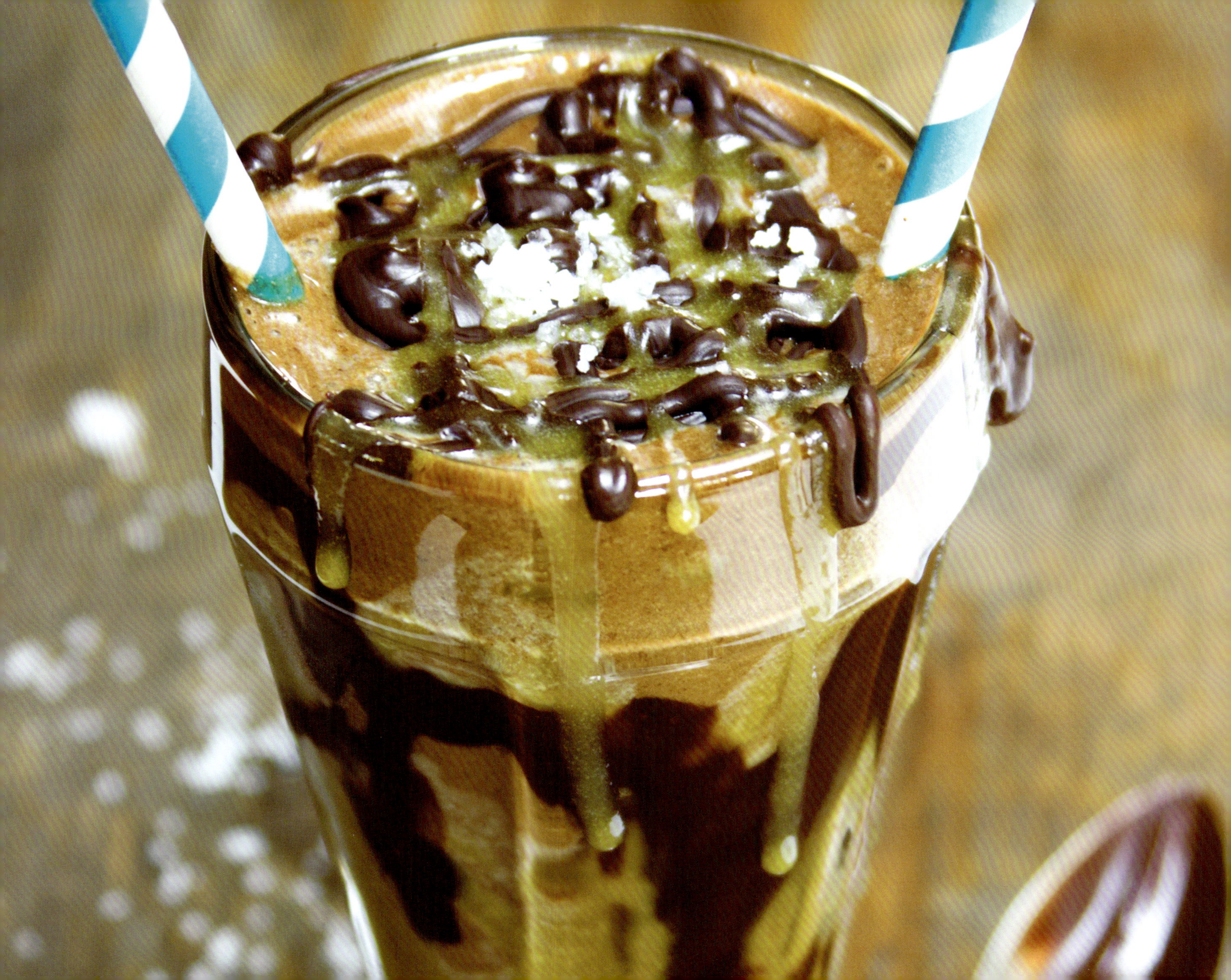

SALTED CARAMEL CHOCOLATE-BANANA MILKSHAKE

MAKES 32 OUNCES (SERVES 4-6)

MILKSHAKE
1 ½ cups coconut cream (see page 74)
2 frozen ripe banana's, peeled
1/4 cup raw cacao powder
3 tablespoons raw light agave
2 teaspoons vanilla extract
1/8 teaspoon sea salt

CARAMEL SAUCE
2 tablespoons coconut butter, melted
2 tablespoons yacon syrup
2 tablespoons raw light agave
1 tablespoon coconut cream (see page 74)
1 tablespoon vanilla extract
1/4 teaspoon sea salt

GARNISH (OPTIONAL)
1/2 cup chocolate sauce (see page 240)
1 tablespoon chunky sea salt

This heavenly chocolate banana milkshake is drizzled with gooey caramel, chocolate sauce and laced with a hint of sea salt. Perfect served with a classic BLAT sandwich.

Make the caramel sauce
1. In a small mixing bowl, whisk together coconut butter, yacon syrup, agave, coconut cream, vanilla and sea salt. Set aside.

Make the milkshake
1. In high-speed blender place coconut cream, frozen bananas, cacao powder, agave, vanilla extract and sea salt. Blend on high for about 1 minute, until totally smooth.

Assemble milkshake
1. Swirl about 2 tablespoons caramel sauce and 2 tablespoons chocolate sauce in each glass. Pour milkshake into glasses of choice and top with drizzles of caramel and chocolate sauce. Sprinkle with chunky sea salt. Serve immediately.

Note: Keeps in refrigerator up to 3 days in airtight container.

C O N D I

M E N T S

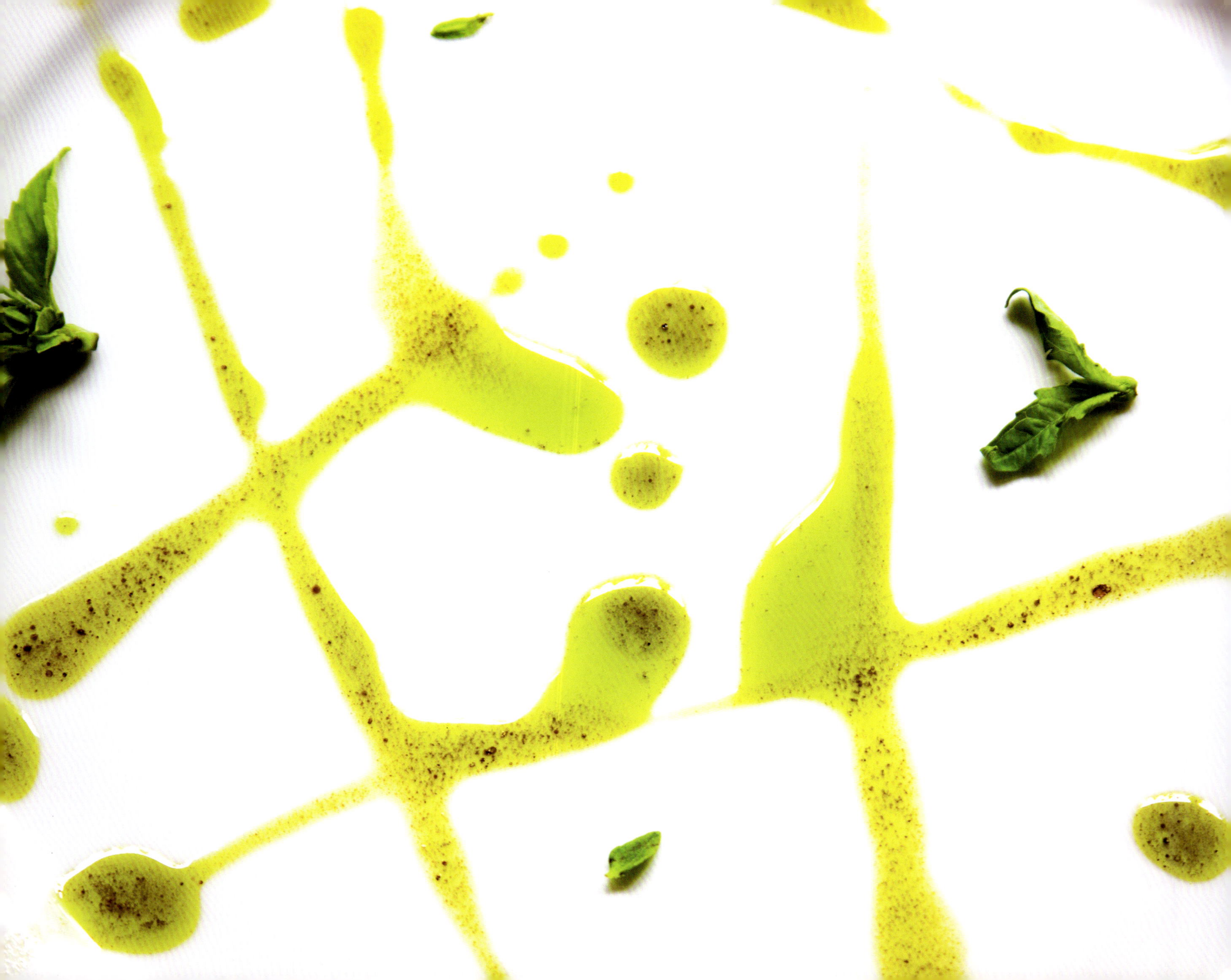

FRESH BASIL OIL

MAKES 12 OUNCES

OIL
1 ½ cups fresh basil, stems removed, tightly packed
1 ½ cups virgin raw olive oil
ice cubes

My talented friend Efrain Gomez, taught me this trick to making the most beautiful bright green basil oil. The key is lightly blanching the basil in hot water and a few seconds later submerging it in ice water. This locks in the chloroform which retains the color. Thanks, Efrain!

Make the oil
1. Blanch basil in hot water (as hot as your tap water will go) for 8–10 seconds. Drain water and immediately put basil in bowl of cold water with ice cubes for 20 seconds.
2. Remove basil from ice water and pat dry with towel. Transfer to high-speed blender
3. Pour olive oil in carafe with basil and blend on high for 15–20 seconds.
4. Strain basil oil through nut-milk bag or triple-lined cheesecloth over bowl, so only a brilliant, bright green oil is left.

Note: Keeps in refrigerator up to 2 weeks in airtight container. Remove 30 minutes before using, so olive oil can liquefy at room temperature.

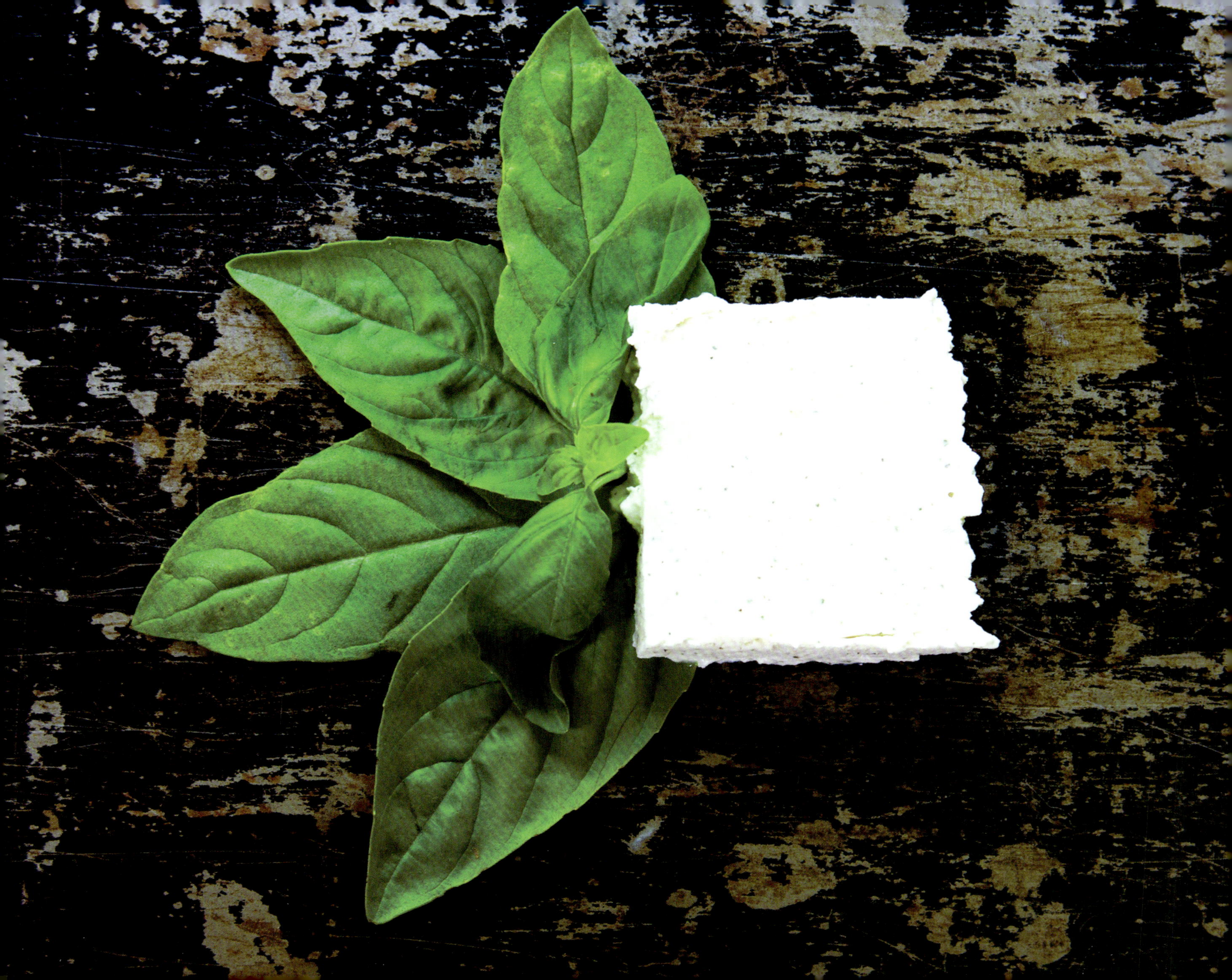

CREAMY CASHEW BASIL MOZZARELLA

MAKES 2 1/2 CUPS

CREAM

1 ½ cups raw cashews, soaked 4–6 hours, drained and rinsed
1 cup water
1/2 cup irish moss gel (see page 102)
1/4 cup raw coconut oil
1 tablespoon dried basil
2 teaspoons lemon juice, fresh-squeezed
1 teaspoon sea salt

I love this semi-soft cheese layered between raw lasagna or stacked between fresh basil leaves and heirloom tomatoes. It's mild in flavor with a brilliant silky structure, making it a versatile cheese for many different recipes.

Make the cheese

1. In high-speed blender place cashews, water, irish moss, lemon juice and sea salt. Blend on high about 2 minutes, until cashews are broken down and cream is a thick, smooth consistency.
2. Add coconut oil and dried basil. Blend another 30 seconds, until coconut oil is well combined.
3. Strain cheese through triple-lined cheesecloth. Squeeze out as much liquid as possible.
4. Remove cheese from cloth and press into an 8-inch x 8-inch baking dish. Cover and place in refrigerator for 4–6 hours to set or until firm to touch.

Note: Keeps in refrigerator up to 5 days in airtight container.

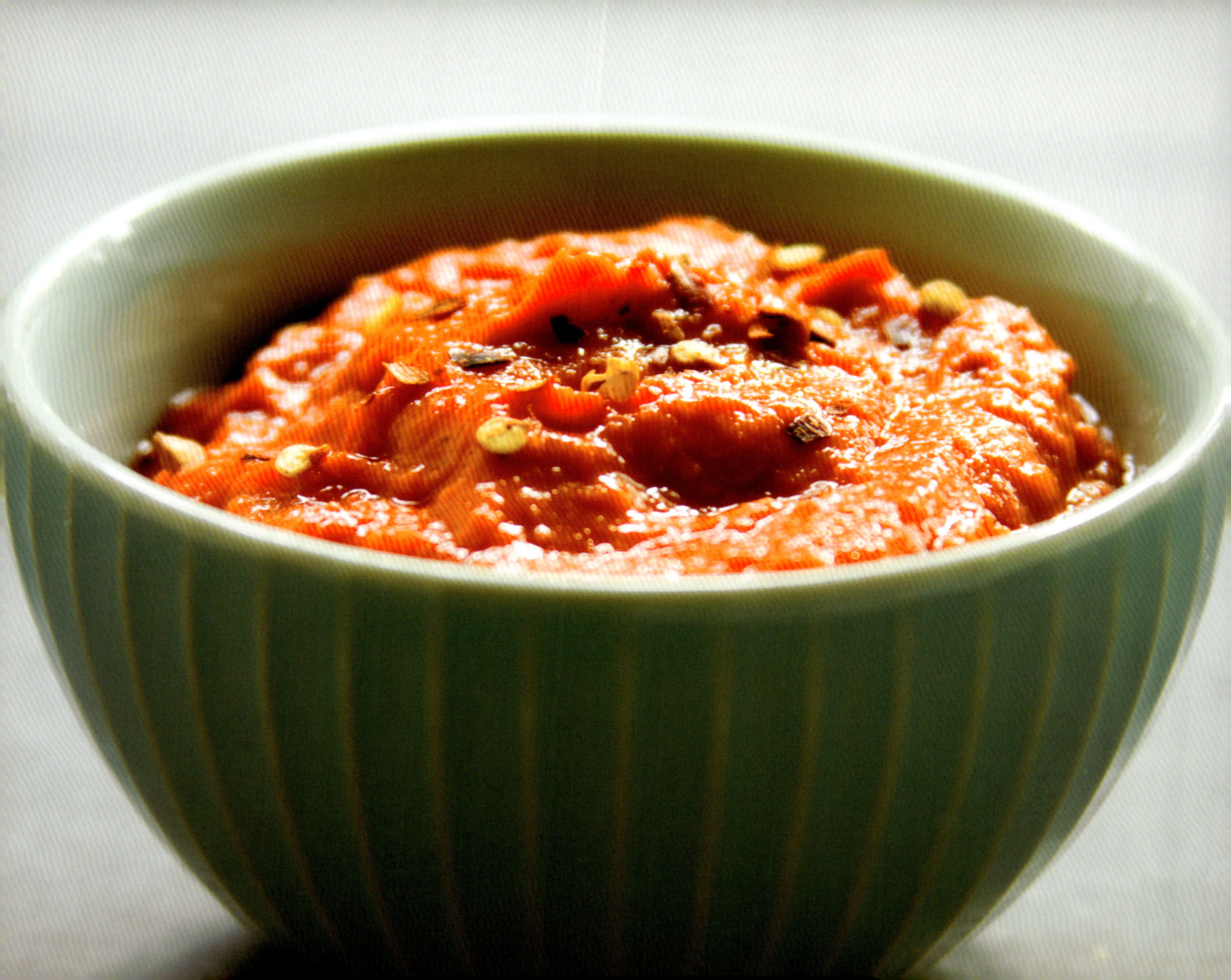

GARLIC CHILI SAUCE

MAKES 1/2 CUP

SAUCE
3/4 cups water
1/2 cup sun-dried tomatoes
4 cloves fresh garlic, peeled
1 tablespoon expeller-pressed grape-seed oil
1 teaspoon raw light agave
1 teaspoon lemon juice, fresh-squeezed
1 teaspoon red pepper flakes
1/2 teaspoon garlic powder
1/4 teaspoon sea salt

This recipe involves little preparation and is the perfect addition to any Asian-inspired dish. The fragrant garlic and spicy red pepper flakes will punch up any recipe.

Make the sauce
1. In high-speed blender place water, sun-dried tomatoes, garlic, grape-seed oil, agave, lemon juice, red pepper flakes, garlic powder and sea salt. Blend on medium speed about 1 minute, until smooth.

Note: Keeps in refrigerator up to 10 days in airtight container.

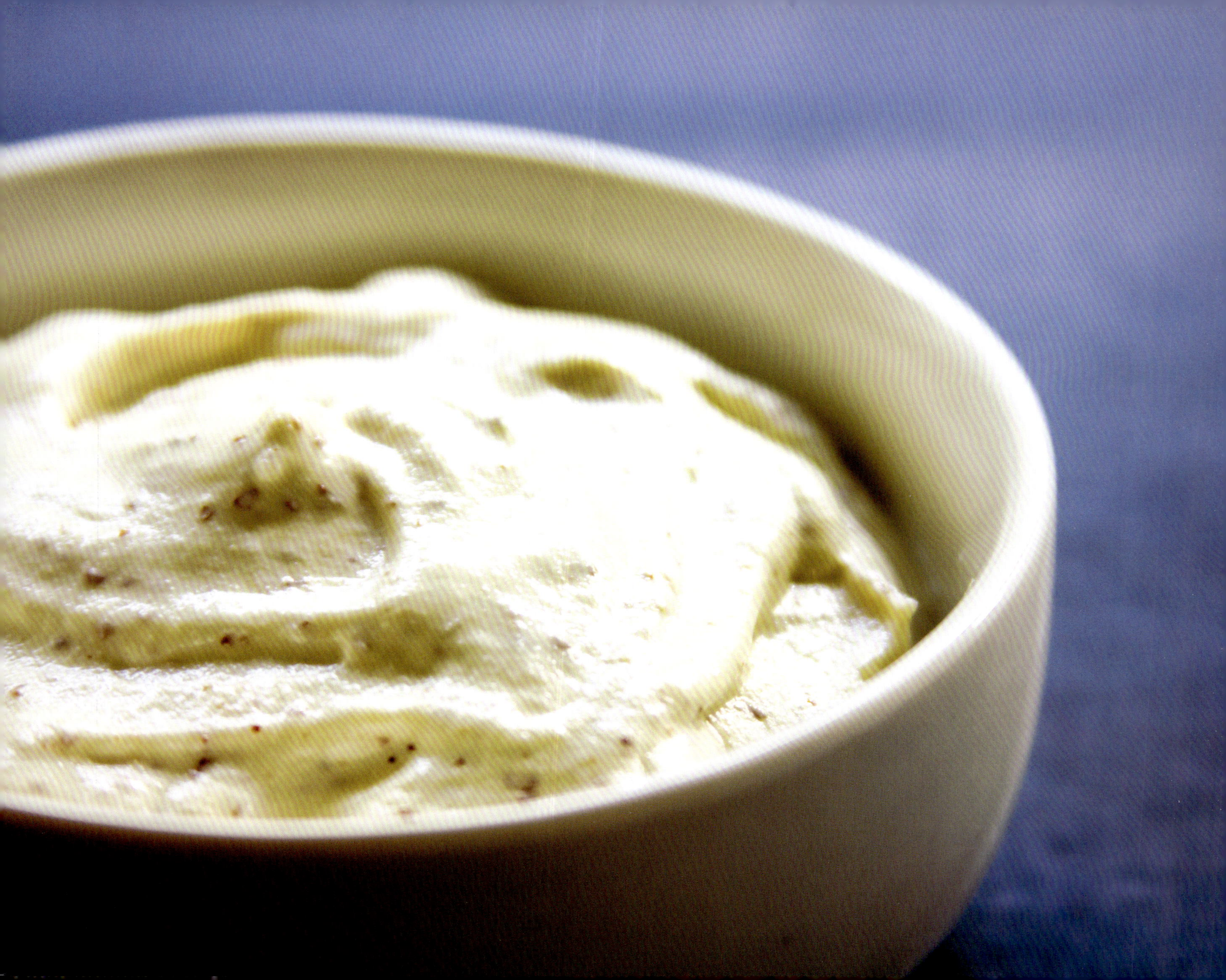

STONE-GROUND MUSTARD WITH CASHEW CREAM, AND LEMON

MAKES 12 OUNCES

SPREAD
1 ¼ cup raw cashews, soaked 4–6 hours, drained and rinsed
1/2 cup water
2 tablespoons stone-ground mustard
2 tablespoons expeller-pressed grape-seed oil
1 ½ tablespoons lemon juice, fresh-squeezed
2 teaspoons apple cider vinegar
1/4 teaspoon sea salt

This recipe is a great creamy base for salad dressing and is excellent spread on sandwiches.

Make the spread
1. In high-speed blender place cashews, water, mustard, grape-seed oil, lemon juice, apple cider vinegar, and sea salt.
2. Blend on high about 2 minutes, until cashews are broken down and spread is a thick consistency.

Note: Keeps in refrigerator up to 7 days in airtight container.

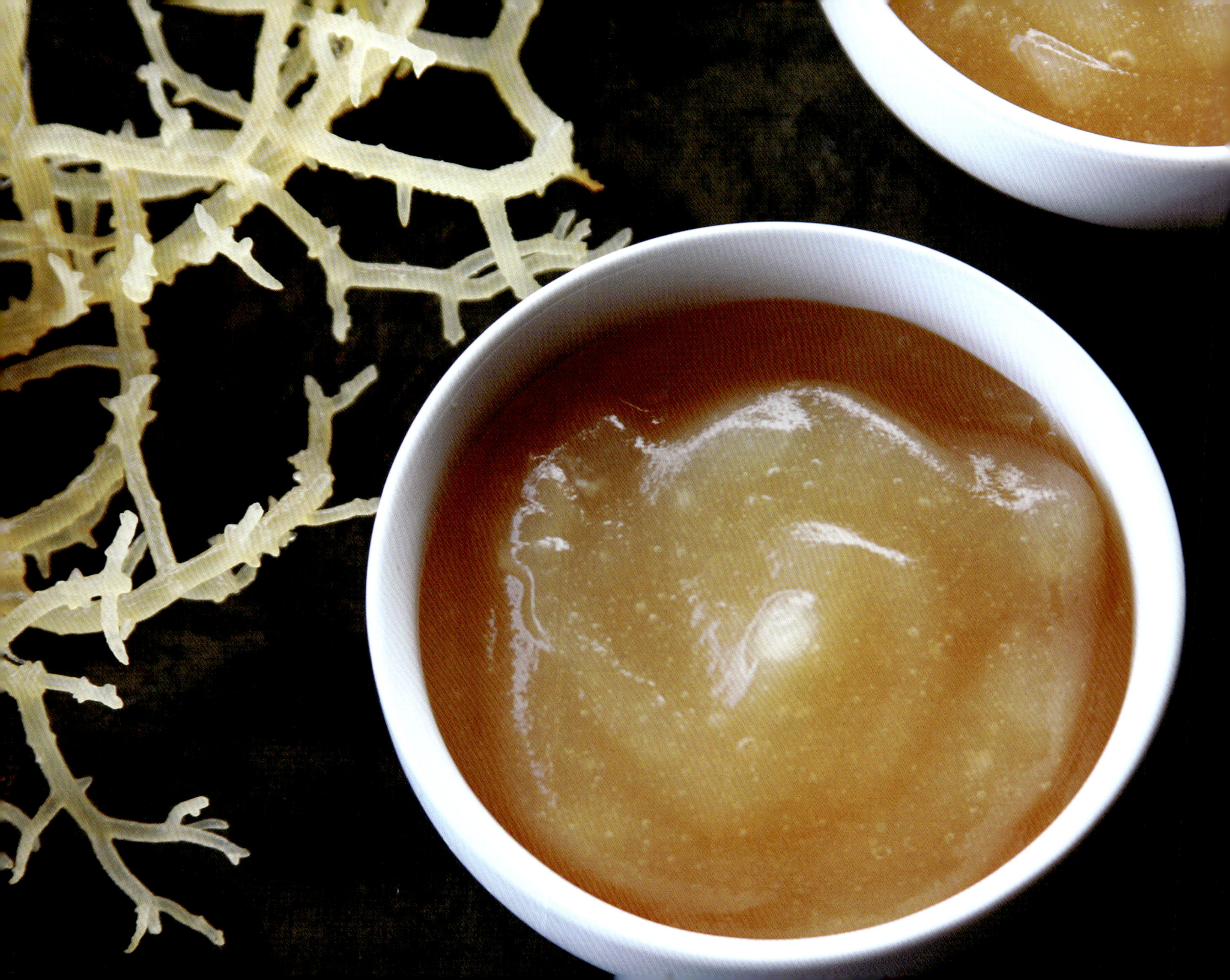

IRISH MOSS
SEA GEL

MAKES 2 CUPS

GEL
1 ½ cups irish moss, soaked 8 hours and rinsed
3/4 cup water

Also known as carrageen or agar-agar, irish moss is commercially used in many products to provide a creamy texture and act as a thickening agent. In this book it is used as a thickener for desserts. What better way to get your sea vegetables than sweet treats? Irish moss is a seaweed that has a very rich history. The Irish considered it to be a good luck charm. Families would harvest the seaweed from shorelines, and it became a main source of food during the Great Potato Famine. I like having this gel in the fridge at all times. It can also make a great face mask, ease sunburns and dermatitis, and moisturize dry skin.

Make the gel
1. In high-speed blender place irish moss, and water. Blend on high for about 2 minutes, until irish moss is broken down into a gel-like consistency.

Note: Keeps in refrigerator up to 7 days in airtight container.

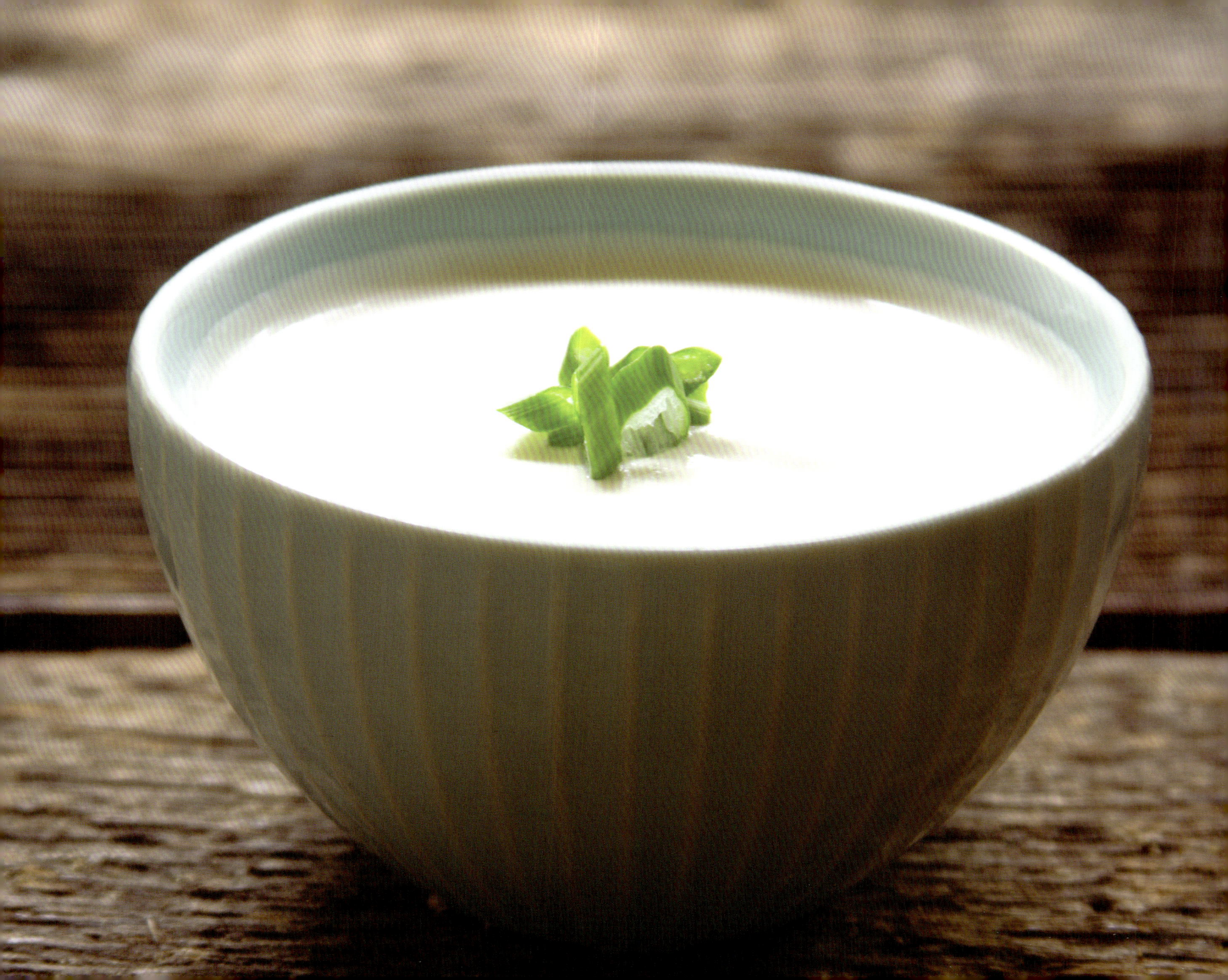

CASHEW CREAM, SOUR LEMON, AND SEA SALT

MAKES 3 CUPS

CREAM
2 cups raw cashews, soaked 4–6 hours, drained and rinsed
1 cup water
3 tablespoons lemon juice, fresh-squeezed
1/2 teaspoon sea salt

Dairy-free, soy-free, sour cream—yes please! This recipe is used a few times throughout the book as a condiment, supplying a wonderful tart, creamy addition to tacos, chili, soups, and more.

Make the cream
1. In high-speed blender place cashews, water, lemon juice, and sea salt.
2. Blend on high about 2–3 minutes, until cashews are broken down and cream is a thick, smooth consistency.

Note: Keeps in refrigerator up to 5 days in airtight container.

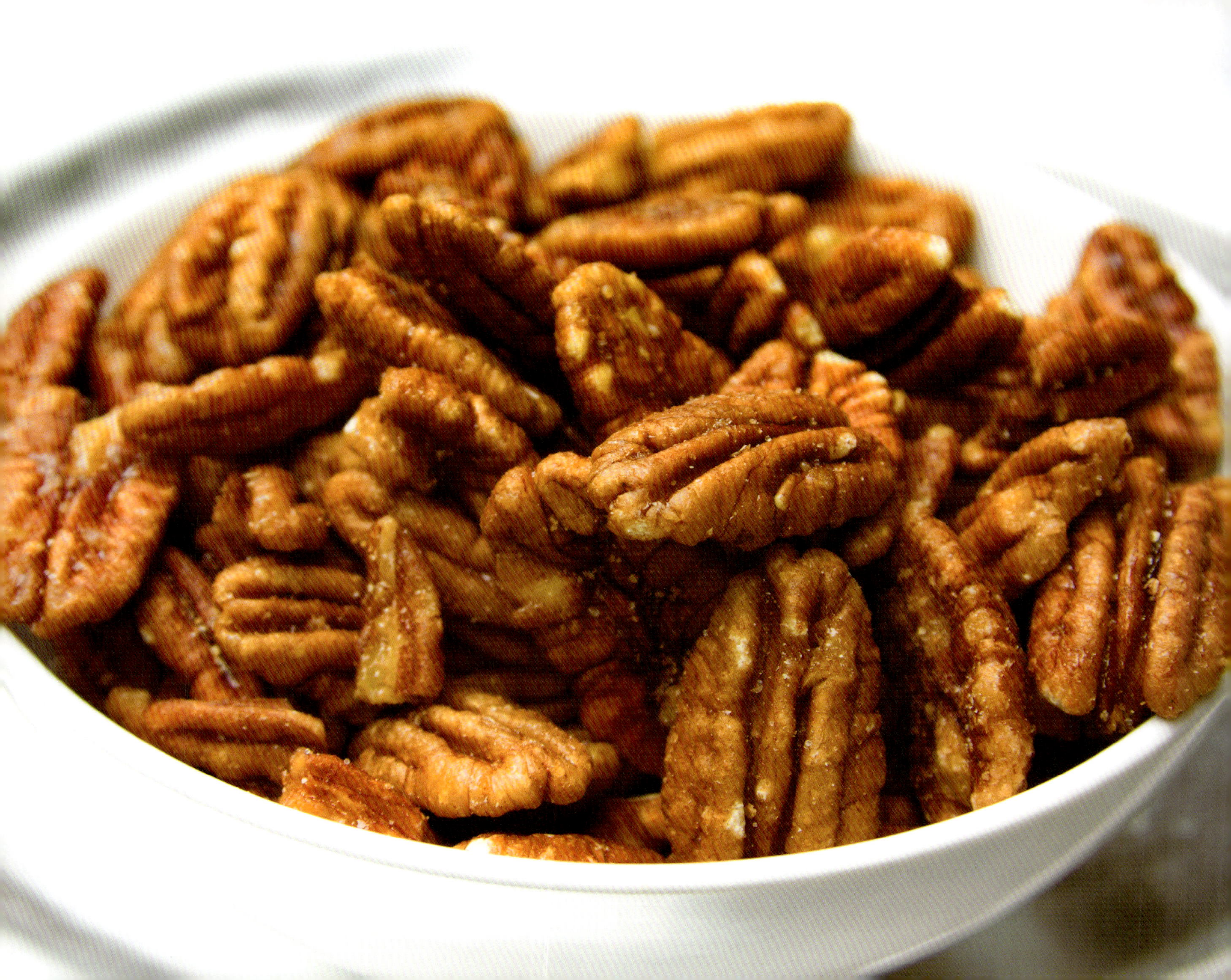

SEA SALT CANDIED PECANS

MAKES 2 CUPS

PECANS

2 cups raw pecans, soaked 4–6 hours, drained and rinsed
3 tablespoons raw coconut sugar
2 tablespoons maple syrup
1 tablespoon raw coconut oil, melted
1/2 teaspoon sea salt
1/2 teaspoon ground cinnamon

Sweet, salty cinnamon coating makes these candied pecans irresistible and addictive. They are great served on desserts, salads, or as a protein-rich snack.

Make the pecans
1. In medium mixing bowl, add coconut sugar, maple syrup, melted coconut oil, sea salt, and ground cinnamon. Whisk until well combined.
2. Add pecans to liquid sauce. Toss until all pecans are evenly coated in sweet candy sauce.
3. On dehydrator tray lined with teflex sheet, spread out pecans. Dehydrate at 115 degrees for 36 hours or until pecans are light and crunchy.

Note: Keeps at room temperature up to 2 months in airtight container.

S   A   L

A D S

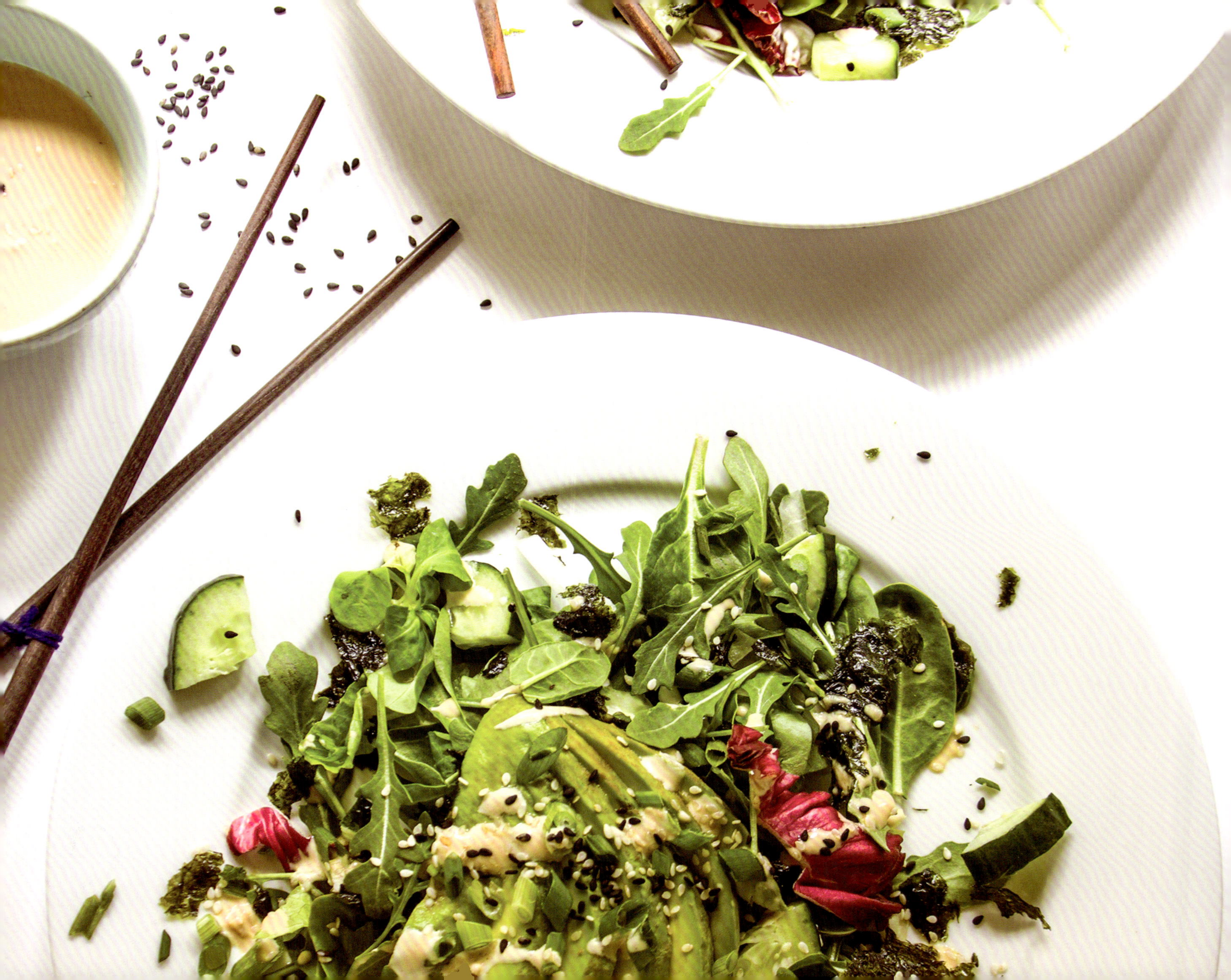

MIXED GREENS, NORI, AVOCADO, AND CUCUMBER WITH CREAMY SESAME GINGER DRESSING

SERVES 4-6

SALAD
8 cups mixed greens
1 cup cucumber, unpeeled and diced
1 large ripe avocado, peeled, pitted and diced
1/2 cup nori, torn into small pieces
1/4 cup green onion, chopped
2 teaspoons black sesame seeds
2 teaspoons white sesame seeds

DRESSING
2 ½ cup water
1/2 cup raw cashews soaked 4–6 hours, drained and rinsed
2 tablespoons rice wine vinegar
2 tablespoons wheat-free tamari
1 ½ tablespoons expeller-pressed sesame oil
1 tablespoon fresh ginger, minced

Crisp mixed greens paired with buttery avocado, crunchy pieces of cucumber and delicate nori flakes are tossed with a light sesame ginger dressing and sprinkled with black-and-white sesame seeds. This salad is great as an entrée and is an excellent source of magnesium and B vitamins.

Make the salad
1. In large salad bowl, add mixed greens, cucumber, avocado, nori, green onion, and black-and-white sesame seeds. Set aside.

Make the dressing
1. In high-speed blender add water, cashews, rice wine vinegar, wheat-free tamari, sesame oil, and ginger. Blend on high about 2 minutes, until totally smooth.
2. Pour dressing over salad and toss lightly to coat. Serve immediately.

Note: Keeps in refrigerator up to 2 days in airtight container.

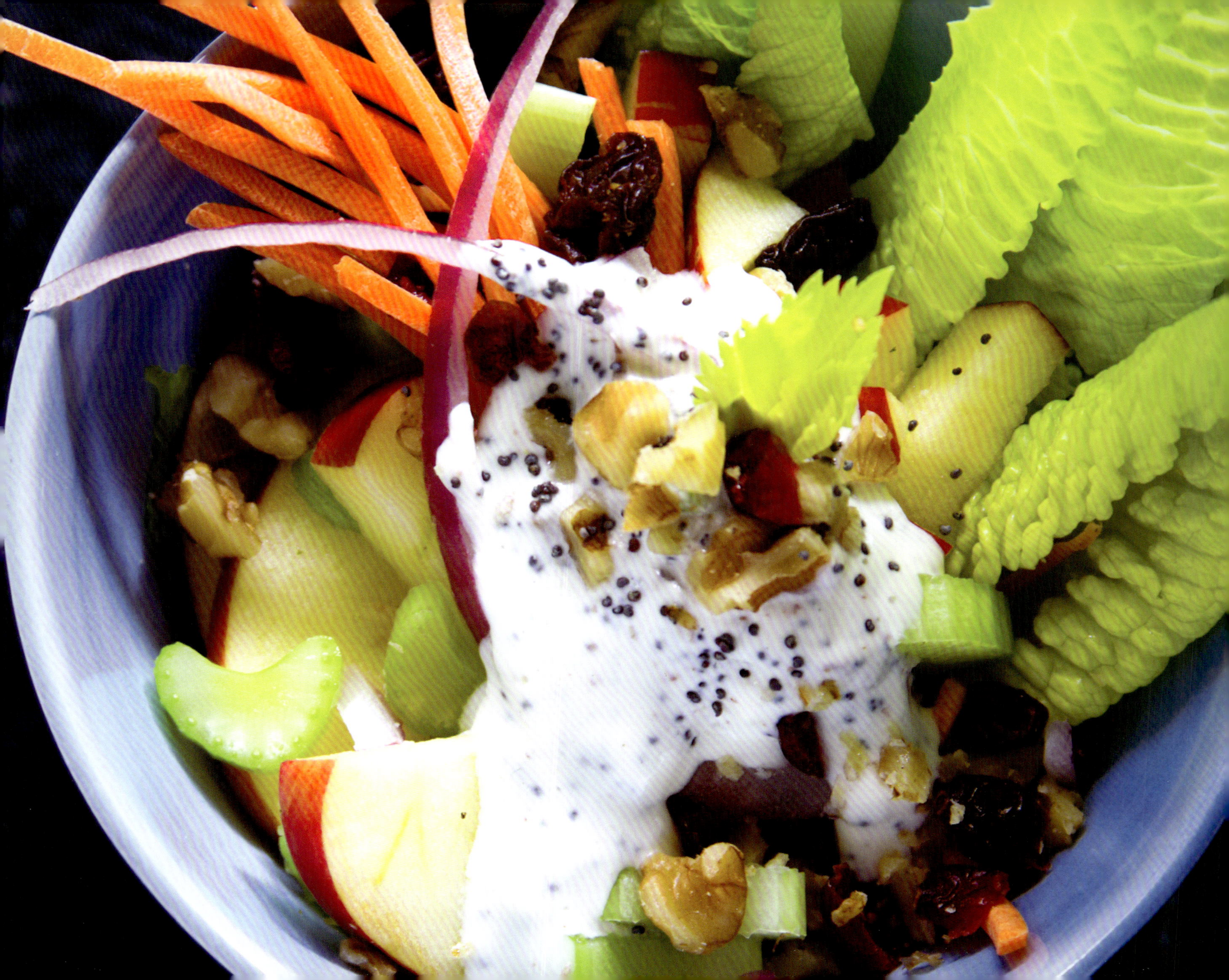

ROMAINE, APPLE, CELERY, CARROT, AND WALNUT WITH LEMON POPPY SEED DRESSING

SERVES 4-6

SALAD

4 cups romaine lettuce, chopped
1 cup carrots, shredded
1/2 cup apple, diced
1/2 cup celery, diced
1/2 cup red onion, diced
1/4 cup raw walnuts, chopped
1/4 cup dried cranberries

DRESSING

1/3 cup expeller-pressed grape-seed oil
1/4 cup cashews soaked 4–6 hours, drained and rinsed
2 tablespoons lemon juice, fresh-squeezed
1 tablespoon poppy seeds
2 teaspoons raw light agave
1 teaspoon stone-ground mustard
1 teaspoon sea salt

Tangy lemon poppy seed dressing tossed with hearty romaine, crisp diced apples, celery, shredded carrots and chopped walnuts then sprinkled with tart dried cranberries. This is substantial enough as an entrée or great served as a starter.

Make the salad
1. In large salad bowl, add romaine, carrots, apple, celery, red onion, walnuts and cranberries. Set aside.

Make the dressing
1. In high-speed blender place cashews, grape-seed oil, lemon juice, agave, mustard, and sea salt. Blend on high for about 2 minutes, until cashews are broken down and dressing is smooth.
2. Add poppy seeds and blend another 10 seconds–just enough to incorporate.
3. Pour dressing over salad and toss gently until well coated. Serve immediately.

Note: Keeps in refrigerator up to 2 days in airtight container.

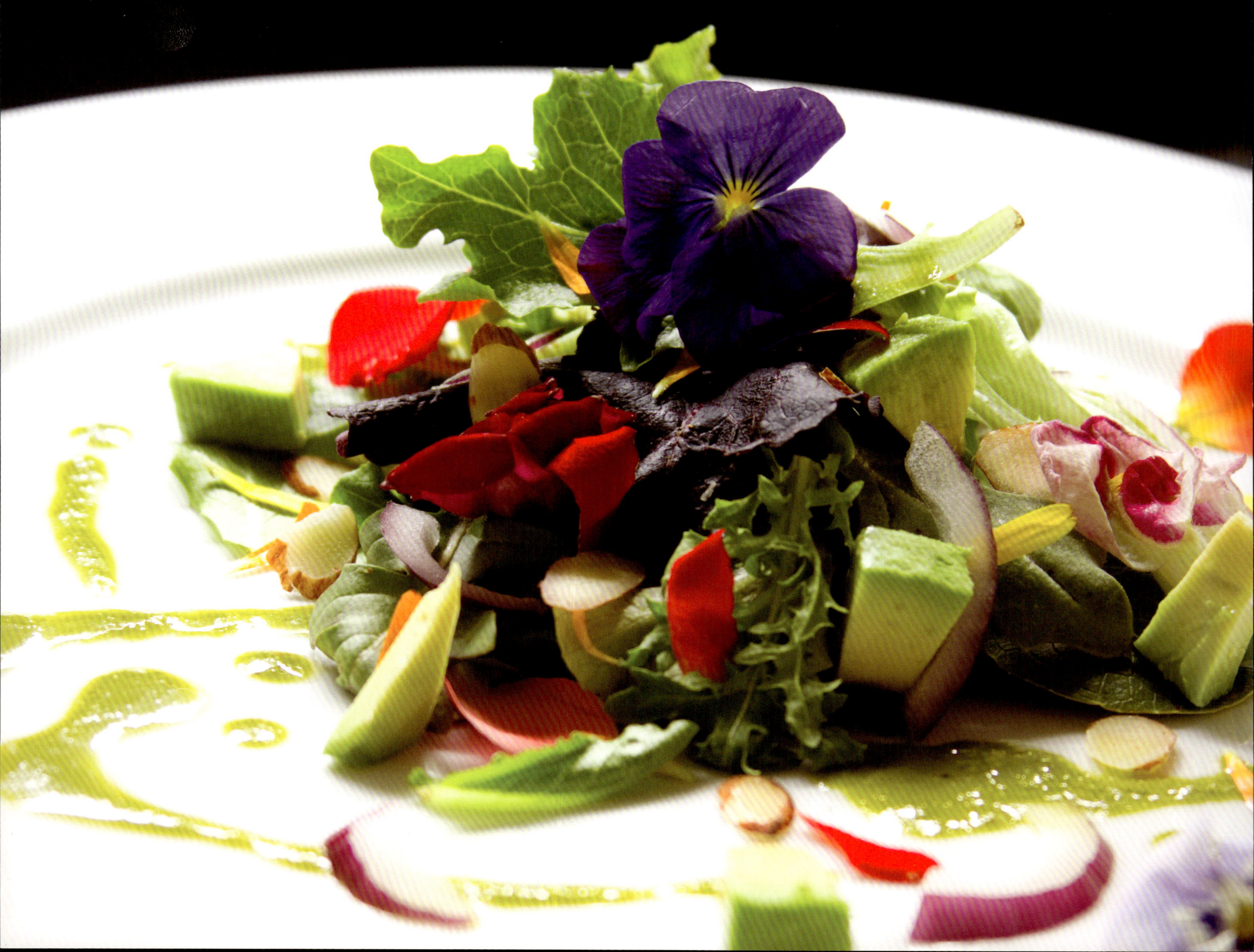

MIXED GREENS, AVOCADO, EDIBLE FLOWERS, AND HERB DRESSING

SERVES 4-6

SALAD
6 cups mixed greens
1/2 cup raw slivered almonds
1/2 cup red onion, diced
1/4 cup edible flowers of choice
1 ripe avocado, peeled, pitted, and cubed

DRESSING
1/2 cup fresh basil, leaves only
1/3 cup virgin raw olive oil
1/4 cup orange juice, fresh-squeezed
2 ½ tablespoons lemon juice, fresh-squeezed
2 tablespoons fresh dill
2 tablespoons fresh thyme
2 tablespoons fresh tarragon
1 tablespoon wheat-free tamari
1 tablespoon raw light agave
1 medium clove garlic, peeled
2 teaspoons sea salt
1/4 cup fresh ground lemon pepper

This was a very popular salad for catering events and dinner parties. It's so beautiful that you just want to stare for a while before consuming—or maybe that's just me. The dazzling spectrum of colors from the edible flowers against the deep green lettuce variety is somewhat mesmerizing. Drizzled in a sweet yet tangy dressing, once you start eating it, you won't be able to stop.

Make the salad
1. In large salad bowl, add mixed greens, slivered almonds, red onion, edible flowers and avocado. Set aside.

Make the dressing
1. In high-speed blender place basil, olive oil, orange juice, lemon juice, dill, thyme, tarragon, wheat-free tamari, agave, garlic, sea salt and lemon pepper. Blend on high for about 1 minute, until herbs are broken down and dressing is smooth.
2. Drizzle dressing over salad. Serve immediately.

Note: Salad keeps in refrigerator up to 2 days in airtight container. Dressing keeps up to 5 days in airtight container.

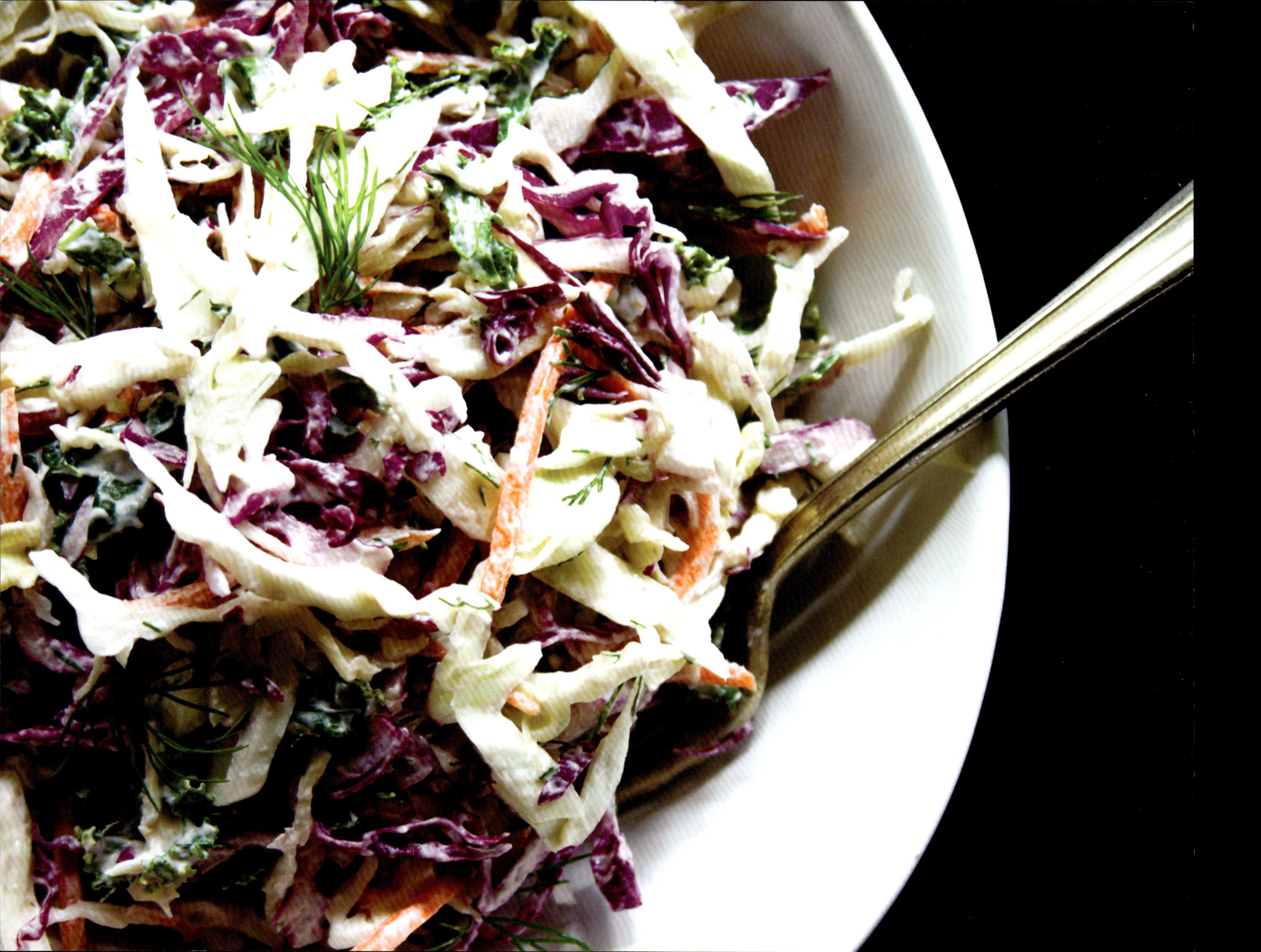

MIXED CABBAGE, CARROT, AND KALE SLAW WITH CREAMY DILL DRESSING

SERVES 4-6

SLAW
2 cups green cabbage, shredded
1 cup purple cabbage, shredded
3/4 cup julienne carrots
1/2 cup green kale, chopped fine
1/4 cup sweet onion, chopped
1 tablespoon fresh dill, stems removed and minced
1/4 teaspoon fresh ground black pepper

DRESSING
1/2 cup cashews soaked 4–6 hours, drained and rinsed
2 tablespoons water
1 ½ tablespoon lemon juice, fresh-squeezed
1 ½ tablespoons apple cider vinegar
1 tablespoon expeller-pressed grape-seed oil
1 teaspoon stone-ground mustard
1/2 teaspoon raw light agave
1/4 teaspoon sea salt

A colorful blend of shredded cabbage, carrots, chopped kale, onion and fragrant dill tossed with a creamy sharp dressing this is perfect for a summer barbecue and a fun, healthy alternative to the American classic.

Make the slaw
1. In large salad bowl, add green cabbage, purple cabbage, carrots, kale, onion, dill, and pepper. Set aside.

Make the dressing
1. In high-speed blender place cashews, water, lemon juice, apple cider vinegar, grape-seed oil, mustard, agave, and sea salt. Blend on high for about 2 minutes, until cashews are broken down and dressing is totally smooth.
2. Pour dressing over slaw. Toss lightly to coat. Serve immediately.

Note: Slaw keeps in refrigerator up to 3 days in airtight container.

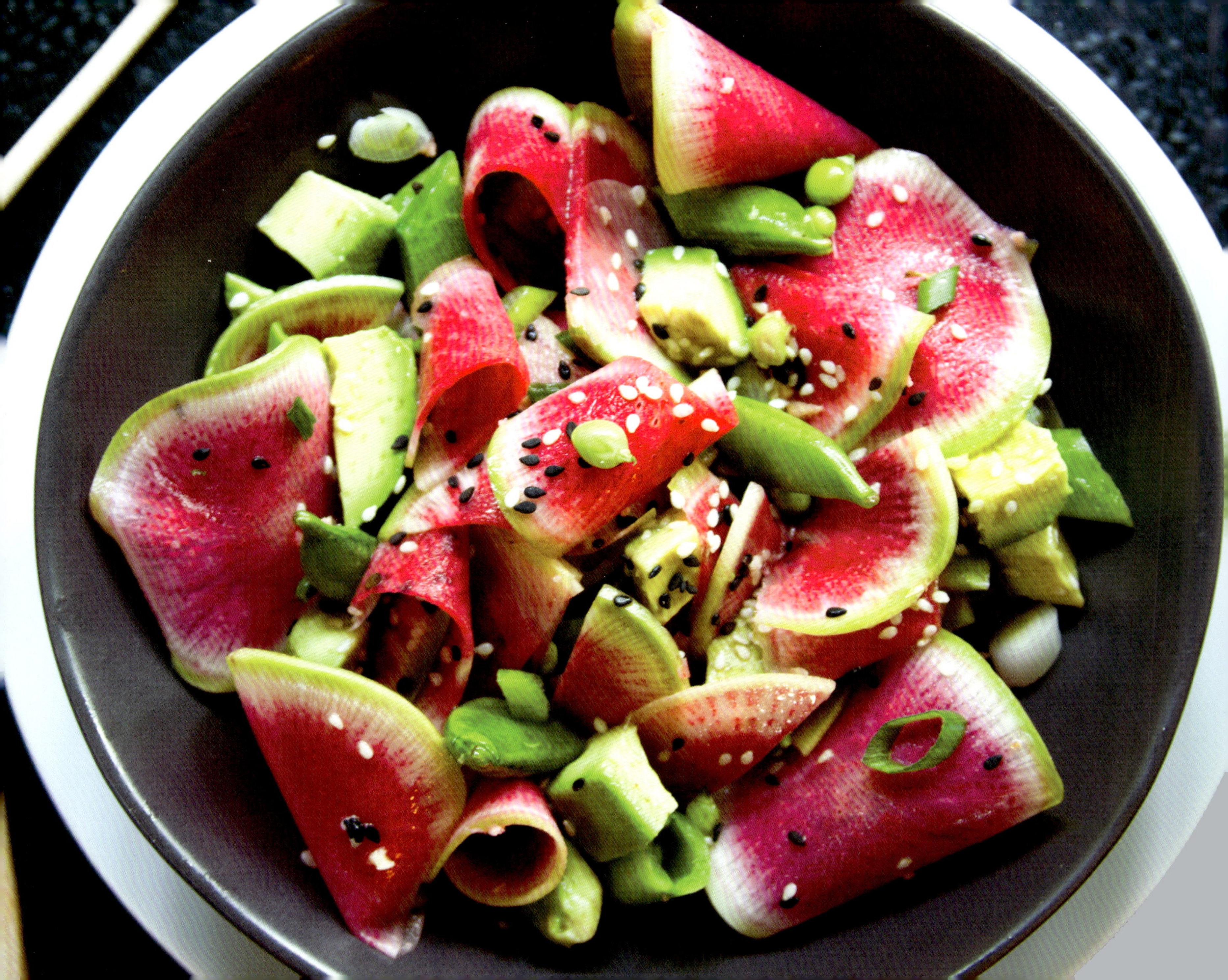

WATERMELON RADISH, AVOCADO, GREEN ONION, AND SWEET SESAME

SERVES 4-6

A stunning explosion of hot pink and mild in flavor, light and crisp watermelon radishes make an unusually colorful display accompanied by creamy avocado, snap peas, crunchy black-and-white sesame seeds, and a delicate Asian dressing. This salad makes a great start to any meal.

Make the salad
1. In medium mixing bowl, add watermelon radishes, snap peas, avocado, green onion, and black-and-white sesame seeds.

Make the dressing
1. In small mixing bowl, add rice wine vinegar, sesame oil, ginger, agave, and sea salt.
2. Whisk until dressing is smooth and oil is well incorporated.
3. Drizzle dressing over salad. Toss lightly to coat. Serve immediately.

SALAD

3 cups watermelon radish, thinly sliced
1 cup fresh sugar snap peas, roughly chopped
1 medium avocado, peeled, pitted and cubed
1/4 cup green onion, green and white parts, chopped
1 teaspoon white sesame seeds
1 teaspoon black sesame seeds

DRESSING

2 tablespoons rice wine vinegar
2 tablespoons expeller-pressed sesame oil
1 tablespoon minced, fresh ginger
1 ½ teaspoons raw light agave
1/4 teaspoon sea salt

Note: Salad keeps in refrigerator up to 2 days in airtight container.

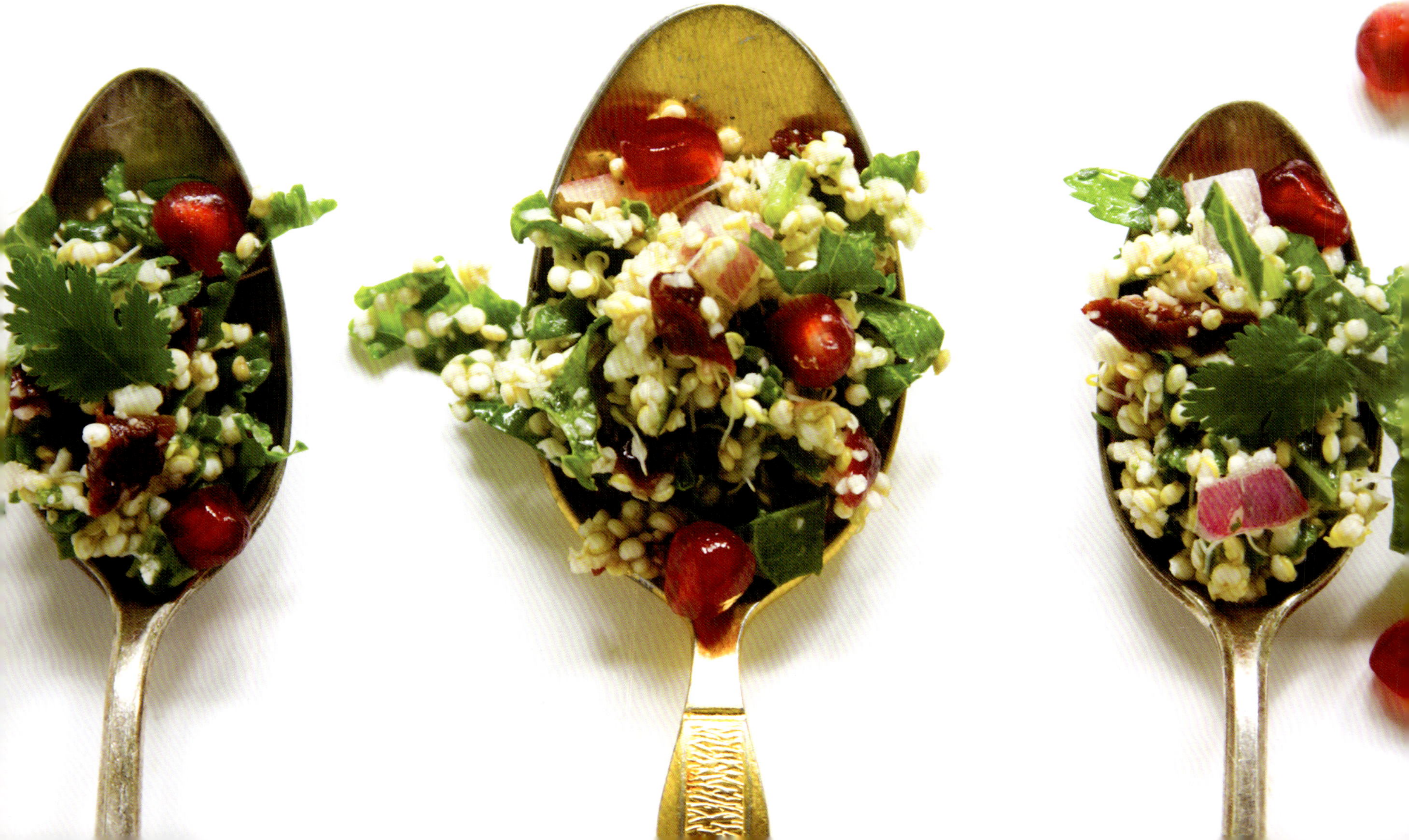

CAULIFLOWER, SPROUTED QUINOA, AND POMEGRANATE SEED SALAD

SERVES 4-6

SALAD

1 cup dry quinoa, soaked 3 hours and rinsed, sprouted 24 hours and rinsed again (makes 2 cups when sprouted)
2 cups raw cauliflower, chopped
2 cups green kale, stems removed and julienne
1/2 cup fresh cilantro, leaves only, chopped
1/2 cup fresh pomegranate, seeds only
1/4 cup red onion, diced
1/4 cup unsweetened dried cherries, chopped

DRESSING

1/3 cup virgin raw olive oil
1/4 cup lemon juice, fresh-squeezed
2 teaspoons raw apple cider vinegar
1½ teaspoons raw honey or agave
1/2 teaspoon sea salt
1/4 teaspoon ground black pepper

This hearty salad has an abundance of flavor and textures. The garnet-like pomegranate seeds add a splash of color, while the lemon honey dressing brings the flavors together. The protein-packed quinoa makes this a great entrée and an ideal dish to bring to a potluck.

Make the salad
1. Make quinoa a day ahead by soaking 1 cup dry quinoa in water. Rinse, place quinoa in sprouting jar, or bowl with perforated cover, this will allow the quinoa to breathe. Sprout for 24 hours. Rinse and place in large salad bowl.
2. In food processor with the S blade, pulse cauliflower for 10 seconds, until it's the consistency of couscous. Add to bowl of sprouted quinoa.
3. Add kale, cilantro, pomegranate, onion, and dried cherries to bowl with quinoa and cauliflower. Mix with wooden spoon until well combined. Set aside.

Make the dressing
1. In a small mixing bowl add olive oil, lemon juice, apple cider vinegar, honey, sea salt, and pepper. Whisk until well combined. Pour over salad. Toss lightly to coat. Serve immediately.

Note: Keeps in refrigerator up to 4 days in airtight container.

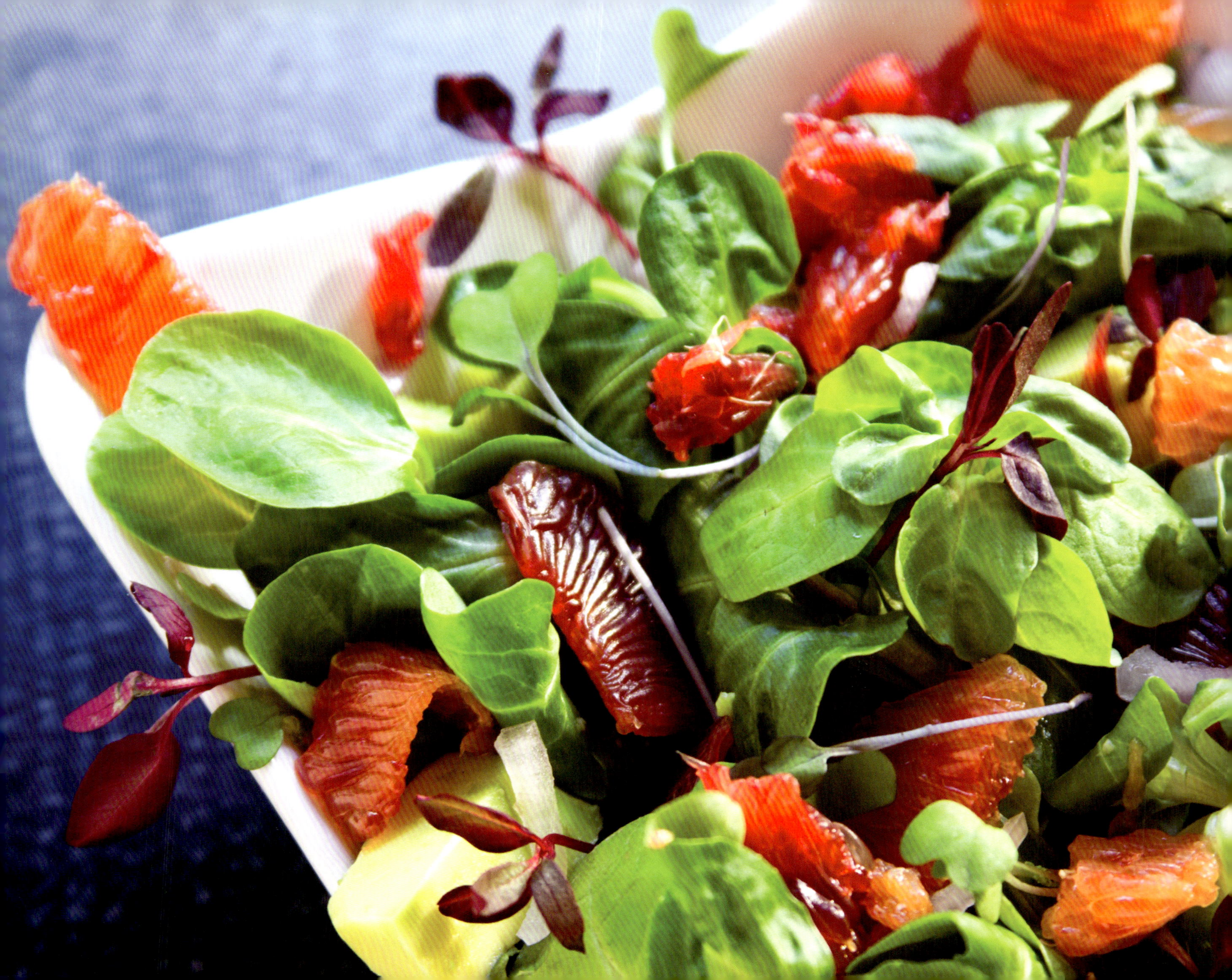

MACHE, AVOCADO, PUMPKIN SEEDS, AND **BLOOD ORANGE** WITH CITRUS DRESSING

SERVES 4-6

Mache, also known as lamb's lettuce, is a very mild, delicate lettuce variety that has a slightly nutty flavor. Blood oranges lend a bright color contrast to this fabulous winter salad, while pumpkin seeds, shallots, and avocado give it texture and depth.

Make the salad
1. In large salad bowl, add mache, micro greens, blood oranges, avocado, pumpkin seeds, and shallots. Set aside.

Make the dressing
1. In a small mixing bowl, add blood orange juice, olive oil, shallots, apple cider vinegar, orange zest, agave, sea salt and pepper. Whisk until oil and juice are well combined.
2. Pour dressing over salad. Toss lightly to coat. Serve immediately.

Note: Keeps in refrigerator up to 2 days in airtight container.

SALAD
3 cups mache lettuce
1 cup micro greens
1½ cups blood orange segments, peeled and halved
1 medium avocado, peeled, pitted and cubed
1/4 cup raw or dehydrated pumpkin seeds
1 tablespoon shallots, peeled and finely chopped

DRESSING
1/4 cup blood orange juice, fresh-squeezed
1/4 cup virgin raw olive oil
2 tablespoons shallots, peeled and finely chopped
2 tablespoons apple cider vinegar
1 ½ tablespoons blood orange zest
1 teaspoon raw light agave
1/4 teaspoon sea salt
1/4 fresh ground black pepper

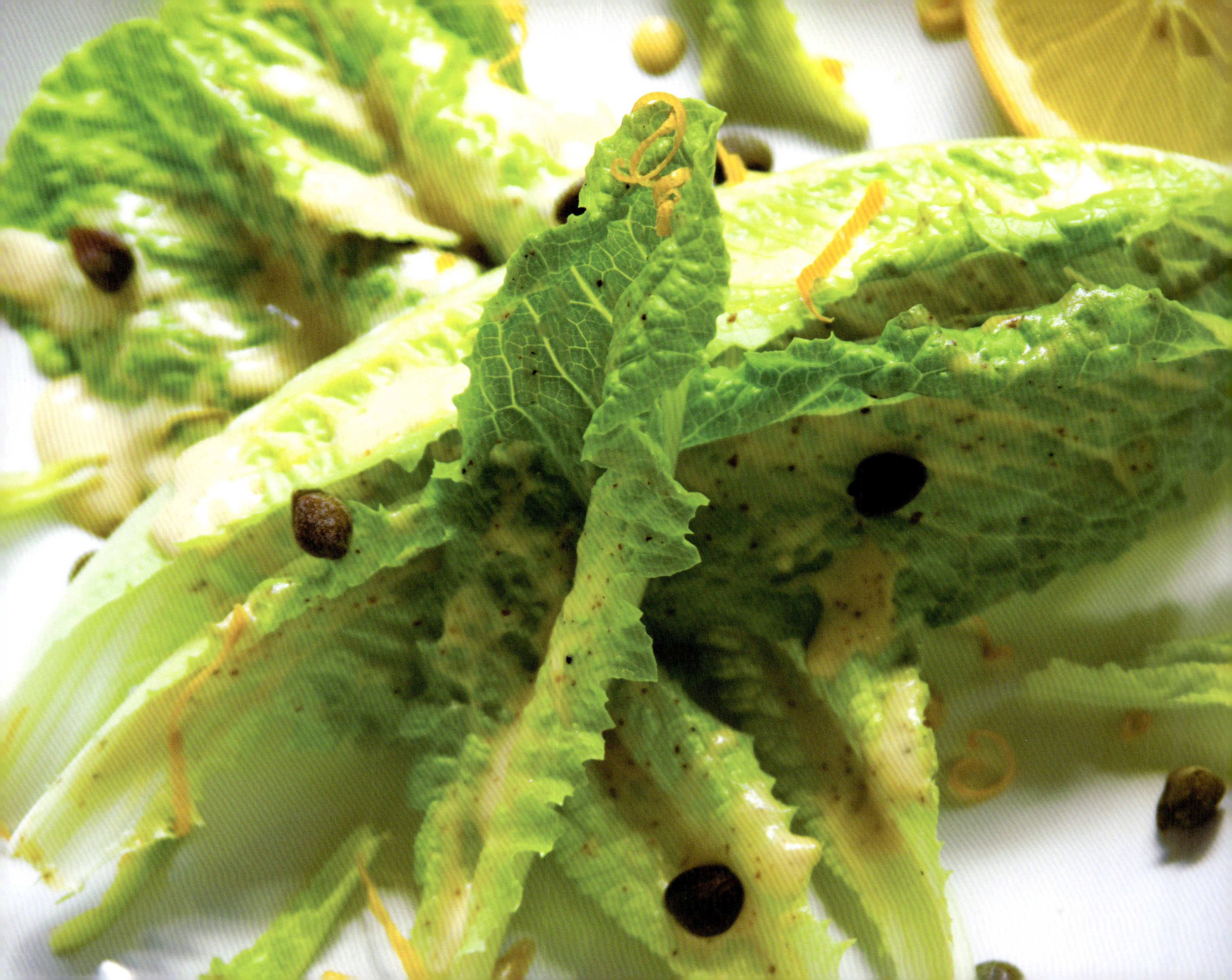

ROMAINE, CAPERS, AND MEYER LEMON CAESAR DRESSING

SERVES 4-6

SALAD
8 cups romaine lettuce, chopped
2 tablespoons caper berries

DRESSING
1¼ cup cashew spread (see page 100)
1/2 cup virgin raw olive oil
1/4 cup caper brine
1/4 cup Meyer lemon juice, fresh-squeezed
4 medium cloves garlic, peeled
2 tablespoons wheat-free tamari
1 tablespoon brown rice miso paste
1 tablespoon nutritional yeast
2 teaspoons raw light agave
1 teaspoon stone-ground mustard
1/2 teaspoon fresh ground black pepper

Caesar salad used to be one of my favorites to order when dining out. I can proudly say that I think this is the best Caesar salad I've ever had. It contains all the components of the famous original with a few extra twists; a thick creamy dressing, crunchy romaine lettuce, and zippy caper berries instead of croutons.

Make the salad
1. In large salad bowl, add romaine and caper berries.

Make the dressing
1. In high-speed blender place cashew spread, olive oil, caper brine, Meyer lemon juice, garlic, wheat-free tamari, miso paste, nutritional yeast, agave, mustard, and pepper. Blend on high for about 2 minutes, until smooth and creamy.
2. Pour dressing over salad and toss lightly to coat. Serve immediately.

Note: Salad keeps in refrigerator up to 2 days in airtight container. Dressing keeps up to 5 days in airtight container.

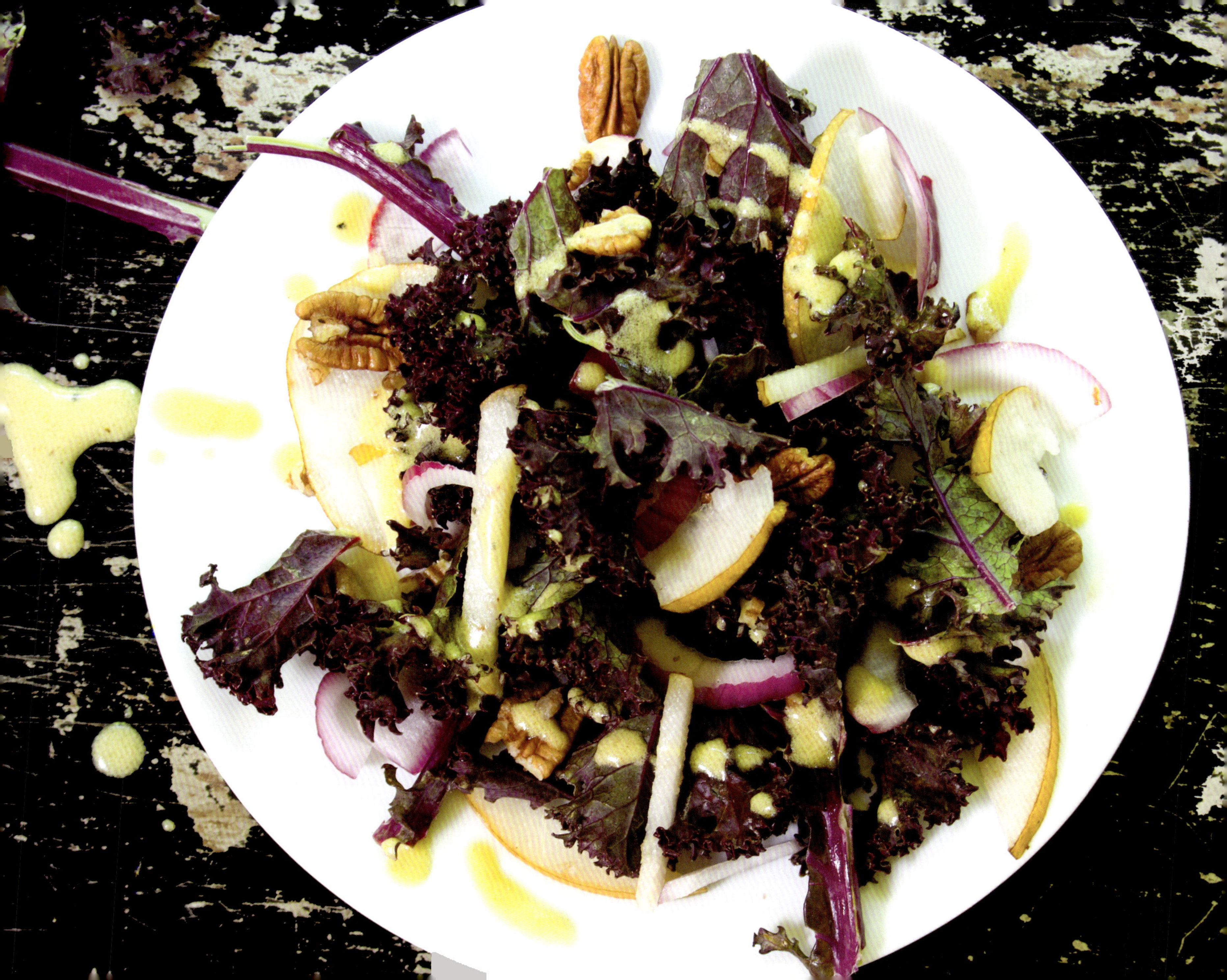

KALE, ASIAN PEAR, RED ONION, **CANDIED PECANS**, AND MUSTARD DRESSING

SERVES 4-6

SALAD
4 cups green and purple kale, chopped
1/2 cup red onion, diced
1/2 cup Asian pear, sliced
1/2 cup candied pecans (see page 106)

DRESSING
1/4 cup expeller-pressed grape-seed oil
2 tablespoons raw apple cider vinegar
2 teaspoons raw light agave
1/4 cup stone-ground mustard
2 tablespoons lemon juice, fresh-squeezed
1/8 teaspoon sea salt
1/8 teaspoon fresh ground black pepper

There are so many options for lettuce when making a salad. Although it's not a lettuce, kale is my favorite green to use. Part of the cabbage family, kale supplies your body with nothing but love.

Make the dressing
1. In small mixing bowl, add grape-seed oil, apple cider vinegar, agave, mustard, lemon juice, sea salt, and black pepper. Whisk until oil is well incorporated, and set aside.

Make the salad
1. In large salad bowl, add kale and red onion.
2. Coat with dressing. Massage dressing into kale for 5 minutes, until leaves start to become darker in color and tender.
3. Add Asian pear and candied pecans. Toss lightly. Serve immediately.

Note: Keeps in refrigerator up to 2 days in airtight container.

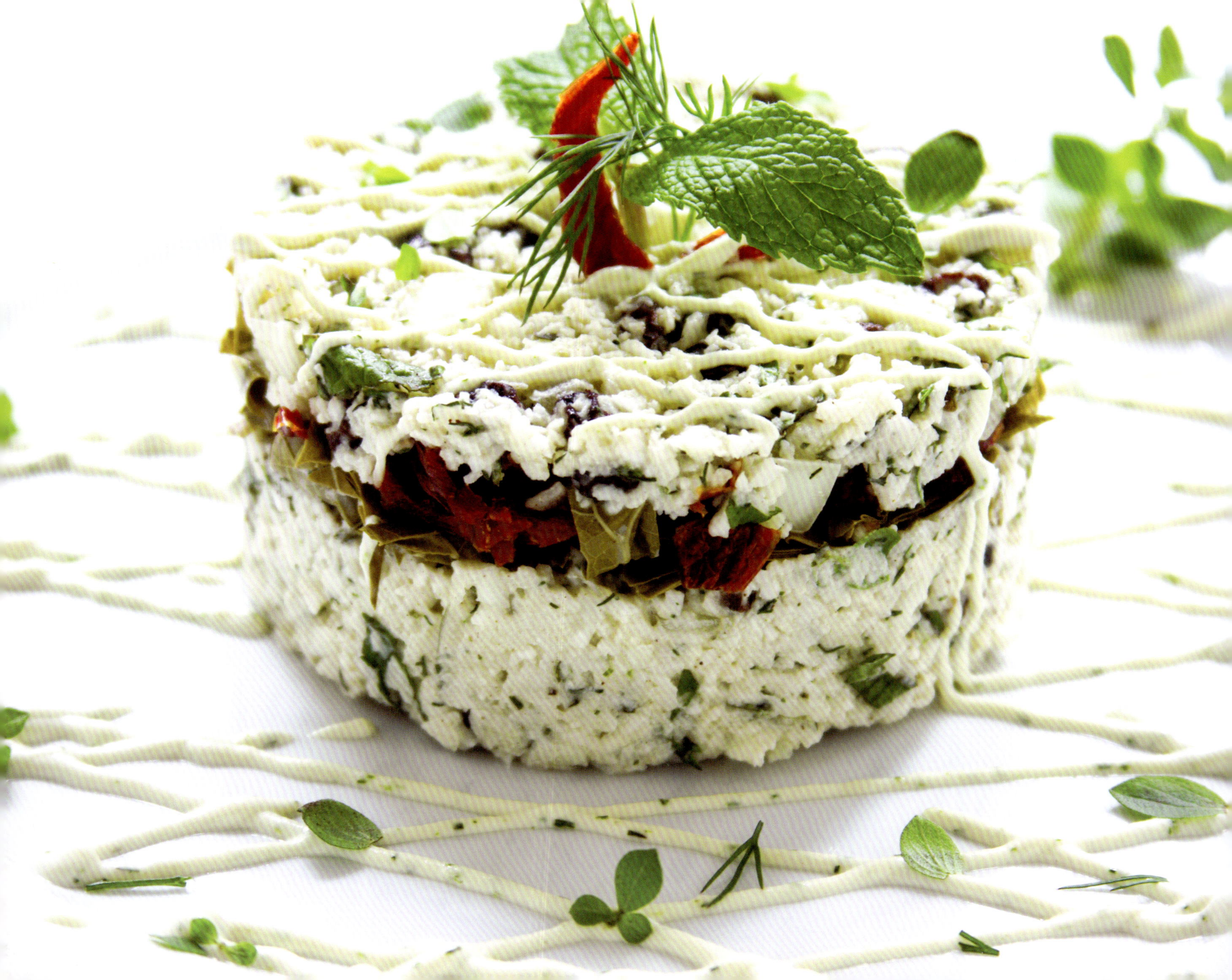

CAULIFLOWER RICE, **GRAPE LEAVES**, SUN-DRIED TOMATO, MINT, AND CREAMY DILL DRESSING

SERVES 4-6

SALAD
4 cups cauliflower, chopped
1 cup grape leaves, chopped
1/2 cup yellow onion, chopped
1/2 cup sun-dried tomatoes
1/2 cup dried currents
2 tablespoons lemon juice, fresh squeezed
2 tablespoons apple cider vinegar
2 tablespoons fresh mint, chopped
2 teaspoons fresh dill, chopped
2 teaspoons fresh oregano, chopped
1/2 teaspoon fresh ground black pepper
1/4 teaspoon ground cinnamon
1/8 teaspoon allspice

DRESSING
1 cup raw cashews, soaked 4–6 hours, drained and rinsed
1/2 cup water
1/4 cup virgin raw olive oil
3 tablespoons lemon juice, fresh-squeezed
2 tablespoons fresh dill
1 tablespoon apple cider vinegar
1/2 teaspoon sea salt

GARNISH
4–6 fresh dill sprigs
4–6 fresh mint sprigs

I was inspired to create this recipe after returning from a trip to Greece, where I indulged in the most amazing stuffed grape leaves. This salad is a deconstructed raw version, lending an explosion of flavors with each bite. With it's cauliflower rice, sun-dried tomatoes accented with tart dried currents, pungent grape leaves, fresh herbs, and a creamy dill dressing, this salad is both refreshing and satisfying enough to serve as an entrée.

Make the salad
1. Using a food processor with S-blade attachment, pulse cauliflower for about 1 minute, until broken down and with a couscous-like consistency. Place in large mixing bowl.
2. Add to bowl grape leaves, onion, sun-dried tomatoes, currents, lemon juice, apple cider vinegar, mint, dill, oregano, black pepper, cinnamon, and allspice. Mix with a spoon until well combined. Cover and set aside.

Make the dressing
1. In high-speed blender add cashews, water, olive oil, lemon juice, apple cider vinegar, and sea salt. Blend on high for about 2 minutes, until totally smooth.
2. Add dill to blender and blend for 5 seconds, until just combined.

Assemble
1. For individual servings, divide salad on serving dishes of choice. Drizzle with about 2 tablespoons of dressing on each plate. Garnish with a sprig of fresh dill and mint.
2. For group serving, pour dressing over salad and gently mix until all ingredients are combined. Garnish with a sprig of dill and mint. Serve immediately.

Note: Keeps in refrigerator up to 3 days in airtight container.

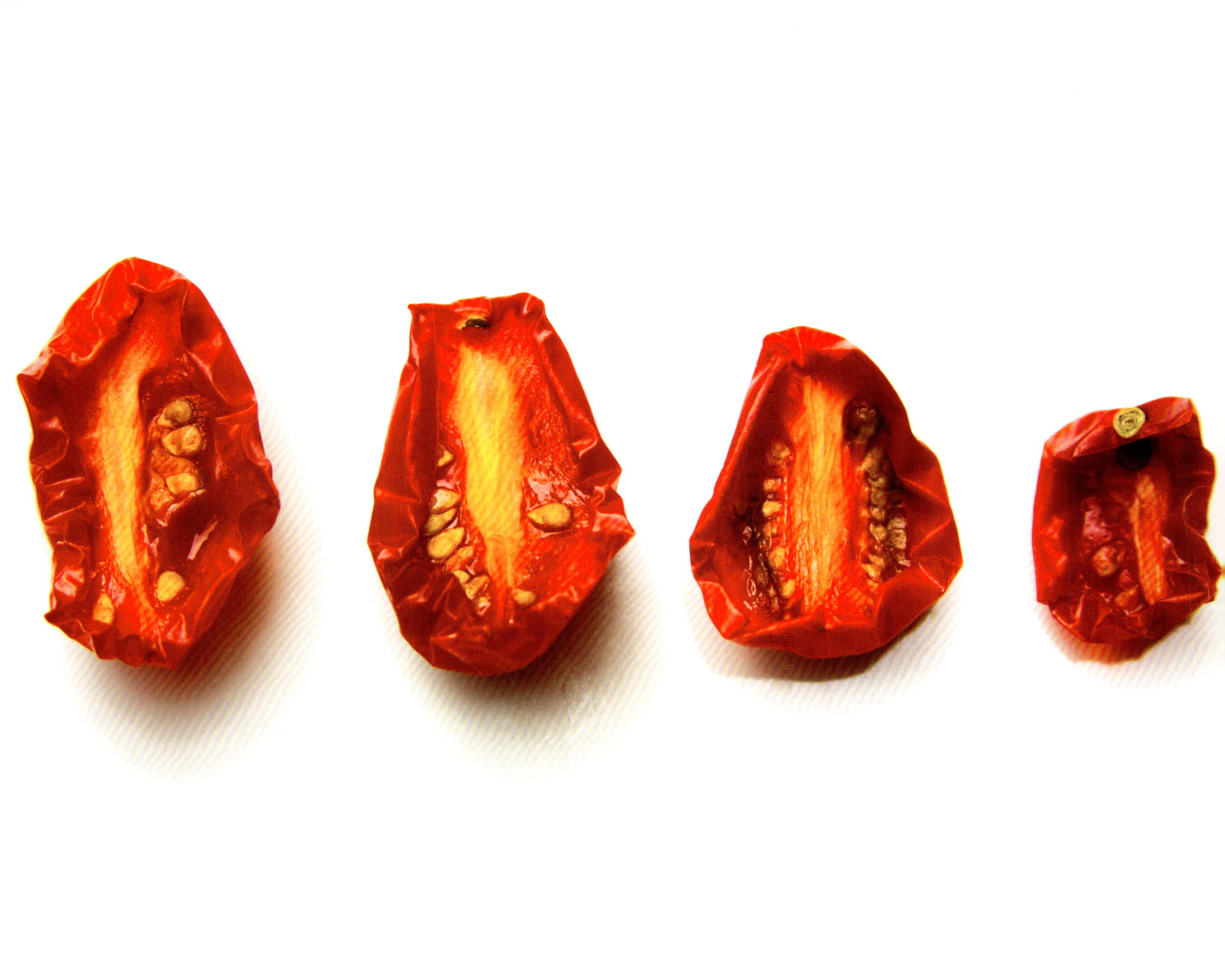

A P P E T

I Z E R S

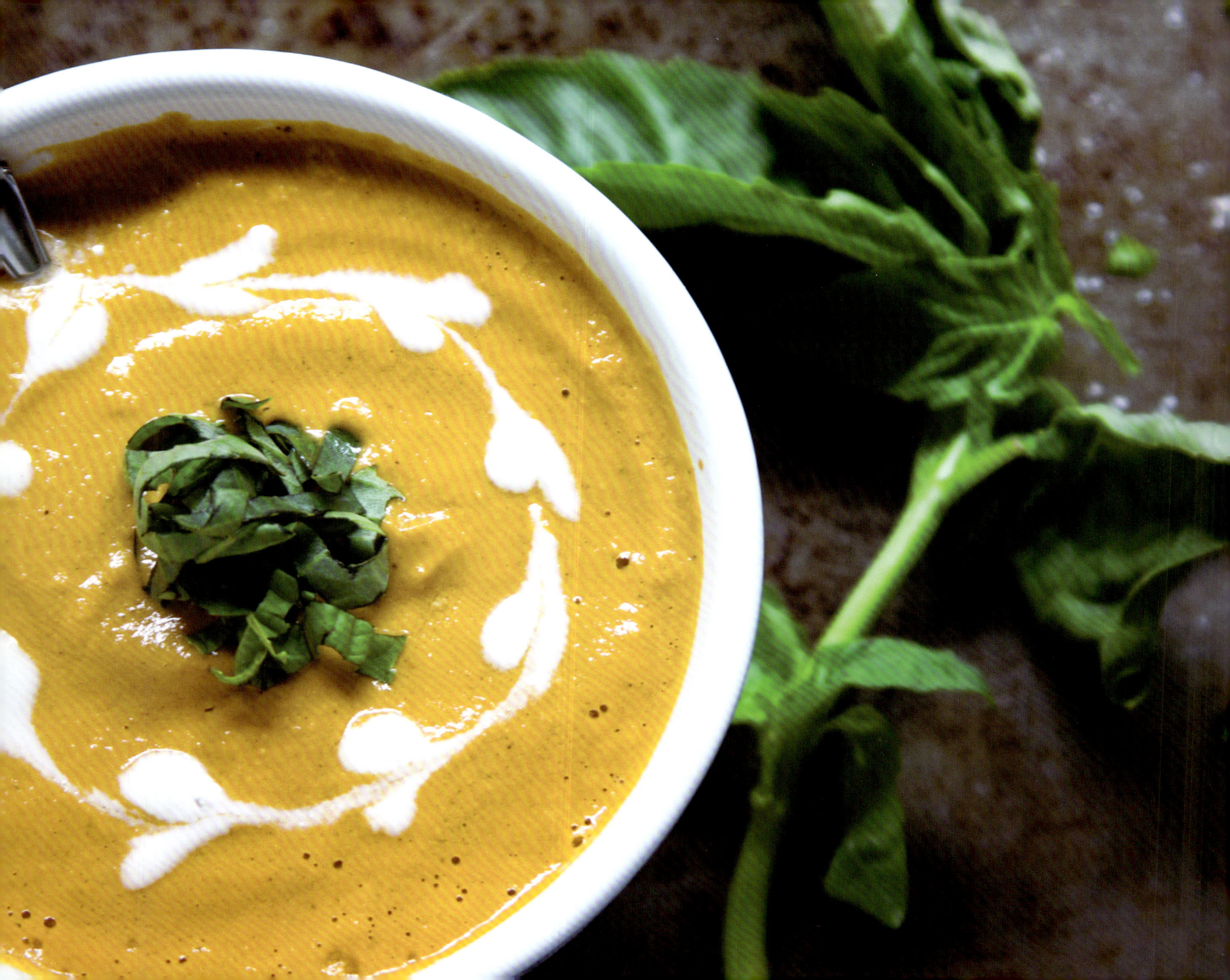

CREAMY TOMATO BISQUE WITH BASIL OIL AND FRESH CRACKED PEPPER

MAKES 32 OUNCES (SERVES 4-6)

SOUP

1¼ cups fresh tomatoes, chopped
1 cup water
1/4 cup fresh sweet onion, chopped
1/4 cup sun-dried tomatoes, chopped
1/4 cup fresh basil, tightly packed
2 tablespoons virgin raw olive oil
2 tablespoons raw tahini
2 medium cloves garlic, peeled
1 tablespoon raw light agave
1 tablespoon apple cider vinegar
1 tablespoon dried basil
1/2 teaspoon sea salt
1/4 teaspoon fresh cracked black pepper

GARNISH

1/4 cup fresh basil leaves, chiffonade
2 tablespoons basil oil (see page 94)
2 tablespoons cashew cream (see page 104)
1 teaspoon fresh cracked black pepper

A creamy tomato bisque with a hint of basil, this soup is great served chilled or slightly warmed in the dehydrator.

Make the soup

1. In high-speed blender place tomatoes, water, onion, sun-dried tomatoes, fresh basil, olive oil, tahini, garlic, agave, apple cider vinegar, dried basil, sea salt, and pepper. Blend on high for about 3 minutes, until all ingredients are broken down and soup is smooth and creamy.
2. Leave soup in blender carafe at room temperature for 20–30 minutes, so the flavors can marinate. This makes a huge difference in taste.
3. Pour soup into bowls of choice and sprinkle with fresh basil in center. Drizzle with basil oil and cashew cream. Serve immediately.

Note: Keeps in refrigerator up to 3 days in airtight container.

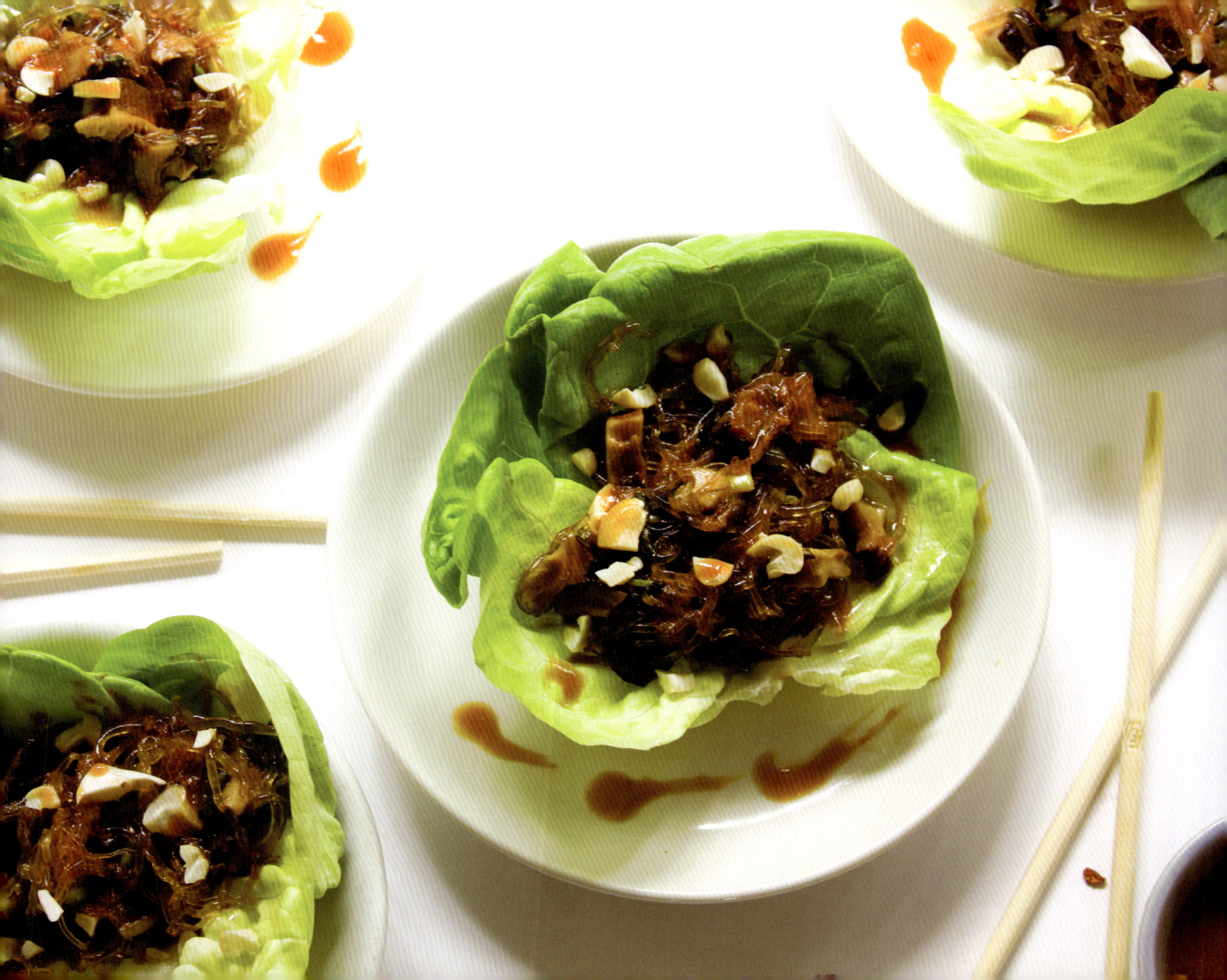

BUTTER LETTUCE CUPS, MARINATED SHITAKES, AND GARLIC CHILI SAUCE

SERVES 4-6

FILLING
8 butter lettuce leaves
1 cup raw clear kelp noodles
1/4 cup fresh cilantro, stems removed
1/4 cup raw cashews, chopped
1/4 cup green onions, chopped
1/4 cup dehydrated shitake mushrooms

MARINADE
1/2 cup expeller-pressed sesame oil
2 tablespoons wheat-free tamari
2 tablespoons rice wine vinegar

SAUCE
1 tablespoon stone-ground mustard
2 tablespoons wheat-free tamari
2 tablespoons raw light agave
2 tablespoons rice wine vinegar
1 ½ tablespoons garlic chili sauce (see page 98)
1 tablespoon lemon juice, fresh-squeezed
1/2 teaspoon expeller-pressed sesame oil

This delicious starter is both easy to make and incredibly satisfying. Soft, marinated kelp noodles sprinkled with crunchy cashews then served in crisp butter lettuce cups. This dish really comes alive with its sweet and tangy chili sauce, adding an intense depth of flavor.

Make the filling
1. In medium mixing bowl, add kelp noodles, cilantro, cashews, green onions, and shitakes. Set aside.

Make the marinade
1. In a small bowl, add sesame oil, wheat-free tamari, and rice wine vinegar. Whisk until combined.
2. Pour marinade over filling and toss lightly until well coated.
3. Place bowl of filling in dehydrator at 115 degrees for 2 hours. This will soften the noodles and speed up the marinating process.

Prepare sauce
1. In a small mixing bowl, whisk mustard, wheat-free tamari, agave, rice wine vinegar, garlic chili sauce, lemon juice, and sesame oil. Set aside.

Assemble lettuce cups
1. Evenly distribute marinated filling in lettuce cups. Drizzle with sweet garlic chili sauce. Serve immediately.

Note: Keeps in refrigerator up to 3 days in airtight container.

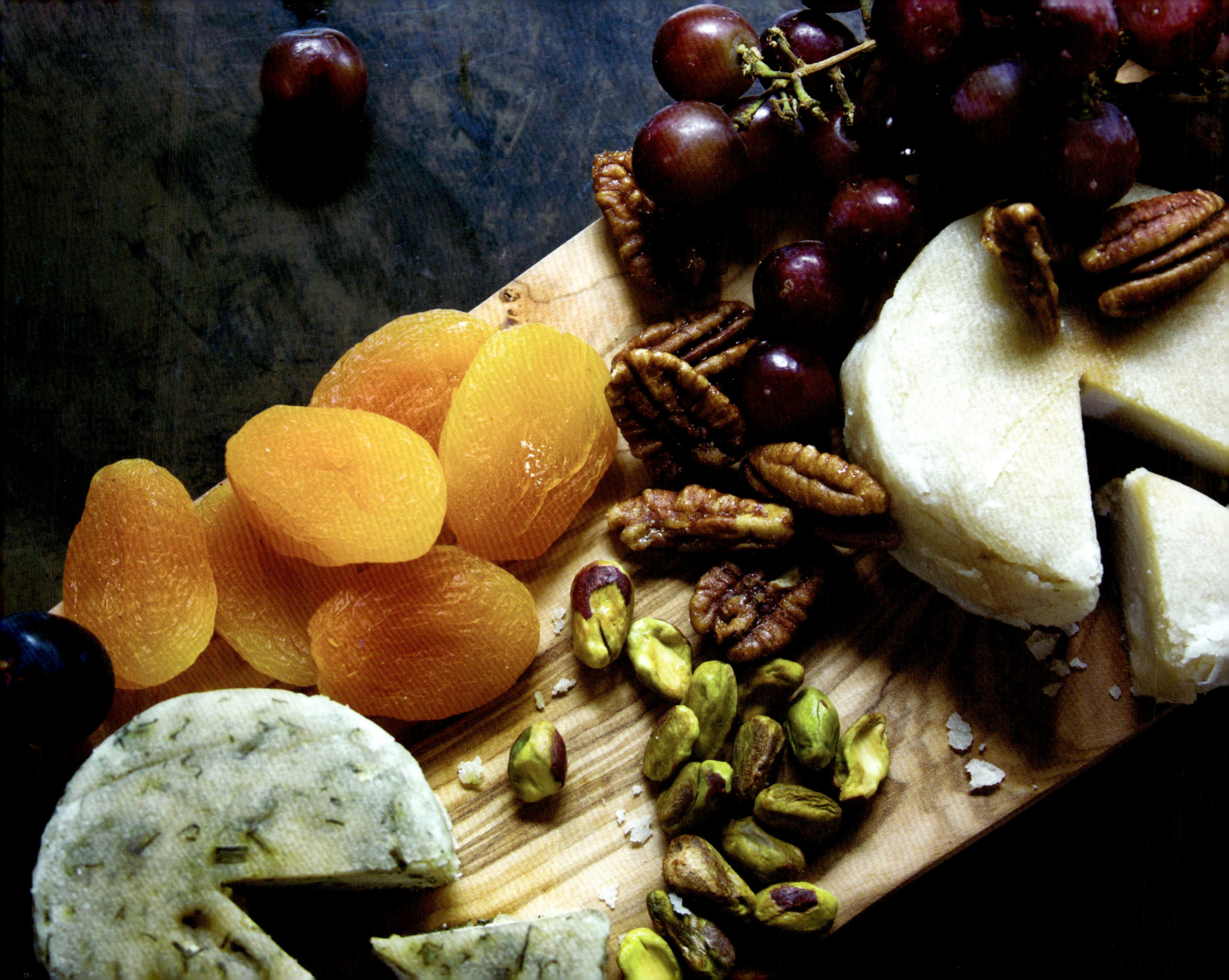

AGED MACADAMIA NUT CHEESE

MAKES 2 3-INCH ROUNDS

CHEESE
1¼ cups water
1 cup raw macadamia nuts
4 capsules vegan probiotics
1/4 teaspoon sea salt

FOR HERB CHEESE
1 tablespoon fresh chives, chopped
2 teaspoons dried parsley
1 teaspoon dried dill

A semi-soft pungent macadamia nut cheese with a sharp sophistication. This cheese works beautifully when arranged with nuts or fresh and dried fruits, or when sprinkled on a raw pizza.

Make the cheese
1. In high-speed blender add water. Pull probiotic caps apart and empty probiotics into water. Let dissolve for 15 minutes.
2. Add macadamia nuts and sea salt to blender. Blend on high for about 2 minutes, until macadamia nuts are broken down and cheese is smooth.
3. Strain cheese through triple-layered cheesecloth, bring all sides together, and squeeze out as much liquid as possible from the cheese.
4. Leave cheese in cloth and tie up with a rubber band. Place between two plates with weights on top (I use rocks). Let the remaining moisture come out for 48 hours.
5. After 48 hours, take the cheese out of cheesecloth. Make sure there are no cloth strings on outer layer of the cheese and, if so, remove.
6. Add desired spices and herbs. Knead in with hands.
7. Divide cheese into two and place in forms or mold of choice. Put in dehydrator for 24–48 hours at 115 degrees, depending on how tangy and hard you want your cheese. The longer you leave it in the dehydrator, the harder and more pungent the cheese will be. The cheese will begin too get slightly darker on the outside. This is good!
8. Remove from dehydrator and wrap cheese in parchment paper.

Note: Keeps in refrigerator up to 3 weeks in airtight container.

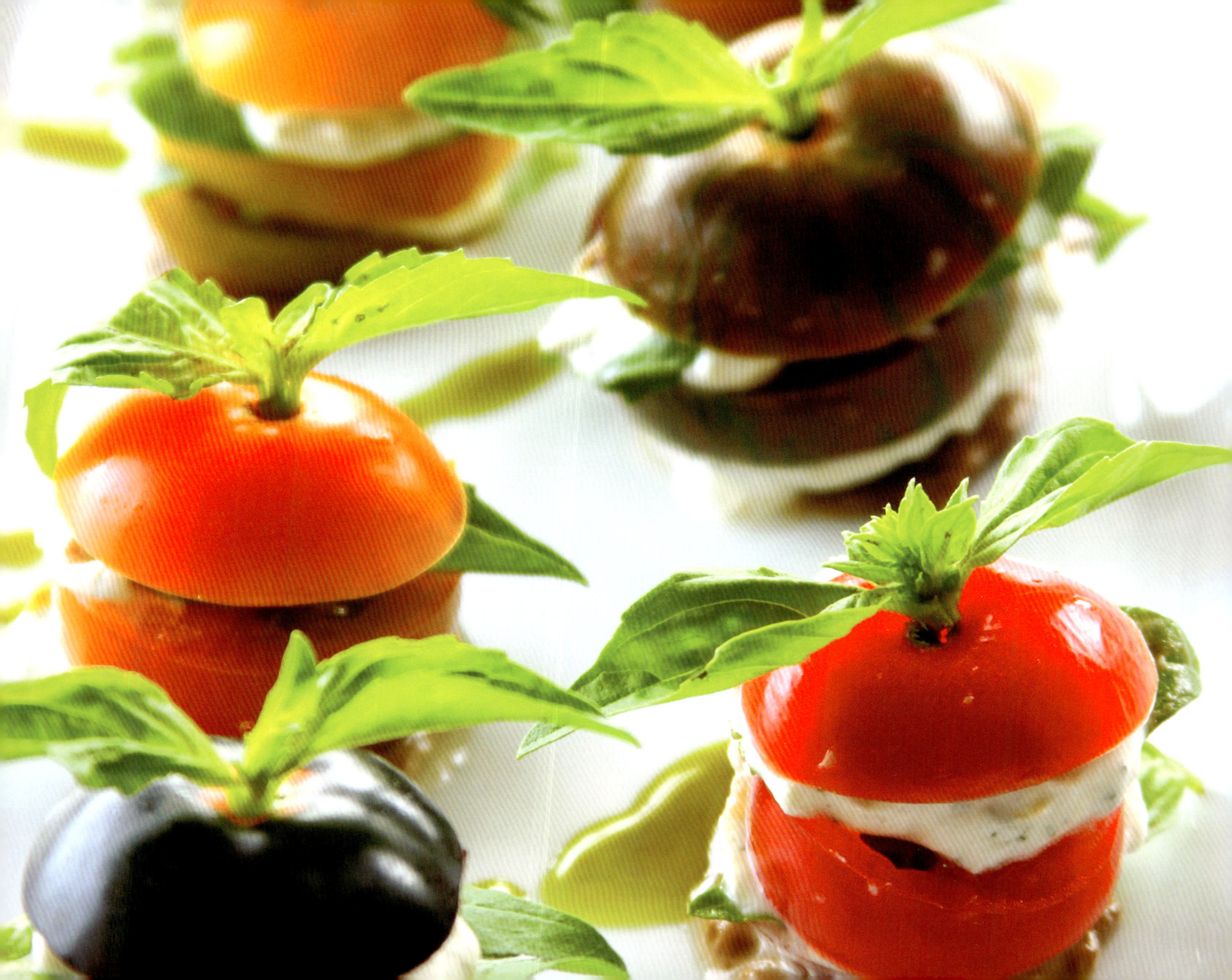

CASHEW BASIL MOZZARELLA, HEIRLOOM TOMATOES, BASIL, AND BALSAMIC FIG SAUCE

SERVES 4-6

FILLING
1¼ cup basil mozzarella cut into 2-inch squares (see page 96)
4 medium heirloom tomatoes, ends removed, cut into 4 equal round slices
24 large fresh basil leaves

SAUCE
5 dried black mission figs
1 cup virgin raw olive oil
1/2 cup balsamic vinegar
2 cloves garlic, peeled
1 teaspoon raw light agave
1/2 teaspoon sea salt
1/2 teaspoon fresh ground black pepper

GARNISH (OPTIONAL)
1/4 cup fresh basil oil (see page 94)

Fresh basil is by far my favorite herb, and there's something undeniable about the combination of ripe tomato, basil, and mozzarella that is perfection! These sophisticated stacks of art are drizzled in a sweet balsamic fig sauce that brings the flavors together beautifully. This traditional dish is great served as an appetizer, at parties, or as a light meal on a warm summer night.

Make the sauce
1. In a high-speed blender, place figs, olive oil, balsamic vinegar, garlic, agave, sea salt, and pepper. Blend on medium-high for about 2 minutes, until fig seeds are broken down and sauce is smooth. There will be a point when the sauce looks really lumpy. Keep blending until the lumps are gone.

Assemble stacks
1. On a clean plate, drizzle fig sauce in zigzag pattern.
2. Layer, tomato, basil leaf, mozzarella square, dollop of fig sauce, and repeat these layers until the last tomato piece is on top.
3. Drizzle with fresh basil oil. Serve immediately.

Note: Keeps in refrigerator up to 3 days in airtight container. These also make great mini stacks using baby heirloom tomatoes, yielding 25–30 small stacks for a party.

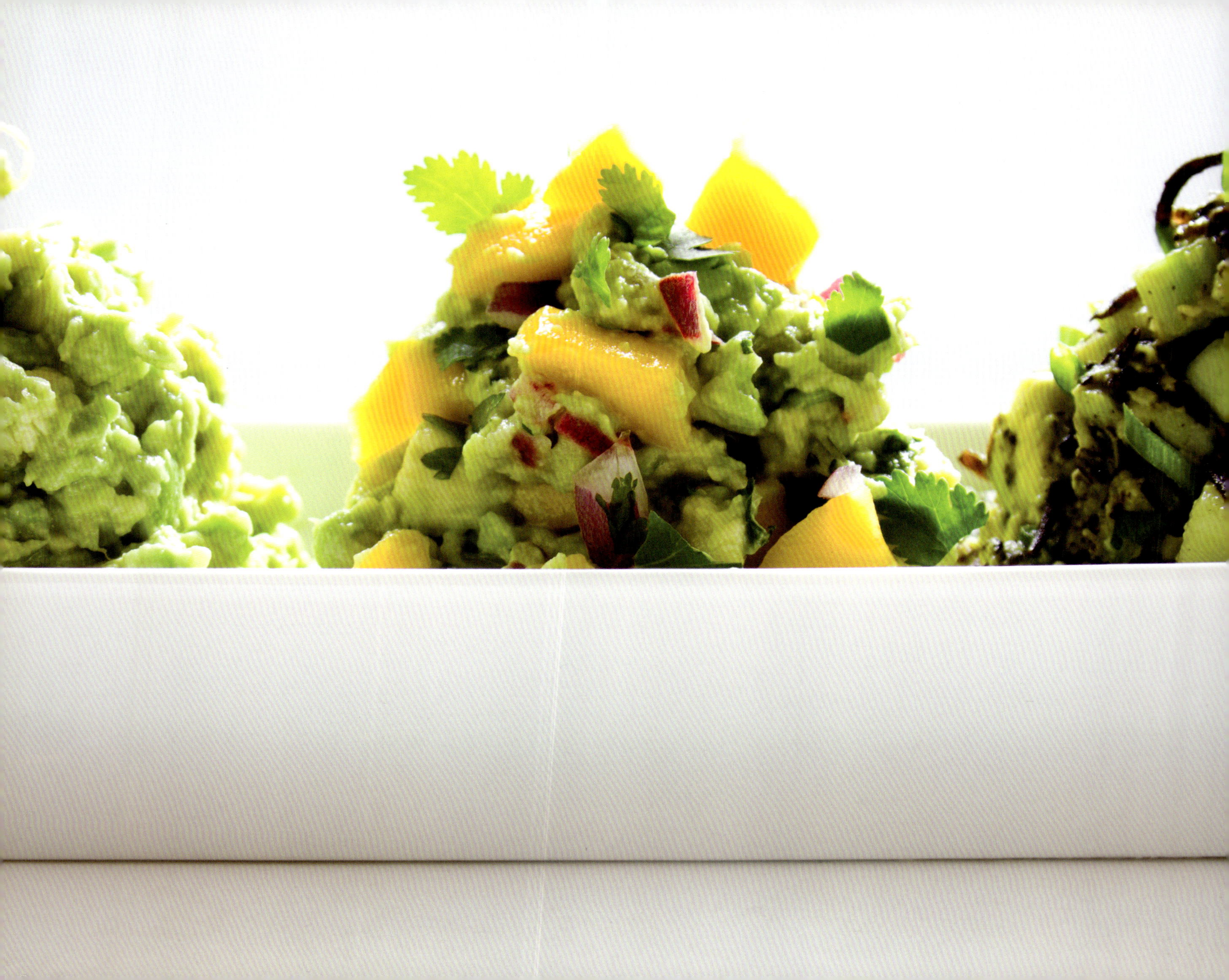

AVOCADO, GARLIC, AND ZESTY LEMON GUACAMOLE

MAKES 1 CUP (SERVES 4-6)

GUACAMOLE

2 small ripe avocados, peeled, pitted and cubed
2½ teaspoons lemon juice, fresh-squeezed
2 large cloves garlic, peeled and minced
1/4 teaspoon sea salt

This guacamole does not skimp on flavor with a fresh squeeze of tart lemon and pungent garlic. Great served with fresh veggies for dipping or as a condiment on tacos, burritos, salads, and more.

Make the guacamole
1. In a small mixing bowl, add avocado, lemon juice, garlic, and sea salt.
2. Mash with fork until combined and avocado is still slightly chunky. Serve immediately.

Note: Keeps in refrigerator up to 3 days in airtight container. If the guacamole browns on top, it's just oxidation. Try putting the pit in with the guacamole. This helps retain the green color.

AVOCADO, GREEN ONION, CUCUMBER, AND **SEAWEED** GUACAMOLE

MAKES 1 CUP (SERVES 4-6)

GUACAMOLE

2 small avocados, peeled, pitted and cubed
1/2 cup English cucumber, peeled and diced
2 tablespoons dried wakame
2 tablespoons green onion, chopped
2½ teaspoons wheat-free tamari

My brother Shane came up with this recipe when we were coming off our first two-week nutritional cleanse. We both had been dreaming of stuffing our faces with all kinds of naughty foods. However, we didn't want to wreak havoc on our bodies after just giving them a good spring cleaning. After pacing back in forth in the kitchen, Shane came up with this and it tasted like heaven. The mild buttery avocado, saltiness from the seaweed, and crunchy bite from the cucumber was incredibly satisfying. Serve with your favorite raw crackers, chips, crudités, or just eat with a spoon straight out of the bowl.

Make the guacamole
1. Briefly rinse wakame in warm water, then soak for 5 minutes in a bowl of water. Drain and pat dry with towel.
2. In a small mixing bowl, add avocado, English cucumber, wakame, green onion, and wheat-free tamari.
3. Mash with fork until combined and avocado is still slightly chunky. Serve immediately.

Note: Keeps in refrigerator up to 2 days in airtight container. If the guacamole browns on top, it's just oxidation. Try putting the pit in with the guacamole. This helps retain the green color.

AVOCADO, LIME, CILANTRO, AND SWEET **MANGO** GUACAMOLE

MAKES 1 CUP (SERVES 4-6)

GUACAMOLE
2 small ripe avocados, peeled, pitted and cubed
1/2 cup mango, peeled, pitted and cubed
1/4 cup red onion, peeled and chopped
2 tablespoons cilantro, stems removed and chopped
1 tablespoon + 1 teaspoon lime juice, fresh-squeezed
2 cloves garlic, peeled and minced
1/4 teaspoon sea salt

I've brought this guacamole to parties over the years and it's always devoured within minutes. A great tropical twist on the classic, avocado and sweet-tart mango are a natural pairing.

Make the guacamole
1. In a small mixing bowl, add avocado, mango, red onion, cilantro, lime juice, garlic, and sea salt.
2. Mash with fork until combined and avocado is still slightly chunky. Serve immediately.

Note: Keeps in refrigerator up to 3 days in airtight container. If the guacamole browns on top, it's just oxidation. Try putting the pit in with the guacamole. This helps retain the green color

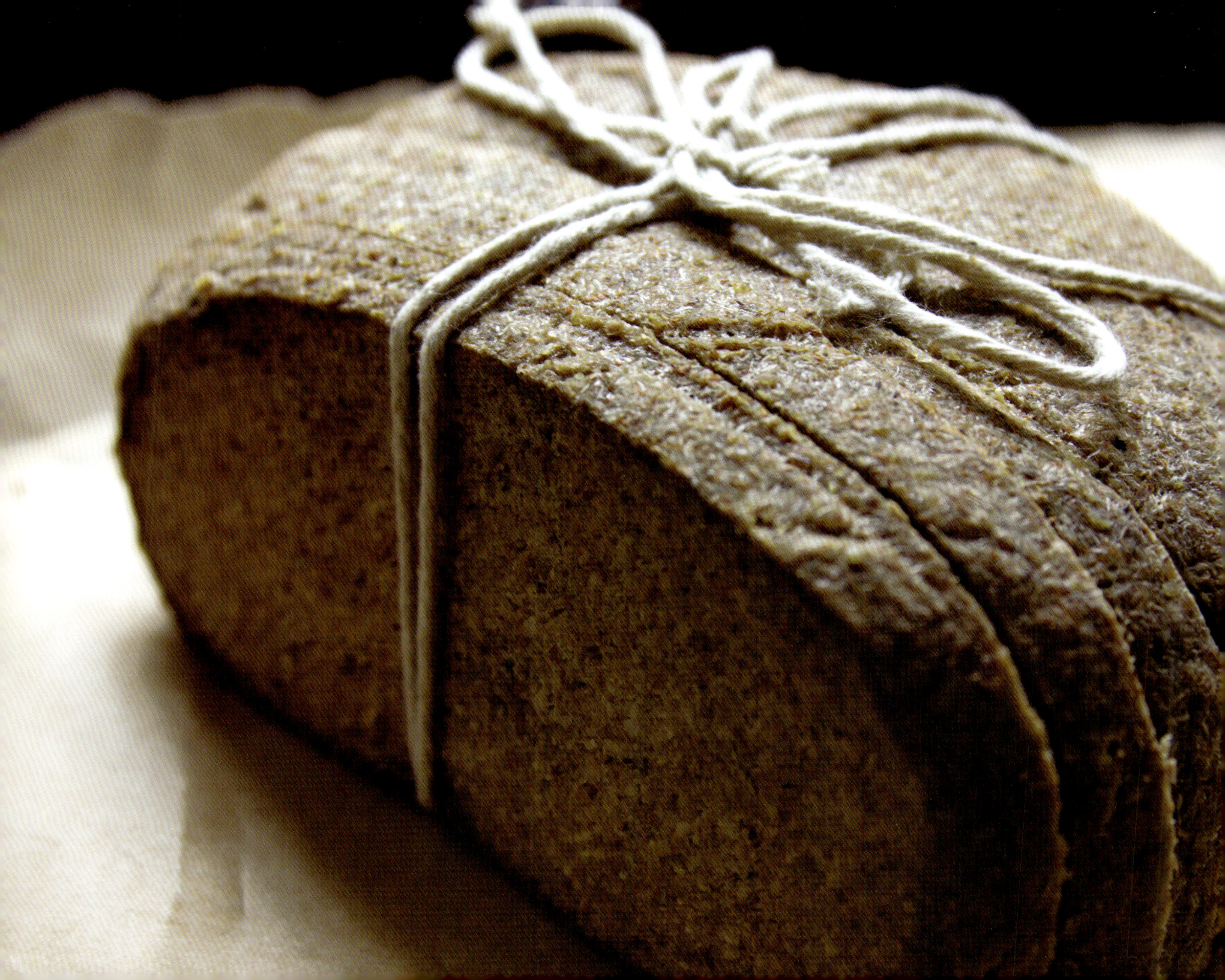

GOLDEN FLAX ALMOND BREAD

MAKES 1 LOAF

BREAD
3 cups almond flour (see page 29)
2 cups zucchini, peeled and chopped
1 cup psyllium husk
3/4 cup golden flax meal
1/4 cup almond milk
2 teaspoons raw light agave
1 teaspoon sea salt
1 teaspoon lemon juice, fresh-squeezed

Finally a raw bread that's edible! It took me years of experimenting in the kitchen to figure out this recipe for a gluten-free, grain-free bread that is easily digestible and mild in flavor. I began researching ancient bread-making techniques along with current gluten-free vegan baked bread recipes. What I discovered was that psyllium husks were often used to help the bread rise and give it a fluffier texture without yeast. I thought I'd give it a try in a raw format, and, to my surprise, it worked! The texture was perfect, but the flavor was off. I tried sprouted buckwheat flour, sprouted oat flour, and many more, but over time it tasted sour and had a very strange aftertaste. Finally, on a last-ditch attempt, I used almond flour and came up with this recipe. It made a beautiful and delicious loaf of raw bread. I am thrilled to be sharing this recipe and hope it will bring you as much joy as it did for me.

Make the bread
1. In high-speed blender place zucchini, almond milk, lemon juice, and agave. Blend on high for about 1 minute, until totally smooth. Set aside.
2. In large mixing bowl, add almond flour, psyllium husk, and sea salt.
3. Pour zucchini and almond milk liquid over flour mixture and knead with hands until well incorporated. The bread should be a doughlike consistency and spring back lightly to touch.
4. Form into round loaf and place on dehydrator tray.
5. Dehydrate at 115 degrees for 24 hours, until crisp on the outside. Slice in half and dehydrate for another 2 hours to ensure that the thickest part of the bread interior is dehydrated all the way through. Enjoy!

Note: Keeps covered in refrigerator up to 7 days.

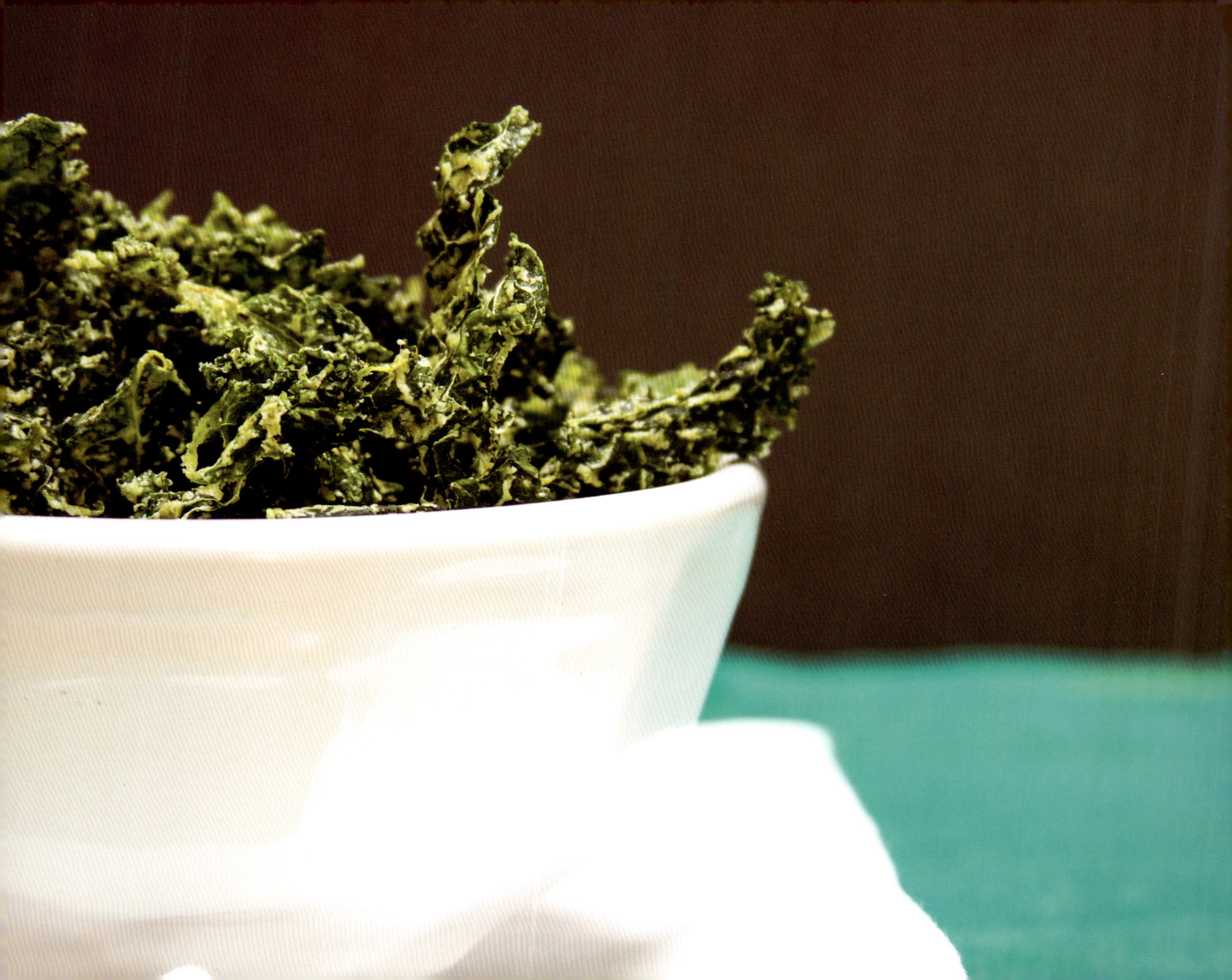

CRISPY HERB KALE CHIPS

MAKES 4 CUPS

CHIPS
8 cups kale, stems removed and roughly chopped
1 cup raw cashews, soaked 4–6 hours, drained and rinsed
1/2 cup water
1/4 cup virgin raw olive oil
2 small garlic cloves, peeled
2 teaspoons dried parsley
2 teaspoons onion powder
1½ teaspoons dried dill
1 teaspoon dried basil
1 teaspoon sea salt

These are a perfect snack when you want to kick that craving for something salty and crunchy. They beat greasy potato chips any day. Plus, they're loaded with vitamins and minerals.

Make the chips
1. In large mixing bowl, add kale and set aside.

Make sauce
2. In high-speed blender add cashews, water, olive oil, garlic, parsley, onion powder, dill, basil, and sea salt. Blend on high for about 1 minute, until cashews are broken down and sauce is smooth.
3. Pour sauce over kale and massage with hands for 5 minutes, until nice and saucy.
4. Put kale chips onto dehydrator trays lined with teflex sheets and spread out evenly. Dehydrate at 115 degrees for 4 hours.
5. Remove teflex sheets and return to dehydrator for another 4 hours, until crisp and crunchy.

Note: These store really well at room temperature in airtight container up to 1 month. If they start to lose crunchiness, put them back in the dehydrator again at 115 degrees to crisp them up.

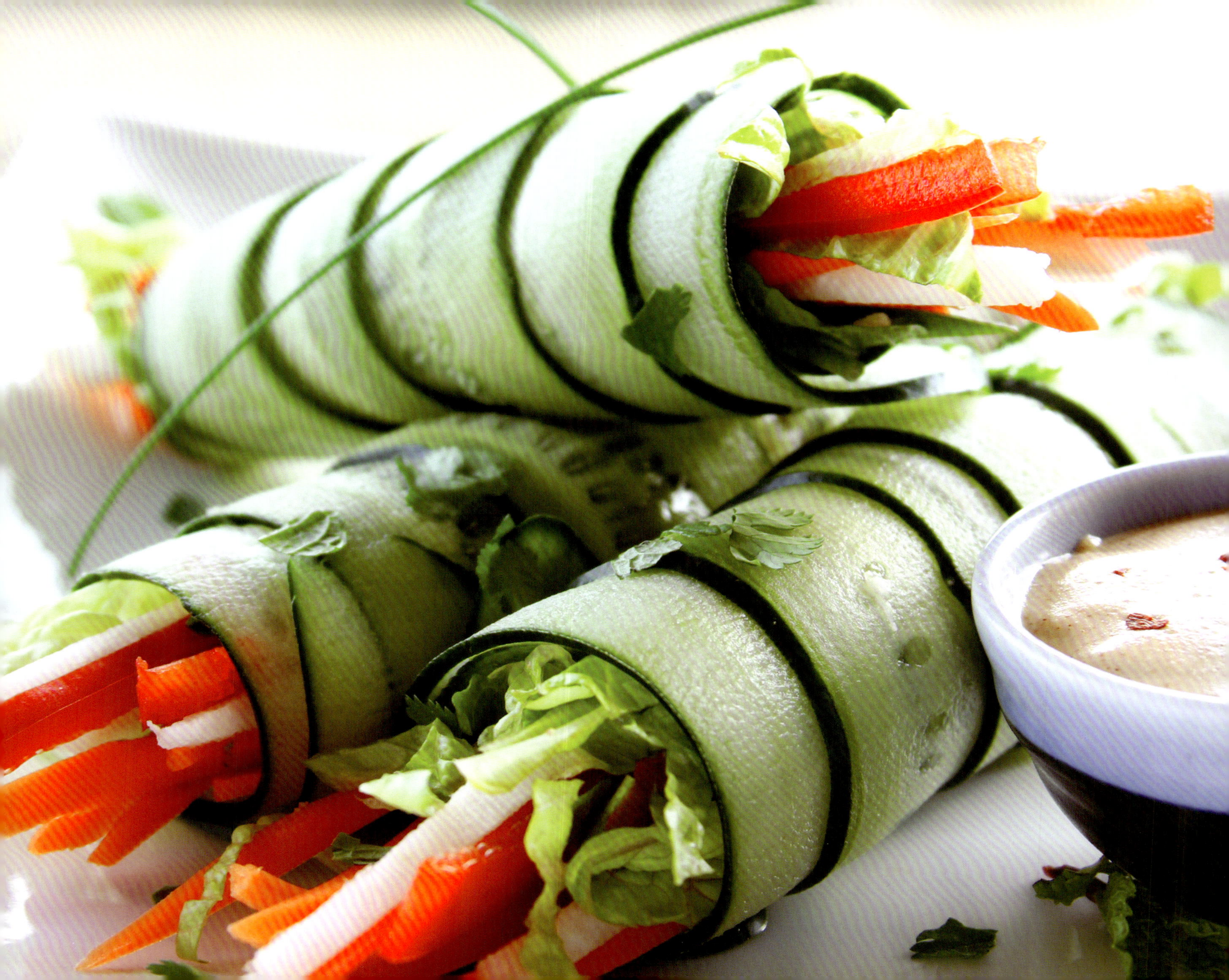

CUCUMBER ROLLS WITH BASIL, MINT, CILANTRO, AND SPICY COCONUT SAUCE

MAKES 8 ROLLS

ROLLS
1½ cups cucumbers, julienne
1 cup romaine lettuce, shredded
1/2 cup carrots, julienne
1/2 cup red pepper, julienne
1/2 cup mung bean sprouts
1/4 cup fresh mint leaves,
1/4 cup fresh basil leaves
1/4 cup fresh cilantro, stems removed
20 fresh chives

SAUCE
1/2 cup young Thai coconut meat
1/2 cup young Thai coconut water
1/3 cup raw almond butter
2½ tablespoons wheat-free tamari
1 tablespoon fresh ginger, peeled and minced
4 medium cloves garlic, peeled
2 teaspoons lime juice, fresh-squeezed
2 teaspoons expeller-pressed sesame oil
1/2 teaspoon red pepper flakes

When dining out at a Thai restaurant, fresh spring rolls are my favorite item to order. I love all the fresh herbs and spices as well as the variations in texture. This recipe is a new spin using thinly sliced cucumber as the wrappers instead of rice, keeping them grain-free. A rainbow of crisp herbs and vegetables peek out the ends while the dipping sauce adds some wild spice, and the cucumber lends a nice crunch when sinking your teeth into these refreshing rolls.

Make the sauce
1. In high-speed blender place coconut meat, coconut water, almond butter, wheat-free tamari, ginger, garlic, lime juice, sesame oil, and red pepper flakes. Blend on high for about 2 minutes, until all ingredients are well combined and sauce is smooth.

Make the rolls
1. Lay out 3 long cucumber slices, one slightly overlapping the next.
2. On side closest to you, layer basil and mint leaves, cilantro, julienne cucumber, carrots, red pepper, mung beans, chives, and shredded lettuce.
3. Roll up like a burrito, leaving some of the vegetables sticking out the ends.

Note: Keeps in refrigerator up to 3 days in airtight container.

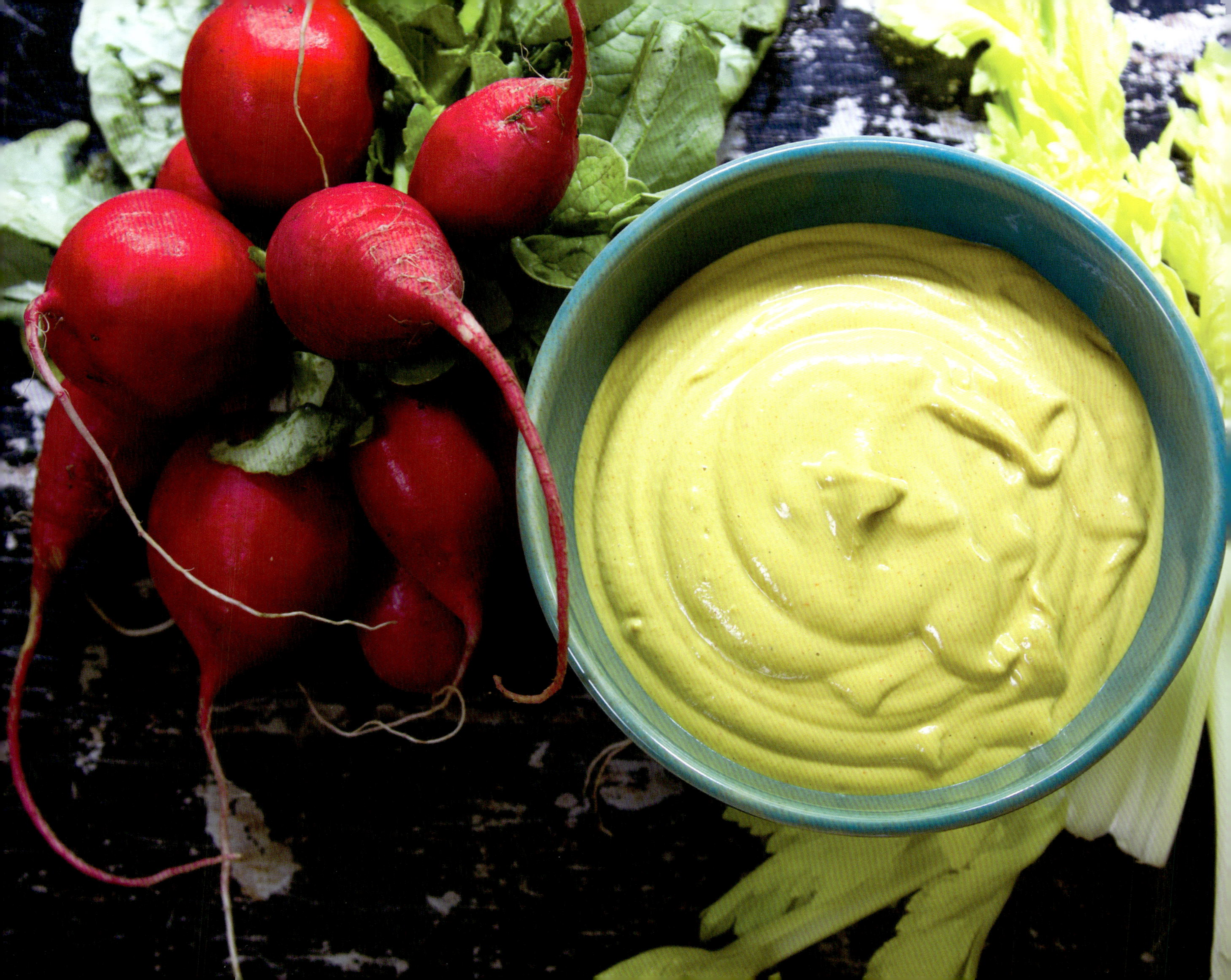

CASHEW CHEESE SAUCE WITH SPICY JALAPENO, TOMATO, AND SWEET ONION

MAKES 3 CUPS

SAUCE

2 ¼ cups raw cashews soaked 4–6 hours, drained and rinsed
1 ½ cups water
3/4 cup nutritional yeast
2 teaspoons raw light agave
2 teaspoons paprika powder
1 teaspoon garlic powder
1 teaspoon onion powder
1 teaspoon sea salt
1/2 teaspoon turmeric powder

TOMATO MIX

1 cup tomatoes, seeds removed and diced
1/2 cup sweet onion, peeled and diced
2 teaspoons jalapeño, seeds removed and finely diced (use more or less, depending on how spicy you'd like it)

Addictive is the first word that comes to mind when I think about this cheesy dip. It's played up with a spicy tomato blend that will have you licking the bowl clean. This is so good drizzled over a taco salad, and as a dip for chips, crackers, crudités, apples, and more. Use your imagination.

Make the tomato mix
1. In a medium mixing bowl, add tomatoes, onion, and jalapeño. Mix with wooden spoon. Cover and set aside.

Make the sauce
1. In high-speed blender place cashews, water, nutritional yeast, agave, paprika powder, garlic powder, onion powder, sea salt, and turmeric powder. Blend on high for about 2 minutes, until the cashews are broken down and sauce is smooth and creamy.
2. Pour cheese over tomato mixture. Stir lightly with a spoon.

Note: Keeps in refrigerator up to 5 days in airtight container.

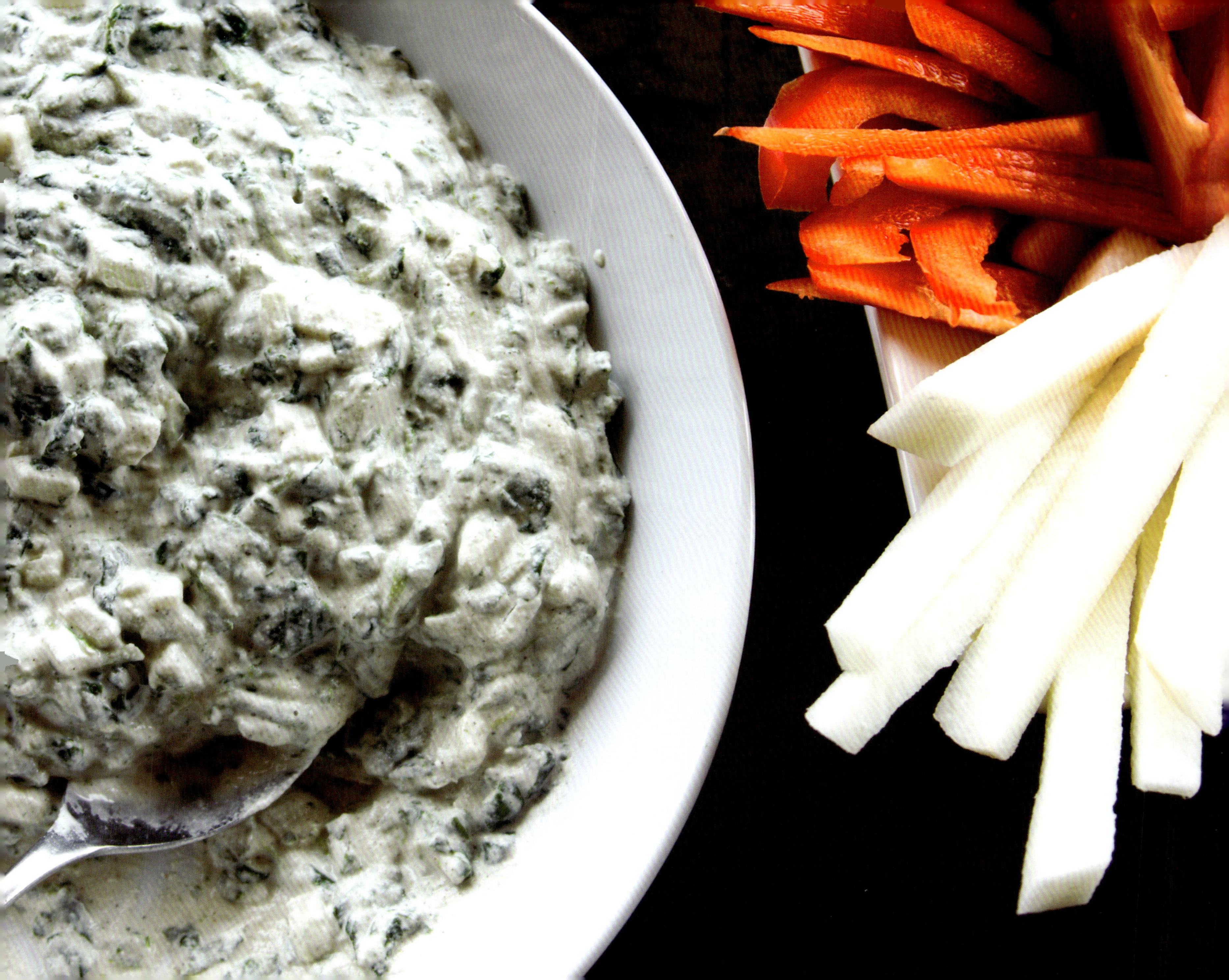

CREAMY CASHEW GARLIC SPINACH DIP

MAKES 2 1/2 CUPS

DIP

2 cups raw cashews soaked 4–6 hours, drained and rinsed
1½ cups thawed frozen spinach
1 cup water
3/4 cup yellow onion, peeled and diced
1/3 cup lemon juice, fresh-squeezed
3 medium cloves garlic, peeled
1 tablespoon onion powder
2 teaspoons garlic powder
1 teaspoon sea salt
1/2 teaspoon fresh ground black pepper

A party classic, this spinach dip is so simple to make and will blow your mind! With a perfect blend of flavors, it's great spread on raw bread or as a dip for raw crackers, chips, crudités, and more. I suggest doubling the recipe—it will disappear very fast.

Make the dip
1. Place thawed spinach in small mesh strainer and squeeze out as much liquid as possible. Place in medium mixing bowl and add onions.
2. In high-speed blender place cashews, water, lemon juice, garlic, onion powder, garlic powder, sea salt and pepper. Blend on high for about 2 minutes, until cashews are broken down and dip is smooth.
3. Pour dip into bowl with spinach and onions. Mix with spoon until spinach mixture is evenly distributed.

Note: Keeps in refrigerator up to 5 days in airtight container.

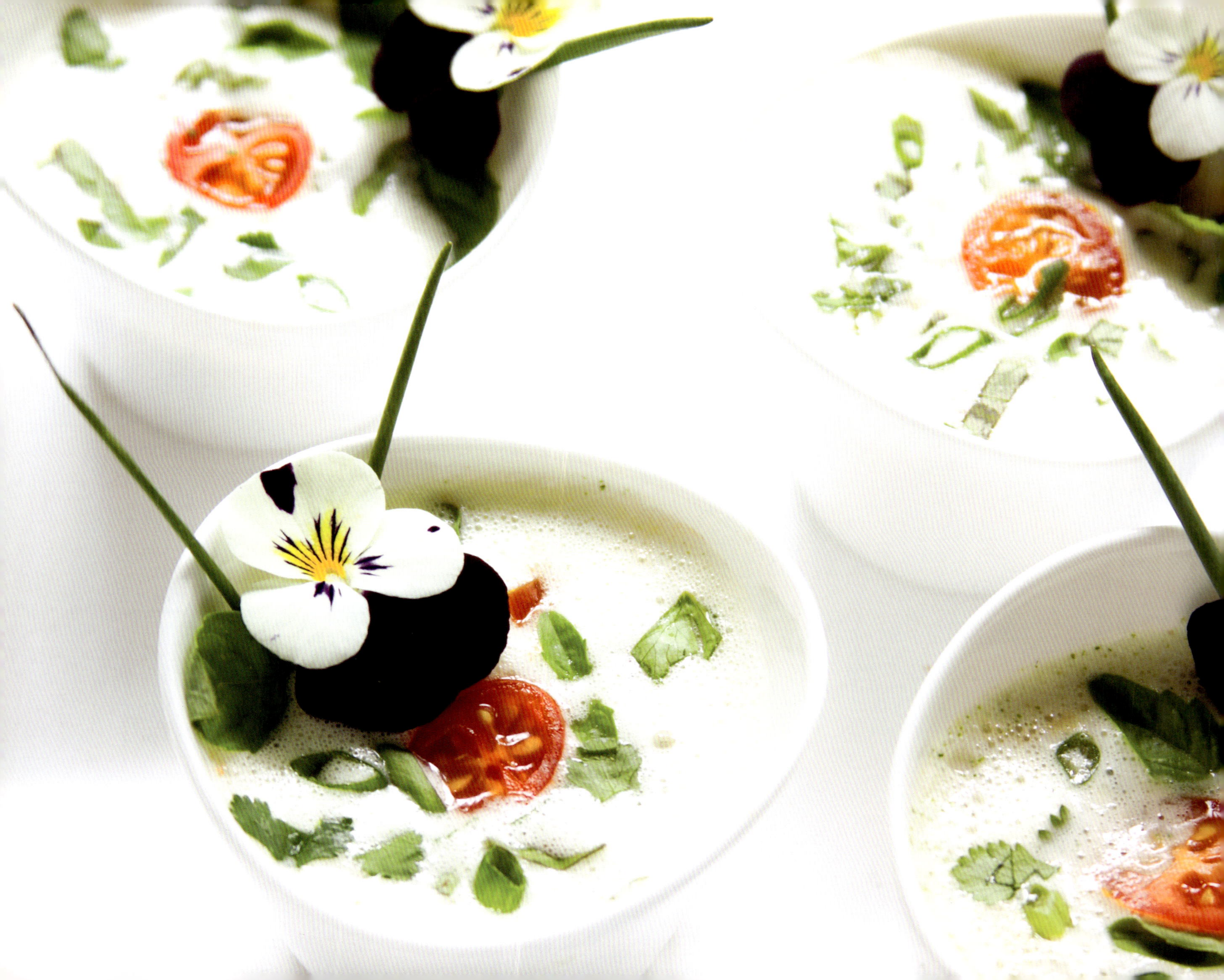

COCONUT LEMONGRASS SOUP WITH BASIL AND KAFFIR LIME LEAVES

MAKES 32 OUNCES (SERVES 4-6)

SOUP

4 cups coconut cream (see page 74)
1/4 cup sweet onion, chopped
2 tablespoons expeller-pressed grape-seed oil
2 tablespoons brown rice miso paste
1 tablespoon wheat-free tamari
1 tablespoon galangal root, peeled and minced
1 tablespoon lemongrass stalk, finely chopped
2 teaspoons raw light agave
2 small cloves garlic, peeled
1 teaspoon kaffir lime leaves, finely chopped
1/4 teaspoon ground ginger

GARNISH

1/4 cup fresh cilantro, leaves only, chopped and loosely packed
1/4 cup fresh basil, leaves only, chopped and loosely packed
1/2 cup cherry tomatoes, quartered
2 tablespoons green onion, chopped

The neutral coconut-milk base of this soup allows the beautiful and complex flavors to shine through. With each bite, your taste buds will be sent on an exotic adventure.

Make the soup
1. In high-speed blender place coconut cream, onion, grape-seed oil, miso paste, wheat-free tamari, galangal root, lemon grass, agave, garlic, lime leaves, and ginger. Blend on high for about 2 minutes, until lemon grass and kaffir lime leaves are broken down and the soup is smooth and creamy.
2. Pour 1 cup of soup into bowls of choice.
3. Distribute 1 tablespoon of cilantro, basil, and cherry tomatoes on top of each bowl of soup. Sprinkle on a few chopped green onions and serve immediately.

Note: Keeps in refrigerator up to 3 days in airtight container.

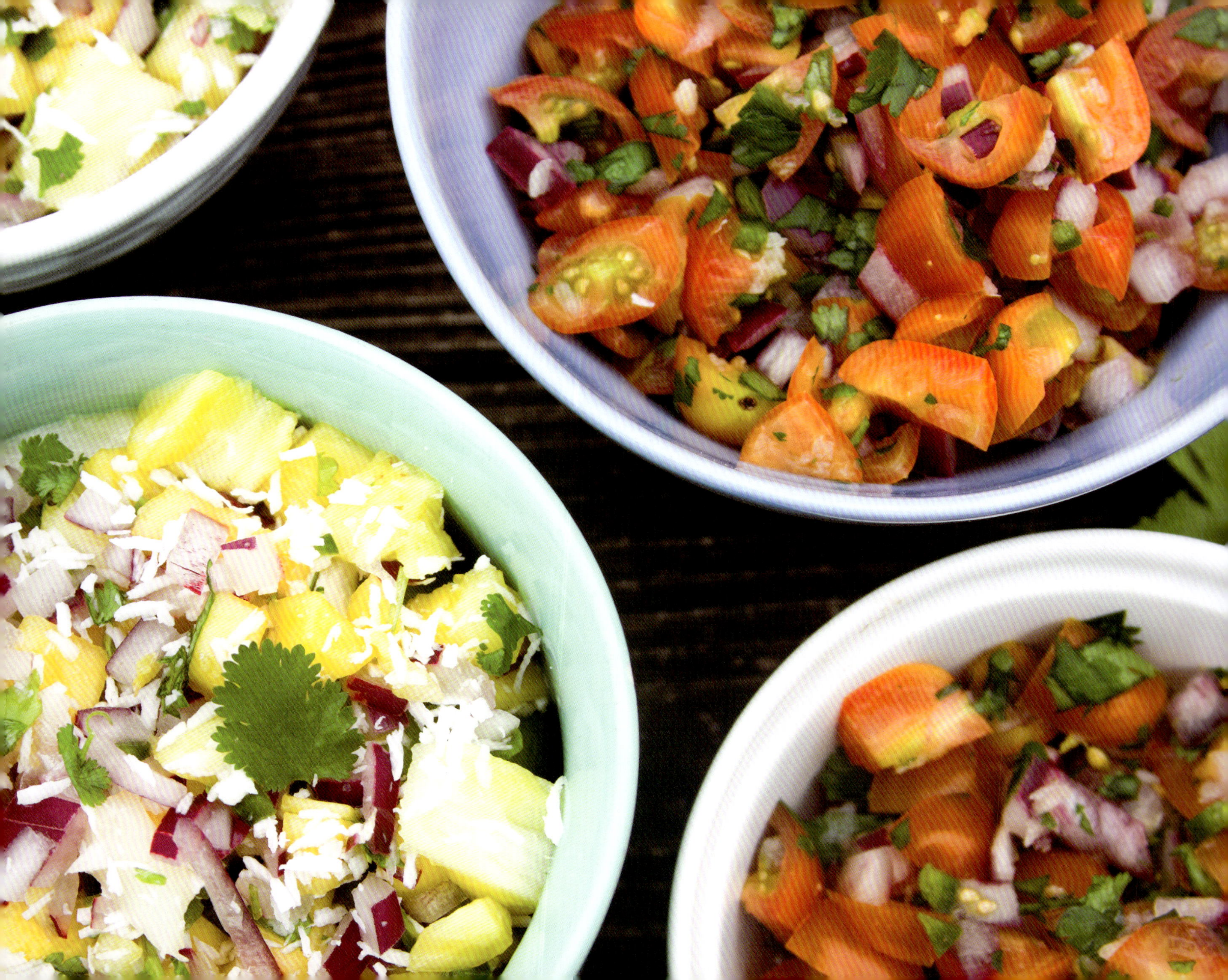

RED ONION, LIME, GARLIC, CILANTRO, AND **CHERRY TOMATO** SALSA

MAKES 2 CUPS

SALSA

1 ½ cups cherry tomatoes, chopped
1/2 cup red onion, diced
1/2 cup fresh cilantro, stems removed and chopped
2 teaspoons jalapeño, seeds removed and chopped
2 teaspoons lime juice, fresh-squeezed
2 cloves garlic, peeled and minced
3/4 teaspoon sea salt

Make the salsa
1. In a small mixing bowl, add tomatoes, onion, cilantro, jalapeño, lime juice, garlic, and sea salt. Mix together with spoon, until all ingredients are well combined.

Note: Keeps in refrigerator up to 3 days in airtight container.

PINEAPPLE, MANGO, LIME, AND SHREDDED COCONUT SALSA

MAKES 2 CUPS

SALSA

3/4 cup fresh pineapple, rind removed and diced
1/4 cup red onion, diced
1/4 cups mango, peeled, pitted and diced
2 tablespoons unsweetened raw coconut, shredded
2 tablespoons fresh cilantro, stems removed and chopped
1 ½ tablespoons lime juice, fresh-squeezed
2 teaspoons jalapeño, seeds removed and diced

Make the salsa
1. In a small mixing bowl, add pineapple, red onion, mango, shredded coconut, cilantro, lime juice, and jalapeño. Mix together with spoon, until all ingredients are well combined.

Note: Keeps in refrigerator up to 2 days in airtight container.

E   N   T   R

E   E   S

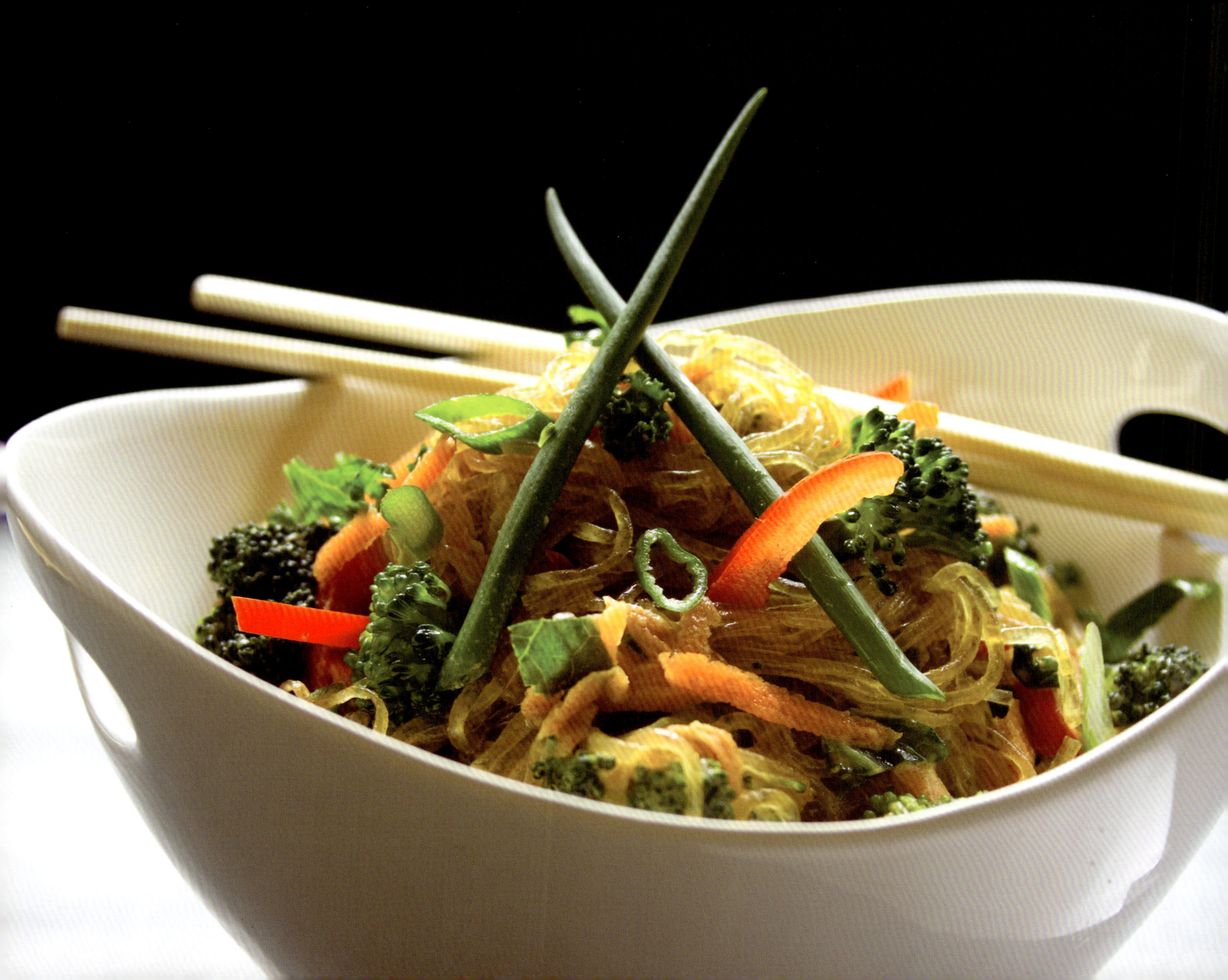

ORANGE TERIYAKI NOODLES, CARROT, BROCCOLI, KALE, AND RED PEPPER

SERVES 4-6

NOODLE BASE

2 12-ounce packs clear kelp noodles
1 cup broccoli florets, chopped
1 cup carrots, shredded
1 cup kale, stems removed and chiffonade
1 cup red bell pepper, seeds removed and cut into thin strips

TERIYAKI SAUCE

1/3 cup orange juice, fresh-squeezed
1/4 cup wheat-free tamari
10 medjool dates, pitted
3 tablespoons brown rice miso paste
2 tablespoons maple syrup
1 tablespoon expeller-pressed sesame oil
2 teaspoons fresh ginger, grated
2 large garlic cloves, peeled

GARNISH

1/4 cup green onions, chopped
1 teaspoon white sesame seeds

This Asian-fusion-inspired dish is composed of a sweet orange teriyaki sauce tossed with crisp marinated vegetables and delicate kelp noodles, creating an exceptionally mouthwatering lunch or dinner.

Make the noodles
1. Rinse kelp noodles in warm water. Pat dry with towel and place in medium mixing bowl.
2. In a different medium mixing bowl, add broccoli, carrots, kale, and red pepper, and toss gently. Set aside.

Make the sauce
1. In high-speed blender place orange juice, wheat-free tamari, dates, miso paste, maple syrup, sesame oil, ginger, and garlic. Blend on high for about 2 minutes, until the dates have broken down and sauce is smooth.

Assemble
1. Pour 1/2 teriyaki sauce over noodles and 1/2 over chopped vegetables. Cover and place in refrigerator for 2-3 hours. This will allow the noodles and vegetables to become soft and more of a cooked-like texture from the salts. The reason the noodles and vegetables are separated is because the water from the vegetables will lessen the flavor of the noodles while marinating, so make sure to marinate these two separately.
2. Once marinated, place vegetables and noodles into strainer and allow excess sauce to drain out, pressing on the mix lightly.
3. Divide into bowls of choice and garnish with green onions and sesame seeds.

Note: Keeps in refrigerator up to 4 days in airtight container.

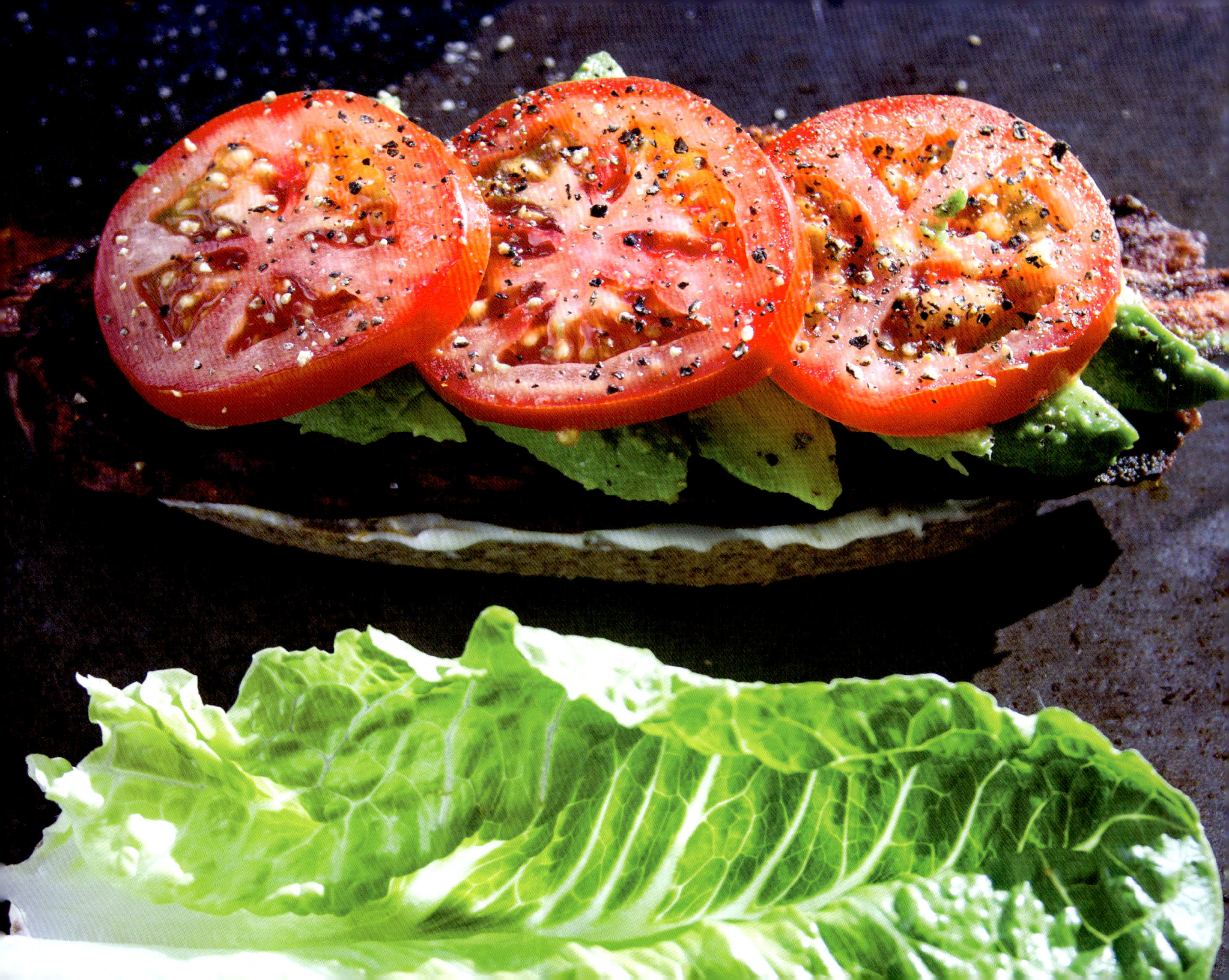

EGGPLANT **BACON**, LETTUCE, AVOCADO, AND TOMATO SANDWICH

MAKES 4 SANDWICHES

SANDWICH

8 slices almond flax bread (see page 146)
24 pieces eggplant bacon (see page 256)
8 large fresh romaine leaves
8 slices ripe tomato
1 medium ripe avocado, peeled, pitted and sliced
1/4 cup cashew spread (see page 100)
sea salt and fresh ground black pepper to taste

Smoky eggplant bacon adds the perfect crunch to this classic sandwich. Complimented by buttery avocado, crisp romaine leaves, and ripe tomato stacked high between two slices of golden flax almond bread and creamy cashew spread this is my favorite sandwich!

Make the sandwich
1. Lay out 8 slices of bread. Spread 1 tablespoon cashew spread on each of the 8 slices of bread.
2. Arrange 6 slices eggplant bacon on top of 4 slices of bread with cashew spread.
3. Top eggplant bacon with a few slices avocado.
4. Top avocado with 2 slices tomato.
5. Top tomatoes with 2 romaine leaves.
6. To finish sandwiches place remaining 4 slices of bread with cashew spread on top of romaine. Serve immediately.

Note: Keeps in refrigerator up to 2 days in airtight container.

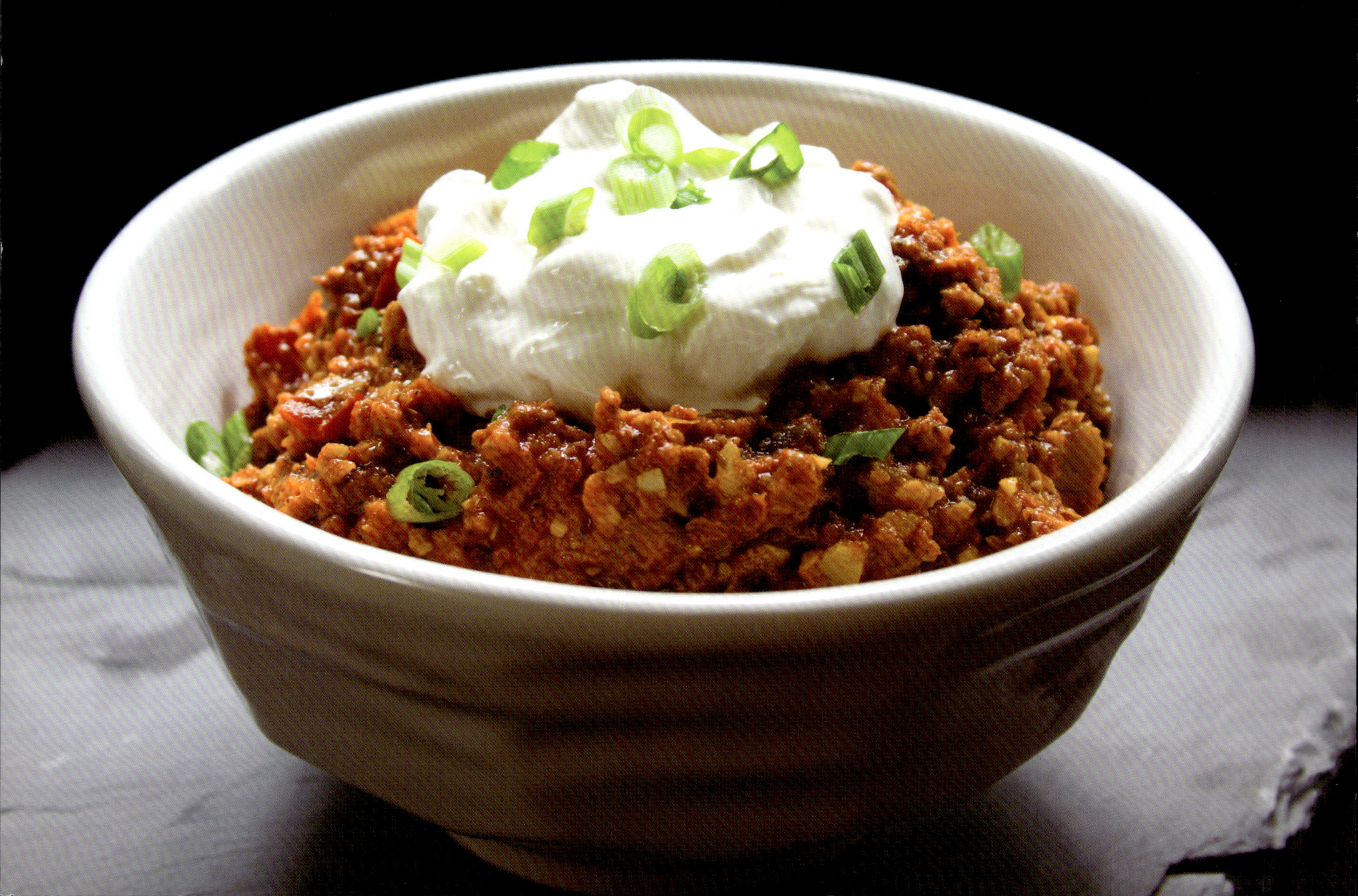

A STORY ABOUT CHILI

    I entered this recipe into the annual Malibu Chili Cook-Off with the hopes of meeting new people in the community and allowing hundreds of people to taste how amazing living food can be. My dear friend and sous chef Yana and I stayed up for twenty-four hours making twenty gallons of chili, so we would be well stocked for the two days of the cook-off. We spray-painted RAW on our T-shirts and designed our navy blue booth with big circus-like strands of lights, oriental rugs, and oversize whimsical paper lanterns in the shapes of stars.
I had never entered my food in a contest before, let alone one that had meat as one of the main ingredients. I went in without expectations and walked away with two first-place awards! One was for the best chili, and the other, for the best-designed booth. We were up against some major players, including some of Malibu's top restaurants and hard-core chili connoisseurs.

Since the chili cook-off began over thirty years ago, this was the first vegetarian chili to ever win the award for best chili, let alone a vegan raw version. Second place was made with filet mignon and Kobe beef. When the judges made their rounds and finally made it to our booth, I didn't know what to expect. As they each took a bite of the chili, I heard oohs and ahhhs. I could tell people were trying to hone in on what exactly they were eating. One judge said, "It's cold and refreshing." Another judge chimed in with, "I could see using this as a sauce on fish, poultry, and even a burger." "Wow, the flavors are constantly changing in my mouth and evolving," said a different judge. At this point I had not described the chili; therefore, no one knew it was vegan and raw. "So what's in this?" one of the judges asked. I listed all the ingredients and described the process in which the chili was made. Some of the judges were smiling with excitement while others had looks of contemplation. You could tell the wheels were turning.

Participating in the Malibu Chili Cook-Off was such a wonderful experience on so many levels. I met some amazing people I'm still in contact with today. I was able to help the Kiwanis foundation by donating proceeds, and in turn they gave me the gift of being able to share my food with the community. I was excited to win first place, but that came last to the feeling of being able to share my passion with so many people.

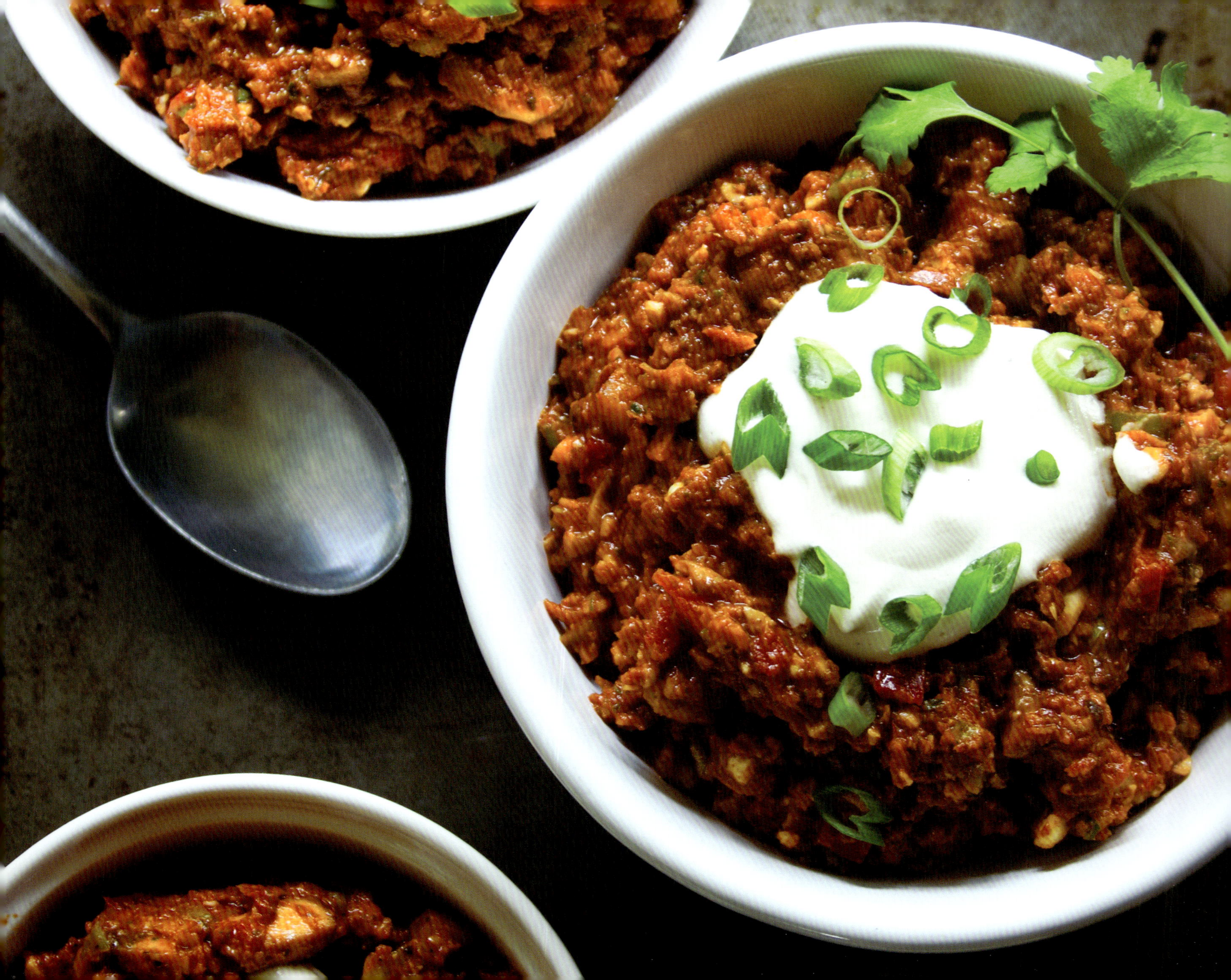

VEGGIE CHILI WITH CASHEW CREAM

MAKES 64 OUNCES (SERVES 4-6)

SAUCE

3 cups sun-dried tomatoes, tightly packed
2 cups water
1/3 cup dried oregano
1/4 cup virgin raw olive oil
1/4 cup wheat-free tamari
1/4 cup raw apple cider vinegar
1/4 cup raw light agave
2 tablespoons chili powder
2 tablespoons cumin powder
2 large garlic cloves, peeled
1 teaspoon sea salt
1/4 teaspoon cayenne powder
1/4 teaspoon ground cinnamon

VEGETABLE BASE

2 ½ cups carrots, chopped
2 ½ cups raw almonds, soaked 8–10 hours, drained and rinsed
2 cups red bell pepper, seeds removed and diced
2 cups portobello mushrooms, finely diced
2 cups celery, diced
1/2 cup red onion, diced

GARNISH

1/2 cup cashew cream (see page 104)
1/4 cup green onions, chopped

Make the sauce
1. In high-speed blender place sun-dried tomatoes, water, oregano, olive oil, wheat-free tamari, apple cider vinegar, agave, chili powder, cumin powder, garlic, sea salt, cayenne, and cinnamon. Blend on low and slowly turn up speed to high for about 2 minutes, or until the mixture is the consistency of chunky marinara sauce. Scrape down sides of blender and add a little more water, if necessary, to blend.
2. Blend about 1 more minute, or until almost smooth. Set aside.

Make the vegetable base
1. In food processor with "S" blade attachment, place soaked almonds and carrots. Pulse until crumbly and slightly chunky in texture.
2. In large mixing bowl, add almond carrot mixture, red peppers, portobellos, celery, and onions.
3. Add sauce to vegetable base. Stir with wooden spoon, until entire base is coated evenly in sauce.
4. Divide into bowls of choice and place a dollop of cashew cream and a sprinkle of chopped green onion on top.

Note: Keeps in refrigerator up to 7 days in airtight container.

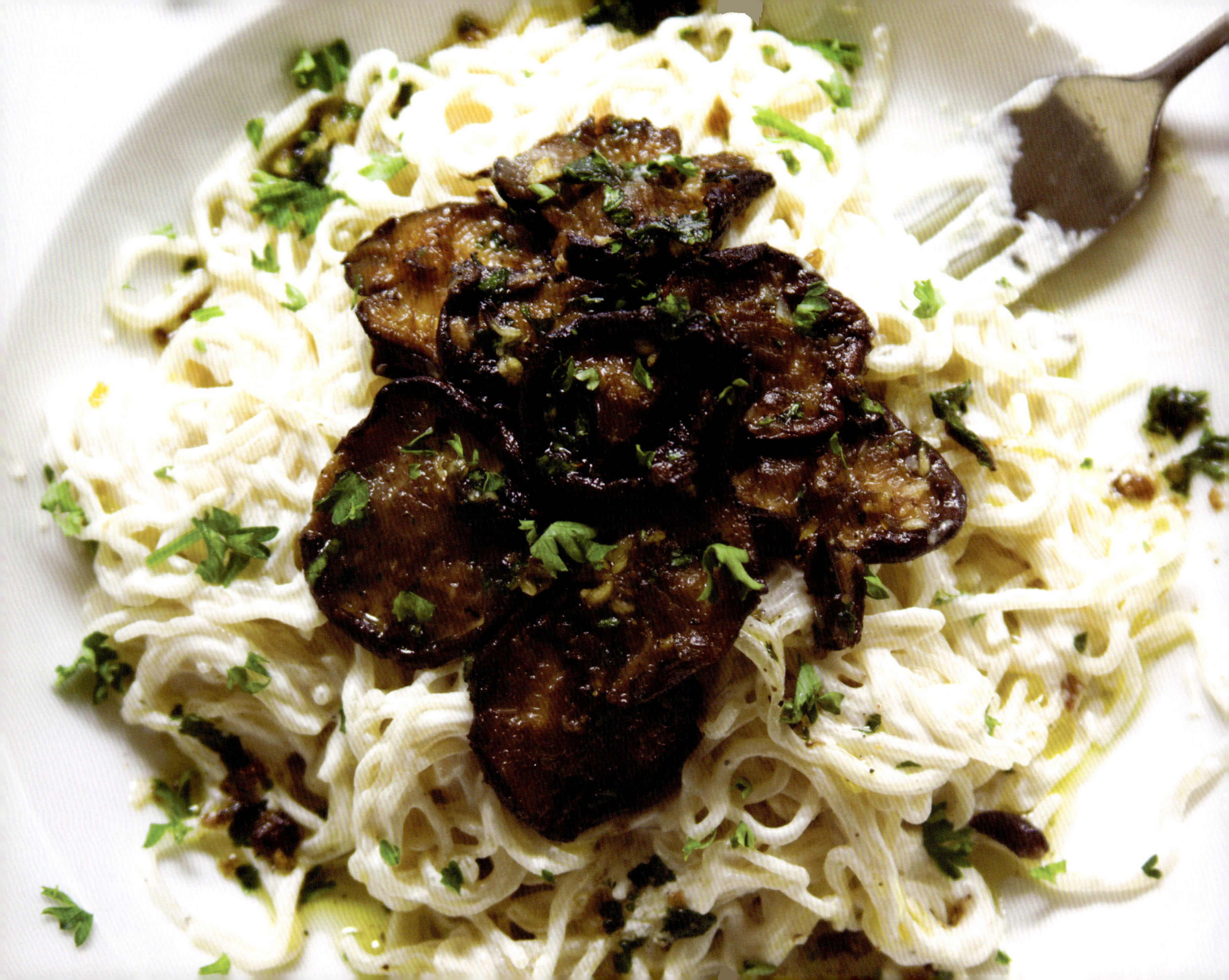

PASTA ALFREDO, GARLIC BUTTER SHITAKES, AND FRESH PARSLEY

SERVES 4-6

PASTA
2 12-ounce packs clear kelp noodles

ALFREDO SAUCE
1 cup raw cashews soaked 4-6 hours, drained and rinsed
1/2 cup water
1 tablespoon shallots, peeled and minced
1 tablespoon virgin raw olive oil
2 teaspoons nutritional yeast
1 teaspoon brown rice miso paste
1 teaspoon raw light agave
1 medium clove garlic, peeled
1/4 teaspoon sea salt
1/8 teaspoon ground nutmeg

SHITAKES
4 cups shitake mushrooms, stems removed
1/2 cup virgin raw olive oil
1 tablespoon fresh parsley leaves, chopped
2 teaspoons garlic, peeled and minced
1/2 teaspoon sea salt

When I was developing this recipe, I was craving something rich, savory, and comforting. I must warn you, these melt-in-your-mouth mushrooms are so good, you may have to restrain yourself from eating them all before they're done. Accompanied by rich creamy alfredo noodles, this is a decadent yet extremely healthy pasta dish that is very low in carbohydrates and sugar.

Prepare the shitakes
1. In medium mixing bowl, add shitakes, olive oil, parsley, garlic, and sea salt. With wooden spoon mix mushrooms until evenly coated with olive oil. Cover and let stand for 1 hour to marinate.

Make the sauce
1. In high-speed blender place cashews, water, shallots, olive oil, nutritional yeast, miso paste, agave, garlic, sea salt, and nutmeg. Blend on high for about 2 minutes, until cashews are broken down and sauce is smooth and creamy.
2. Pour alfredo sauce over kelp noodles, and toss. Make sure all noodles are coated in sauce. Cover and refrigerate for 2 hours, so noodles can soften while the mushrooms are dehydrating.

Dehydrate the shitakes
1. After an hour of marinating, spread mushroom mixture onto dehydrator tray lined with a teflex sheet.
2. Dehydrate at 115 degrees for 6-7 hours, or until edges are slightly crispy and center is buttery and soft.

Assemble
1. If you want a warm dish, place the noodles in a bowl into the dehydrator for 2 hours with mushrooms before serving.
2. When ready place alfredo pasta noodles on desired serving dishes and top with shitakes, fresh ground black pepper, and a sprinkle of fresh parsley.

Note: Keeps in refrigerator up to 3 days in airtight container.

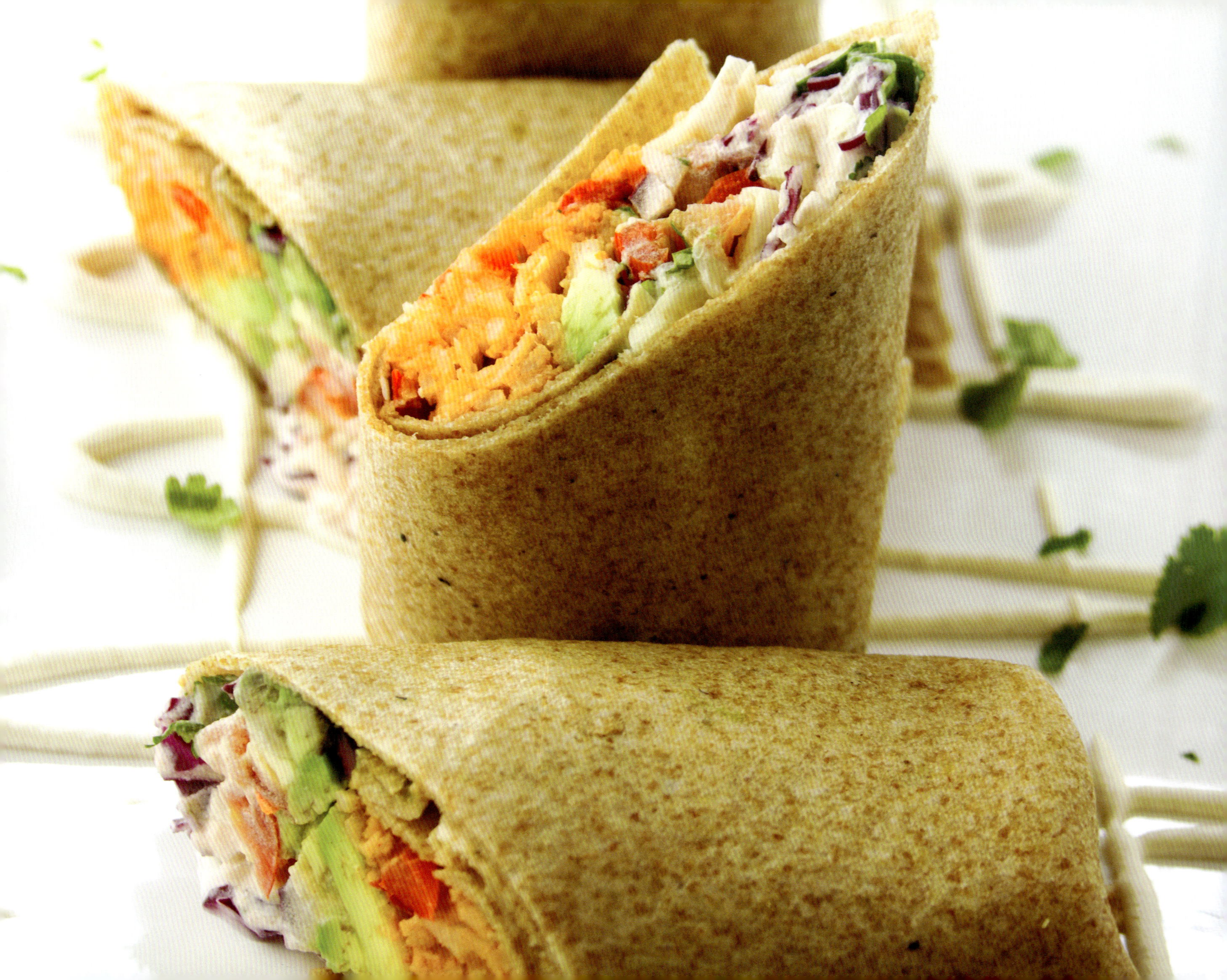

SPANISH RICE, BURRITO WITH CABBAGE, SALSA, AVOCADO, AND LIME CREAM

SERVES 4

TORTILLA
3 cups young Thai coconut meat
1 ¾ cups water
3/4 cup golden flax meal
1 teaspoon cumin powder
1/4 teaspoon sea salt

SPANISH RICE
3 cups jicama, peeled and shredded
1/2 cup sweet onion, peeled and diced
1/2 cup red bell pepper, seeds removed and diced
2 tablespoons sun-dried tomatoes, diced
1 ½ tablespoons lime juice, fresh-squeezed
1 tablespoon virgin raw olive oil
1 tablespoon onion powder
2 teaspoons garlic powder
1 teaspoon cumin powder
1 teaspoon chili powder
1 teaspoon paprika
1/4 teaspoon sea salt
1/8 teaspoon cayenne powder

TOPPINGS
1 medium avocado, peeled, pitted and sliced into 16 pieces
1 cup green and purple cabbage, shredded
1/2 cup cherry tomato salsa (see recipe 158)
1/4 cup fresh cilantro, leaves only, chopped

LIME CREAM
1 cup raw cashews soaked 4–6 hours, drained and rinsed
1/2 cup water
2 tablespoons lime juice, fresh-squeezed
1/2 teaspoon garlic powder
1/4 teaspoon cumin powder
1/4 teaspoon sea salt

Shredded jicama stands in for the base of this zesty spanish rice. Topped with avocado, shredded cabbage, fresh cilantro and salsa, then drizzled in tart lime cream and tightly wrapped in a golden tortilla with a rainbow of bold color and flavor. This burrito makes a refreshing lunch or dinner. If you're short on time, use collard greens or butter lettuce leaves for the tortilla.

Make the tortilla
1. In high-speed blender place coconut meat, water, flax meal, cumin, and sea salt. Blend on high for about 1 minute, until coconut meat is broken down and smooth.
2. Pour tortilla mixture onto dehydrator trays lined with teflex sheets. Spread out evenly with spatula thickly enough that there are no transparent spots. If there are, there will be holes in the tortillas.
3. Dehydrate at 105 degrees for 4 hours.
4. After 4 hours flip over tortilla and slowly peel away teflex sheet. Return to dehydrator for another 8 hours.
5. Tortillas should be firm but still pliable. Transfer to cutting board. Cut both sheets into 2 sections, creating 4 tortillas. If tortillas get too dry, don't worry! Wet your hands with a little water, and flick them over tortillas. Let stand for 15 minutes. If they're still too dry, continue process until they're pliable.

Make spanish rice
1. In food processor with a shredding disc attachment, shred jicama (or shred by hand with a cheese grater).
2. Transfer shredded jicama to a layer of paper towels and let stand for 1/2 hour to absorb the liquid. Goal is to remove as much liquid as possible from the jicama.
3. In a medium mixing bowl, add jicama, onion, red pepper, sun-dried tomatoes, lime juice, olive oil, onion powder, garlic powder, cumin powder, chili powder, paprika, sea salt, and cayenne. Mix with wooden spoon, until vegetables are evenly coated with spices.

Make lime cream
1. In high-speed blender place cashews, water, lime juice, garlic powder, cumin and sea salt. Blend on high for about 2 minutes, until cashews are broken down and cream is smooth.

Assemble
1. Lay out tortilla. On the side closest to you, top with 1/4 cup spanish rice.
2. Arrange 4 avocado slices on top of spanish rice.
3. Spoon 2 tablespoons fresh salsa on top of avocado.
4. Sprinkle on a few tablespoons of cabbage on top of avocado.
5. Drizzle 1–2 tablespoons lime cream on cabbage.
6. Sprinkle 1 tablespoon cilantro on lime cream.
7. Roll like a burrito by folding in both outer sides and rolling away from you, so there are no openings in the tortilla and all the filling is secured. Serve immediately.

Note: Keeps in refrigerator up to 3 days in airtight container.

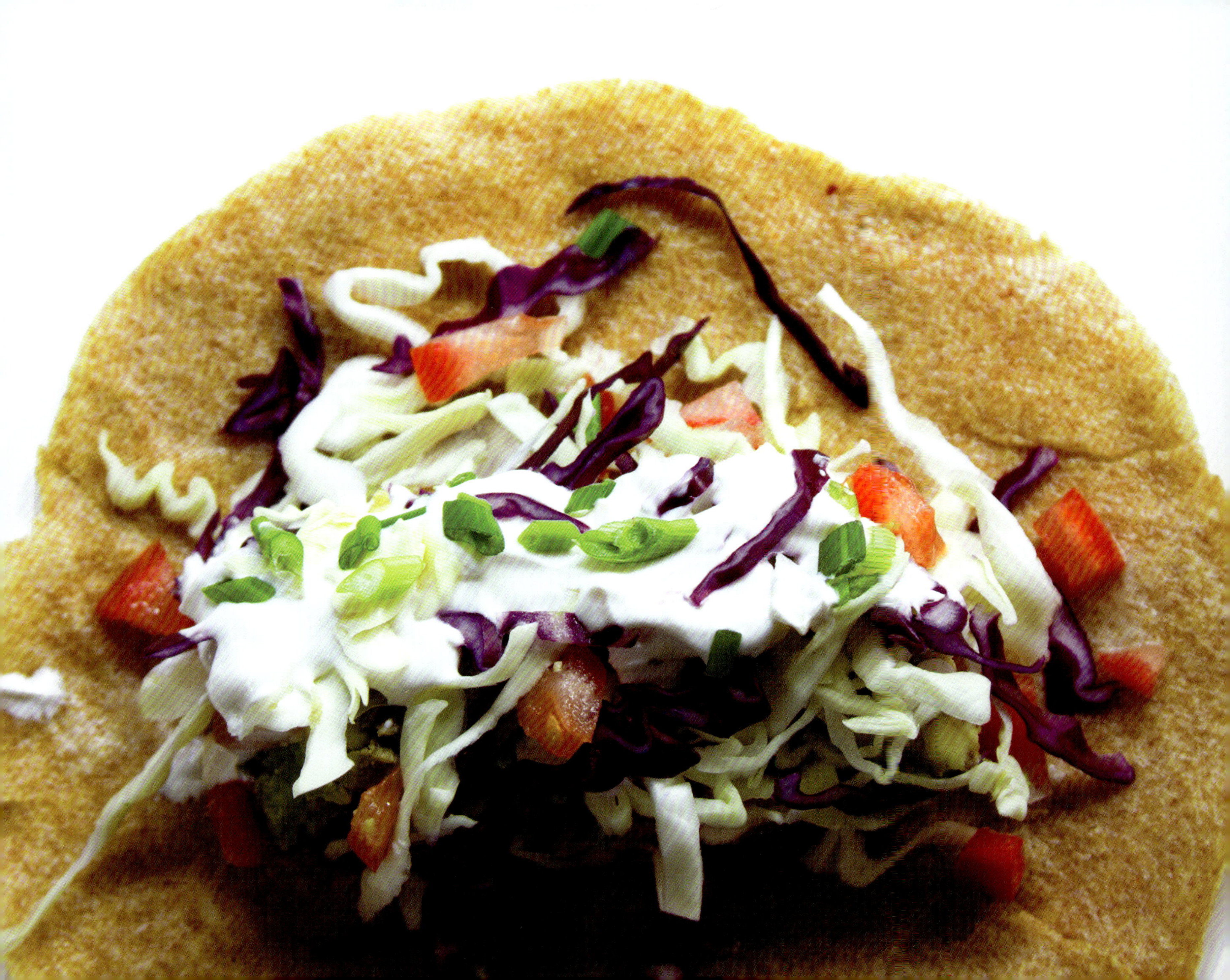

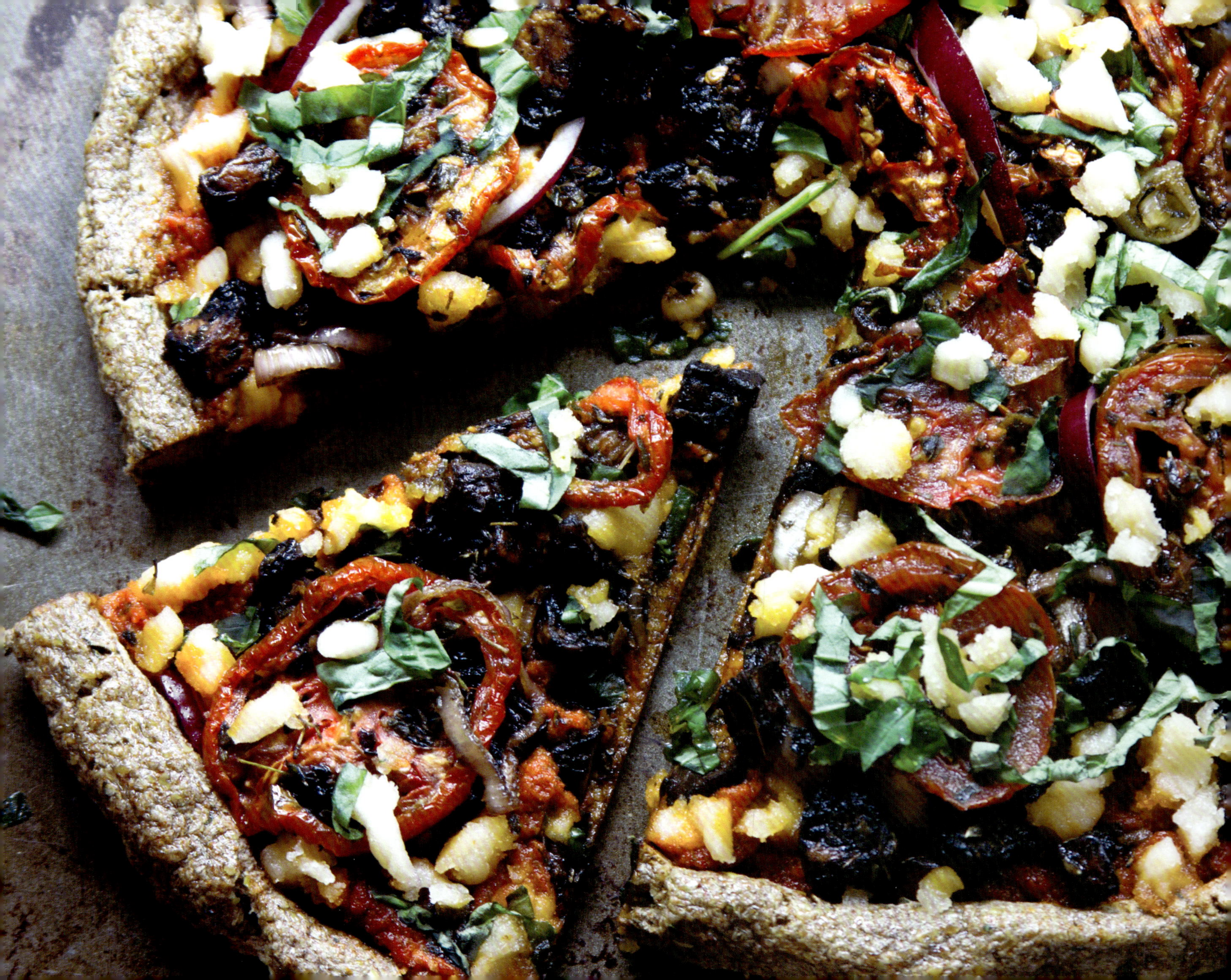

MARINATED VEGETABLE HERB PIZZA

MAKES 8-10 SLICES

DOUGH
1 ½ cups almond flour (see page 29)
1 cup zucchini, peeled and chopped
3/4 cup psyllium husk
1/2 cup golden flax meal
2 tablespoons almond milk
1 tablespoon virgin raw olive oil
1 ½ teaspoons italian seasoning
1 teaspoon lemon juice, fresh-squeezed
1/2 teaspoon sea salt

PIZZA SAUCE
1/2 cup sun-dried tomatoes
1/2 cup water
1/4 cup ripe tomato, chopped
2 tablespoons virgin raw olive oil
1 tablespoon yellow onion, peeled and chopped
2 teaspoons dried oregano
2 teaspoons dried basil
2 teaspoons lemon juice, fresh-squeezed
1 teaspoon maple syrup
1 teaspoon apple cider vinegar
1/2 teaspoon sea salt

TOPPINGS
2 cups portobello mushrooms, chopped
1 cup macadamia nut cheese (see page 138)
1 cup tomatoes, thinly sliced
1/2 cup red onion, peeled and thinly sliced
1/2 cup marinara sauce
1/4 cup fresh basil, leaves only, minced
1/4 cup virgin raw olive oil
2 tablespoons fresh oregano, leaves only, minced
1 teaspoon garlic, peeled and minced
1/2 teaspoon sea salt

Just like the bread recipe, this pizza totally rocked my world! Finally a raw pizza crust that's chewy, mild and tasty. This pizza will rival the traditional greasy one any day. The possibility for toppings is endless. If you don't like one of the toppings listed below, switch it out for something you love. If you really want to impress your friends and family, make a few of these and throw a pizza party. People will be begging for more.

Make the dough
1. In a high-speed blender, place zucchini, almond milk, lemon juice, and agave. Blend on high about 30 seconds, until zucchini is broken down and smooth.
2. In medium mixing bowl, add almond flour, psyllium husk, seasoning, and sea salt. Pour liquid zucchini mix over dry flour mix. Knead with hands until ingredients are totally combined and doughy. Dough should spring back when lightly touched.
3. Mold dough into 12-inch round pizza crust. Brush 1 tablespoon olive oil on the bottom and edges of the crust.
4. Place on dehydrator tray and dehydrate at 115 degrees for 12–14 hours. Bottom layer should be firm and edges slightly doughy.

Make marinara
1. In high-speed blender place sun-dried tomatoes, water, tomato, olive oil, onion, oregano, basil, lemon juice, maple syrup, apple cider vinegar, and sea salt. Blend on medium-high speed for about 1 minute. Stop blender and scrap down sides with spatula.
2. Continue blending on high until sun-dried tomatoes are broken down and sauce is almost smooth. If you desire a thinner sauce, add more water and blend until smooth. Use remaining sauce for another pizza or over kelp noodles for pasta.

Make toppings
1. In medium mixing bowl, toss portobellos, tomatoes, onion, olive oil, oregano, garlic, and sea salt until evenly coated.
2. Place toppings on dehydrator tray lined with teflex sheet. Dehydrate at 115 degrees for 4 hours. If you're around, every few hours toss vegetables so they can dehydrate and soften evenly. This will create a cooked-like texture that is very flavorful.

Assemble
1. Remove crust from dehydrator. Brush 1 tablespoon olive oil on bottom layer and edges of pizza crust one more time.
2. Pour marinara sauce evenly over crust. Top with about 1/4 cup thick layer of crumbled aged cheese.
3. Place marinated vegetables over cheese and sprinkle on fresh basil. Top with remaining 1/4 cup cheese. Slice and serve.

Note: Keeps in refrigerator up to 5 days in airtight container. Keeps in freezer up to 2 months in airtight container.

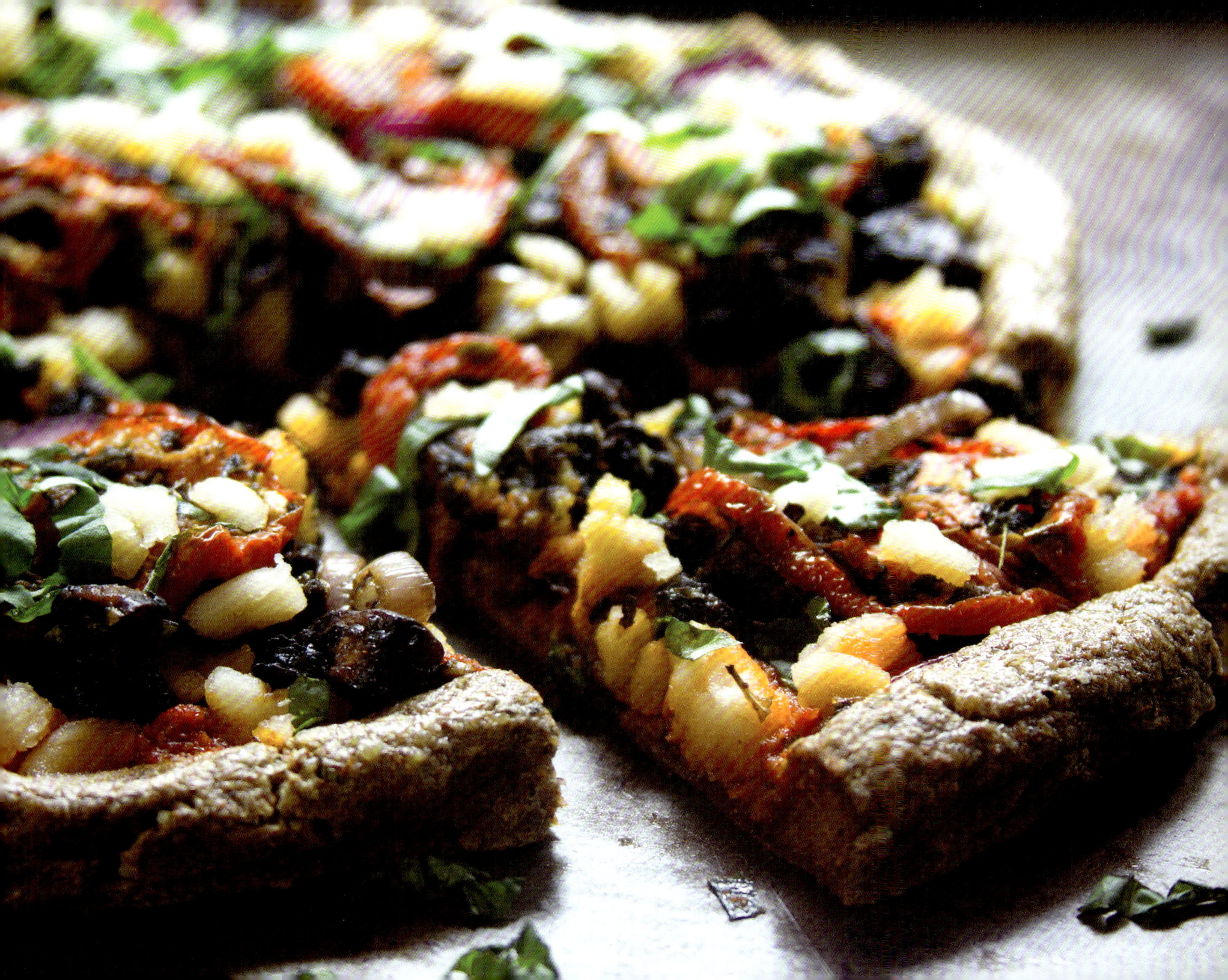

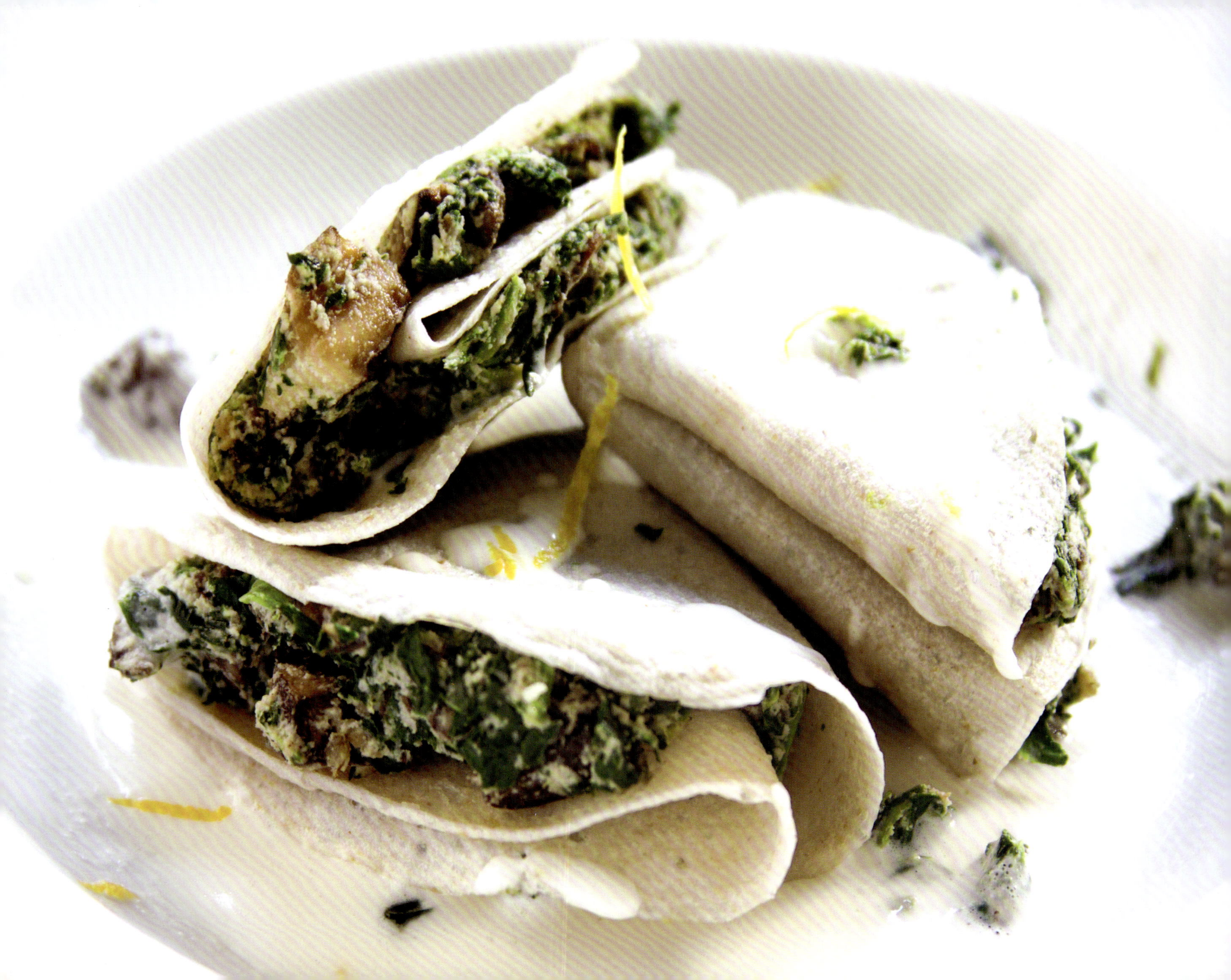

WILD MUSHROOM SPINACH CREPES WITH MACADAMIA RICOTTA AND LEMON CREAM SAUCE

MAKES 8 CREPES (SERVES 4)

CREPES
3 cups young Thai coconut meat
1 cup water
1/4 teaspoon sea salt

CHEESE
2 cup raw macadamia nuts
1 ¼ cup water
2 teaspoons lemon juice, fresh-squeezed
1/4 teaspoon sea salt

MUSHROOMS + SPINACH
1 cup wild mushrooms of choice (portobello, porcini, chanterelles, and oyster are a few ideas) roughly chopped
1 cup frozen spinach, thawed and drained well
3 tablespoons virgin raw olive oil
1 teaspoon garlic, peeled and minced
1/2 teaspoon sea salt

LEMON CREAM SAUCE
3/4 cup leftover macadamia nut cream from cheese
1 tablespoon lemon juice, fresh-squeezed
2 teaspoons raw light agave
1 teaspoon lemon zest
1/8 teaspoon sea salt

GARNISH (OPTIONAL)
2 teaspoons lemon zest

I've always had a weak spot for crepes, sweet or savory. This rich and savory recipe combines wilted spinach, marinated mushrooms, and creamy macadamia cheese drizzled in a tart lemon cream sauce. Transport yourself to Paris when enjoying these rich and decadent crepes.

Make the crepes
1. In a high-speed blender, place coconut meat, water, and sea salt. Blend on high for about 1 minute, until coconut meat is broken down and liquid is thick and smooth.
2. Using 2 dehydrator trays lined with teflex sheets, pour 8 thick dollops of mixture on sheets. With back of spoon, evenly spread out crepes, using circular motion from the inside out and creating 6-inch circles. Make sure there is no transparency in the crepes, as this will create holes in them.
3. Dehydrate at 105 degrees for 4 hours. Flip over and slowly peel away teflex sheets. Return to dehydrator for another 8 hours (for a total of 12 hours).
4. Crepes should be firm but still pliable. If crepes get too dry, don't worry! Wet hands with water and flick them over crepes to soften. Let stand for 15 minutes. If they're still dry, continue process until pliable.

Make the cheese
1. In high-speed blender place macadamia nuts, water, lemon juice, and sea salt. Blend on high for about 2 minutes, until macadamia nuts are broken down and cheese is almost smooth.
2. Over small mixing bowl, place a triple-lined cheesecloth. Pour cheese into cloth. Gather all 4 sides and twist until tight. Keeping the cheesecloth over the bowl, squeeze out liquid.
3. Remove cheese from cheesecloth and reserve liquid for the lemon cream sauce. Cover and place in refrigerator.

Make the mushrooms and spinach
1. In medium mixing bowl, toss mushrooms, olive oil, garlic, and sea salt. Let marinate for 1/2 hour. Transfer to dehydrator trays lined with teflex sheets.
2. Dehydrate at 115 degrees for 3 hours, until slightly crisp on the outside and soft and buttery on the inside.
3. In medium mixing bowl, add macadamia cheese, thawed spinach, and dehydrated mushrooms. Mix with spoon until all elements are just combined.

Make the lemon cream
1. In small mixing bowl, add macadamia cheese cream, lemon juice, agave, lemon zest, and sea salt. Whisk until well combined.

Assemble
1. Lay out 8 crepes. Spread 2 tablespoons filling on each crepe.
2. Fold the crepe in half once.
3. Fold the semicircle in half.
4. Place 2 crepes on each serving dish of choice.
5. Drizzle lemon cream sauce around and over crepes.
6. Sprinkle with fresh parsley leaves and lemon zest. Serve immediately.

Note: Keeps in refrigerator up to 3 days in airtight container.

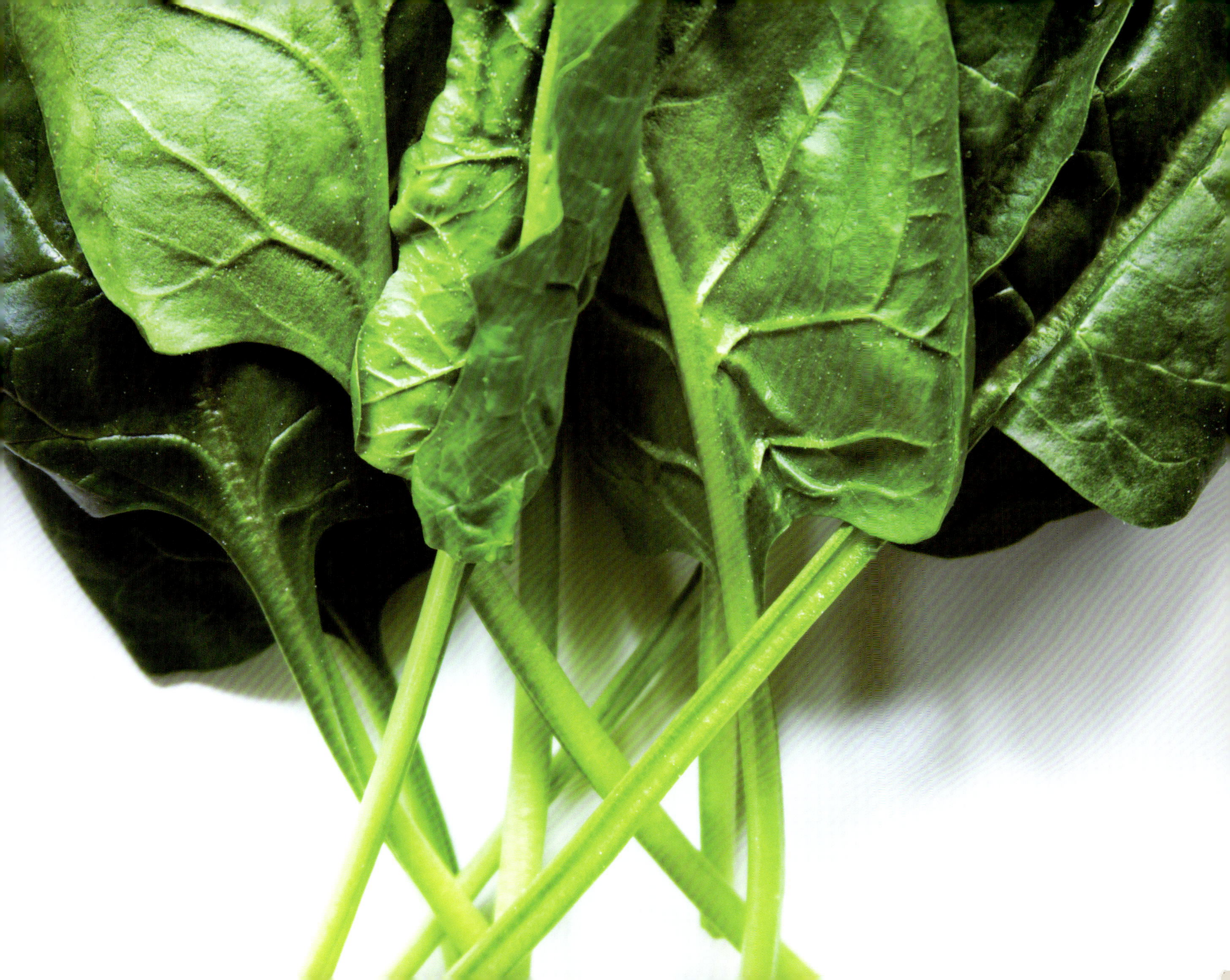

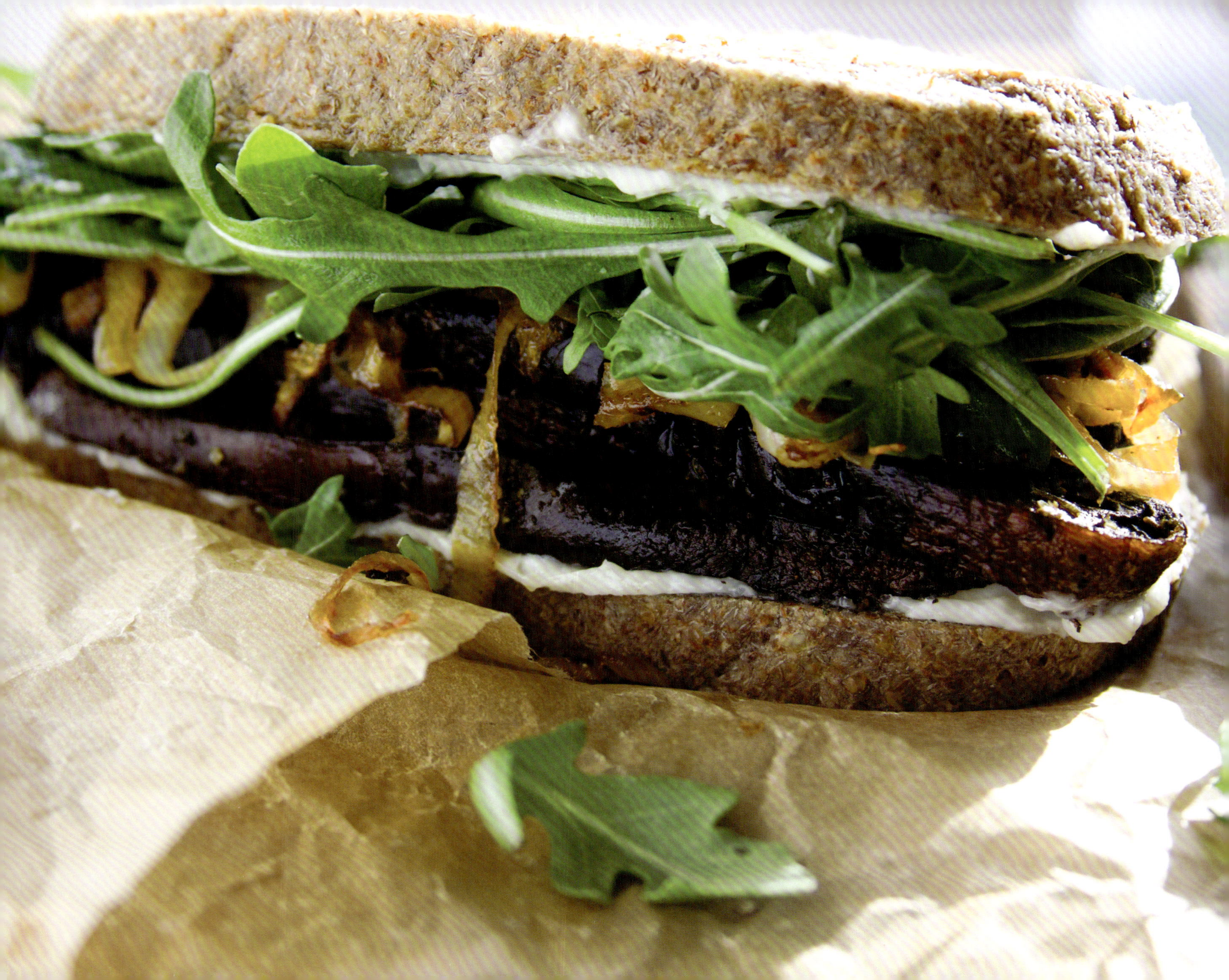

MARINATED MUSHROOM, CARAMELIZED ONIONS, GARLIC AIOLI, AND ARUGULA SANDWICH

MAKES 4 SANDWICHES

SANDWICH
8 slices almond flax bread (see page 146)
2 cups fresh arugula

MUSHROOMS
2 large portobello mushrooms, stems removed, cut into 1/4–inch thick slices
1/2 cup virgin raw olive oil
4 medium cloves garlic, peeled and minced
2 tablespoons balsamic vinegar
1/2 teaspoon dried basil
1/2 teaspoon sea salt
1/4 teaspoon fresh ground black pepper

GARLIC AIOLI
1 cup raw cashews soaked 4–6 hours, drained and rinsed
1/2 cup water
3 medium cloves garlic, peeled
1 tablespoon lemon juice, fresh-squeeezed
1 tablespoon apple cider vinegar
1/4 teaspoon sea salt

CARAMELIZED ONIONS
2 cups sweet onion, thinly sliced
2 tablespoons virgin raw olive oil
1 teaspoon raw light agave

A meaty portobello-mushroom sandwich generously topped with sweet caramelized onions, peppery arugula, and smothered in garlic aioli. This is a great sandwich to pack for a picnic.

Make the mushrooms
1. In a small mixing bowl, toss mushrooms, olive oil, garlic, balsamic vinegar, basil, sea salt, and pepper. Toss, until most the olive oil is soaked up from the mushrooms.
2. On dehydrator tray lined with teflex sheet, spread out mushrooms. Dehydrate at 115 degrees for 4–6 hours until mushrooms are dark and very soft on the inside.

Make the onions
1. In a small mixing bowl, add onions, olive oil, and agave. Toss to coat.
2. On dehydrator tray lined with teflex sheet, spread out onions. Dehydrate with mushrooms at 115 degrees for 4 hours. Some of the onions might get slightly crispy, but this will add great texture to the sandwich.

Make the aioli
1. In high-speed blender add cashews, water, garlic, lemon juice, apple cider vinegar, and sea salt. Blend on high for about 2 minutes, until cashews are broken down and aioli is smooth and creamy.

Assemble
1. Lay out slices of bread. Spread 1 tablespoon aioli on each slice off bread.
2. On 4 slices of the bread, top aioli with 1/2 cup dehydrated mushrooms.
3. Top mushrooms with 1/4 cup caramelized onions.
4. Top caramelized onions with 1/2 cup arugula.
5. Finish sandwich with top layer of bread. Serve immediately.

Note: Keeps in refrigerator up to 2 days in airtight container.

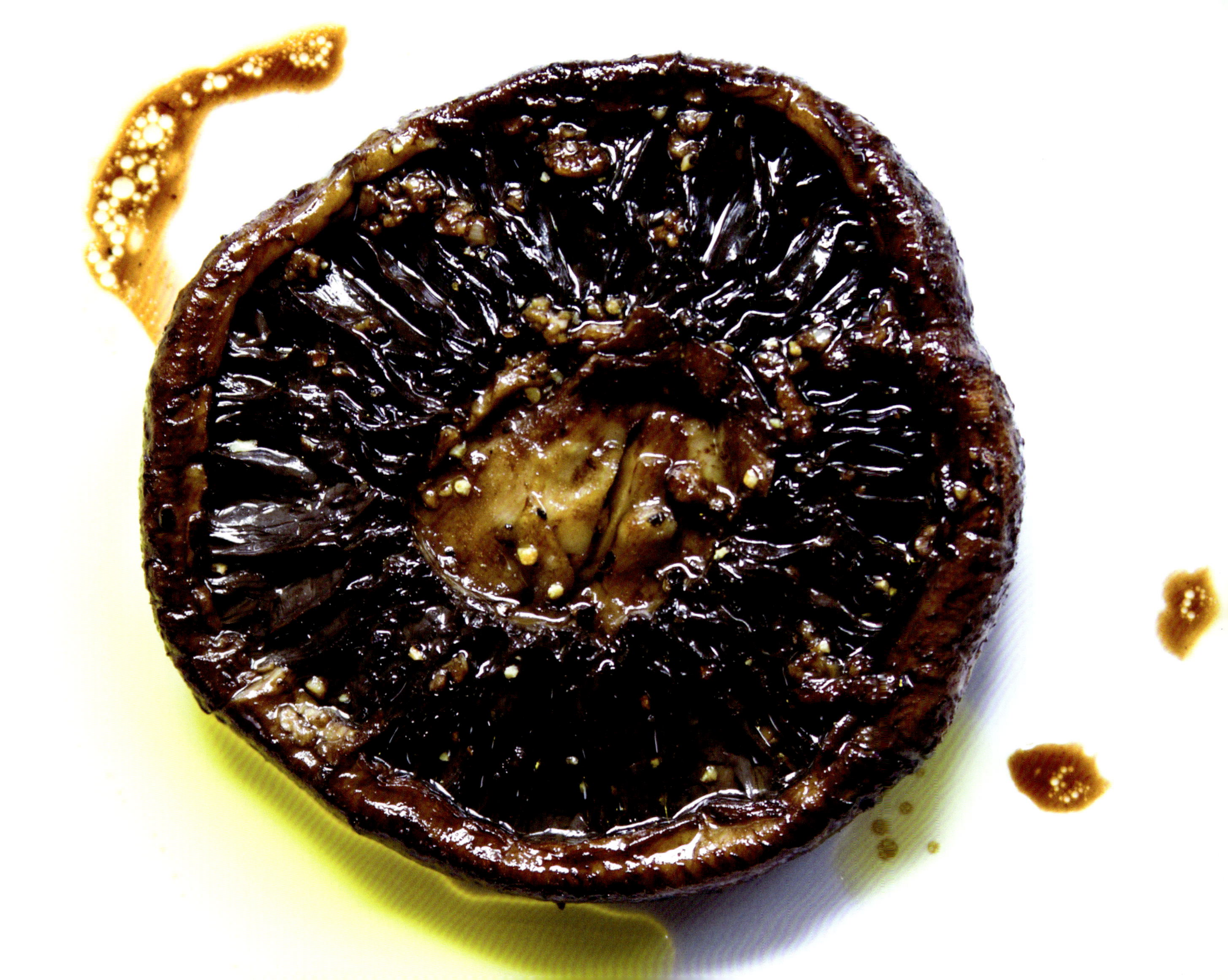

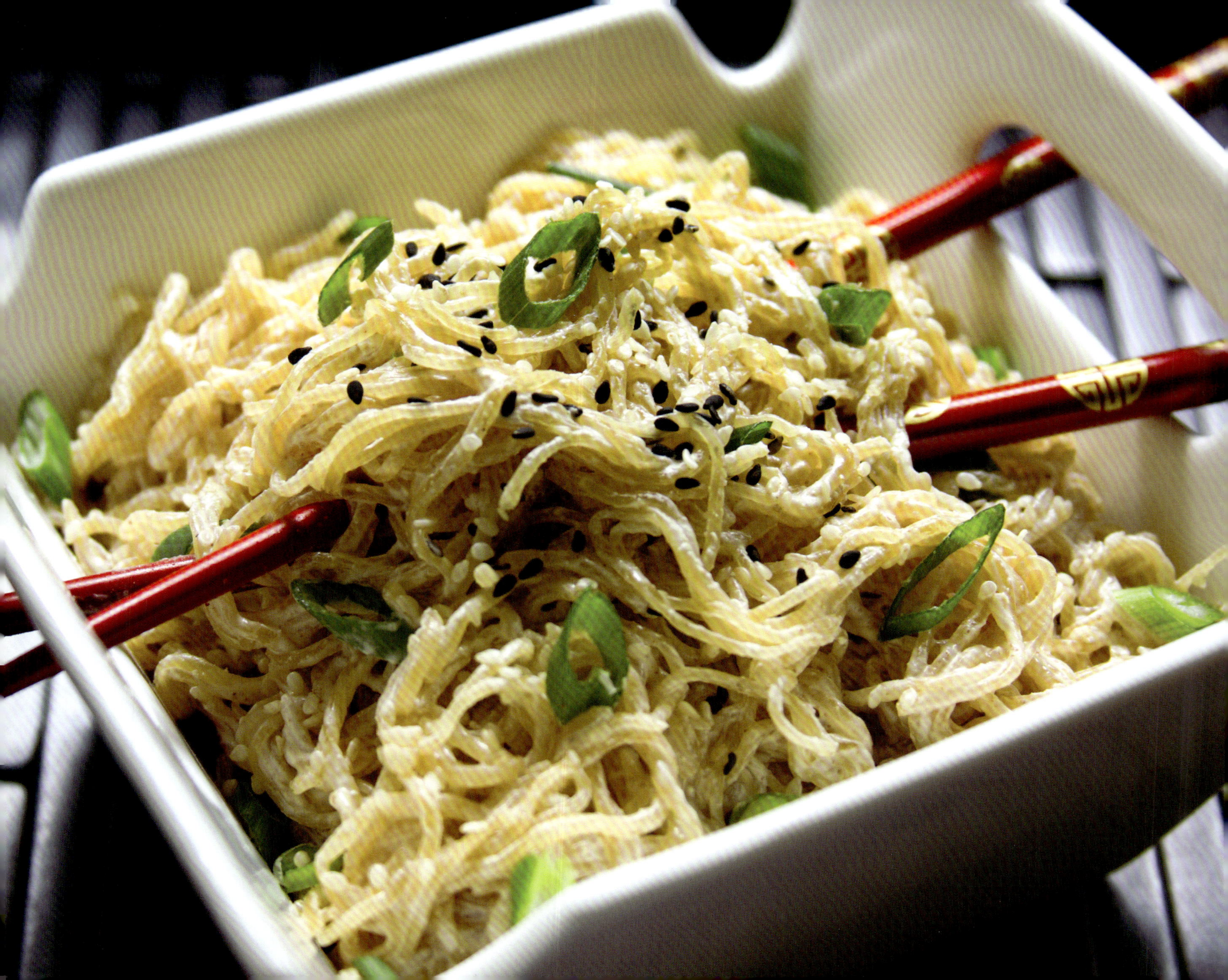

TOSSED SESAME NOODLES WITH GREEN ONION AND CRUSHED RED PEPPER FLAKES

SERVES 4-6

NOODLES
2 12-ounce packs clear kelp noodles

SAUCE
1/4 cup raw tahini
1/4 cup expeller-pressed sesame oil
1/4 cup rice wine vinegar
1/4 cup wheat-free tamari
2 tablespoons raw almond butter
2 tablespoons water
1 tablespoon + 1 teaspoon raw light agave
2 teaspoons lime juice, fresh-squeezed
2 teaspoons fresh ginger, peeled and minced
2 small cloves garlic, peeled

GARNISH
1/4 cup green onions, chopped
2 teaspoons black and white sesame seeds
1 teaspoon crushed red pepper flakes

This recipe was one of those beautiful disasters. My intention was to make something totally different, but it evolved into this scrumptious recipe composed of delicate kelp noodles bathed in a creamy white sesame sauce, crisp green onions, then sprinkled with black-and-white sesame seeds and crushed red pepper for some kick.

Make the noodles
1. Rinse kelp noodles in warm water. Pat dry with towel, then lay out noodles on cutting board. Using a sharp knife, cut the noodles horizontally then vertically. Place in medium mixing bowl, cover and set aside.

Make the sauce
1. In high-speed blender place tahini, sesame oil, rice wine vinegar, wheat-free tamari, almond butter, water, agave, lime juice, ginger, and garlic. Blend on high for about 1 ½ minutes until sauce is smooth and creamy.
2. Pour sauce over noodles, and toss with serving spoons until all noodles are coated evenly with sauce. Cover and place in refrigerator for 1 ½ hours. This will allow the noodles to marinate and soften from the salts.

Assemble
1. After the noodles are done marinating, place them on serving dishes of choice and garnish with a few sprinkles of green onion, black-and-white sesame seeds, and crushed red pepper flakes. Serve with chopsticks.

Note: Keeps in refrigerator up to 4 days in airtight container.

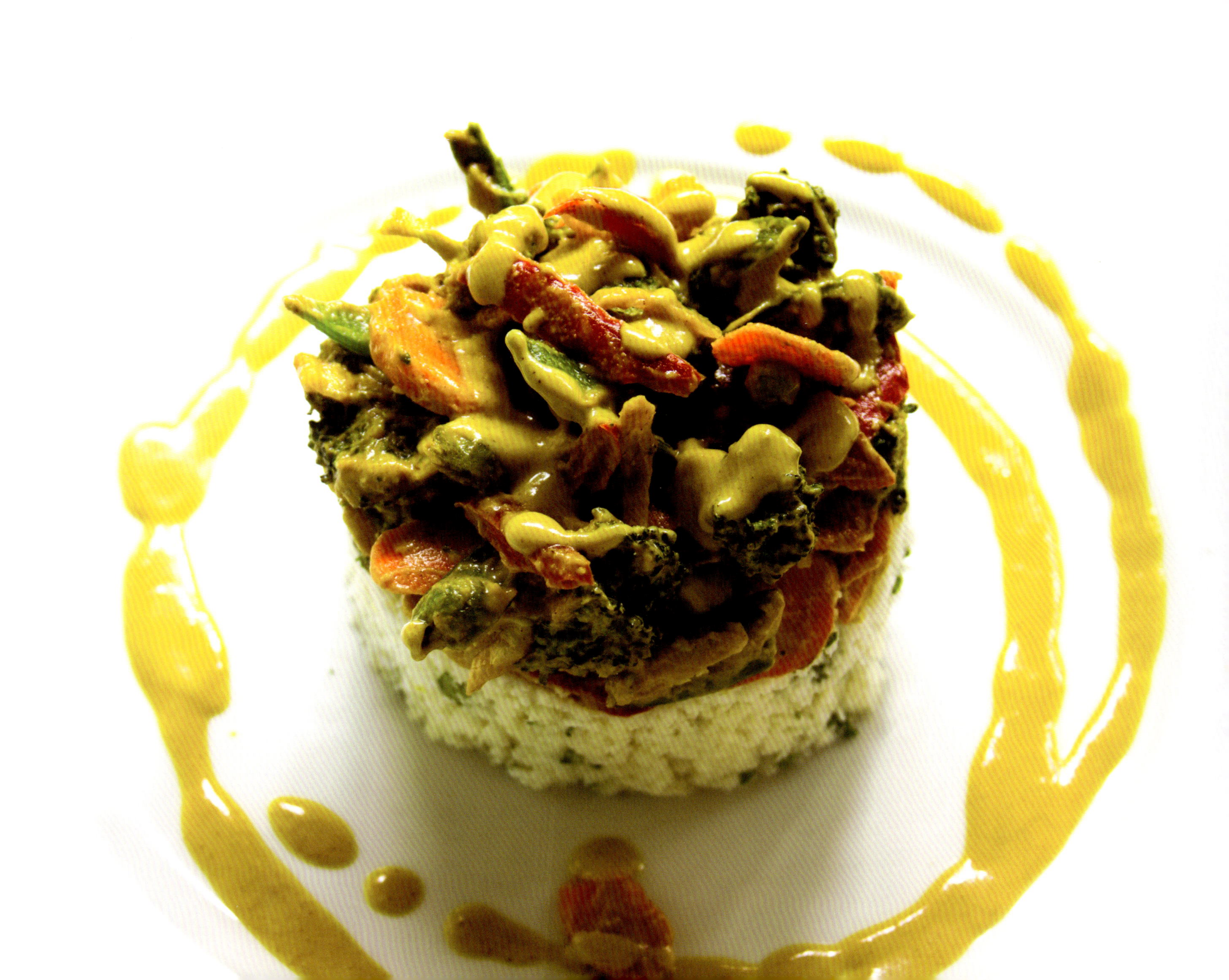

COCONUT CURRY VEGETABLES WITH CAULIFLOWER SCENTED RICE

SERVES 4-6

CURRY SAUCE

1 cup young Thai coconut meat
3/4 cup young Thai coconut water
1/4 cup raw cashews soaked 4–6 hours, drained and rinsed
2 tablespoons wheat-free tamari
2 tablespoons coconut butter, melted
2 tablespoons curry powder
1 large clove garlic, peeled
1 teaspoon fresh ginger, peeled and minced
1 teaspoon raw light agave
1 teaspoon lemon juice, fresh-squeezed
1/2 teaspoon turmeric powder
1/2 teaspoon onion powder
1/8 teaspoon ground cinnamon

VEGETABLES

3 cups broccoli florets, chopped
1 ½ cups sweet onion, thinly sliced
1 cup snap peas
1 cup carrots, thinly sliced into circles
1 cup red pepper, seeds removed and chopped

RICE

5 cups cauliflower, chopped
1/2 cup unsweetened raw coconut, shredded
1/4 cup fresh cilantro, leaves only, chopped
2 tablespoons coconut butter, melted
1 teaspoon garlic, peeled and minced
1/4 teaspoon sea salt

I am obsessed with curry, especially when it's paired with my other food obsession, coconut. The two ingredients work beautifully together, creating an exotic golden sauce that's tossed with a colorful blend of vegetables and served with fluffy cilantro coconut rice.

Make the sauce
1. In high-speed blender place coconut water, coconut meat, cashews, coconut butter, wheat-free tamari, curry powder, garlic, ginger, agave, lemon juice, turmeric powder, onion powder, and cinnamon. Blend on high for about 2 minutes, until cashews and coconut meat are broken down and curry sauce is smooth, and creamy.

Make the vegetables
1. In medium bowl, add broccoli, sweet onion, snap peas, carrots, and red pepper. Pour 1 ½ cups curry sauce over vegetables and mix together with spoon until all vegetables are well coated.
2. Spread vegetables on dehydrator tray lined with teflex sheet. Dehydrate at 115 degrees for 4 hours. This will soften and marinate the vegetables to perfection! In the meantime make the rice, do the dishes, and set the table.

Make the rice
1. In food processor with "S" blade attachment, add cauliflower. Pulse until consistency of cooked rice.
2. Add shredded coconut, garlic, and sea salt. Pulse another 10–20 seconds, until just combined.
3. Transfer to a medium mixing bowl. Stir in melted coconut butter and fresh cilantro.

Assemble
1. On dishes of choice, place 1 cup coconut cilantro rice and 1/2 cup warm curried vegetables. Drizzle with remaining curry sauce. Sprinkle on a few cilantro leaves. Serve immediately.

Note: Keeps in refrigerator up to 3 days in airtight container.

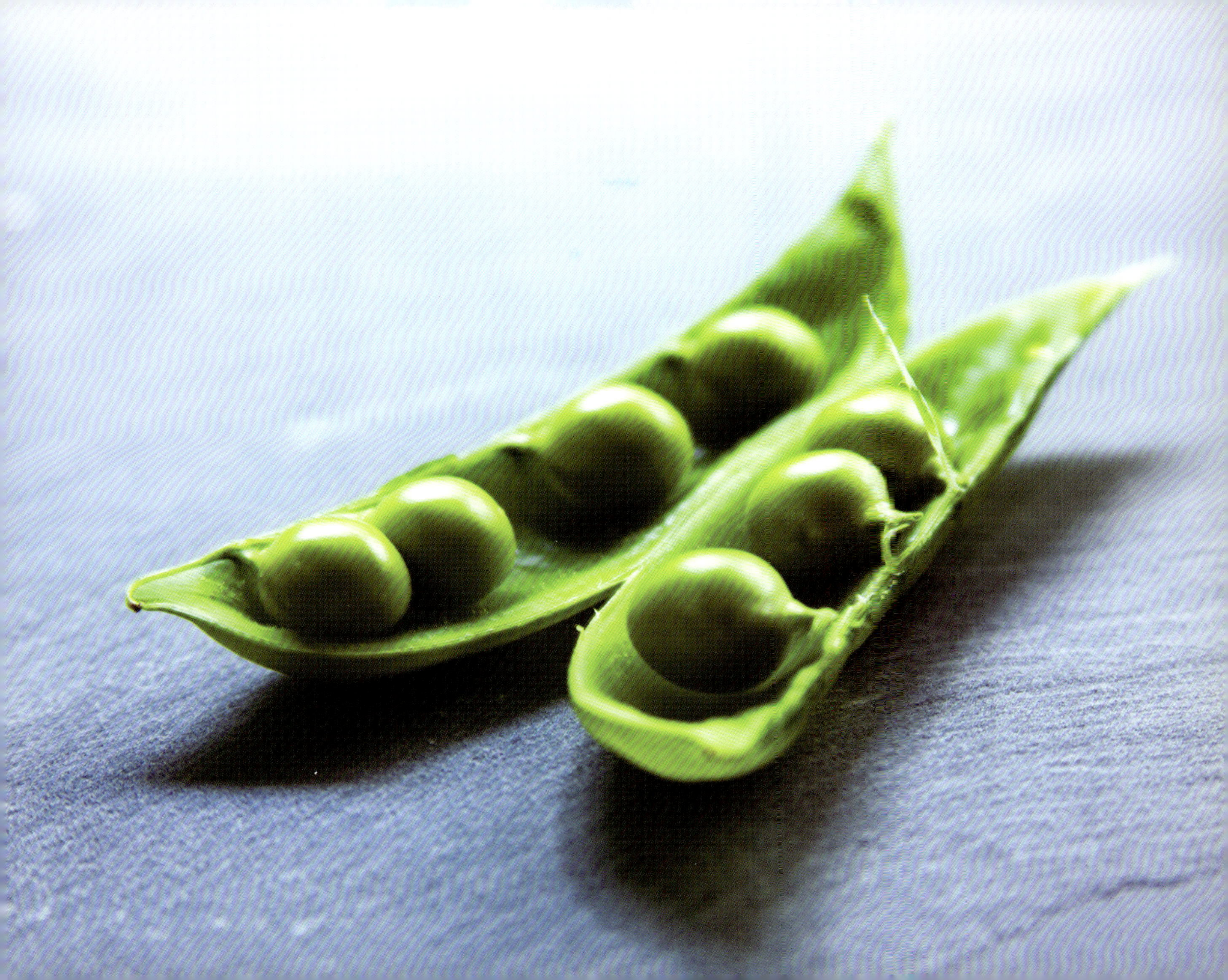

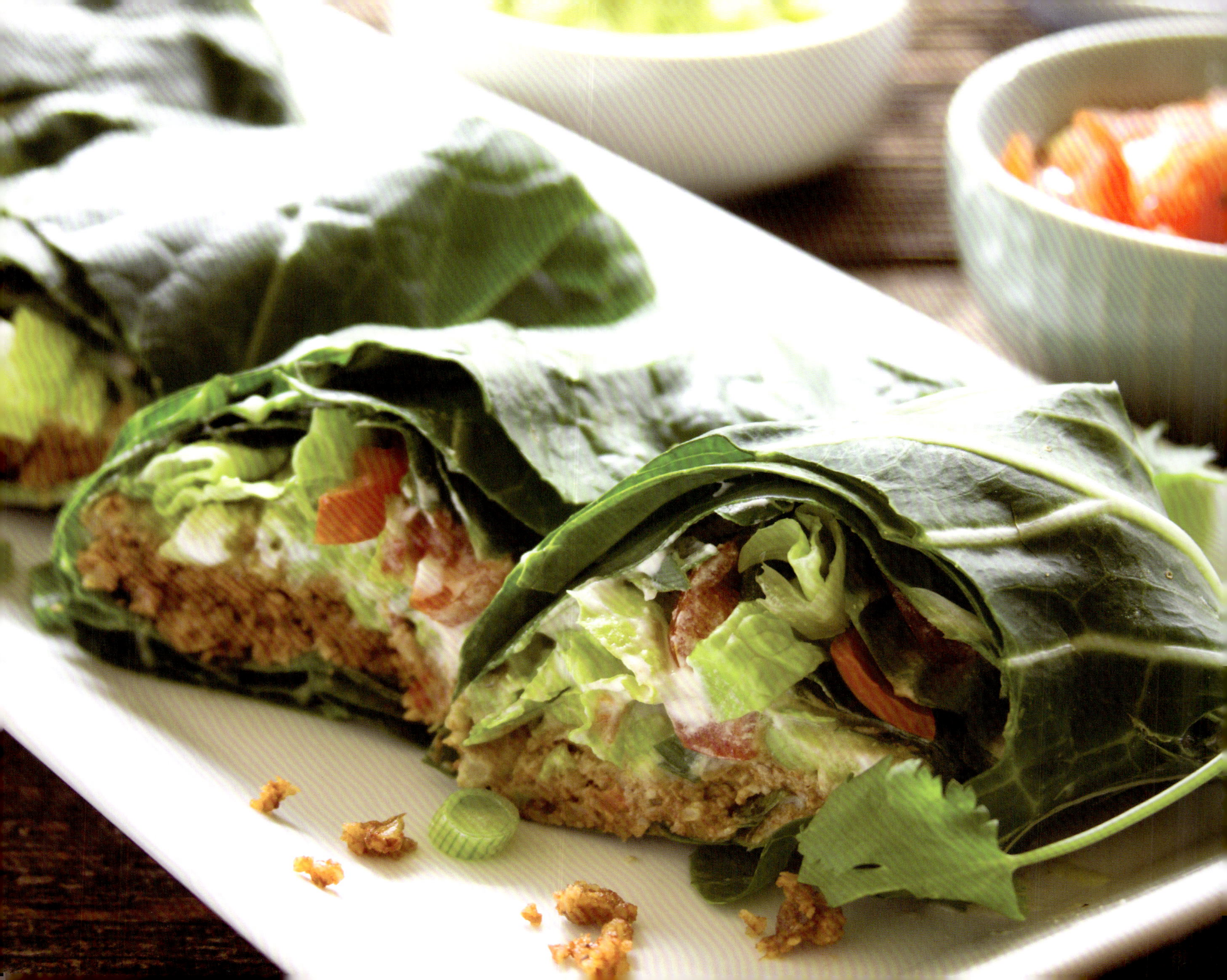

COLLARD LEAF TACOS WITH SEASONED NUT MEAT, CASHEW CREAM, GUACAMOLE, AND FRESH SALSA

SERVES 4-6

FILLING

4 large collard leaves, washed and thick stems removed
1 cup nut meat
1 cup lettuce, shredded
1/2 cup cherry tomato salsa (see page 158)
1/2 cup lemon guacamole (see page 142)
1/2 cup cashew cream (see page 104)
1/4 cup green onions, chopped

NUT MEAT

1 cup raw walnuts soaked 4 hours, drained and rinsed
2 tablespoons expeller-pressed grape-seed oil
2 tablespoons yellow onion, chopped
2 teaspoons cumin powder
2 teaspoons chili powder
1 teaspoon onion powder
1 teaspoon garlic powder
1/4 teaspoon sea salt

This was one of the first recipes I developed as a raw food chef. The complexity of flavor and textures take these tacos to a whole different level, yet they are simple and quick to make. I have brought these to multiple parties and events that I've catered, and they always end up being devoured and the star of the party.

Make the nut-meat
1. In a food processor with "S" blade attachment, add walnuts, grape-seed oil, yellow onion, cumin powder, chili powder, onion powder, garlic powder and sea salt. Pulse for about 30 seconds, until slightly chunky but well combined.

Assemble
1. Lay out collard leaves. On side closest to you, top each leaf with 1/4 cup nut meat.
2. Top nut meat with guacamole.
3. Top guacamole with shredded lettuce.
4. Top shredded lettuce with cashew cream.
5. Top cashew cream with green onion.
6. Top green onions with fresh salsa.
7. Fold in ends and roll away from you, just as if you were wrapping a burrito. Slice in half. Repeat until you have wrapped all 4 collards.

Note: Keeps in refrigerator up to 2 days in airtight container.

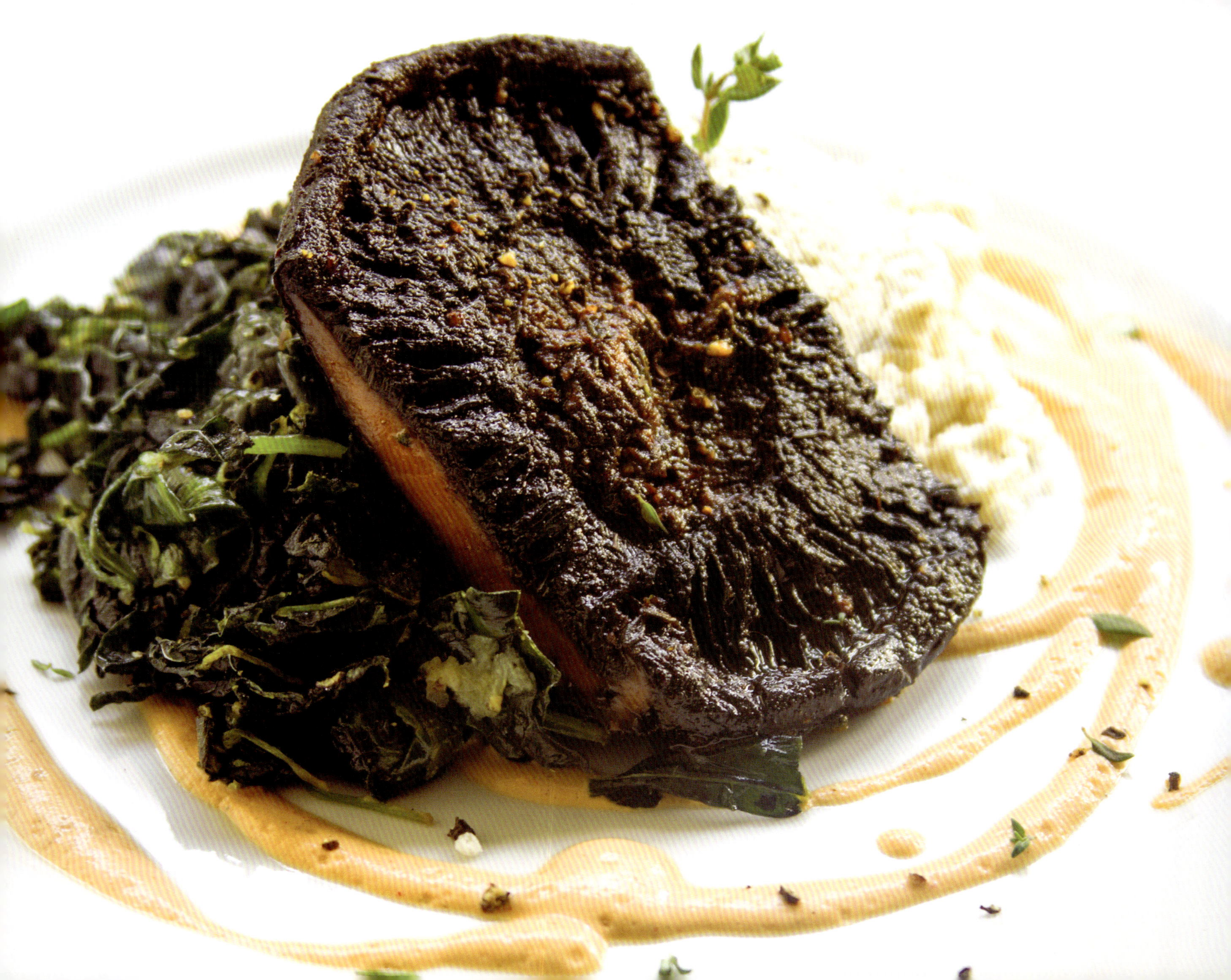

SMOKED PORTOBELLO, JICAMA PUREE, GARLIC GREENS, AND SMOKED PAPRIKA CREAM

SERVES 4

PORTOBELLO
4 medium portobello mushrooms
1/2 cup virgin raw olive oil
1 tablespoon fresh thyme, stems removed
2 teaspoons smoked paprika powder
1 teaspoon natural liquid smoke (optional for added smoky flavor)
1 teaspoon fresh ground black pepper
1/2 teaspoon sea salt

GREENS
3 cups fresh baby spinach leaves
3 cups green kale, stems removed and chopped
3 medium cloves garlic, peeled
2 tablespoons virgin raw olive oil
1 tablespoon lemon juice, fresh-squeezed
1 teaspoon fresh ground black pepper
1/2 teaspoon onion powder
1/2 teaspoon garlic powder
1/8 teaspoon sea salt

JICAMA PUREE
6 cups jicama, peeled and chopped
1 cup raw cashews soaked 4–6 hours, drained and rinsed
1 cup water
2 tablespoons expeller-pressed grape-seed oil
2 medium cloves garlic, peeled
2 teaspoons lemon juice, fresh-squeezed
1 teaspoon sea salt
1/4 teaspoon fresh ground black pepper

PAPRIKA CREAM
1 ½ cups cashew cream
1/2 cup water
1 tablespoon yellow onion, finely chopped
2 ½ teaspoons smoked paprika powder
2 teaspoons expeller-pressed grape-seed oil
2 medium cloves garlic, peeled

This gourmet Southern-inspired meal gets a boost of flavor with smoked paprika marinated portobello mushrooms, buttery jicama mash, and wilted garlic greens all surrounded by a creamy smoked cashew cream.

Make the portobello
1. In medium mixing bowl, add portobellos, olive oil, thyme, smoked paprika, liquid smoke (optional), black pepper, and sea salt. Toss until portobellos have soaked up most the oil. Cover and let marinate for 2 hours.
2. Spread mushrooms out on dehydrator tray lined with a teflex sheet. Dehydrate at 115 degrees for 8 hours. If you're around, turn portobellos after 4 hours for even dehydration.

Make the greens
1. In medium bowl, add baby spinach, kale, garlic, olive oil, lemon juice, black pepper, onion powder, garlic powder, and sea salt. Massage kale and spinach for 3–5 minutes until leaves are evenly coated and start to turn a darker shade of green.
2. Transfer greens to dehydrator tray line with teflex sheet. Dehydrate with mushrooms at 115 degrees for 3 hours. Some greens may get a little crispy around the edges, which will add extra texture to the dish.

Make the jicama
1. In food processor with "S" blade attachment, add jicama. Pulse about 1 minute, until broken down and jicama resembles mashed potatoes.
2. Place jicama in nut-milk bag or triple-lined cheesecloth and squeeze out all the liquid. It will shrink down a lot once liquid is out. Place jicama back in food processor with "S" blade.
3. In high-speed blender place cashews, water, grape-seed oil, garlic, lemon juice, sea salt and black pepper. Blend on high for about 2 minutes, until cashews are broken down, smooth and creamy.
4. Reserve 1 ½ cups cashew cream for paprika cream.
5. Add 1/2 cup cashew cream to jicama in food processor and puree for about 1 minute, until well combined.

Make the paprika cream
1. In high-speed blender place reserve cashew cream, water, yellow onion, smoked paprika powder, grape-seed oil, and garlic. Blend on high for about 1 minute, until onions are broken down and sauce is smooth.

Assemble
1. Using an ice cream scooper, scoop about 1/2 cup puree onto each plate.
2. Place 1/2 cup garlic greens next to jicama puree.
3. Remove portobellos from dehydrator and cut into rectangles. Place in front of jicama and greens.
4. Drizzle a generous amount of paprika cream on the outside rim of plate.
5. Garnish with a sprinkle of fresh thyme. Serve immediately.

Note: Keeps in refrigerator up to 3 days in airtight container.

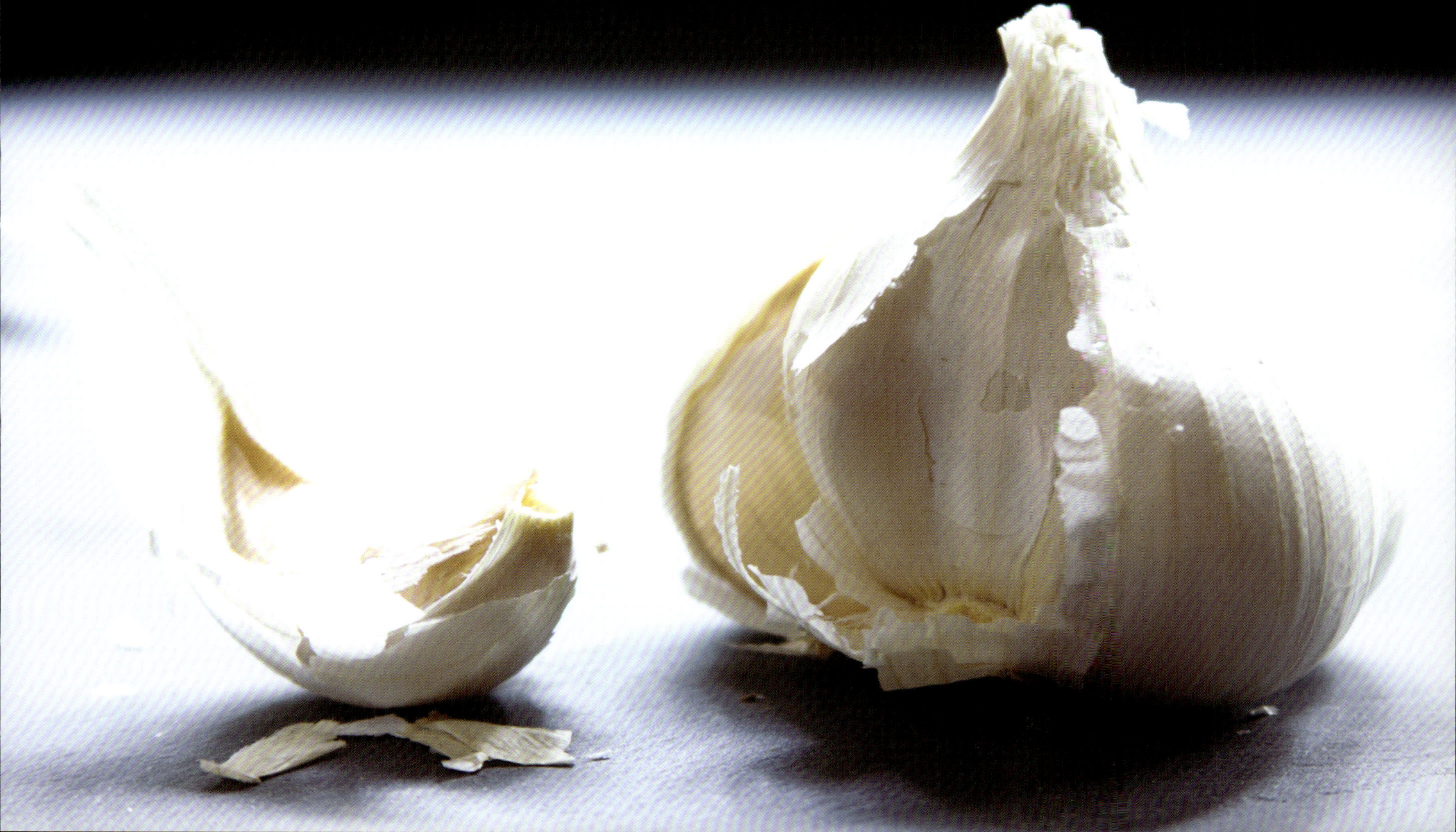

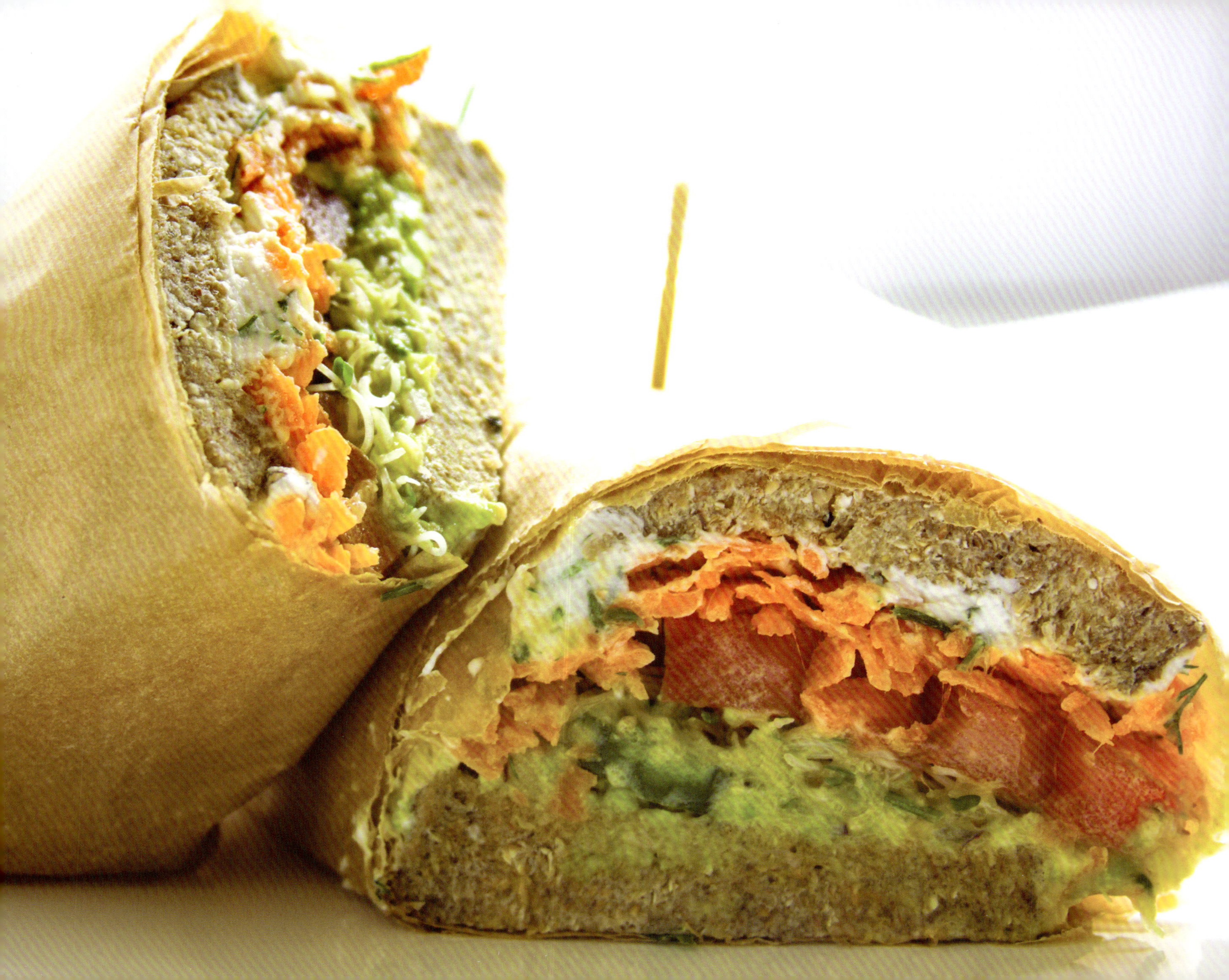

HERB CASHEW CREAM CHEESE, CARROTS, TOMATO, CUCUMBER, AND AVOCADO SPROUT **SANDWICH**

SERVES 4

SANDWICH

8 slices almond flax bread (see page 146)
16 thin round cucumber slices
8 slices ripe tomato
1 cup herb cream cheese
1 medium ripe avocado, peeled, pitted and mashed with fork
1/2 cup carrots, shredded
1/2 cup alfalfa sprouts
1/4 cup cashew spread (see page 100)

CASHEW CREAM CHEESE

2 ¼ cups cashews soaked 4–6 hours drained and rinsed
3/4 cup warm water
1 tablespoon minced fresh chives
2 teaspoons vegan probiotic powder
2 teaspoons lemon juice, fresh-squeezed
3/4 teaspoon sea salt
1/2 teaspoon dried oregano
1/2 teaspoon dried parsley

I adore a good sandwich! They're quick, easy, filling, and have endless possibilities. The herb cream cheese is packed with protein and the vegetables lend extra nutrition, rich flavor, color, and texture. Feel free to add or substitute any ingredients to create your own perfect veggie sandwich.

Make herb cream cheese
1. In high-speed blender, add water and probiotics. Let stand for 5 minutes. Add cashews, lemon juice, and sea salt. Blend on high for about 2 minutes, until cashews are broken down and smooth.
2. Pour cheese into small mixing bowl to culture. Cover and let stand at room temperature for 24 hours. If you would like to speed up the culturing process, place cheese in dehydrator at 105 degrees for 12 hours.
3. After cheese is done culturing stir in chives, oregano, and parsley. Cover and place in refrigerator for about 2 hours, or until chilled.

Assemble
1. Lay out 8 slices of bread. Top 4 slices with 1/4 cup herb cream cheese.
2. Top cream cheese with 2 tablespoons shredded carrots.
3. Top shredded carrots with 2 tomato slices.
4. Top tomato slices with 2 tablespoons sprouts.
5. Top sprouts with 4 cucumber slices.
6. Spread 1 tablespoon cashew spread on other 4 slices bread.
7. Top cashew spread with 2 tablespoons mashed avocado.
8. To finish sandwich, place avocado side of bread on top of cucumber side. Secure with deli toothpick. Serve immediately.

Note: Keeps in refrigerator up to 2 days in airtight container.

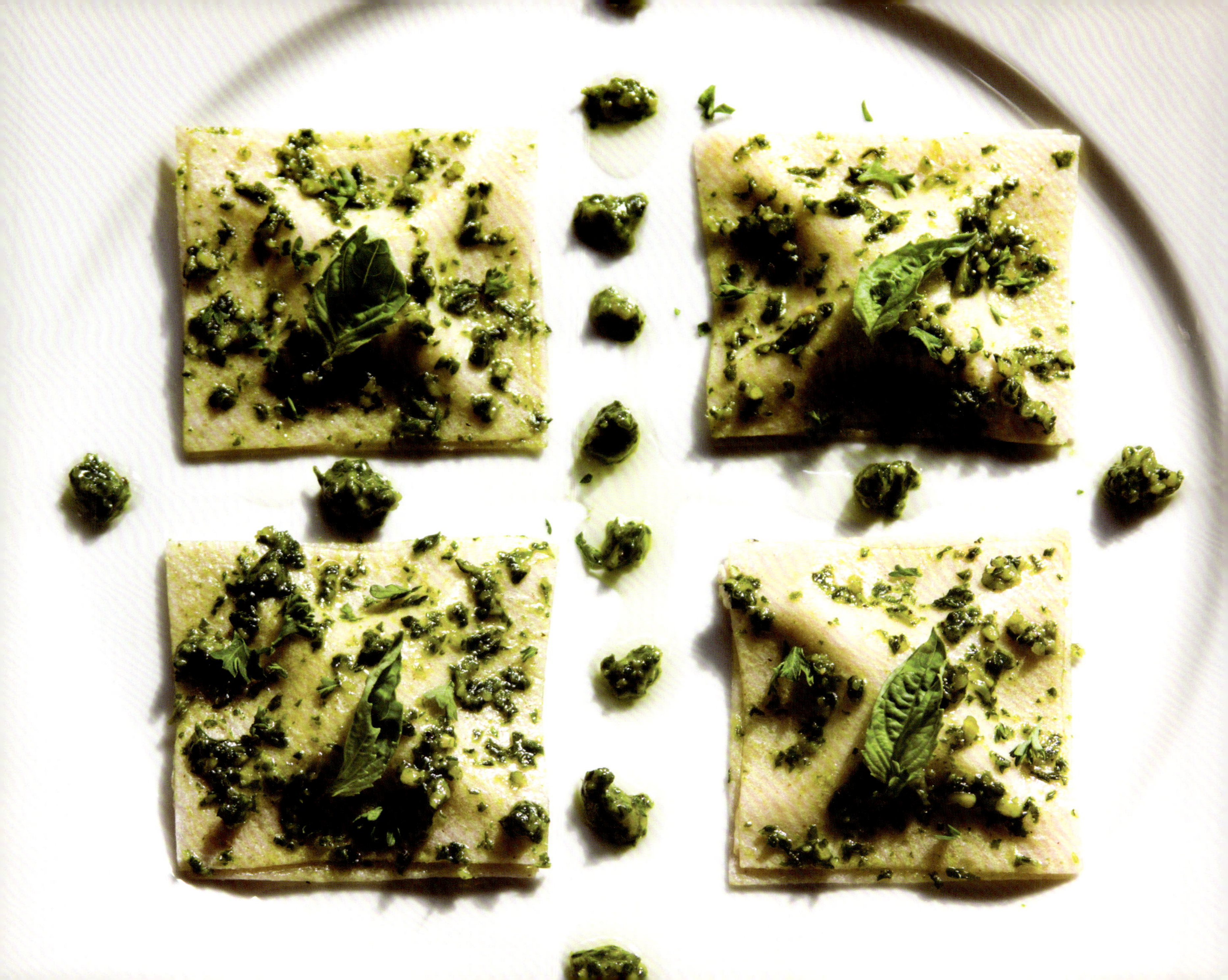

RAVIOLIS, CASHEW CHEESE, AND **TRUFFLE** INFUSED PESTO

MAKES 16 (SERVES 4-6)

RAVIOLIS
3 cups young Thai coconut meat
1 ½ cups water
1/4 teaspoon sea salt

CASHEW CHEESE
1 cup raw cashews soaked 4–6 hours, drained and rinsed
1/2 cup water
1/4 cup irish moss gel (see page 102)
2 tablespoons raw coconut oil
1 ½ teaspoons lemon juice, fresh-squeezed
1/2 teaspoon sea salt

TRUFFLE PESTO
2 cups fresh basil leaves, stems removed and tightly packed
1/4 cup virgin raw olive oil
1/4 cup fresh parsley, stems removed and tightly packed
1/4 cup raw hulled pumpkin seeds
2 tablespoons white truffle oil
2 medium cloves garlic, peeled
1 tablespoon nutritional yeast
1 teaspoon lemon juice, fresh-squeezed
1/4 teaspoon sea salt
1/4 teaspoon fresh ground black pepper

Delicate cashew cheese is carefully stuffed into ravioli shells and dressed with fragrant truffle-oil-infused basil pesto. This impressive entrée is earthy, light, and loaded with flavor.

Make the raviolis
1. In high-speed blender place coconut meat, water, and sea salt. Blend on high for about 1 minute, until coconut meat is broken down and smooth.
2. Pour coconut liquid onto dehydrator trays lined with teflex sheets. Spread thick with spatula, until evenly spread across sheet. Make sure there is no transparency in the liquid.
3. Dehydrate at 105 degrees for 6 hours. Remove from dehydrator and flip onto other side. Slowly, peel away teflex sheet. Return to dehydrator for another 6 hours at 105 degrees.
4. Remove ravioli sheet and transfer to cutting board. Cut into 2inch x 2inch squares.

Make the cheese
1. In high-speed blender place cashews, water, irish moss, lemon juice and sea salt. Blend on high about 2 minutes, until cashews are broken down and cream is a thick and smooth.
2. Add coconut oil. Blend another 30 seconds, until coconut oil is well combined.
3. Strain cheese through triple-lined cheesecloth. Squeeze out as much liquid as possible and tie up with rubber band. Place in refrigerator for 4–6 hours to set or until firm to touch.

Make the pesto
1. In food processor with "S" blade attachment, place basil, olive oil, parsley, pumpkin seeds, truffle oil, garlic, nutritional yeast, lemon juice, sea salt, and black pepper. Pulse for about 30 seconds, or until pesto is mixed thoroughly yet slightly chunky.

Assemble
1. Lay out half the ravioli squares and brush them with warm water. Place 1 teaspoon cashew cheese in center of each.
2. Top each one with another square, mirroring the lower square. Wet fingers with water and press around edges of raviolis until they're well sealed. Keep dipping fingers in water if needed.
3. Coat raviolis with pesto and drizzle with white truffle oil.

Note: Keeps in refrigerator up to 3 days in airtight container.

D E S S

E R T S

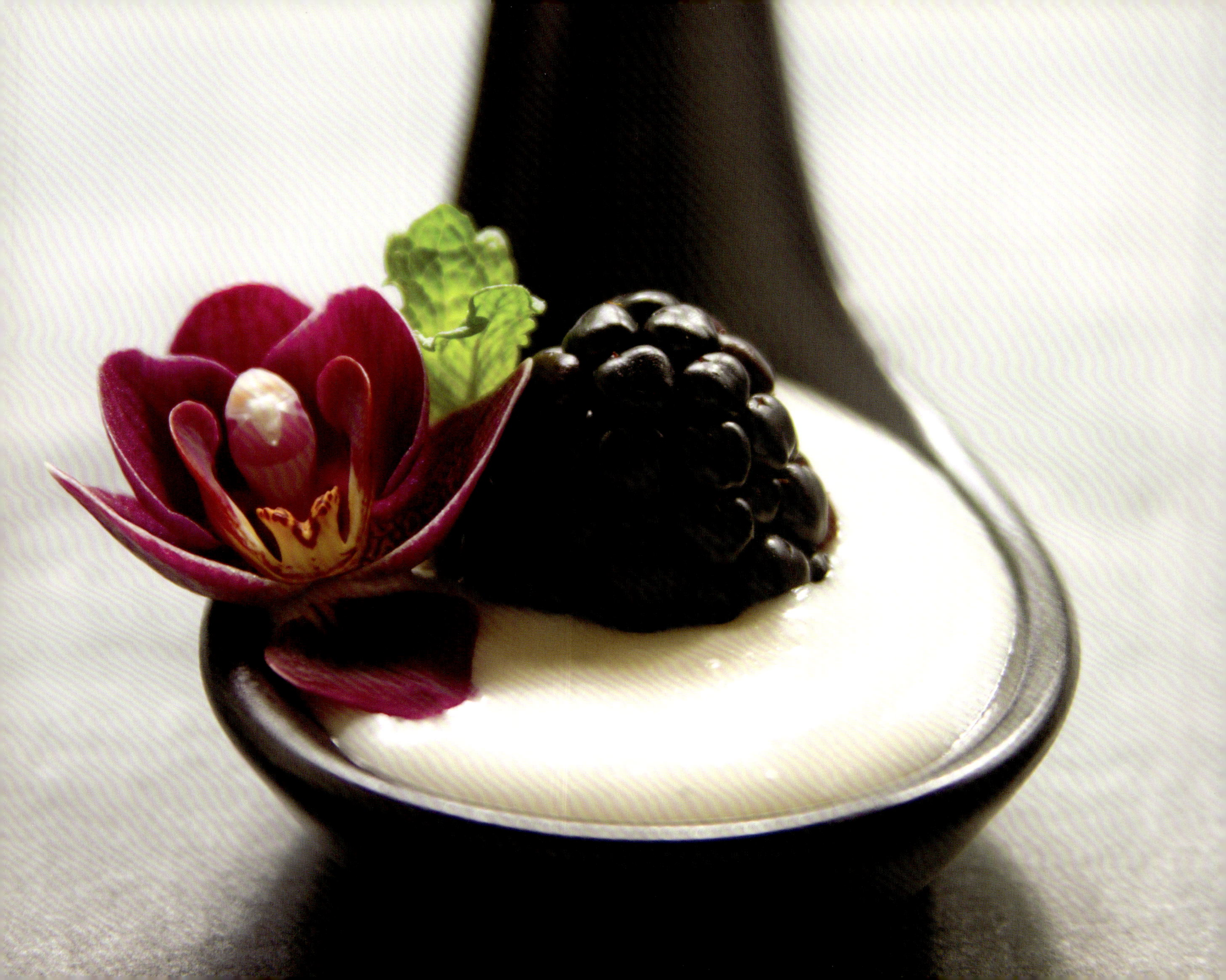

VANILLA BEAN PUDDING, BLACKBERRY, AND EDIBLE ORCHID

MAKES 2 CUPS (SERVES 4)

PUDDING
1 cup young Thai coconut meat
1/2 cup young Thai coconut water
3 tablespoons raw light agave
2 tablespoons coconut butter, melted
1 tablespoon vanilla extract
1/2 vanilla bean, scraped, seeds only
1/8 teaspoon sea salt

GARNISH
4 large fresh blackberries
4 fresh edible micro orchid flowers
4 small mint leaves, stems removed

This visually stunning dessert is very light and a wonderful way to end any meal. A sophisticated play on the classic vanilla pudding it is garnished with fresh, plump blackberries and succulent edible orchid flowers.

Make the pudding
1. In high-speed blender place coconut meat, coconut water, agave, coconut butter, vanilla extract, vanilla bean, and sea salt. Blend on high for about 2 minutes until coconut meat is broken down and pudding is smooth and creamy.
2. Pour 1/2 cup pudding into dishes of choice. Cover and refrigerate 2–3 hours to set.
3. Before serving top with a fresh blackberry, orchid, and mint leaf.

Note: Keeps in refrigerator up to 4 days in airtight container.

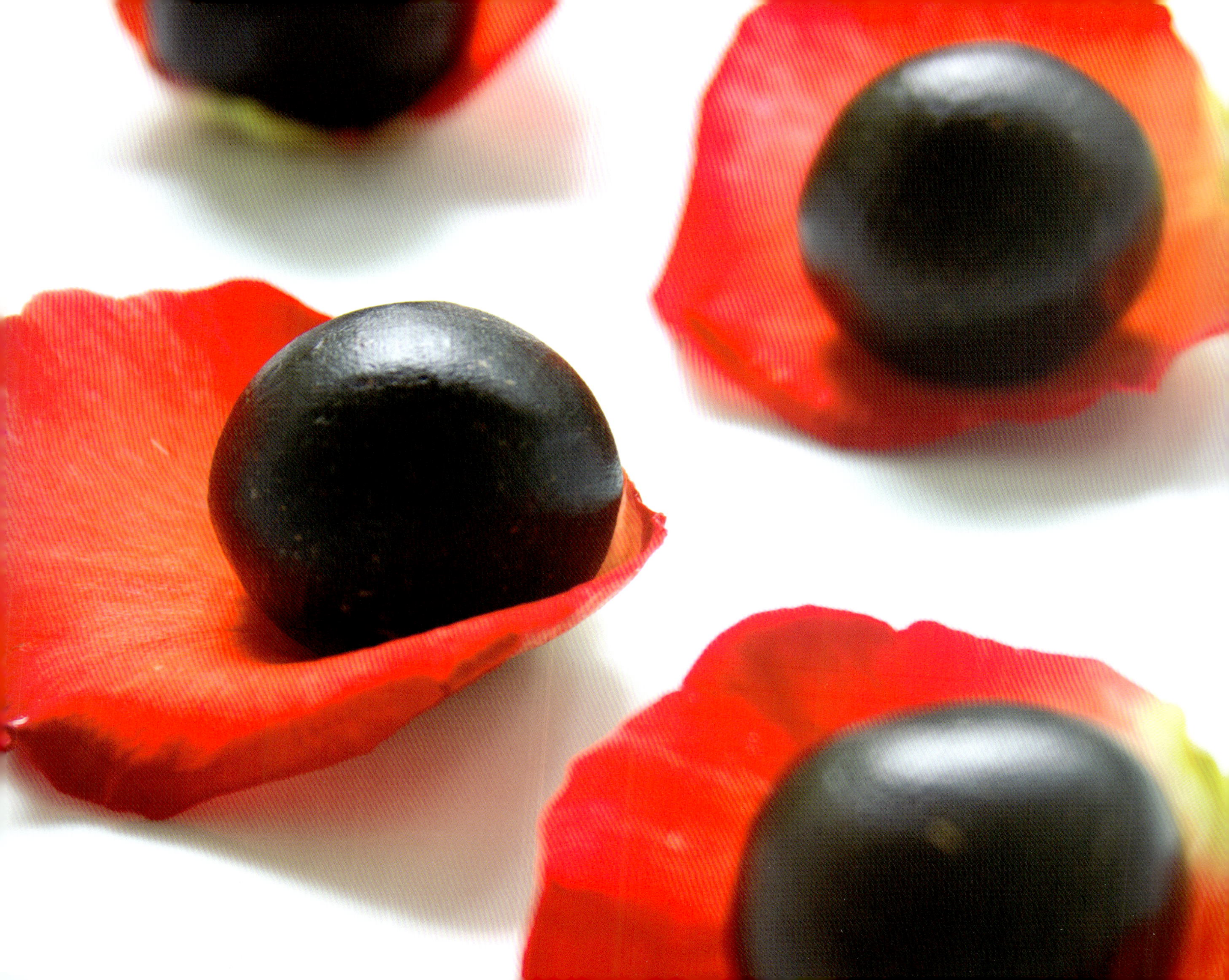

ALMOND BUTTER, HONEY, COCONUT OIL, SPIRULINA, AND CAROB

SERVES 4-6

TRUFFLES

1/4 cup raw almond butter
2 tablespoons raw carob powder
2 tablespoons raw coconut oil
1 tablespoon raw honey or raw light agave
1 ½ tablespoons spirulina powder
1/4 teaspoon sea salt

These are the best snacks before or after workouts, on hikes, or when you need a quick pick-me-up, and are also great if you have a sweet tooth and need something to satisfy a craving. Beautifully presented in rose petals, these make a great alternative to chocolate truffles.

Make truffles

1. In small mixing bowl, add almond butter, carob powder, coconut oil, honey, spirulina powder, and sea salt. Mash together with fork until all carob powder is broken down, with no clumps.
2. Roll into symmetrical balls. Set on parchment paper. Transfer to refrigerator for about 15 minutes to harden and hold shape. Take out and place each one on a rose petal. Serve immediately.

Note: Keeps in refrigerator up to 7 days in airtight container.

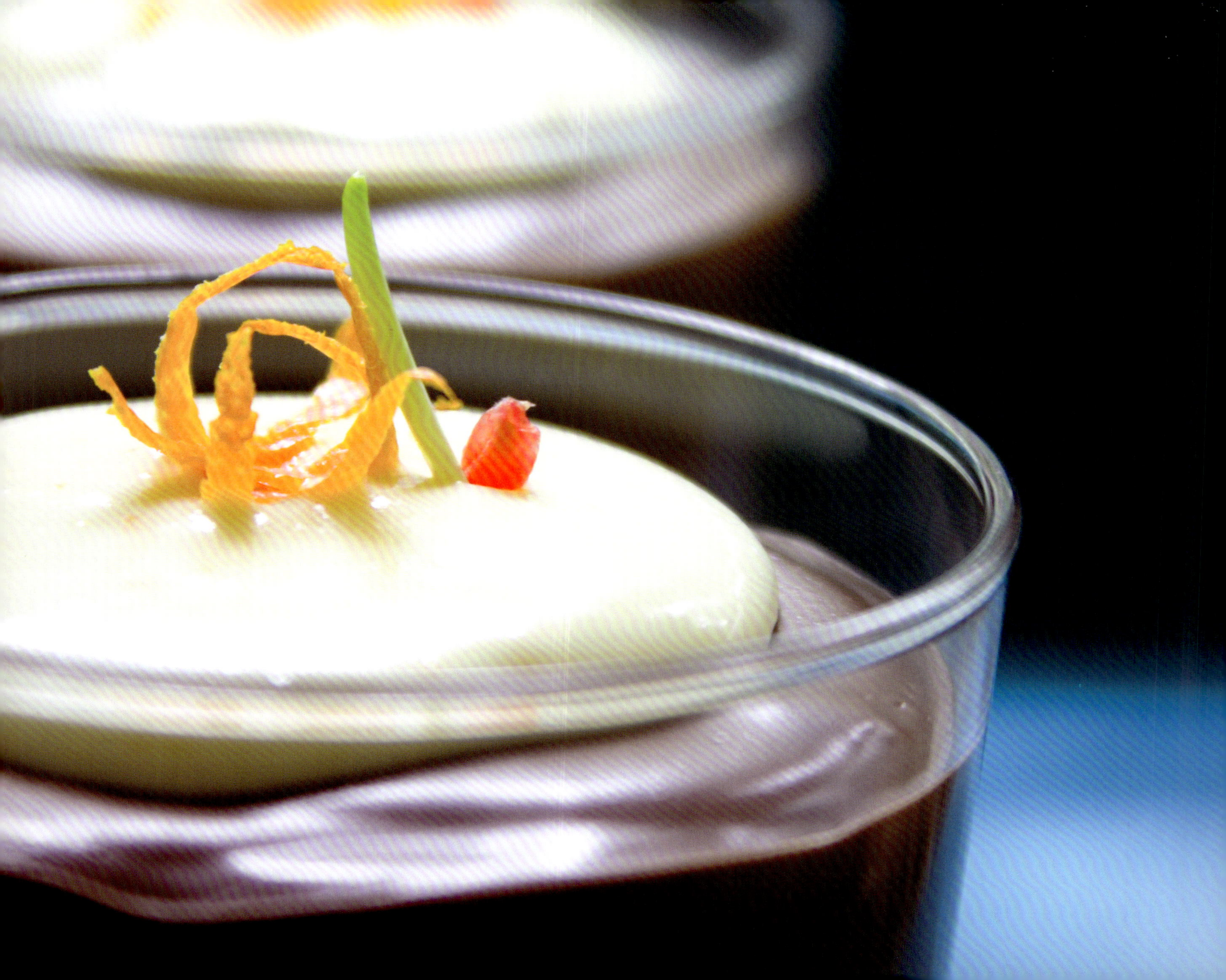

DARK CHOCOLATE MOUSSE WITH TANGELO CREME AND ZEST

SERVES 4-6

MOUSSE
1 ½ cups young Thai coconut meat
3/4 cup young Thai coconut water
3/4 cup raw cacao powder
1/3 cup maple syrup
1/3 cup raw coconut oil
2 tablespoons raw light agave
1 tablespoon vanilla extract
1/4 teaspoon sea salt

TANGELO CREME
1/2 cup young Thai coconut meat
1/4 cup young Thai coconut water
2 tablespoons tangelo juice, fresh-squeezed
2 tablespoon raw coconut oil
1 tablespoons raw light agave
3/4 teaspoon tangelo zest
1/8 teaspoon sea salt

GARNISH
1 tablespoon tangelo zest

Composed of velvety smooth chocolate mousse topped with a dollop of citrus-infused tangelo créme, luxurious in taste and texture, this is great dessert to serve when entertaining.

Make the mousse
1. In high-speed blender place coconut meat, coconut water, cacao powder, maple syrup, agave, vanilla extract, and sea salt. Blend on high for about 2 minutes, until coconut meat is broken down and mousse is smooth.
2. Add coconut oil to mousse and blend on high for 30 seconds, until just combined.
3. Pour mousse into serving dishes of choice. Place in refrigerator for 2 hours or until set. Should be firm to touch.

Make the créme
1. In high-speed blender place coconut meat, coconut water, tangelo juice, agave, tangelo zest, and sea salt. Blend on high for about 1 minute, until coconut meat is broken down.
2. Add coconut oil, and blend another 30 seconds, until well combined.

Assemble
1. Remove mousse from refrigerator. Place 1 or 2 tablespoons tangelo créme on top of mousse. Garnish with tangelo zest. Serve immediately.

Note: Mousse keeps in refrigerator up to 7 days in airtight container. Tangelo créme keeps 1 day in airtight container. The combination of young Thai coconuts, and some citrus fruits, create a bitter aftertaste after 24 hours. Try and make the tangelo créme the same day you will be serving it. It is delicious!

DESSERTS

210

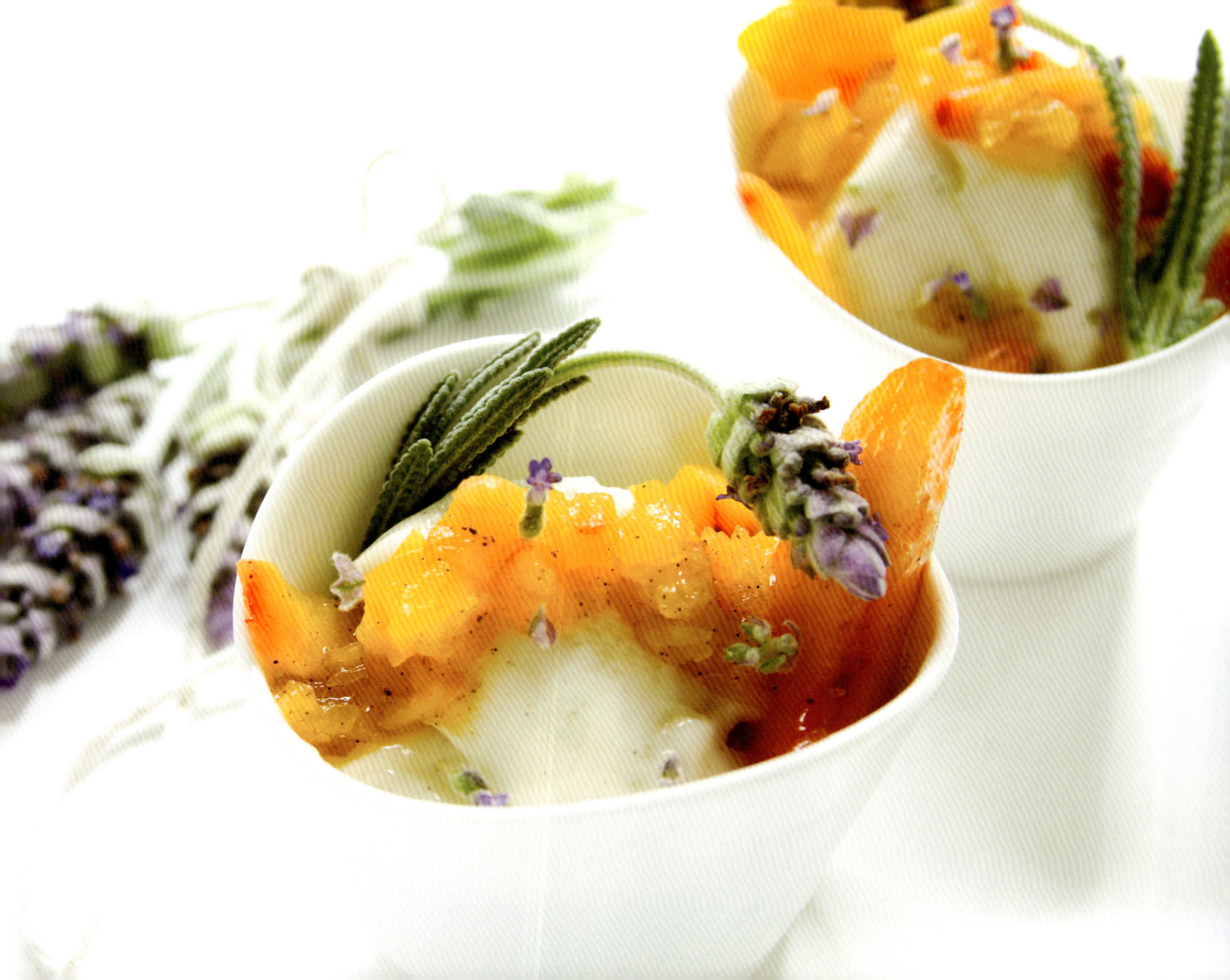

LAVENDER ICE CREAM, PEACHES, VANILLA BEAN, AND CINNAMON

MAKES 1 PINT (SERVES 4-6)

ICE CREAM
1 ½ cups coconut cream (see page 74)
1/2 cup raw coconut oil
1/3 cup raw light agave
2 ½ teaspoons edible dried lavender
1/2 teaspoon vanilla extract
1/4 teaspoon sea salt

PEACH COMPOTE
2 cups peaches, pitted and roughly chopped
2 tablespoons raw light agave
1 tablespoon lemon juice, fresh-squeezed
1 vanilla bean, scraped, seeds only
1/4 teaspoon cinnamon

GARNISH (OPTIONAL)
fresh or dried lavender flowers

Fragrant lavender blossom ice cream is complemented perfectly by the floral essence of ripe peaches—a delectable summertime treat.

Make ice cream
1. In high-speed blender place coconut cream, coconut oil, agave, dried lavender, vanilla extract, and sea salt. Blend on high for about 2 minutes, until coconut oil is broken down and not chunky or frothy. You want the ice cream to be totally smooth.
2. Transfer to ice-cream maker of choice and follow directions as if making traditional ice cream.

Make the peach compote
1. In small mixing bowl, add peaches, agave, lemon juice, vanilla bean, and cinnamon. Mash with fork, until combined but still chunky.
2. Using an ice-cream scooper, scoop out ice cream into serving dishes of choice. Top with peach compote and a few sprinkles of fresh or dried lavender.

Note: Ice cream keeps in freezer up to 1 month in airtight container.

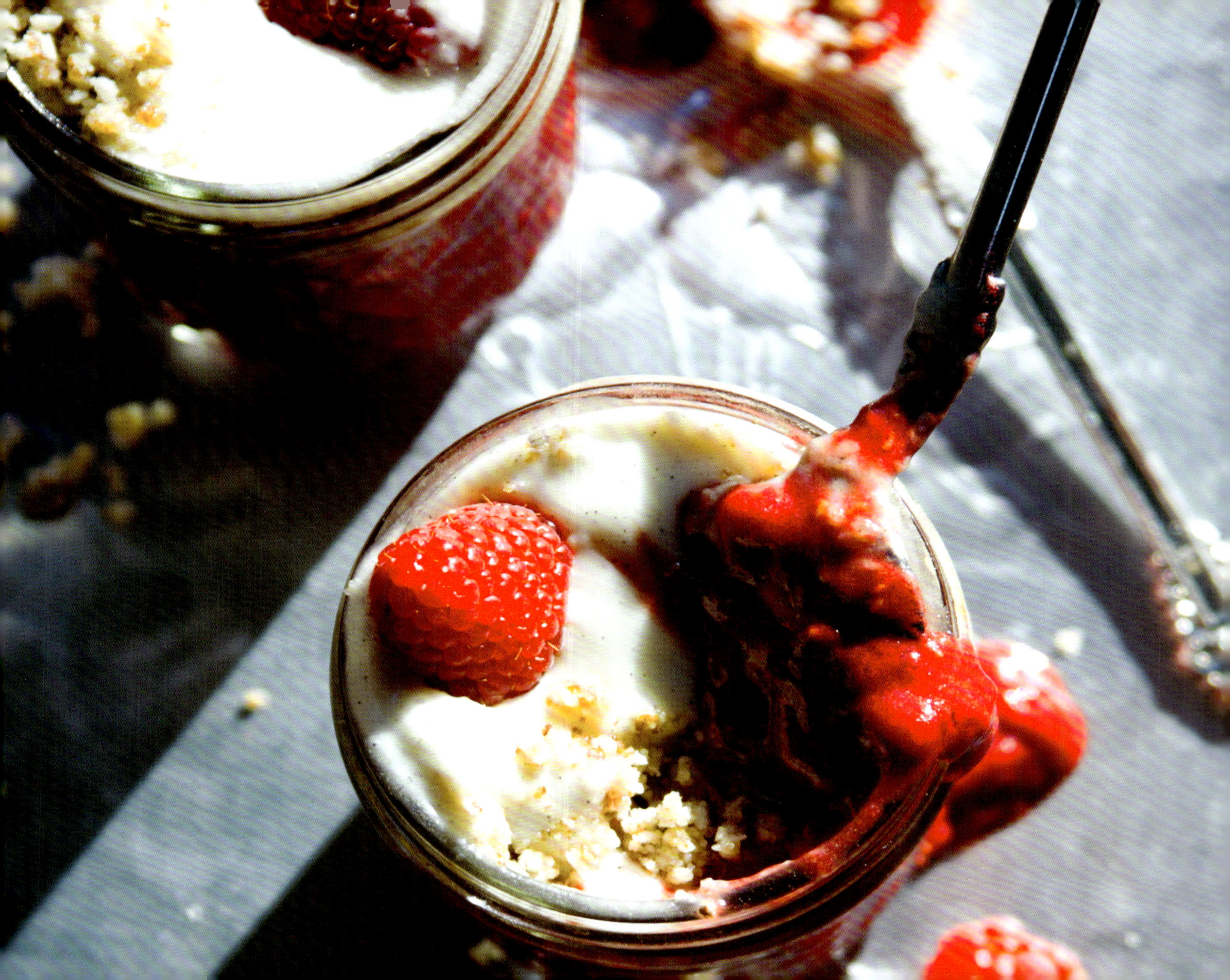

COCONUT, PECANS, RASPBERRIES, AND TAHITIAN VANILLA BEAN

SERVES 6-8

RASPBERRY FILLING
5 cups thawed frozen raspberries
2 cups fresh raspberries
1/2 cup medjool dates, pitted
2 tablespoons raw light agave
1 tablespoon lemon juice, fresh-squeezed
1 tablespoon lecithin granules
2 teaspoons ground cinnamon
1 teaspoon vanilla extract
1/4 teaspoon sea salt

CRUMBLE
1 ¼ cup raw pecans
1 ¼ cup unsweetened raw coconut, shredded
5 medjool dates
1 tablespoon raw coconut oil
1/2 teaspoon sea salt
1/8 teaspoon cayenne powder

VANILLA CREAM
1 cup young Thai coconut meat
1 cup young Thai coconut water
1/4 cup raw coconut oil
2 tablespoons raw light agave
1 Tahitian vanilla bean, scraped, seeds only
1 teaspoon vanilla extract
1/4 teaspoon sea salt

This dessert has always been a top seller and major hit at dinner parties and events—a great summer recipe when raspberries are abundantly in season, ripe, and falling off the vines. The sweet-tart filling is topped with pecan coconut crumble and drenched in a creamy vanilla-bean sauce. Layer these in mason jars for the perfect picnic dessert to share.

Make the filling
1. In food processor with "S" blade attachment, add 4 cups frozen raspberries, dates, agave, lemon juice, lecithin, cinnamon, vanilla extract, and sea salt. Pulse for about 3 minutes, until dates are broken down and filling is almost smooth.
2. In medium bowl, add raspberry mixture from food processor, remaining 1 cup frozen raspberries, and fresh raspberries. Stir with spoon until well combined. Cover and set aside. Clean out food processor for crumble.

Make the crumble
1. In food processor with "S" blade attachment, add pecans, shredded coconut, dates, coconut oil, sea salt, and cayenne. Pulse for about 20 seconds, until a nice crumbly mixture is achieved.

Make the cream
1. In high-speed blender place coconut meat, coconut water, agave, vanilla bean, vanilla extract, and sea salt. Blend on high for about 1 minute, until coconut meat is broken down and cream is smooth.
2. Add coconut oil and blend on high for another 30 seconds, until well combined.

Assemble
1. Place raspberry filling in 8-inch x 8-inch baking dish or use 4 to 6 mason jars for individual servings.
2. Sprinkle on pecan-coconut crumble.
3. Drizzle with vanilla sauce. Serve immediately.

Note: Keeps in refrigerator up to 5 days in airtight container.

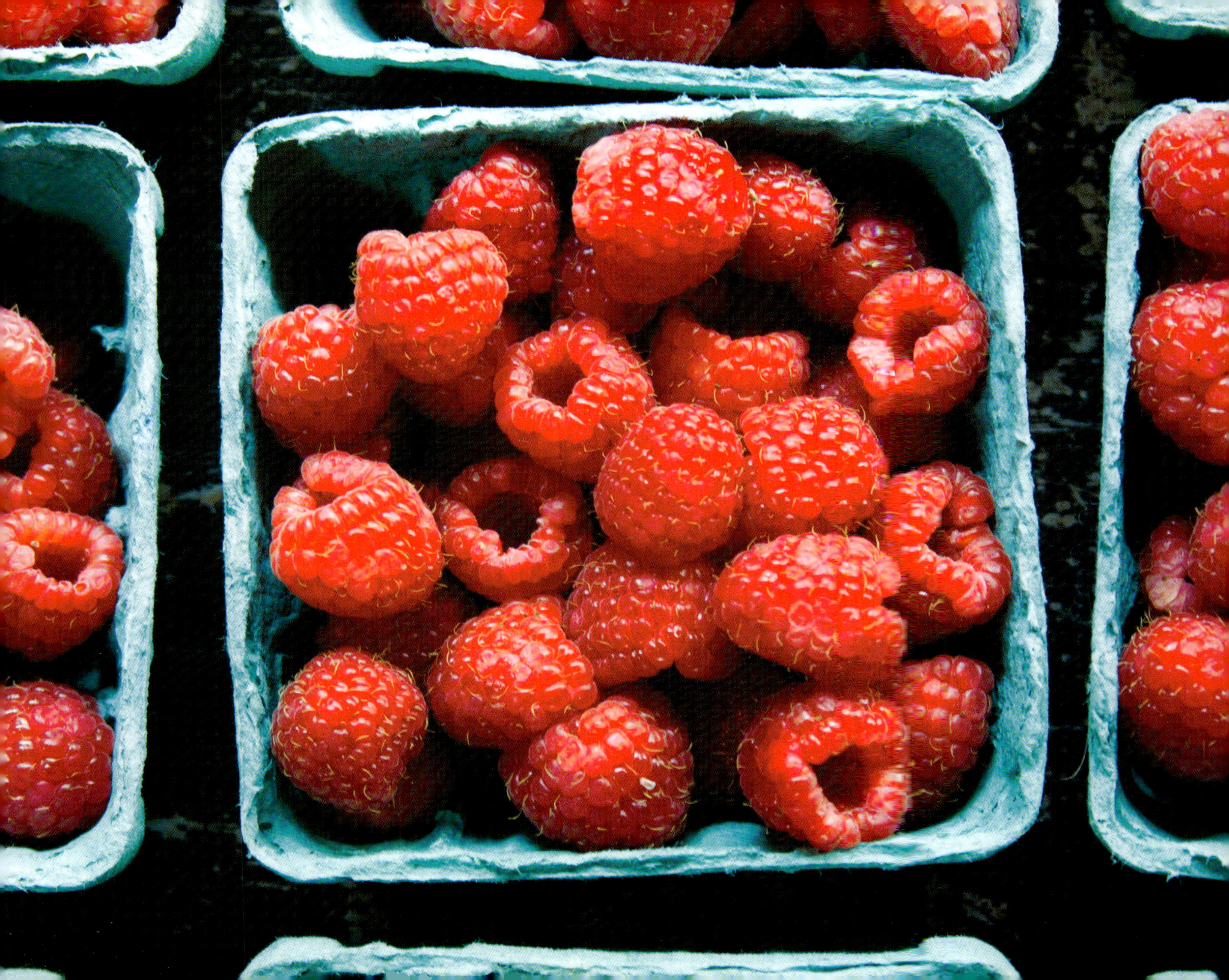

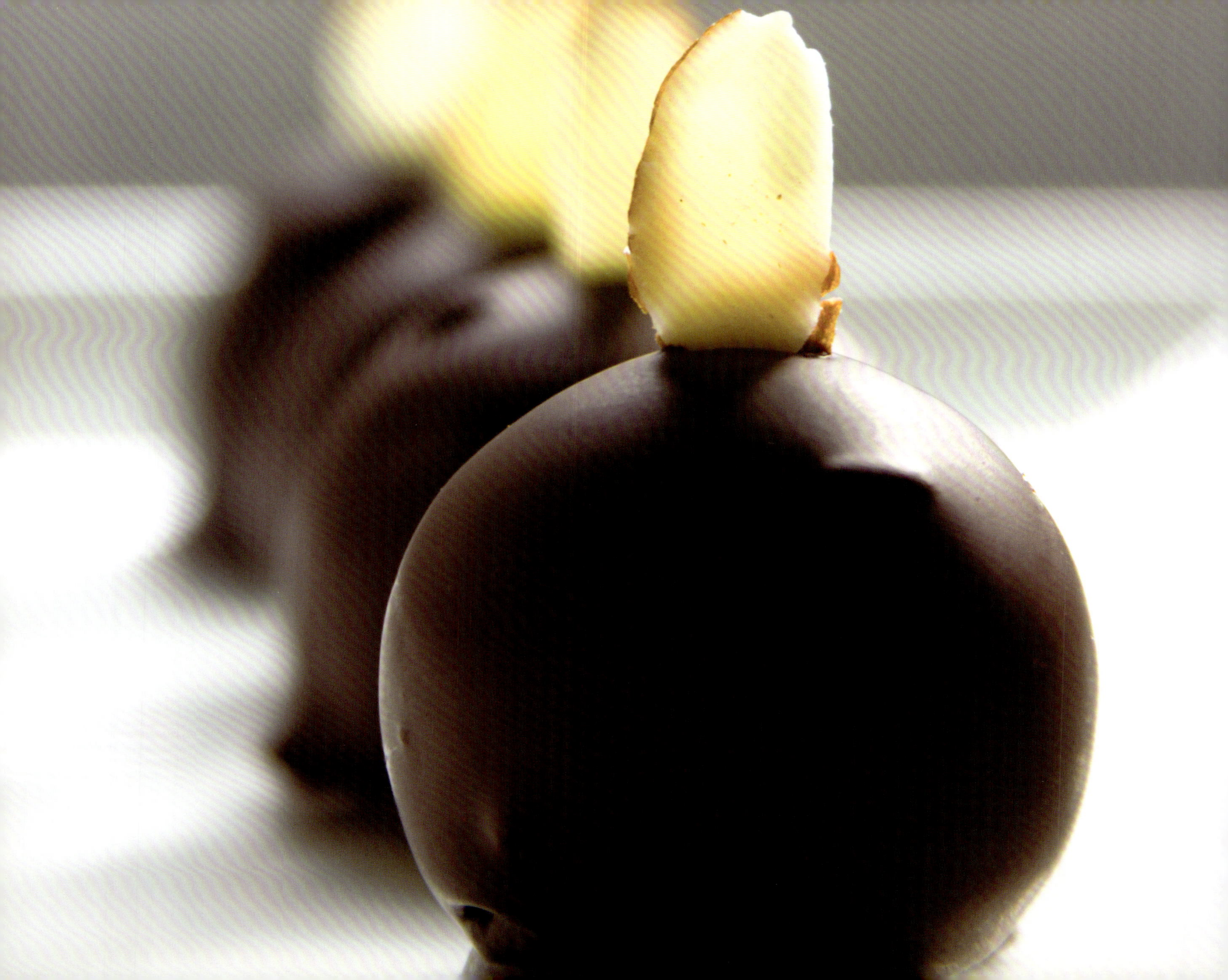

DARK CHOCOLATE AMARETTO TRUFFLES

MAKES 6 LARGE TRUFFLES

CHOCOLATE COATING
1/2 recipe tempered dark chocolate base (see page 246)

TRUFFLES
1/2 cup raw cacao powder
1/3 cup raw light agave
1/4 cup coconut butter, melted
1 teaspoon vanilla extract
1 teaspoon almond extract
1/8 teaspoon sea salt

GARNISH
1 tablespoon raw slivered almonds for topping truffles

Velvety chocolate almond ganache enveloped in a delicate dark chocolate coating, these truffles will melt in your mouth with each bite. For a beautiful presentation, I like to place these truffles on a silver tray lined with white rose petals.

Make the truffles
1. In small mixing bowl, add cacao powder, agave, coconut butter, vanilla extract, almond extract, and sea salt. Mash together with fork until cacao powder is no longer chunky and filling is thick and smooth.
2. With palm of hands, roll into 6 large balls. Transfer to parchment paper. Set in freezer for 15 minutes, until slightly hard.
3. Remove from freezer and reroll filling into more-symmetrical balls. Place back in freezer for 30 minutes, and work on tempered chocolate base.
4. Once base is ready, remove truffles from freezer and dip into tempered chocolate one at a time, coating heavily. Place back on parchment paper. Top with slivered almonds.
5. Return to freezer one last time for 15 minutes, until chocolate coating is hard.

Note: Keeps in refrigerator or at room temperature up to 4 weeks in airtight container.

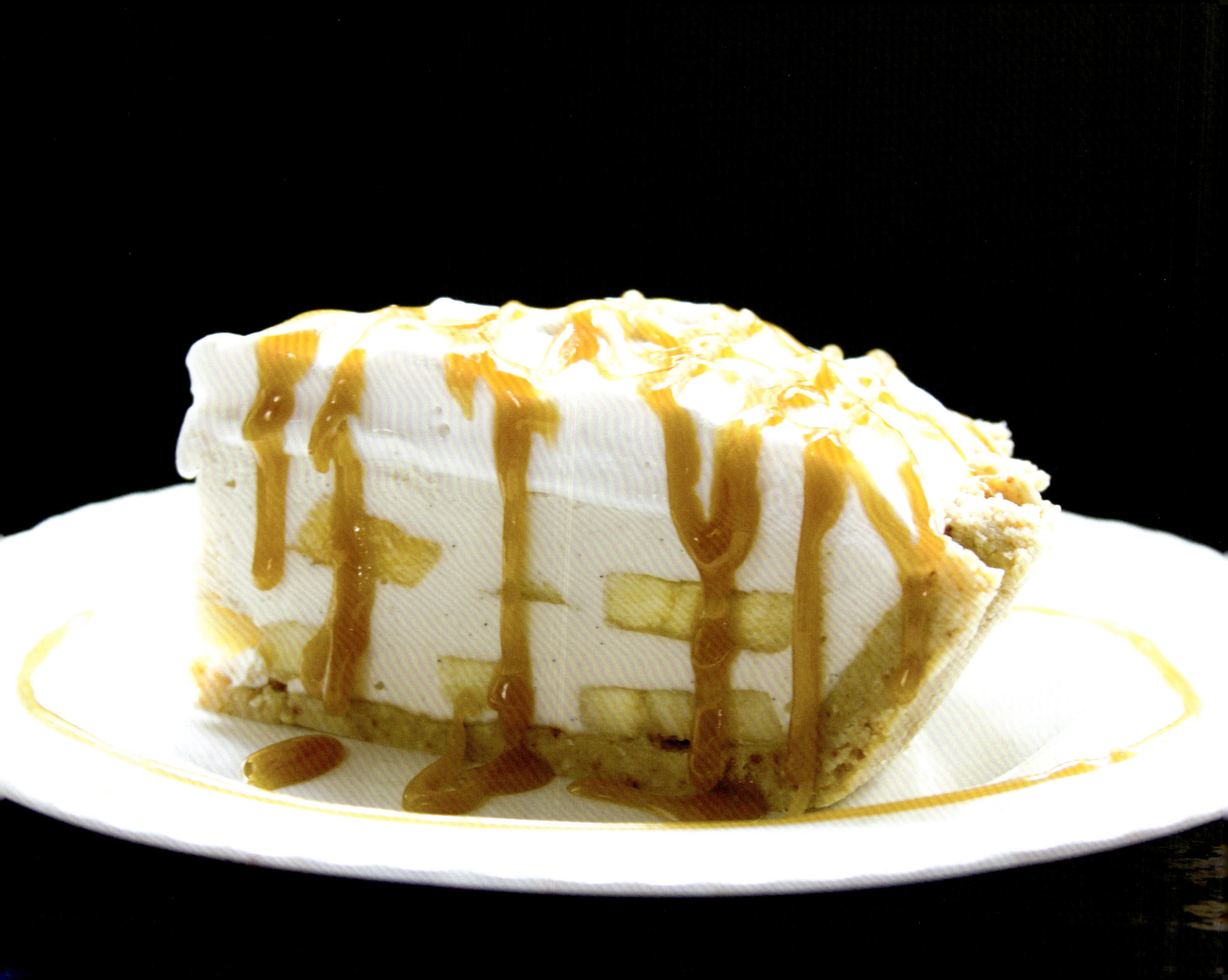

BANANA CREAM PIE DRIZZLED IN CARAMEL RUM SAUCE

MAKES 1 9-INCH PIE

CRUST

3 cups raw cashew flour (see page 29)
2 tablespoons raw coconut oil, melted
2 tablespoons raw coconut sugar
1 tablespoon water
1/2 teaspoon sea salt

FILLING

3 medium ripe bananas, peeled and sliced into 1/4-inch rounds
1 cup young Thai coconut meat
1 cup young Thai coconut water
1 cup raw cashews soaked 4–6 hours, drained and rinsed
3/4 cup raw coconut oil
1/2 cup raw light agave
2 ½ tablespoons lecithin granules
1 ½ tablespoons vanilla extract
1 vanilla bean, scraped, seeds only

WHIPPED TOPPING

1 ½ cups young Thai coconut meat
1/2 cup young Thai coconut water
1/2 cup raw coconut oil
1/4 cup raw light agave
1/2 teaspoon vanilla extract
1/8 teaspoon sea salt

CARAMEL RUM SAUCE

2 tablespoons coconut butter, melted
2 tablespoons yacon syrup
2 tablespoons raw light agave
1 tablespoon almond milk
1 teaspoon rum extract
1/2 teaspoon vanilla extract
1/8 teaspoon sea salt

Banana cream pie was developed in the early 1900s and is still considered one of America's favorite pies, and here's my version: cashew shortbread crust, filled with velvety smooth vanilla custard layered with fresh sliced banana, and smothered in whipped topping then polished off with gooey rum caramel sauce.

Make the crust

1. In medium mixing bowl, add cashew flour, melted coconut oil, coconut sugar, water, and sea salt. With a fork mix until it molds into a slightly wet dough.
2. Coat 9-inch pie plate with coconut oil and pat in piecrust. Flute edges using thumb and forefinger.
3. Place piecrust in dehydrator at 115 degrees for 8–12 hours, until crust in slightly flaky around edges.

Make the filling

1. In high-speed blender place coconut meat, coconut water, cashews, agave, vanilla extract, and vanilla bean. Blend on high for about 1 minute, until coconut meat is broken down and smooth.
2. Add coconut oil and lecithin. Blend another 30 seconds, until well combined.
3. After 8–12 hours remove crust from dehydrator and line bottom of crust with overlapping sliced bananas, circling from outside in, until covered.
4. Pour 1/2 the filling over banana slices.
5. Place another layer of sliced bananas over cream, and pour the remaining filling over sliced bananas. Cover and set in freezer for 30 minutes or until slightly firm to touch.

Make the whipped topping

1. In high-speed blender place coconut meat, coconut water, agave, vanilla extract, and sea salt. Blend on high for about 1 minute, until coconut meat is broken down and cream is smooth.
2. Add coconut oil and blend another 30 seconds, until well combined.
3. Take pie out of freezer and slowly pour whipped topping over filling.
4. Cover and place in freezer for 1 hour to begin firming process. Transfer to refrigerator for 4 hours before serving, so pie has time to set.

Make the caramel rum sauce

1. In small mixing bowl, add melted coconut butter, yacon syrup, agave, almond milk, rum extract, vanilla extract, and sea salt. Whisk until all ingredients are well combined and sauce is thick and smooth.

Assemble

1. When ready to serve, drizzle pie in caramel rum sauce and top with fresh sliced bananas. Serve immediately.

Note: Pie keeps in refrigerator up to 4 days in airtight container. Bananas may turn a little brown, but they are still good. Caramel sauce keeps up to 3 weeks in refrigerator in airtight container.

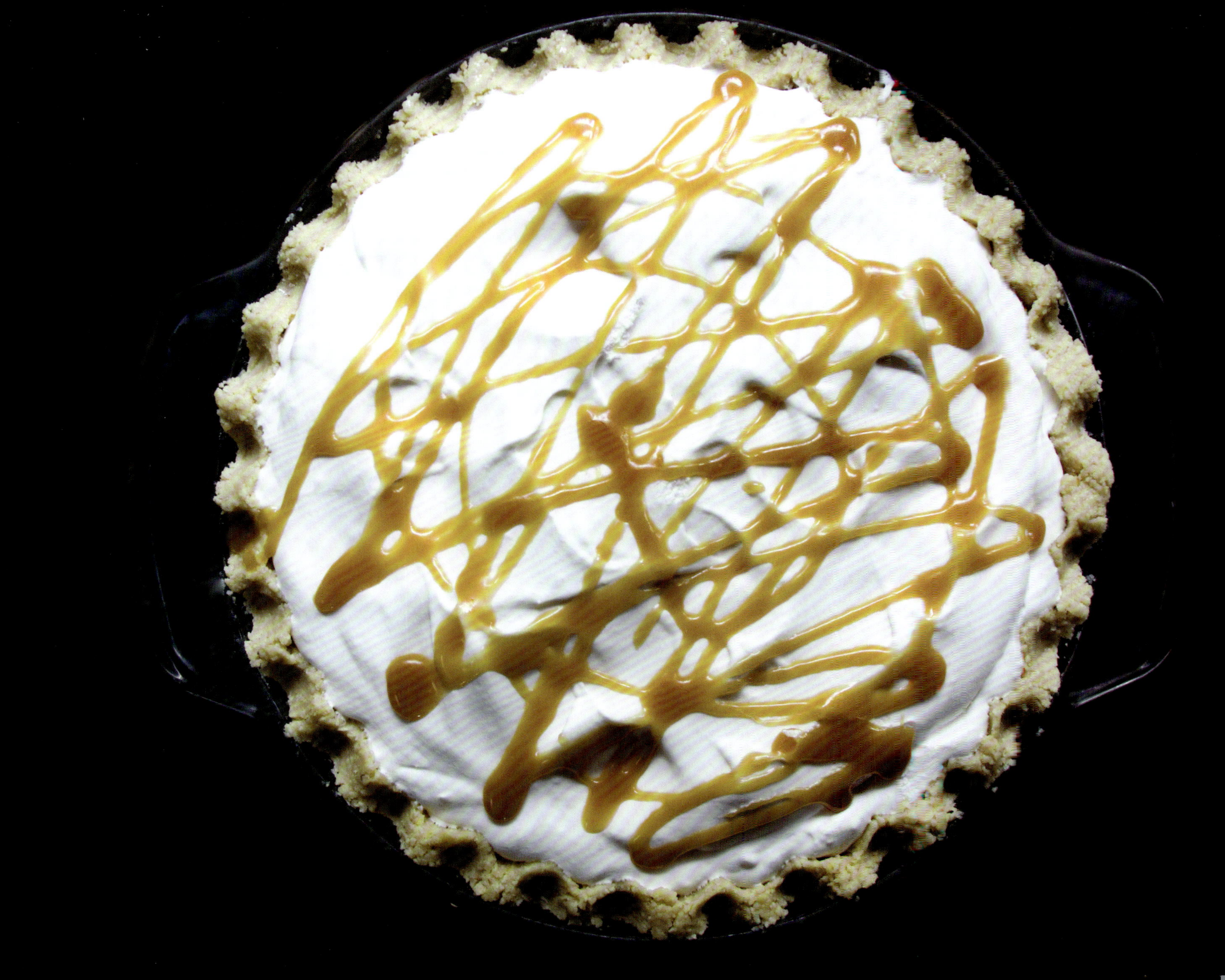

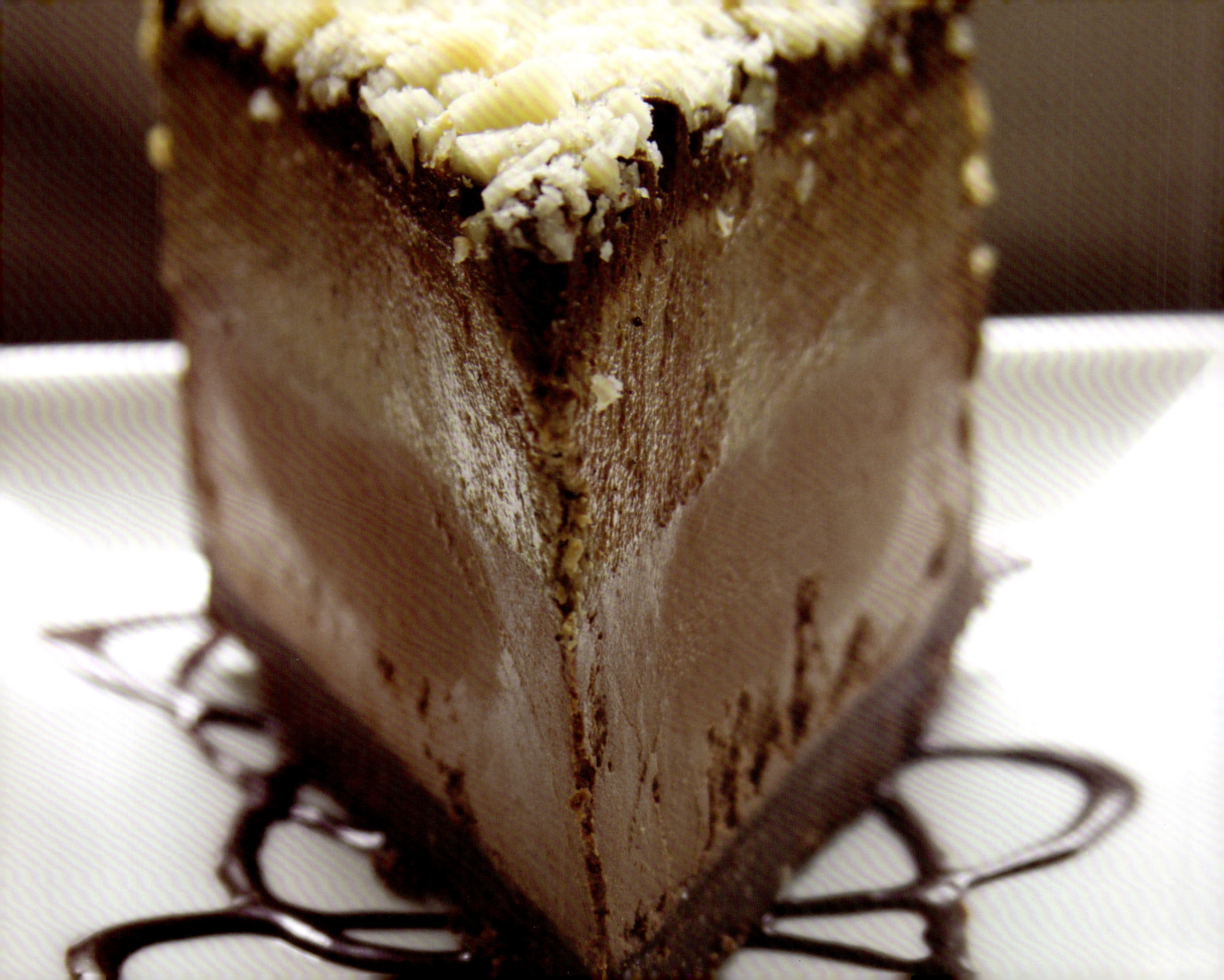

KONA COFFEE MACADAMIA NUT CHEESECAKE WITH MOCHA FUDGE SAUCE

MAKES 1 9-INCH CHEESECAKE

CRUST

1 ½ cups dry almond flour (see page 29)
3/4 cup raw cacao powder
1/3 cup date paste (see page 22)
3 tablespoons raw coconut oil
2 tablespoons Kona coffee, finely ground
1/2 teaspoon sea salt

CHOCOLATE FILLING

1 ½ cups raw cashews soaked 4–6 hours, drained and rinsed
1 ¼ cup raw cacao powder
1 cup young Thai coconut meat
1 cup young Thai coconut water
1 cup raw coconut oil
1/2 cup maple syrup
1/3 cup raw light agave
2 tablespoons vanilla extract
2 tablespoons lemon juice, fresh-squeezed
1 ½ tablespoons lecithin granules
1/4 teaspoon sea salt

COFFEE FILLING

1 ½ cups cashews soaked 4–5 hours, drained and rinsed
1 cup young Thai coconut meat
1 cup Kona coffee espresso
1/2 cup raw coconut oil
1/2 cup + 1 tablespoon raw light agave
2 tablespoons vanilla extract
2 tablespoons Kona coffee, finely ground
1 tablespoon lemon juice, fresh-squeezed
1 tablespoon lecithin granules
1/4 teaspoon sea salt

MOCHA FUDGE SAUCE

1/4 cup almond milk
1/2 cup raw light agave
1/2 cup raw cacao powder
1/4 cup coconut butter, melted
1 tablespoon vanilla extract
1 ½ teaspoons Kona coffee, finely ground
1/4 teaspoon sea salt

GARNISH

1 ½ cups raw macadamia nuts, chopped

On a trip to Hawaii a few years ago, I was in the beginning stages of brainstorming ideas for this book. It was the perfect place to be for inspiration. An abundance of fresh food grows everywhere on the islands. After visiting some local coffee and macadamia nut farms, I was inspired to write this recipe. It's an explosion of taste and textures, rich and extremely decadent. A small slice goes a long way.

Make the crust
1. In medium mixing bowl, add almond flour, cacao powder, date paste, coconut oil, ground coffee, and sea salt. Mix with spoon, until well combined and formed into a thick dough. Use your hands if you need to.
2. Coat 9–inch springform cheesecake pan with coconut oil. Pat down crust firmly, going 1 inch up the sides of the pan.

Make the chocolate filling
1. In high-speed blender place cashews, cacao powder, coconut meat, coconut water, maple syrup, agave, vanilla extract, lemon juice, and sea salt. Blend on high for about 2 minutes, until cashews and coconut meat are broken down.
2. Add coconut oil and lecithin. Blend another 30 seconds, until well combined.
3. Pour over crust. Cover and set in freezer for 1 hour.

Make the coffee filling
1. In high-speed blender place cashews, coconut meat, espresso, agave, vanilla extract, ground coffee, lemon juice, and sea salt. Blend on high for about 2 minutes, until cashews and coconut meat are broken down and filling is smooth.
2. Add coconut oil and lecithin. Blend another 30 seconds, until well combined
3. Remove cheesecake from freezer and pour coffee filling over chocolate filling. Cover and return to freezer for 2 hours to set and harden.

Make the mocha fudge sauce
1. In high-speed blender place almond milk, agave, cacao powder, coconut butter, vanilla extract, ground coffee, and sea salt. Blend on high for about 1 minute, until sauce is smooth and creamy.
2. Remove cheesecake from freezer and top with 1 ½ cups mocha fudge sauce. Keep remaining 1/4 cup for drizzling on plate and cheesecake.

Garnish
1. Sprinkle 1/2 cup chopped macadamia nuts on mocha fudge sauce and press down lightly.
2. Place cheesecake in refrigerator for 8 hours or overnight to firm completely.
3. After 8 hours remove cheesecake from refrigerator. Take cheesecake out of springform pan and pat remaining 1 cup chopped macadamia nuts around entire outside of cheesecake.
4. Slice and plate on desired serving dishes. Drizzle each plate with leftover mocha fudge sauce and serve immediately.

Note: Cheesecake keeps in refrigerator up to 5 days in airtight container. Mocha fudge sauce keeps up to 3 weeks in refrigerator in airtight container.

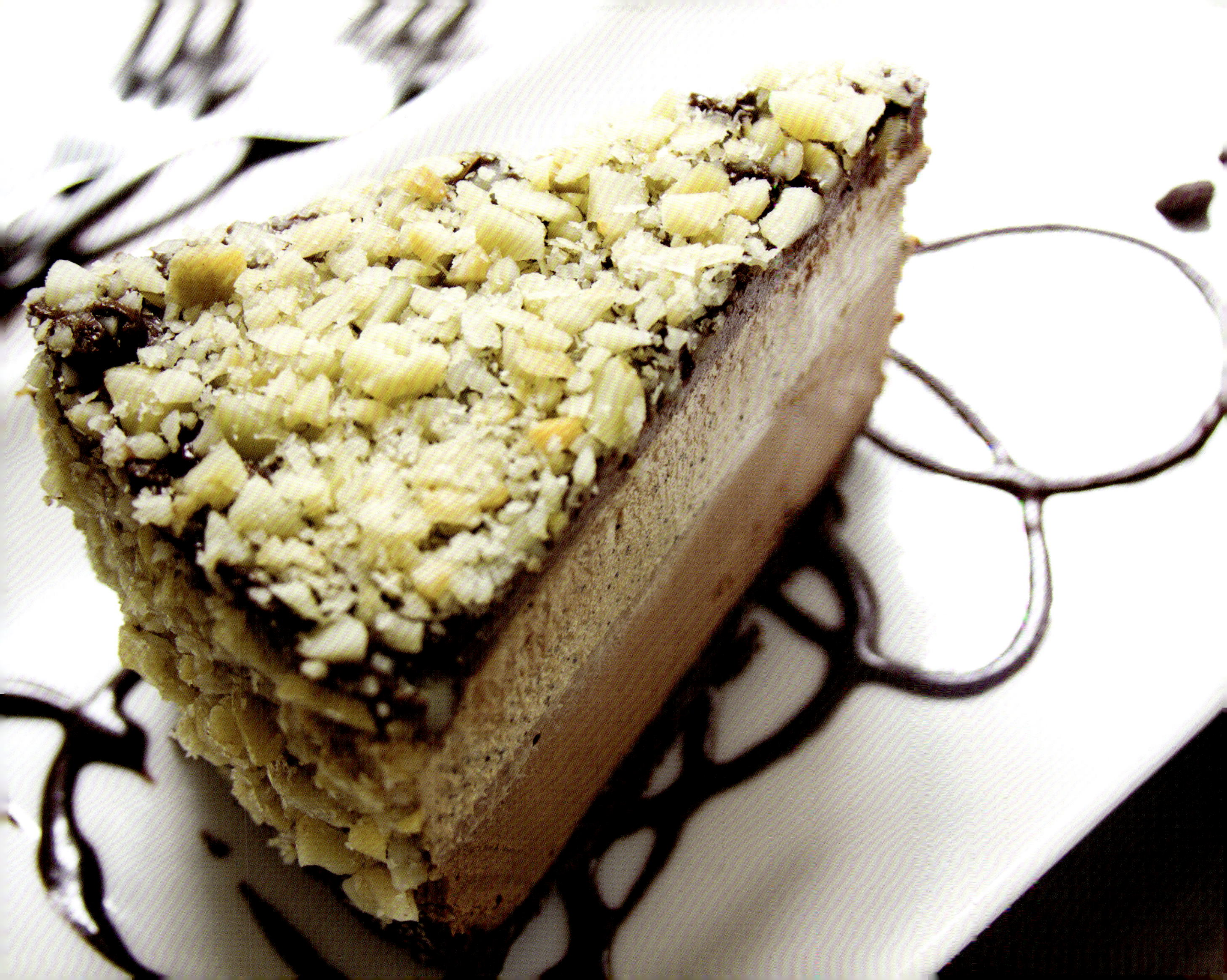

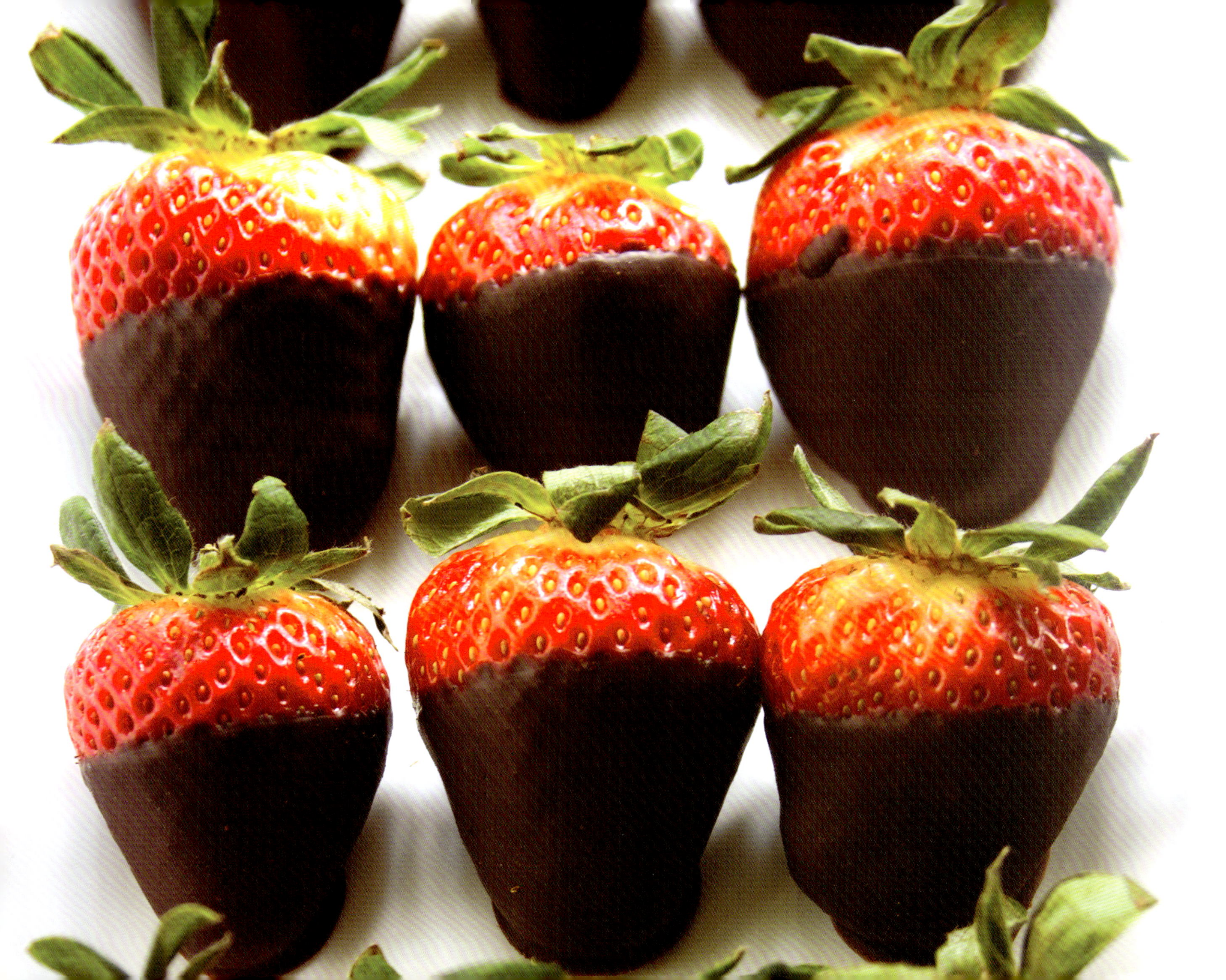

DARK CHOCOLATE HAND-DIPPED STRAWBERRIES

MAKES 24 STRAWBERRIES

CHOCOLATE COATING
1 recipe tempered dark chocolate base (see page 246)

STRAWBERRIES
24 fresh sweet strawberries

Juicy ripe and hand-dipped in chocolate, these strawberries are an elegant yet simple dessert to prepare and great served at a party any time of the year.

Make the strawberries
1. Hold strawberries by stems. Dip halfway into melted chocolate. Repeat 4 times to really coat the berries.
2. After the 4th dip, let excess chocolate drizzle off, and place strawberry on wax or parchment paper to cool. Repeat until all strawberries are coated.
3. Allow to cool for 2–3 hours at room temperature before serving.

Note: Keeps in refrigerator up to 3 days in airtight container.

DESSERTS

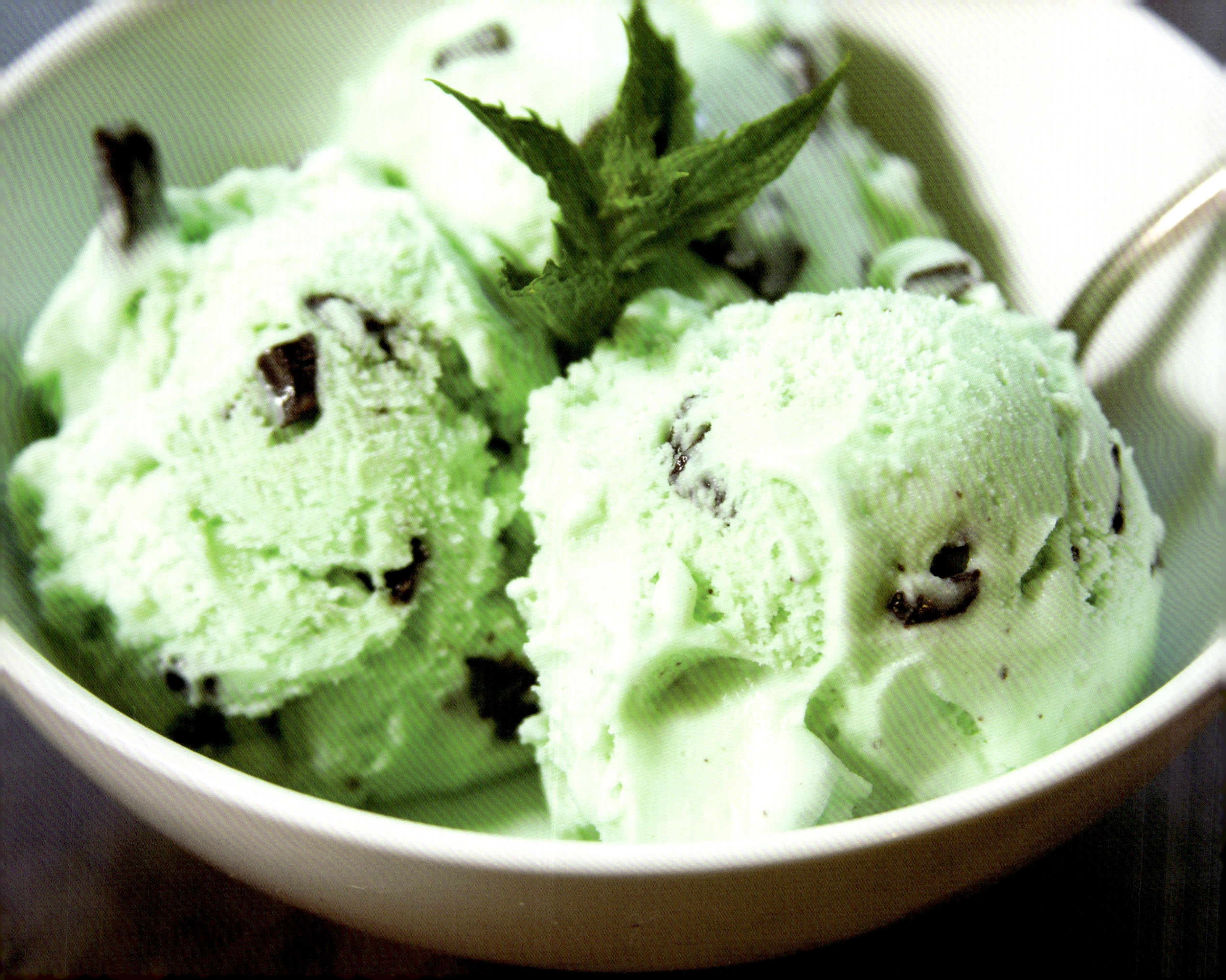

FRESH MINT CHOCOLATE CHIP ICE CREAM

MAKES 2 CUPS (1 PINT)

MINT CHIP ICE CREAM

1 ½ cups coconut cream (see page 74)
1 ½ cups fresh mint leaves, stems removed
1/3 cup raw light agave
1/4 cup + 2 tablespoons raw coconut oil
1/4 cup chopped raw tempered chocolate (see page 246)
15 drops food-grade mint essential oil
2 teaspoons lecithin granules
1/4 teaspoon spirulina powder (optional for darker green)
1/8 teaspoon sea salt

Cool and creamy mint ice cream swirled with chunky pieces of dark chocolate, this is the perfect accompaniment to the chocolate molten cake or eaten right out of the container.

Make the ice cream

1. In high-speed blender place coconut cream, mint leaves, agave, mint oil, spirulina, and sea salt. Blend on high for about 1 minute, until mint leaves are broken down and ice cream is totally smooth.
2. Add coconut oil and lecithin. Blend about 30 seconds, until coconut oil is well combined.
3. Pour into small mixing bowl and stir in pieces of tempered dark chocolate.
4. Transfer to ice cream maker of choice and follow directions as if making traditional ice cream.

Note: Keeps in the freezer up to 1 month in airtight container.

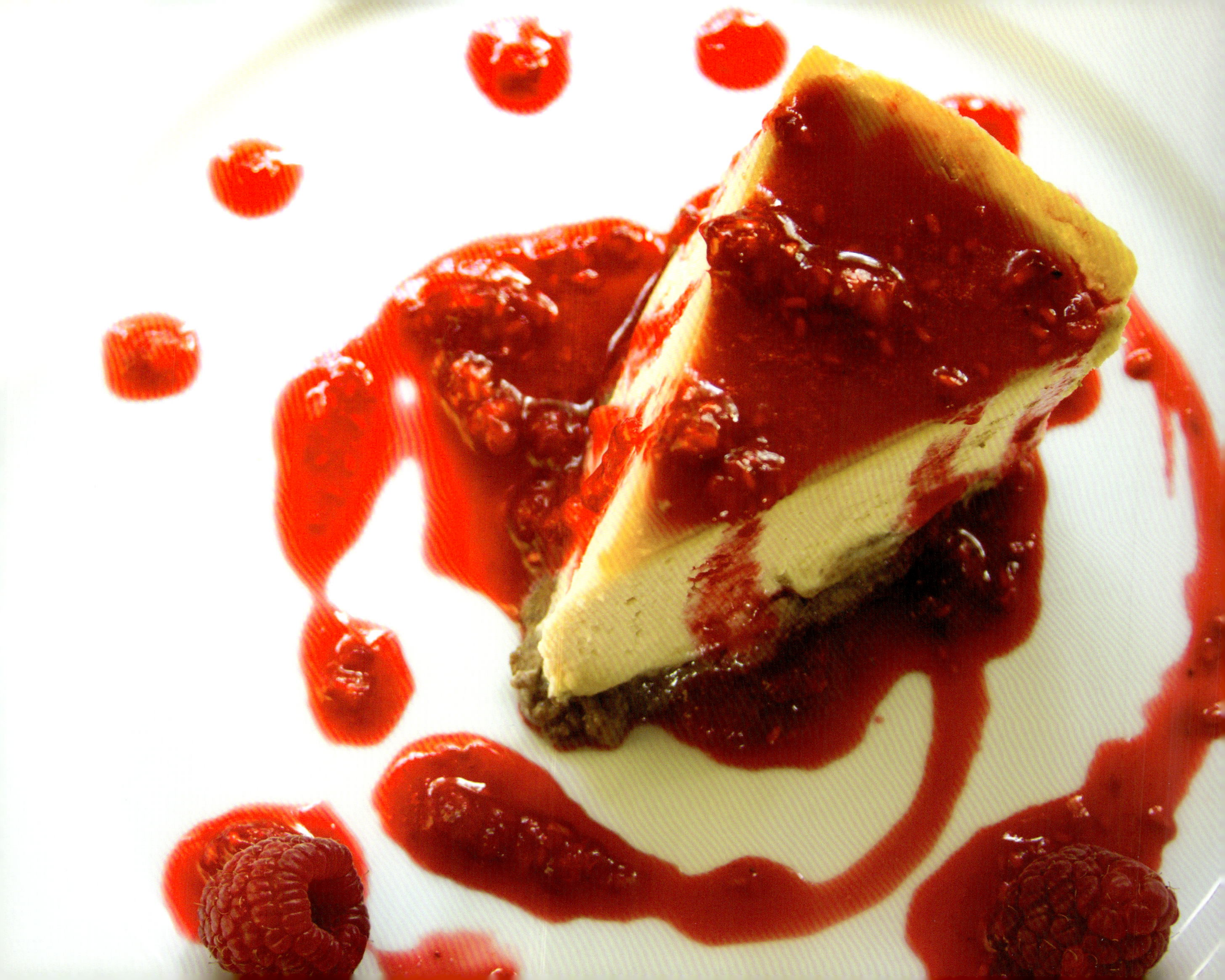

CLASSIC CHEESECAKE WITH PECAN GRAHAM CRUST AND RED RASPBERRY SAUCE

MAKES 1 9-INCH CHEESECAKE

CRUST

2 ½ cups pecan flour (see page 29)
1/2 cup raw coconut sugar
1/4 teaspoon ground cinnamon
1/4 teaspoon sea salt

CHEESE FILLING

2 ½ cups raw cashews soaked 4–6 hours, drained and rinsed
1 ½ cups warm water
1 ½ cups raw coconut oil
3/4 cup raw light agave
1/4 cup lemon juice, fresh-squeezed
10 capsules vegan probiotic powder
1 tablespoon lecithin granules
1/2 teaspoon vanilla extract
1/2 teaspoon sea salt

RASPBERRY SAUCE

1 cup fresh raspberries
1 ½ tablespoons raw light agave
1 tablespoon lemon juice, fresh-squeezed

I LOVE cheesecake! It's been a mission of mine to develop a raw version that goes above and beyond the dairy version. Finally, success; a rich cheesecake complemented by a crushed pecan graham crust is dehydrated to give it the perfect texture. The raspberry sauce adds a layer of dazzling colors and a subtle hint of tartness. Delicious!

Make the crust
1. In medium mixing bowl, add pecan flour, coconut sugar, cinnamon and sea salt. Mix with spoon until well combined and formed into a thick dough
2. Coat 9-inch springform cheesecake pan with coconut oil. Pat down crust, firmly going 1 inch up the sides of the pan. Cover and place in refrigerator.

Make the cheese filling
1. In high-speed blender place contents of probiotic caps and warm water. Let stand for 5 minutes.
2. Add cashews, agave, lemon juice, vanilla extract, and sea salt. Blend on high for about 2 minutes, until cashews are broken down and filling is smooth.
3. Add coconut oil and lecithin. Blend another 30 seconds, until well combined.
4. In medium mixing bowl, pour cheese filling and cover. Let sit at room temperature for 12 hours, to culture.
5. After 12 hours remove crust from refrigerator and pour cheese filling over crust.
6. Place cheesecake in dehydrator at 115 degrees for 24 hours. This will allow the cheese filling to culture and remove some of the moisture for a more cheese-like texture.
7. After 24 hours remove cheesecake from dehydrator and transfer to refrigerator for 4 hours or until firm to touch.

Make the raspberry sauce
1. In small mixing bowl, add raspberries, agave, and lemon juice. Using a fork, mash berries until sauce is well combined but slightly chunky. Drizzle over cheesecake and serve immediately.

Note: Cheesecake keeps in refrigerator up to 5 days in airtight container. Sauce keeps up to 3 days in airtight container.

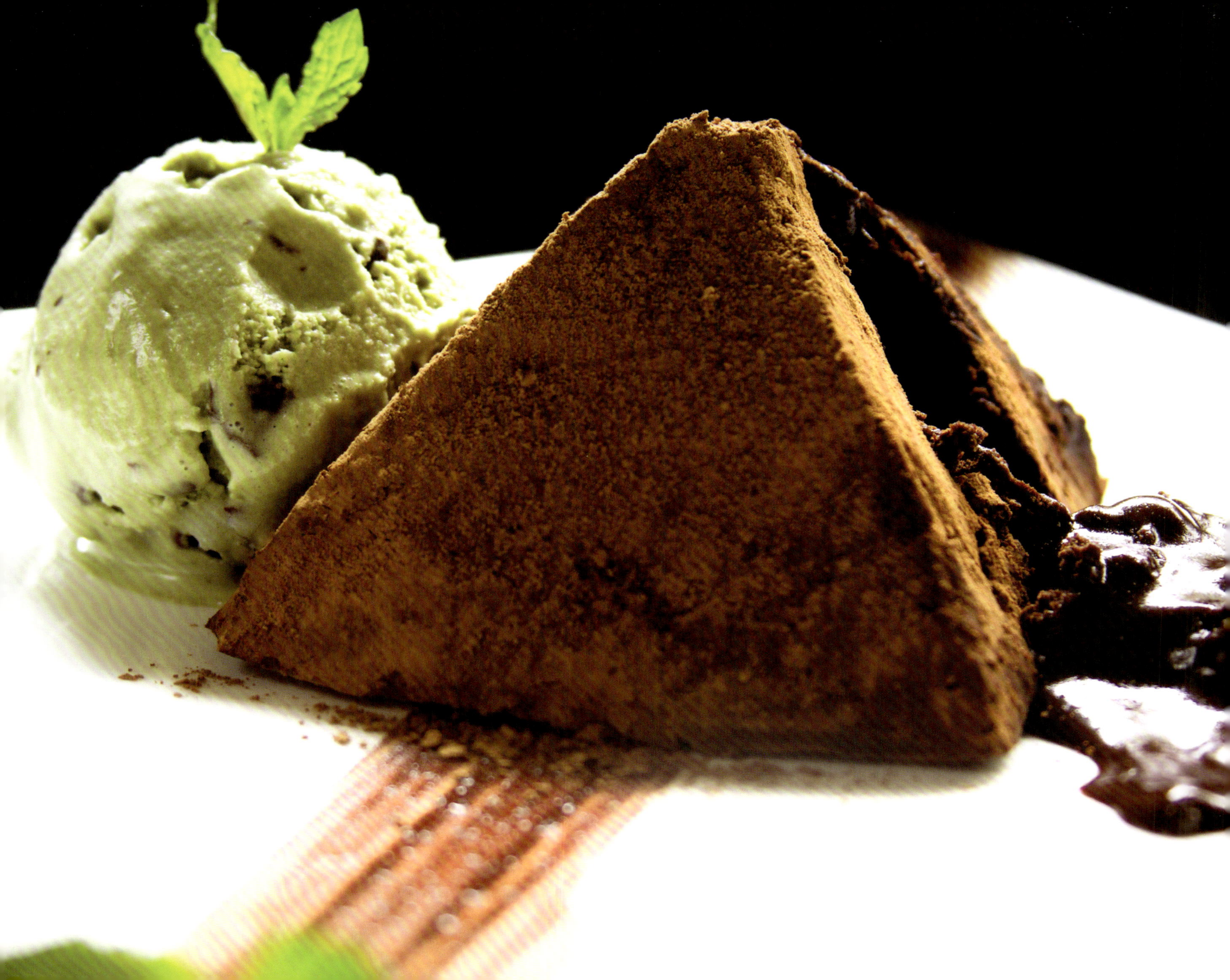

CHOCOLATE MOLTEN PYRAMID CAKE, LIQUID FUDGE, AND MINT CHIP ICE CREAM

MAKES 6 2-INCH PYRAMID CAKES

CAKE

5 cups raw almond flour (see page 29)
2 cups raw cacao powder
1 cup date paste (see page 22)
1/4 cup raw coconut oil
3 tablespoons raw light agave
2 tablespoons almond milk
2 teaspoons vanilla extract
1 vanilla bean, scraped, seeds only
1/2 teaspoon sea salt

LIQUID FUDGE

3/4 cup raw light agave
1/2 cup coconut butter, melted
1/2 cup raw cacao powder
1 tablespoon vanilla extract
1 vanilla bean, scraped, seeds only
1/4 teaspoon sea salt

GARNISH

1 cup mint ice cream (see page 230)
6 fresh mint sprigs
2 tablespoons raw cacao powder

Inspired by flipping through the pages of *Bon Appetite* magazine, this exquisite pyramid cake has a gooey chocolate molten fudge center that flows out when cut into. Matched with refreshing mint-chip ice cream, this dessert is equally as impressive as it is delicious.

Make the cake
1. In medium mixing bowl, add date paste, coconut oil, vanilla extract, and sea salt. Using an electric mixer, whip for about 5 minutes, until light and fluffy.
2. In a separate medium mixing bowl, add almond flour, cacao powder, and vanilla bean. Mix with spoon until dry ingredients are well combined.
3. Slowly add flour mix to date paste. Add in almond milk and agave and beat with electric mixer for about 4 minutes or until fluffy, cake-like consistency and all ingredients are well combined. Scrape down sides of bowl with spatula, if necessary.
4. Using coconut oil, grease inside of all six molds. Press 3/4 cup cake base into stainless steel medium pyramid molds, so each side is about 1/2-inch thick with cake and center is hollowed out for liquid fudge.

Make the liquid fudge
1. In a small mixing bowl, add agave, coconut butter, cacao powder, vanilla extract, vanilla bean, and sea salt. Whisk until sauce is thick and totally smooth.

Assemble
1. Pour 2 tablespoons liquid fudge into center of each chocolate cake pyramid form. Place in freezer upside down for 1/2 hour to set the fudge sauce.
2. Remove from freezer and pat 1/4 cup cake base onto the bottom of each cake, covering liquid fudge.
3. With a spatula or butter knife, smooth out base of cake so it's even all the way across.
4. Transfer back to freezer for 1–2 hours to set. This will make it easier to remove cakes from molds.
5. When ready to serve, remove each cake from pyramid form by running a butter knife around inside edges of cake. Flip pyramid right side up onto plate and lightly press around edges to remove. It should come out fairly easily.

6. For liquid fudge to ooze out when cut into, place in dehydrator at 115 degrees for 2 hours prior to serving.
7. Once all cakes are out of forms and dehydrator, sift 2 tablespoons cacao powder over tops right before serving.
8. Plate on serving dishes of choice. Place a scoop of mint-chip ice cream on side of cake and a fresh mint sprig. Serve immediately.

Note: Keeps in refrigerator up to 5 days in airtight container.

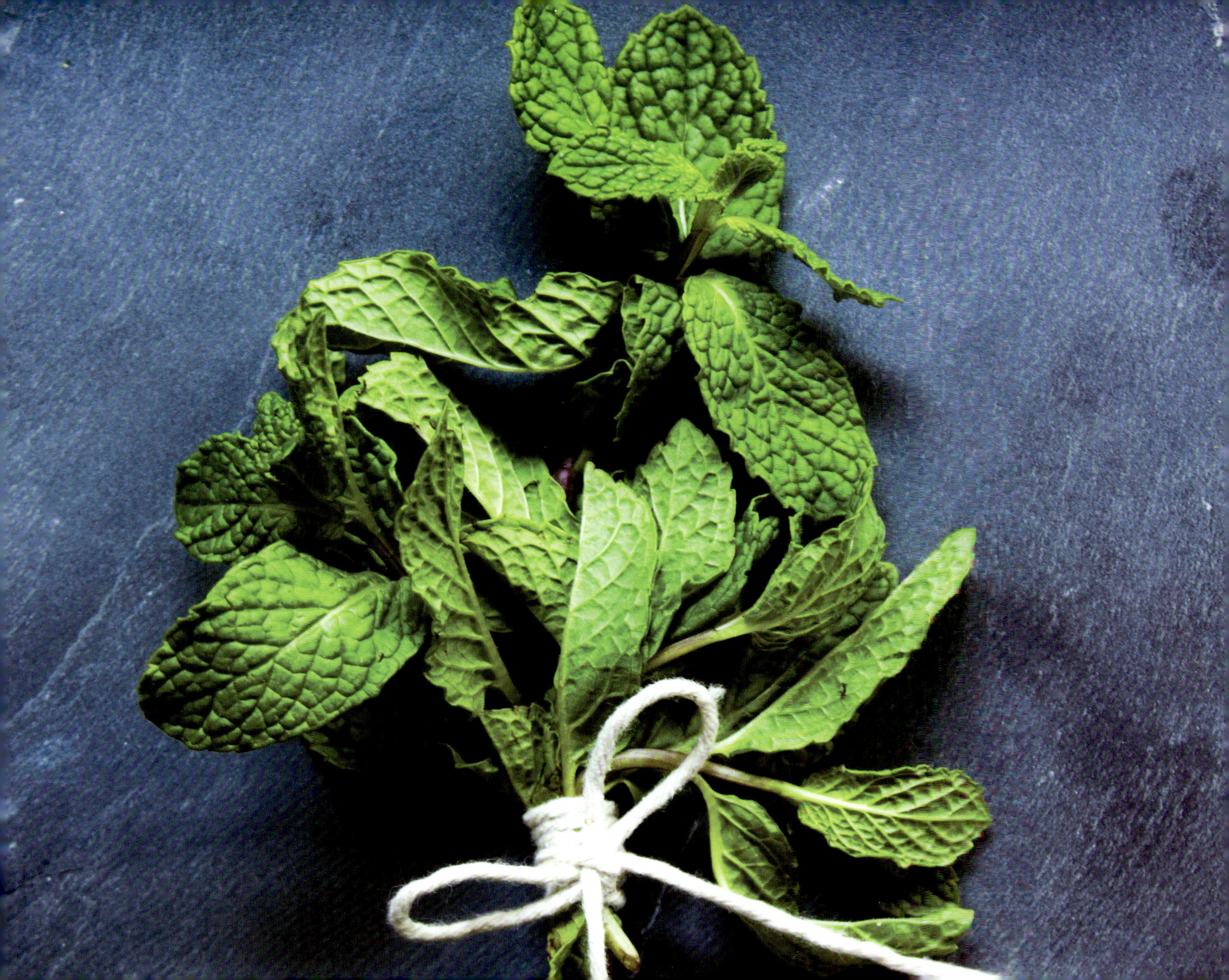

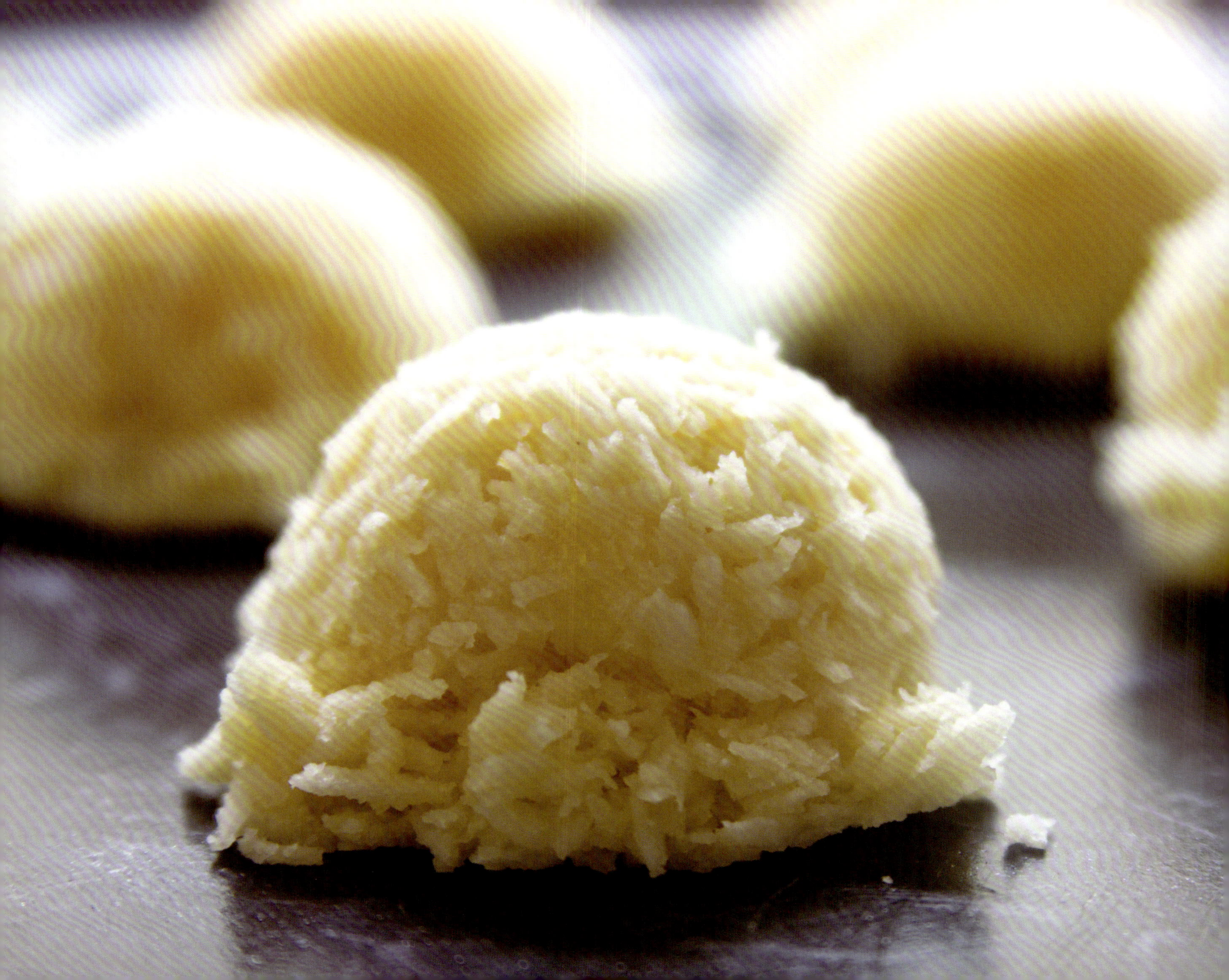

ORANGE BLOSSOM SHREDDED COCONUT MACAROONS

MAKES 24 MACAROONS

MACAROONS
4 cups unsweetened raw coconut, shredded
1/2 cup coconut butter, melted
1/2 cup light raw agave
1/3 cup orange juice, fresh-squeezed
3 tablespoons orange blossom water
1/2 teaspoon sea salt

Citrus-scented orange blossom paired with light and fluffy coconut create a delicate macaroon that is slightly crisp on the outside with a moist and chewy center. I like serving these macaroons alongside a hot pot of tea.

Make the macaroons
1. In large mixing bowl, add shredded coconut, coconut butter, agave, orange juice, orange blossom water, and sea salt. Mix with spoon, stirring until all ingredients are well combined.
2. Using an ice cream scooper, shape macaroons into 2-inch rounds.
3. Drop onto dehydrator tray. Dehydrate at 115 degrees for 8–10 hours. Macaroons should be crisp on outside and soft and chewy on inside

Note: Keeps at room temperature up to 5 days in airtight container. These freeze really well up to 2 months in airtight container.

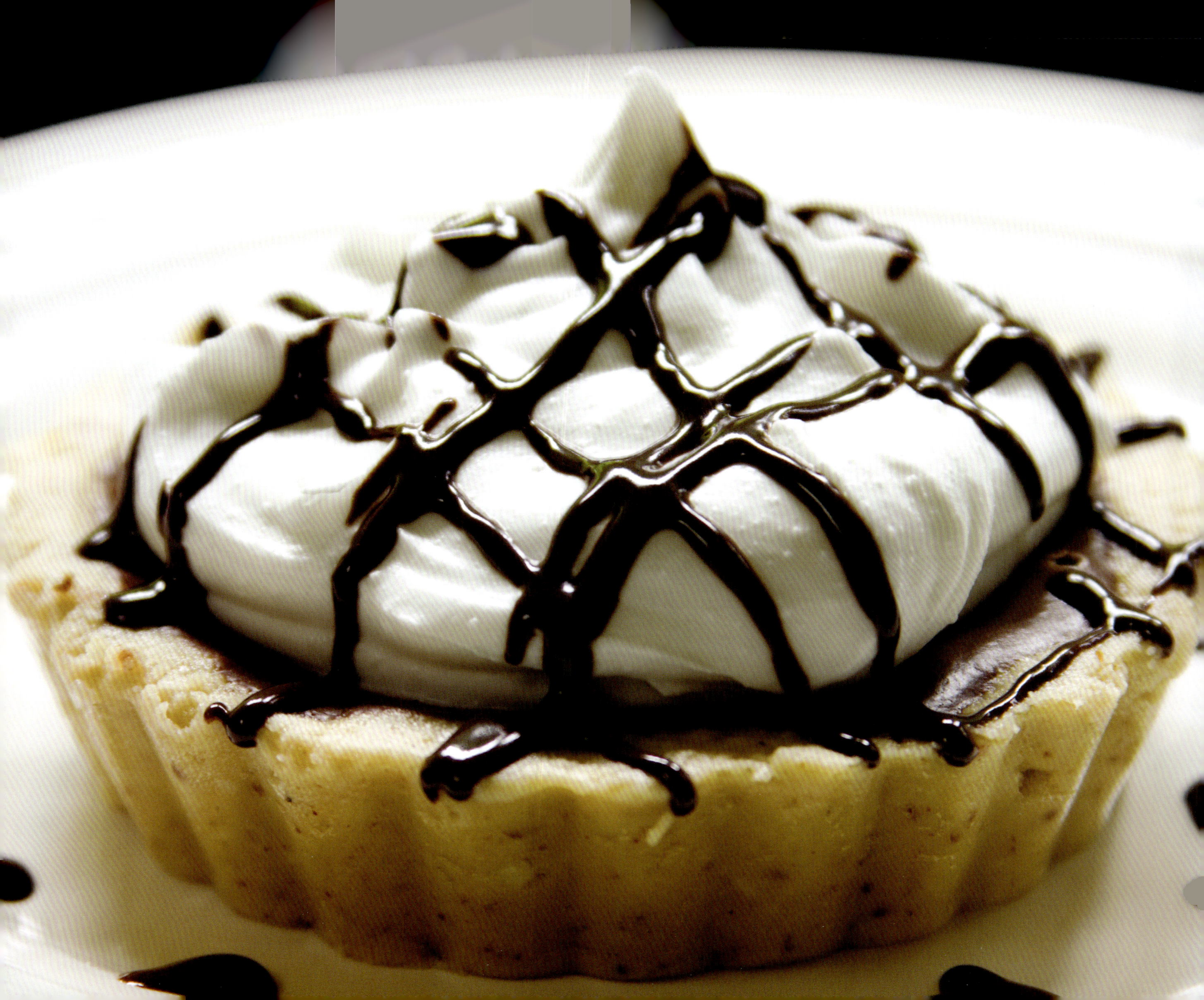

CHOCOLATE CREAM TARTLETS WITH FLAKY CASHEW CRUST AND WHIPPED CREAM

MAKES 6 TARTLETS OR 1-9-INCH PIE

CRUST
3 cups raw cashew flour (see page 29)
2 tablespoons raw coconut oil, melted
2 tablespoons raw coconut sugar
1/2 teaspoon sea salt

FILLING
2 cups young Thai coconut meat
1 cup raw cacao powder
3/4 cup young Thai coconut water
1/2 cup maple syrup
1/2 cup raw coconut oil
1/4 cup raw light agave
2 tablespoons lecithin granules
1 ½ tablespoons vanilla extract
1/2 vanilla bean, scraped, seeds only
1/4 teaspoon sea salt

WHIPPED CREAM
1 ½ cups young Thai coconut meat
1/2 cup young Thai coconut water
1/2 cup raw coconut oil
1/4 cup raw light agave
1/4 cup irish moss gel (see page 102)
1/2 teaspoon vanilla extract
1/8 teaspoon sea salt

CHOCOLATE SAUCE (OPTIONAL)
1/2 cup almond milk
1/2 cup raw light agave
1/2 cup raw cacao powder
1/4 cup coconut butter, melted
1 tablespoon vanilla extract
1/4 teaspoon sea salt

Light and flaky cashew crusts filled with silky, dark chocolate mousse are generously topped with light whipped coconut cream making these tartlets a standout and one of my favorite recipes.

Make the crust
1. In medium mixing bowl, add cashew flour, melted coconut oil, coconut sugar, water, and sea salt. With a fork, mix until crust forms into a slightly wet dough.
2. Coat 6 tartlet pans or 9-inch pie plate with coconut oil and pat in piecrust. Flute edges using thumb and forefinger.
3. Place tartlet pans or piecrust in dehydrator at 115 degrees for 8–12 hours, until crust in slightly flaky around edges.

Make the filling
1. In high-speed blender place coconut meat, cacao powder, coconut water, maple syrup, agave, vanilla extract, vanilla bean, and sea salt. Blend on high for about 2 minutes, until coconut meat is broken down and smooth.
2. Add coconut oil and lecithin. Blend another 30 seconds, until well combined.
3. Remove tartlets or piecrust from dehydrator after 8–12 hours. Pour 1 cup filling into each tartlet over crust or all filling over 9-inch piecrust. Cover and place in freezer to set.

Make the whipped cream
1. In high-speed blender place coconut meat, coconut water, agave, irish moss, vanilla extract, and sea salt. Blend on high for about 1 minute, until coconut meat is broken down and cream is smooth.
2. Add coconut oil and blend another 30 seconds, until well combined.
3. Take tartlets or pie out of freezer and slowly pour 1/2 cup whipped cream over each chocolate-filled tartlet or all whipped cream over chocolate-filled pie. Cover and place back in freezer for 1 hour to begin firming process. Transfer to refrigerator for 4 hours to set.

Assemble
1. To serve, pop tartlets out of pans and place on serving dishes of choice. Drizzle with chocolate sauce. Serve immediately.

Note: Keeps in refrigerator up to 5 days in airtight container. These freeze well up to 1 month in airtight container.

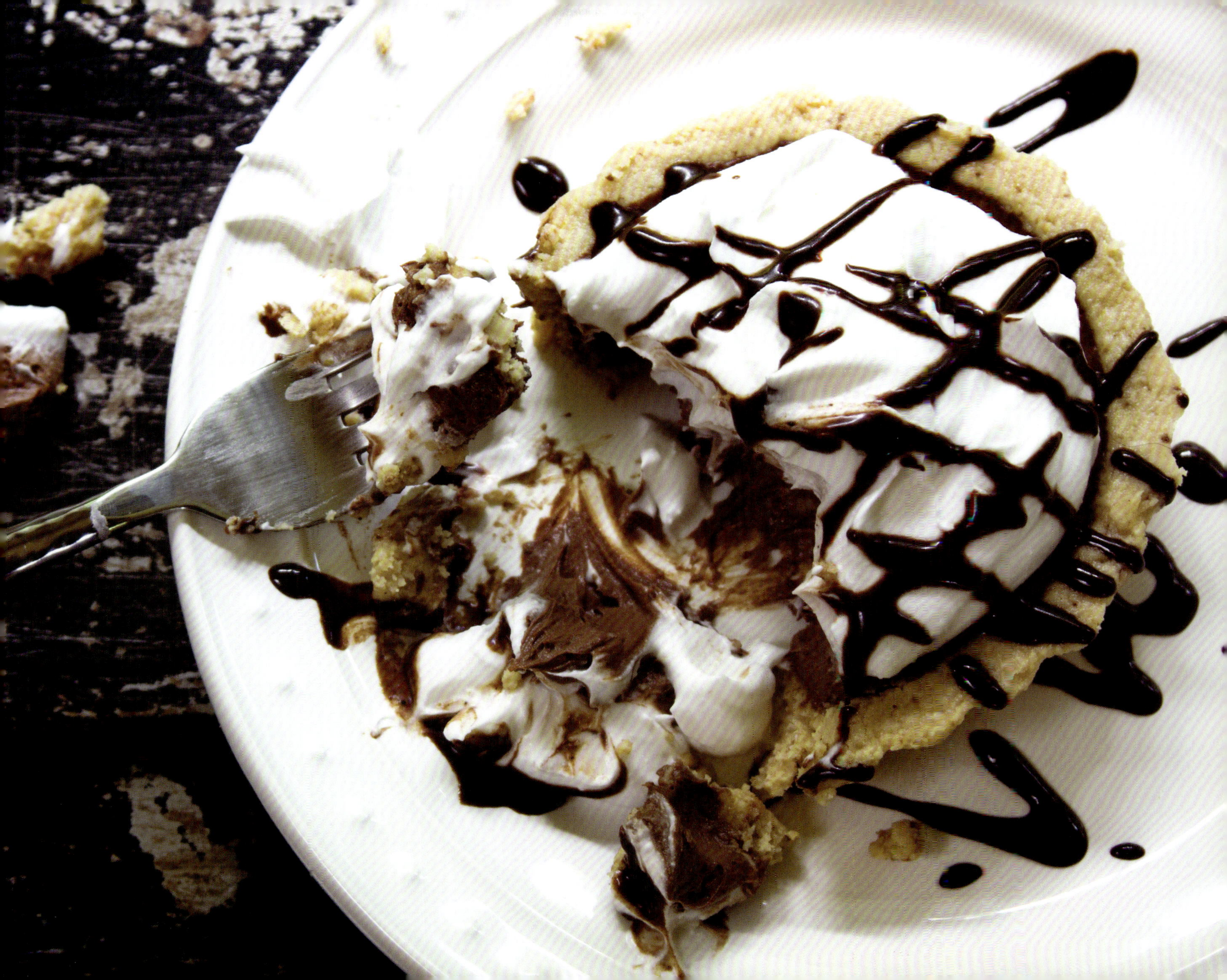

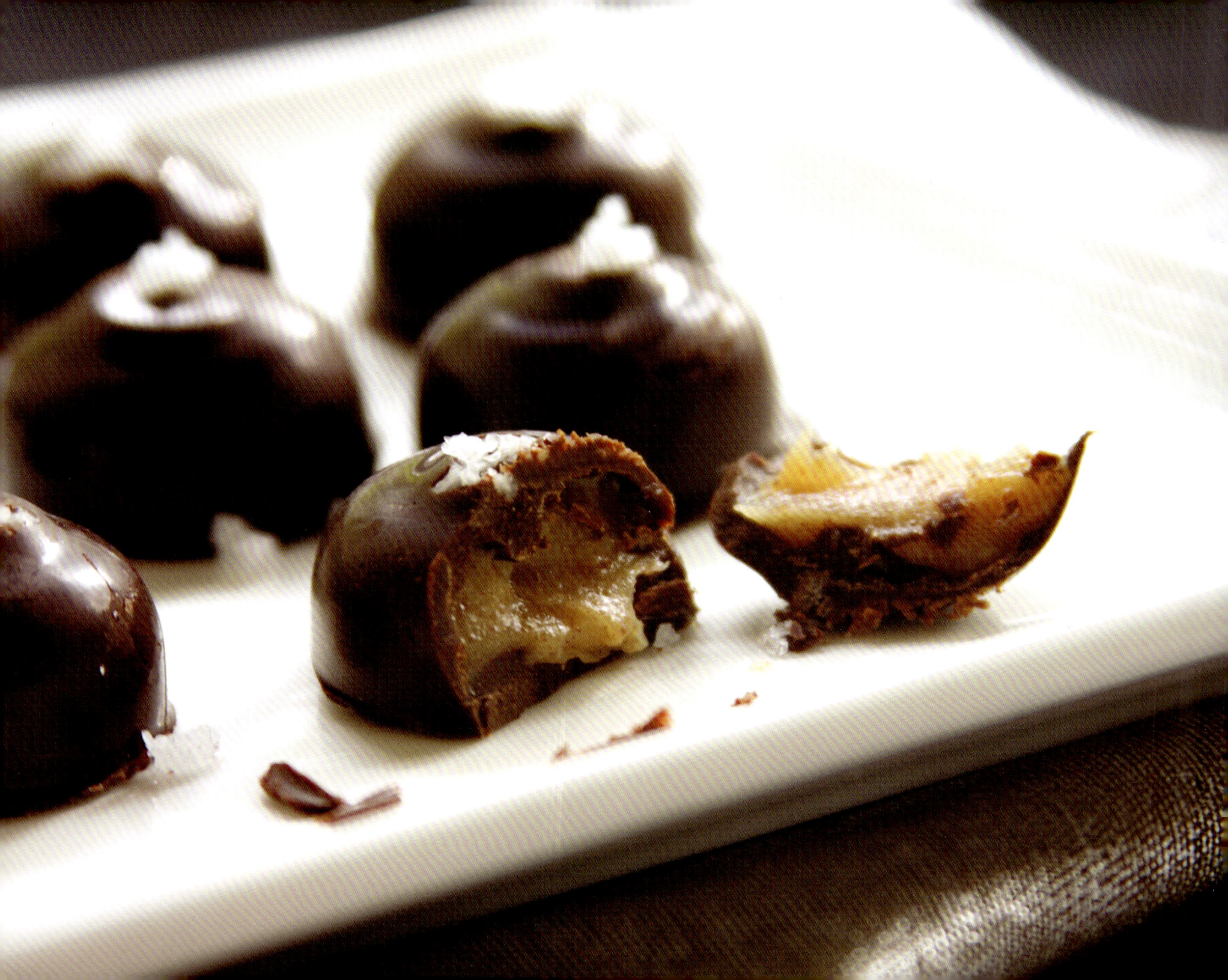

BUTTERY CARAMEL, CELTIC SALT, AND DARK CHOCOLATE TRUFFLES

MAKES 6 LARGE TRUFFLES

CHOCOLATE COATING
1/2 recipe tempered dark chocolate base (see page 246)

CARAMEL
1/2 cup coconut butter, melted
1/2 cup raw light agave
1/3 cup yacon syrup
3 large medjool dates, pitted
1 tablespoon vanilla extract
1/2 teaspoon sea salt

GARNISH
2 teaspoons course celtic sea salt

Soft buttery caramel-filled dark chocolates are sprinkled with chunky celtic sea-salt crystals creating a sweet yet bold contrast. These are great to give as gifts around the holidays.

Make the caramel
1. In high-speed blender place coconut butter, agave, yacon, dates, vanilla, and sea salt. Blend on high for about 2 minutes, until dates are broken down and caramel is smooth and creamy. Since caramel is so thick, use spatula to scrape down blender, if needed.

Assemble
1. Sprinkle a few celtic sea-salt crystals on bottom of chocolate mold.
2. Pour about 1 teaspoon chocolate base into molds. With a small culinary paintbrush or back side of measuring spoon, brush chocolate up the sides of molds. This will be the outer shell. After all molds are filled, place in freezer for about 10 minutes to cool and set.
3. Remove from freezer. Pour caramel into pastry piping bag or garnishing bottle with small tip. Fill each chocolate mold 3/4 full with caramel.
4. Spoon chocolate base over caramel filling until mold is filled to top. When all molds are filled, tap entire mold on counter to release air bubbles.
5. Place in freezer for 15 minutes to set. Remove and serve.

Note: Keeps at room temperature up to 4 weeks in airtight container.

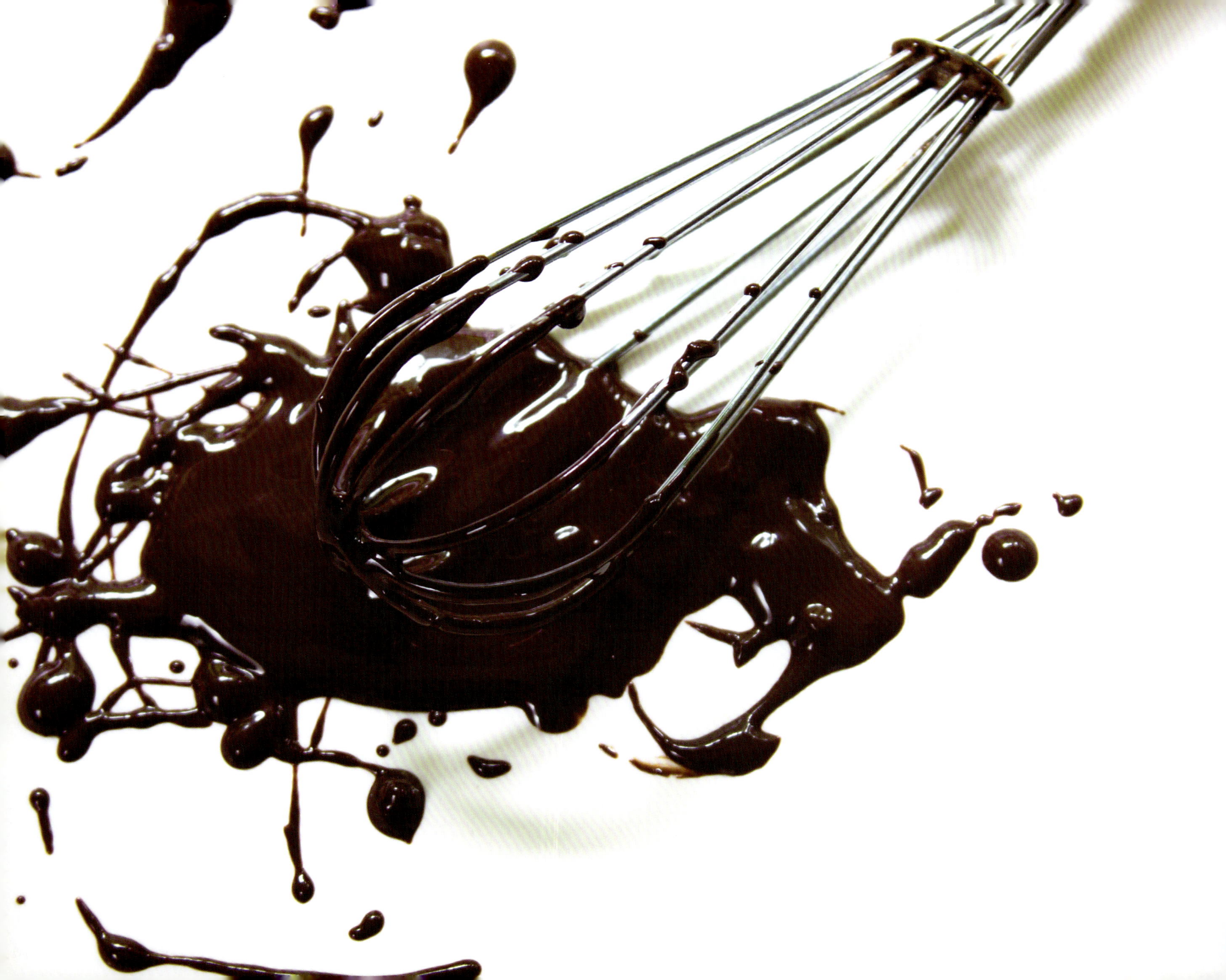

RAW TEMPERED CHOCOLATE BASE

MAKES 2 1/2 CUPS

CHOCOLATE

1 ¼ cup raw cacao paste (also called raw cacao liquor)
1 cup raw cacao butter
1/4 cup raw light agave
2 teaspoons vanilla extract
1/8 teaspoon sea salt

It took me years in the kitchen to perfect this delicate chocolate base. The secret to the shiny, smooth texture is the tempering process which allows the chocolate to be stable at room temperature for months. Make sure to follow the recipe precisely, and you will have a great chocolate base for all your candy and truffle creations

Make the chocolate
1. In medium mixing bowl, melt cacao paste and cacao butter. The easiest way to do this is to place in denydrator at 118 degrees for about 45 minutes, until almost all the cacao paste and butter is melted.
2. Remove from dehydrator and stir in agave, vanilla, and sea salt until well combined. Place back in dehydrator and warm for about 10 minutes. This is the final and most important part of tempering chocolate. During this 10 minutes you DO NOT want the chocolate to go above 88 degrees. Using a candy thermometer, check every 2 or 3 minutes to ensure the chocolate is staying at or below 88 degrees.
3. Once it hits 88 degrees, remove from dehydrator and use for truffles, candies, chocolates, fondue, and anything you want to dip in chocolate. Tempering will create a raw chocolate that is stable to keep at room temperature for quite a few months.

Note: Keeps at room temperature up to 1 month in airtight container. It is very important that all equipment when tempering chocolate is totally dry and gets no water in it. Water will compromise the integrity of the chocolate.

B R E A K

F A S T S

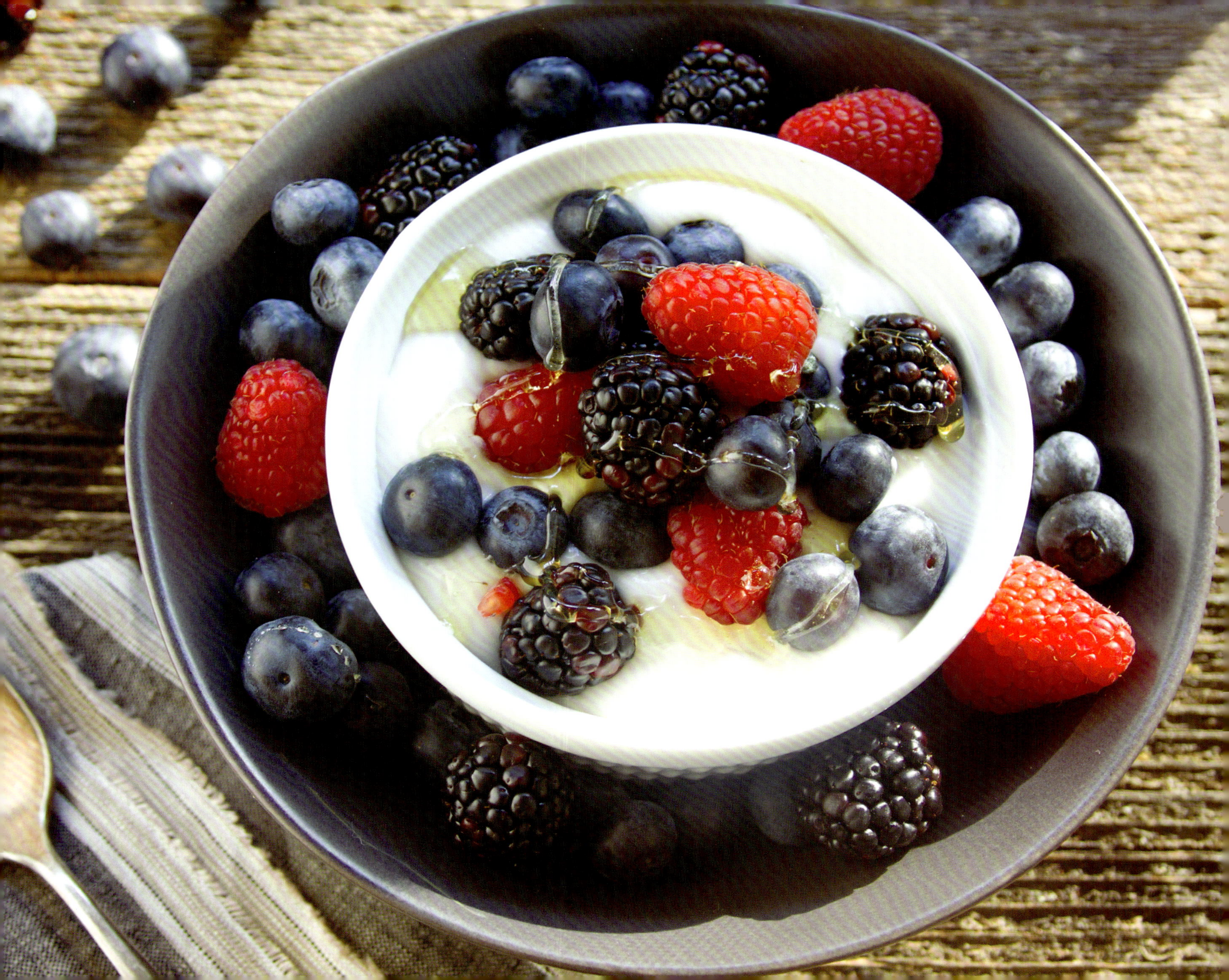

COCONUT YOGURT, SUMMER BERRIES, AND HONEY

MAKES 4 CUPS (SERVES 4)

YOGURT
3 cups young Thai coconut meat
1 ½ cups young Thai coconut water
6 vegan probiotic caps

GARNISH
1 cup fresh blueberries
1 cup fresh blackberries
1 cup fresh raspberries
2 tablespoons raw honey or raw light agave

Finally, a yogurt without all the additives and sugar! This yogurt is really easy to make, has all the healthy benefits of coconut, and is loaded with probiotics. Topped with fresh antioxidant-rich summer berries and raw honey, this recipe is an excellent way to start the day.

Make the yogurt
1. In high-speed blender place coconut meat, coconut water, and contents of probiotic caps. Blend on high for about 2 minutes, until coconut meat is broken down and yogurt is smooth. The small amount of heat from blending will start the culturing process.
2. In small mixing bowl, pour yogurt and cover. Set on counter at room temperature for 12 hours to culture. If you want a more-tangy yogurt, increase culturing time until desired taste is achieved.
3. After culturing is complete, chill yogurt in refrigerator for 1–2 hours before serving.

Assemble
1. Scoop 1 cup yogurt into 4 serving bowls of choice.
2. Top each bowl with 1/4 cup blueberries, 1/4 cup blackberries, and 1/4 cup raspberries, and drizzle with honey for a touch of sweetness

Note: Keeps in refrigerator up to 3 days in airtight container.

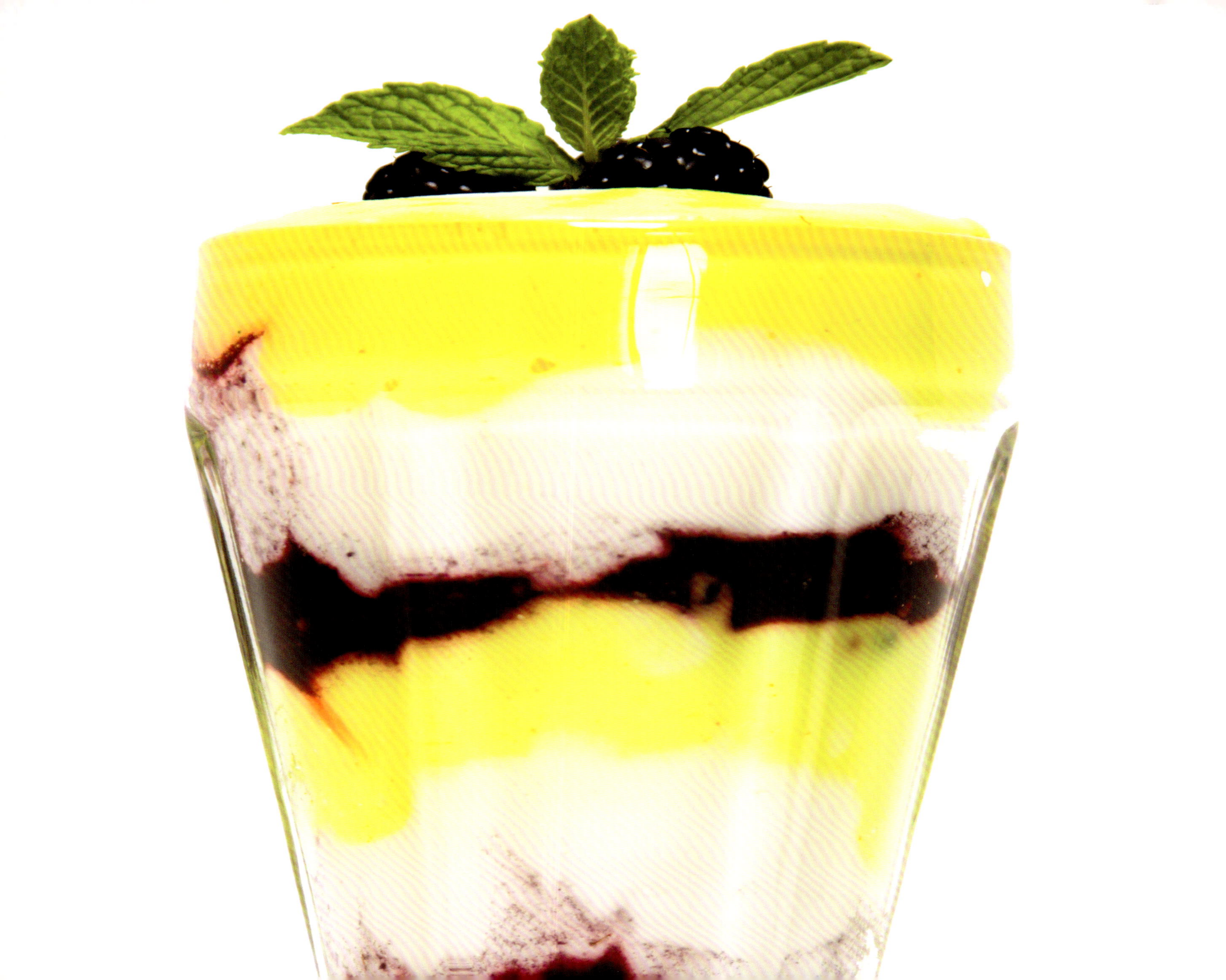

MASHED BLACKBERRY, WHIPPED CREAM, AND LEMON CUSTARD PARFAIT

MAKES 4 16-OUNCE PARFAITS

LEMON CUSTARD

1 ½ cups young Thai coconut meat
1/2 cup young Thai coconut water
1/2 cup raw light agave
1/2 cup lemon juice, fresh-squeezed
1/4 cup raw coconut oil
1 ½ tablespoons irish moss gel (see page 102)
1 tablespoon lecithin granules
1/4 teaspoon turmeric powder
1/8 teaspoon sea salt

WHIPPED CREAM

1 ½ cups young Thai coconut meat
1/2 cup young Thai coconut water
1/4 cup raw light agave
1/4 cup raw coconut oil
2 tablespoons irish moss gel (see page 102)
1/2 teaspoon vanilla extract
1/8 teaspoon sea salt

BLACKBERRY COMPOTE

3 cups fresh blackberries
2 teaspoons lemon juice, fresh-squeezed
2 teaspoons raw light agave
1 teaspoon fresh lemon zest

GARNISH

1/4 cup fresh blackberries
4 mint sprigs

Layers of blackberry compote, fluffy vanilla whipped cream and tangy lemon custard will have your taste buds dancing. I was inspired to create this recipe after seeing a photo in *Bon Appetite* magazine featuring a colorful lemon parfait set against an aqua blue backdrop. This version is free of dairy, sugar, and nuts, making it allergen-friendly.

Make the blackberry compote
1. In small mixing bowl, add blackberries, lemon juice, agave, and lemon zest. Mash with fork until well combined but leaving blackberries slightly chunky.

Make the lemon custard
1. In high-speed blender place coconut meat, coconut water, agave, lemon juice, irish moss gel, turmeric, and sea salt. Blend on high for about 2 minutes, until coconut meat is broken down and smooth.
2. Add coconut oil and lecithin. Blend another 30 seconds, until well combined.

Make the whipped cream
1. In high-speed blender place coconut meat, coconut water, agave, irish moss, vanilla extract, and sea salt. Blend on high for about 1 minute, until coconut meat is broken down and cream is smooth.
2. Add coconut oil and blend another 30 seconds.

Assemble
1. In 16–ounce parfait cups, layer 2 tablespoons blackberry compote.
2. Top compote with 1/4 cup whipped cream
3. Top whipped cream with 1/4 cup lemon custard.
4. Repeat blackberry, whipped cream, lemon one more time. Garnish with a few fresh blackberries and mint leaves.

Note: Keeps in refrigerator up to 3 days in airtight container.

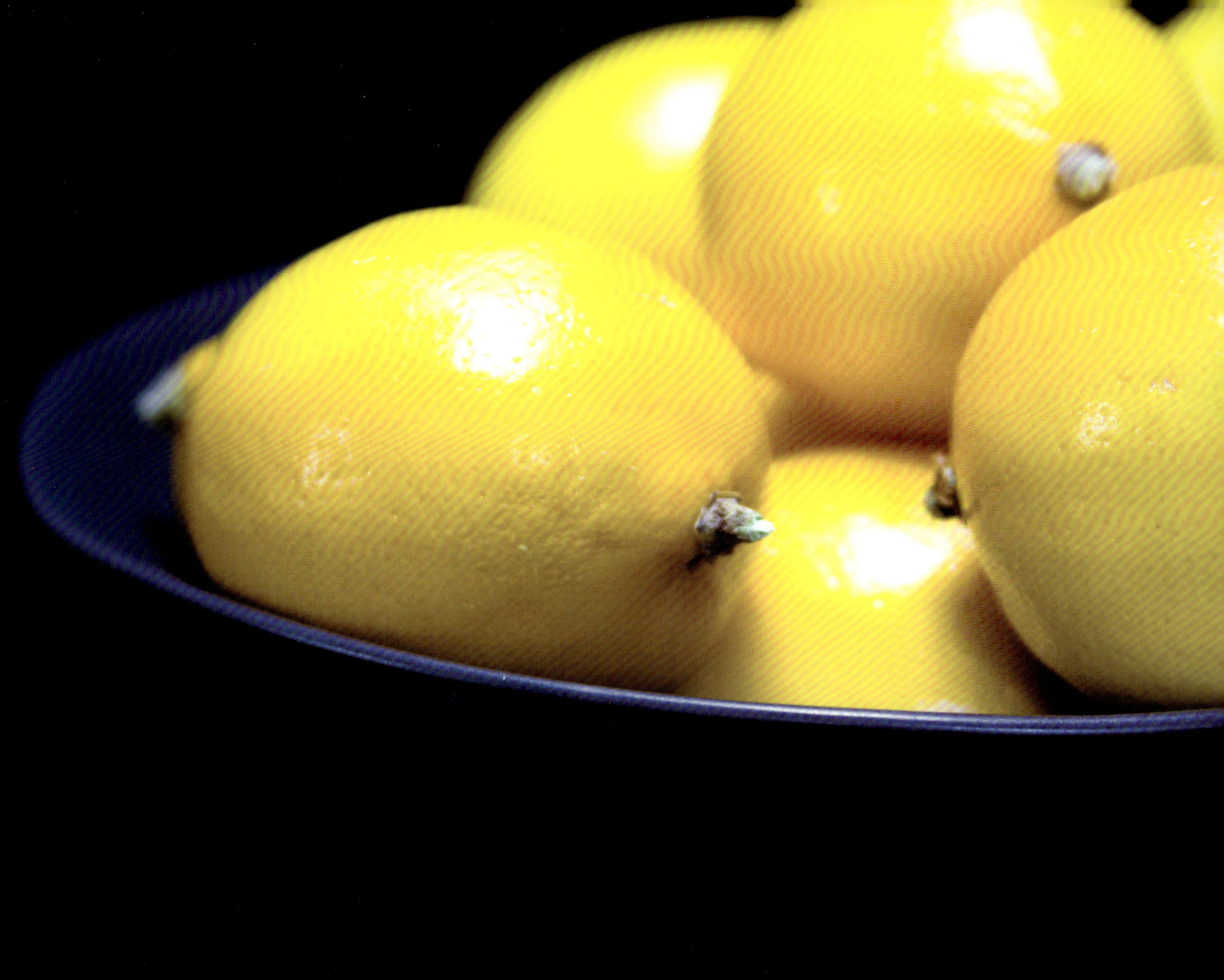

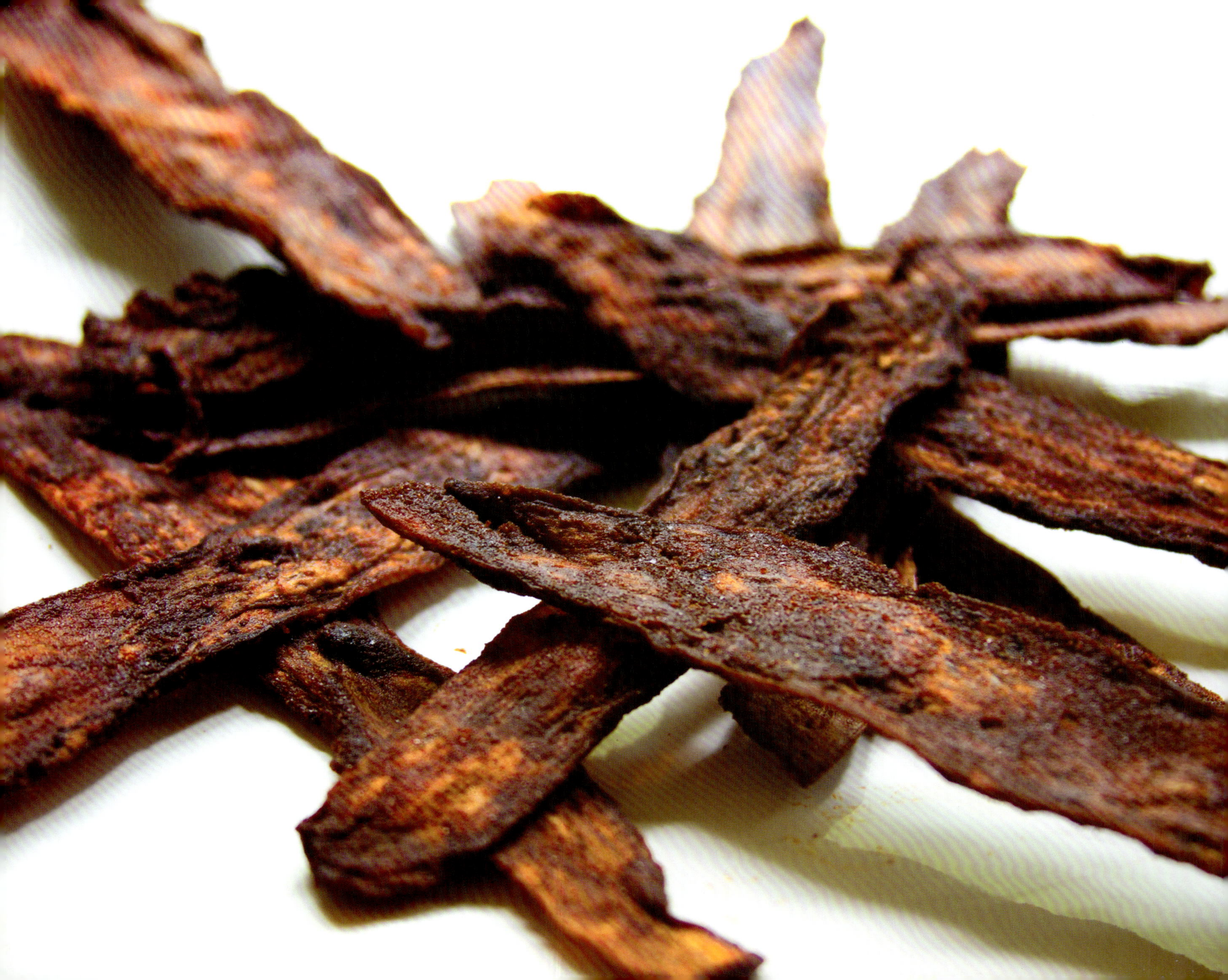

EGGPLANT BACON WITH APPLE AND SMOKED PAPRIKA

MAKES ABOUT 30 STRIPS

BACON STRIPS
1 large or 2 small eggplants, peeled and cut in half lengthwise
1/2 teaspoon sea salt

MARINADE
1/4 cup wheat-free tamari
1/4 cup smoked paprika
1/4 cup expeller-pressed grape-seed oil
1/4 cup apple juice, fresh-pressed
2 tablespoon maple syrup

Smoky with apple undertones, this eggplant bacon adds nice texture to salads and a great crunchy addition to any sandwich. I've tried various raw "bacon" recipes over the years using both coconut meat and zucchini, but I have to say eggplant is my favorite. It creates perfect crispy strips.

Make the marinade
1. In small mixing bowl, add wheat-free tamari, smoked paprika, grape-seed oil, apple juice, and maple syrup. Whisk until well combined.

Make the bacon
1. Using a mandoline slicer, set on the thinnest setting, slice eggplant.
2. In large mixing bowl, add sliced eggplant and sea salt. Cover and let stand 1/2 hour. This will allow excess water from the eggplant to come out.
3. Pour any water out of bowl and pat eggplant with paper towels to collect any excess liquid and return to bowl.
4. Pour marinade over eggplant strips and toss lightly to coat. Cover and let stand for 1 ½ hours, so eggplant can soak up all the marinade.
5. Spread strips out on dehydrator tray lined with teflex sheet. Space about 1/4-inch apart from one another. Dehydrate at 115 degrees for 4 hours.
6. Remove bacon from teflex sheets and return to dehydrator tray. Place back in dehydrator at 115 degrees for another 20 hours. Should be light and crispy when done.

Note: Keeps up to 2 weeks at room temperature in airtight container.

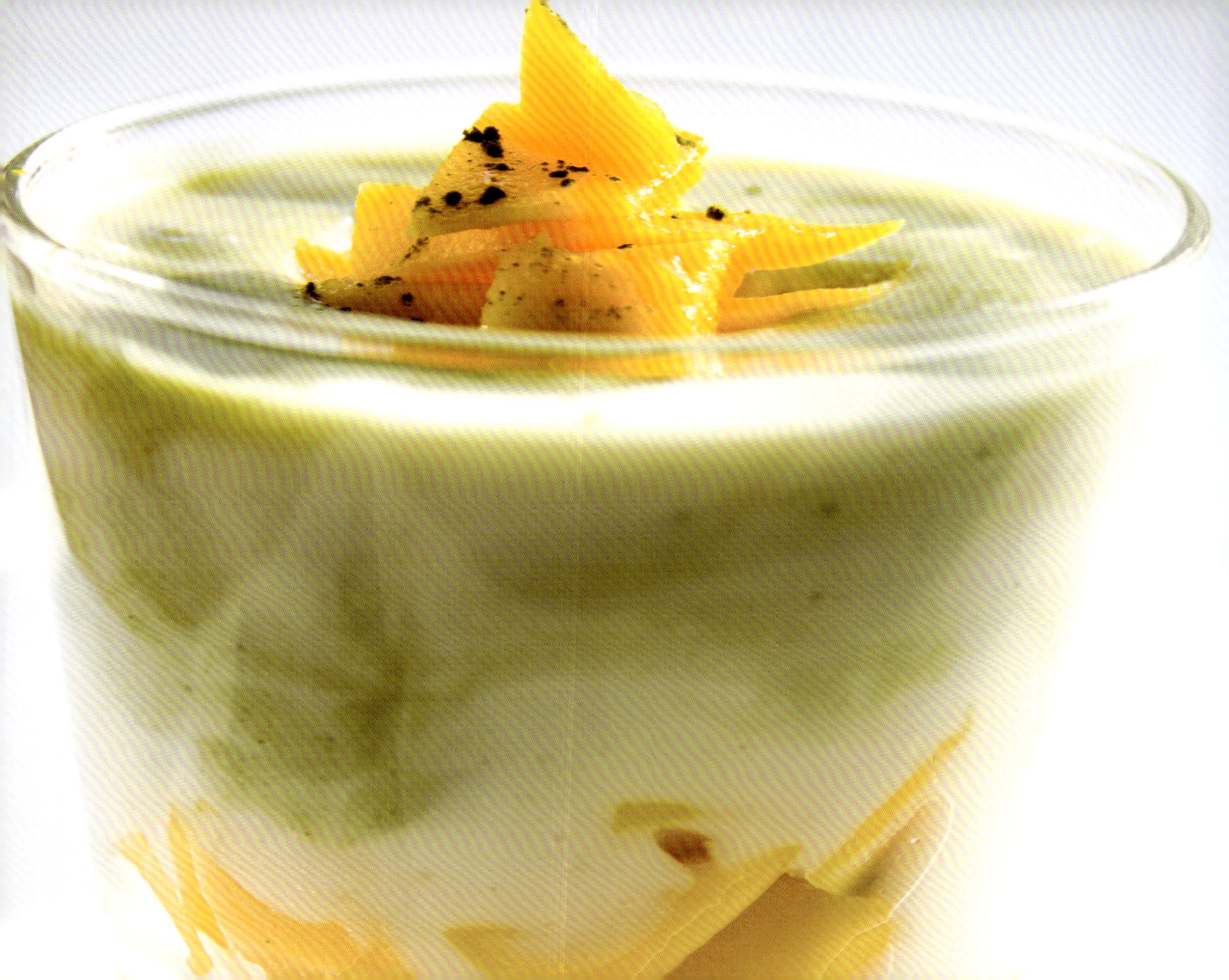

COCONUT YOGURT WITH SENCHA GREEN TEA SWIRL AND RIPE MANGO

MAKES 4 12-OUNCE CUPS

SENCHA YOGURT

2 ¼ cup plain coconut yogurt (see page 250)
1 tablespoon raw honey or raw light agave
1/2 teaspoon sencha powder

GARNISH

2 cups ripe mango, peeled, pitted and cubed
1 ½ tablespoons raw honey or raw light agave

Aromatic sencha green tea paired with sweet ripe mango and creamy coconut yogurt. This breakfast is rich in healthy fats, antioxidants, and catenins and is absolutely delicious.

Make the sencha yogurt
1. In small mixing bowl, add 1/4 cup plain coconut yogurt, sencha powder, and honey. Stir with spoon until green-tea powder has dissolved.

Assemble
1. In 4–12 ounce serving dishes of choice, layer 1/2 cup cubed mango.
2. Top mango with 1/2 cup plain coconut yogurt.
3. Top yogurt with 1 tablespoon sencha yogurt. With a spoon, swirl into plain yogurt.
4. Top sencha swirl with a few mango cubes. Drizzle with 1 teaspoon honey. Serve immediately.

Note: Keeps up to 3 days in refrigerator in airtight container.

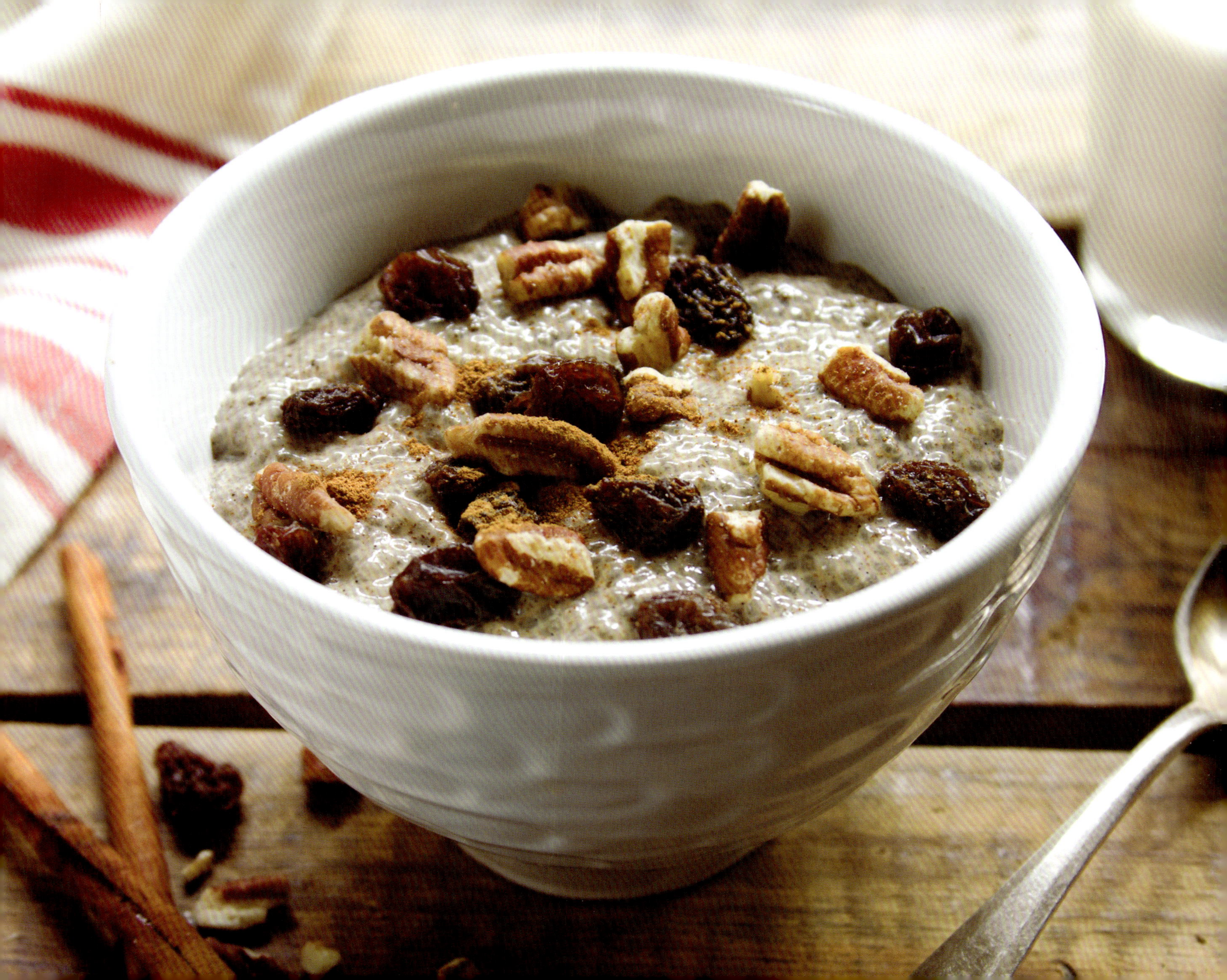

CHAI-INFUSED CHIA SEED PORRIDGE WITH APPLE, RAISINS, AND PECANS

MAKES 3 CUPS (SERVES 4)

CHIA PORRIDGE

2 chai tea bag
1 cup vanilla almond milk (see page 76)
1/2 cup raw chia seeds
1/2 cup boiling water
2 tablespoon raw light agave or raw honey
1 teaspoon ground cinnamon
dash of sea salt to taste

GARNISH

1/2 cup raw pecans, chopped
1/2 cup apple, diced
1/4 cup raisins
1 tablespoon raw agave or raw honey
4 cinnamon sticks (optional)

Native Americans used chia seeds medicinally as well as for food during long journeys. Chia seeds are rich in omega fatty acids, protein, and calcium. This porridge is a great energizing way to start your day.

Make the porridge
1. Steep chai tea bags in 1/2 cup boiling water for 10–15 minutes.
2. In medium mixing bowl, add almond milk, chia seeds, agave, cinnamon, and sea salt. Stir with spoon until well combined and chia seeds are covered in liquid and clump-free.
3. Remove tea bags from water and pour chai tea into chia porridge. Gently stir until all ingredients are well combined. Let stand for 20 minutes. The chia seeds will soak up all the liquid, leaving a thick porridge.

Assemble
1. In serving bowls of choice, spoon 3/4 cups porridge into each bowl.
2. Sprinkle with chopped pecans, apple and raisins. Drizzle with agave or honey and place cinnamon sticks on edge of bowl. Serve immediately.

Note: Keeps up to 3 days in refrigerator in airtight container.

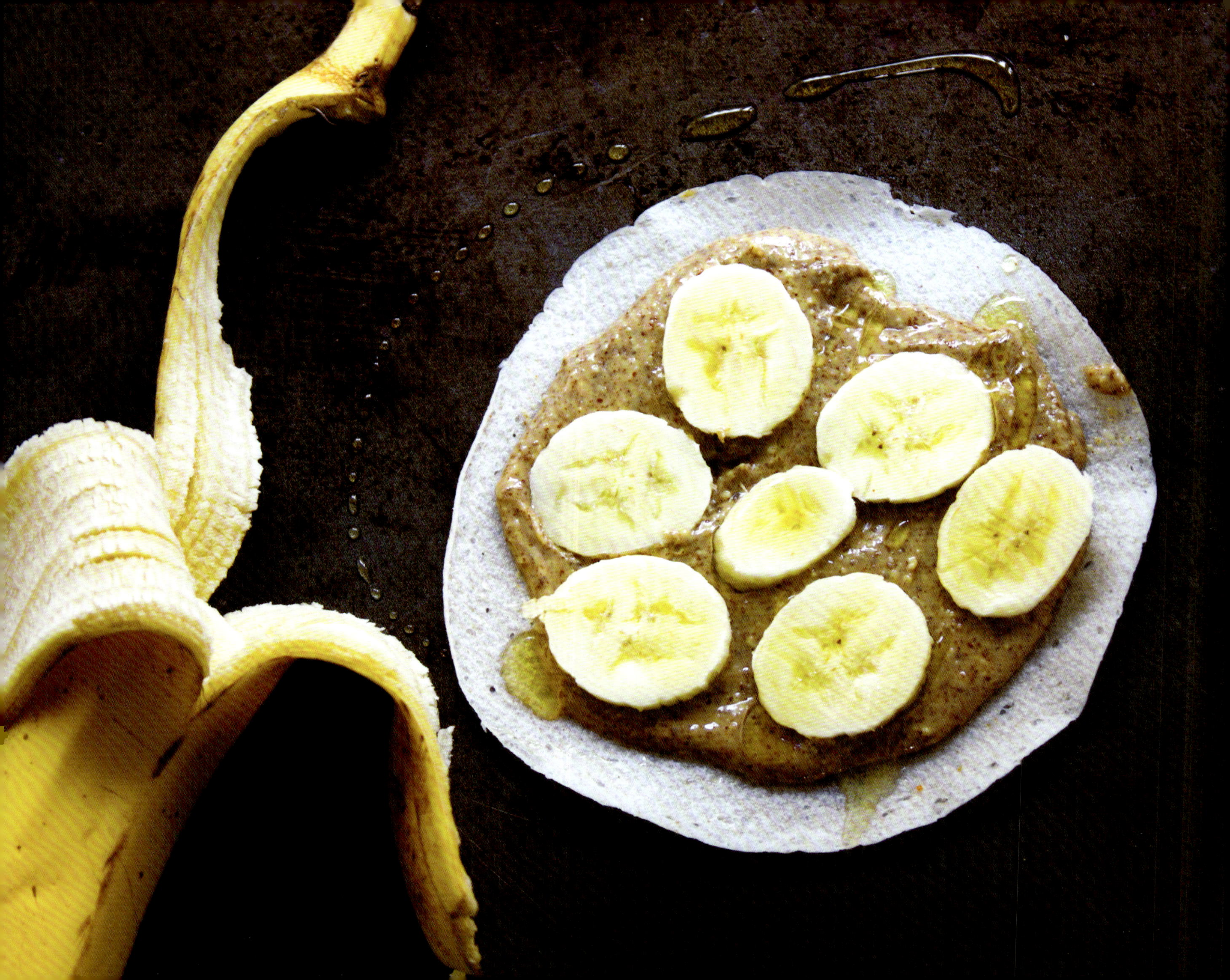

COCONUT CREPES ALMOND BUTTER, VANILLA HONEY, AND SLICED BANANA

SERVES 4

CREPES
1 ½ cups young Thai coconut meat
1/2 cup water
1/8 teaspoon sea salt

FILLING
1/2 cup raw almond butter
2 ripe bananas, peeled and sliced in 1/4–inch rounds
2 tablespoons raw honey or raw light agave
1 vanilla bean, scraped, seeds only

Creamy almond butter drizzled in vanilla honey and slices of sweet ripe banana are rolled up in a light coconut crepe. These are great for a breakfast on the go or midday snack.

Make the crepes
1. In a high-speed blender place coconut meat, water, and sea salt. Blend on high for about 1 minute, until coconut meat is broken down and liquid is thick and smooth.
2. Using dehydrator trays lined with teflex sheets, pour 4 thick dollops of mixture on sheets. With back of spoon, evenly spread out crepes, using circular motion from the inside out and creating 6-inch circles. Make sure there is no transparency in the crepes, as this will create holes.
3. Dehydrate at 105 degrees for 4 hours. Flip over and slowly peel away teflex sheets. Return to dehydrator for another 8 hours.
4. Crepes should be firm but still pliable. If crepes get too dry, don't worry! Wet hands with water and flick over crepes to soften. Let stand for 15 minutes. If they're still dry, continue process until pliable.

Make the vanilla honey
1. In small mixing bowl, add honey and vanilla bean. Stir with spoon until combined.

Assemble
1. Spread 2 tablespoons almond butter on each crepe.
2. Top almond butter with 1/2 sliced banana.
3. Drizzle banana slices with vanilla honey.
4. Roll up. Serve immediately.

Note: Keeps up to 2 days in refrigerator in airtight container.

BREAKFASTS

262

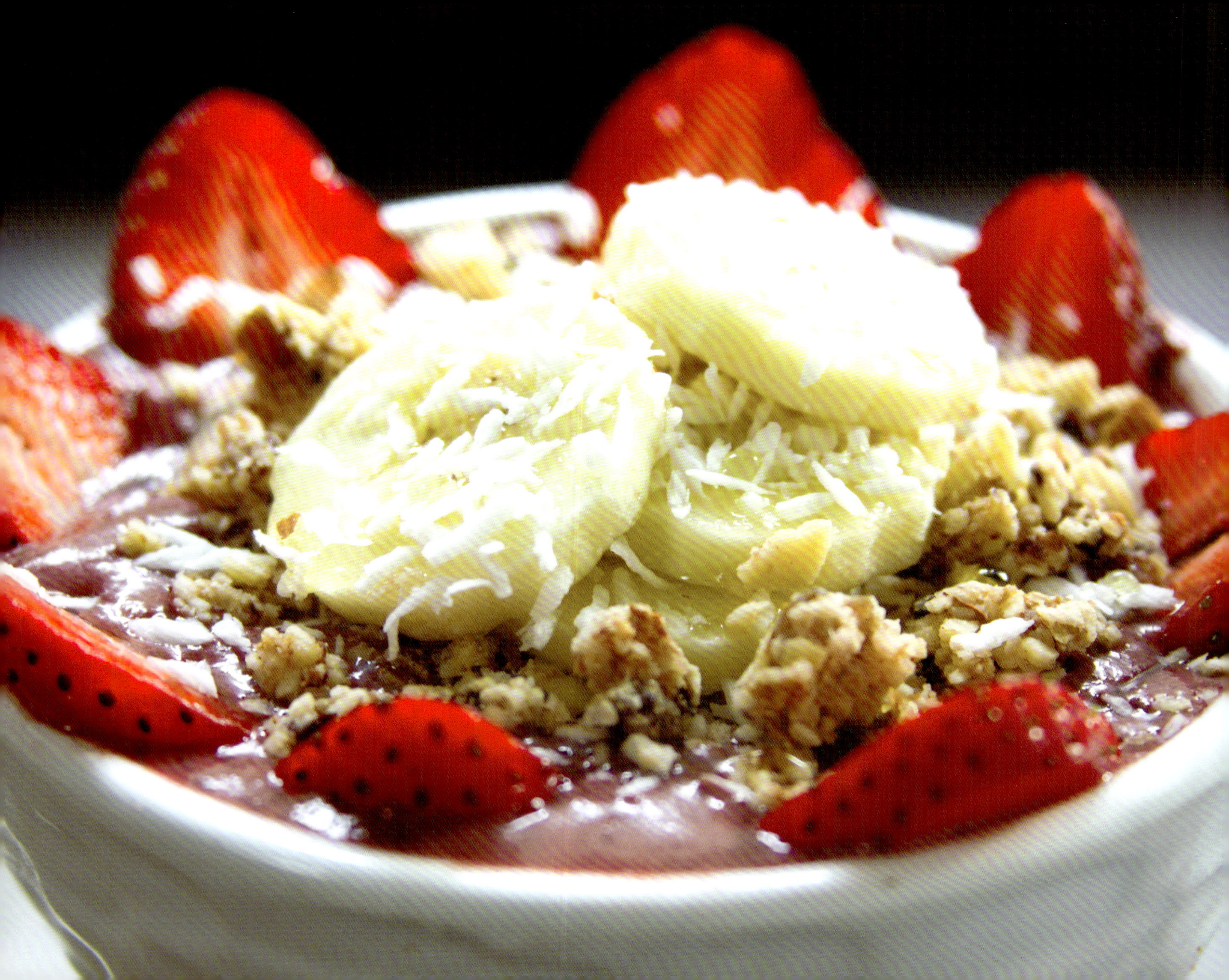

ACAI BOWL WITH GRANOLA, FRESH STRAWBERRIES, BANANA, COCONUT, AND HONEY

SERVES 4

BOWL

4 cups acai smoothie (see page 64)
1 cup cherry almond granola (see page 266)
1 cup fresh strawberries, stems removed and sliced
1 medium ripe banana, peeled and sliced into 1/4–inch rounds
1/4 cup unsweetened raw coconut, shredded
1/4 raw honey or raw light agave

A beautiful deep purple, antioxidant-packed smoothie topped with crunchy granola, an array of fresh fruit, and drizzled in honey. When I was on the Big Island of Hawaii, I heard about these amazing breakfast bowls that gave you superhero energy all day. So of course I had to hunt one of these magical breakfast bowls down. Let's just say when I found one, it was inhaled within minutes. I had to re-create this as soon as I returned to the mainland and share it with everyone. So here is my version of the magical acai breakfast bowl. Enjoy!

Assemble
1. Pour 1 cup acai smoothie into each serving bowl of choice.
2. Top smoothie with 1/4 cup granola.
3. Top granola with 1/4 cup strawberries.
4. Top strawberries with banana slices.
5. Top banana slices with 1 tablespoon shredded coconut.
6. Drizzle coconut with honey or agave. Serve immediately.

Note: Keeps up to 2 days in refrigerator in airtight container but best served immediately.

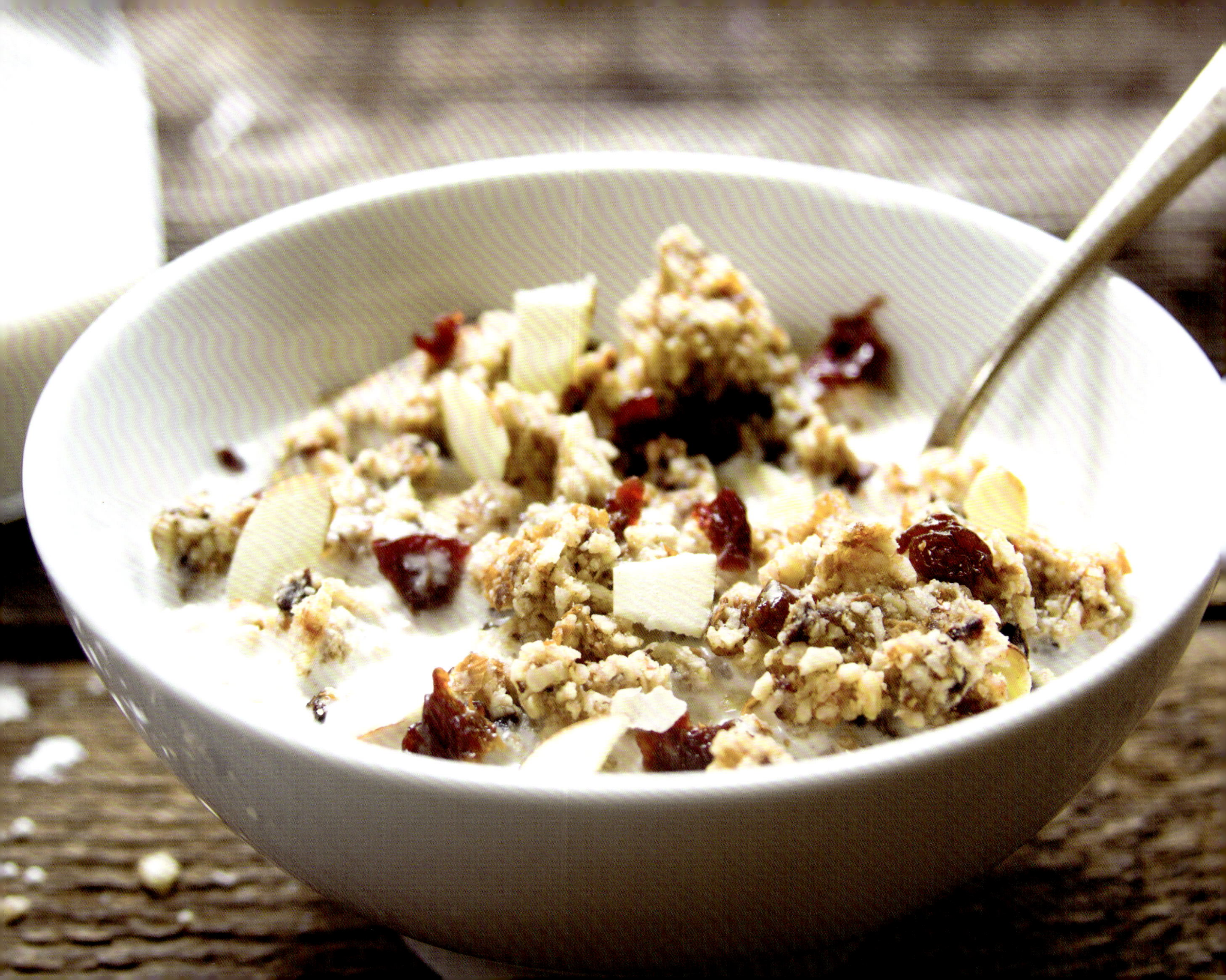

CHERRY ALMOND GRANOLA

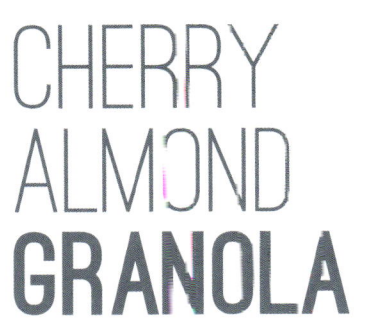

MAKES 6 CUPS

GRANOLA

15 medjool dates, pitted
2 cups unsweetened raw coconut, shredded
2 cups raw almonds soaked 8–10 hours, drained and rinsed
1/2 cup dried cherries, chopped
1/4 cup raw coconut oil
2 tablespoons raw light agave
2 tablespoons almond extract
1 teaspoon vanilla extract
1 teaspoon ground cinnamon
3/4 teaspoon sea salt

Cherry and almond together is a great flavor combination. This grain-free granola makes an awesome breakfast served with vanilla almond milk, as a snack on the go, or layered in parfaits. I always like to keep a bag of it in my pack when traveling for a quick protein-packed pick-me-up. If you're not a fan of cherry and almond, substitute with 1/2 cup raisins and one tablespoon ground cinnamon.

Make the granola
1. In food processor with S blade attachment, add dates, shredded coconut, almonds, dried cherries, coconut oil, agave, almond extract, vanilla extract, cinnamon, and sea salt. Pulse for about 30 seconds, until well combined but slightly chunky.
2. Spread out granola on dehydrator tray lined with teflex sheet. Dehydrate at 115 degrees for 24 hours or until slightly crisp and dry.

Note: Keeps at room temperature up to 2 months in airtight container.

ACKNOWLEDGMENTS

SPECIAL THANKS

My heartfelt thanks to **TOM SHADYACK** you are an inspiration in all you do. Your spirit and zest for life are contagious. You've contributed to this book with heart and faith. You believed in me and offered a means so I could have creative control and share these love-filled recipes with the world. You are such a gift—I AM eternally grateful. Thank you!

MOM AND DAD first of all, thank you for being patient; letting me turn your kitchen into a photography studio and ruin all your dish towels; and being my taste-testers, even when you were stuffed and cheering me on when I thought I just couldn't make one more dessert. You are both my mentors through this life and my best friends. You exposed me from an early age to the wondrous elements of our world. You taught me how to see the beauty in everything and raised me in an environment to respect our mother earth—a place where I became connected to the land and understood where my food came from. Giving me the space to get dirty and use nature as my playground, you always kept me well fed with organic nourishing foods and educated me on health and spiritual well-being. I thank you every day for raising me in such a loving, artistic, supportive, and communicative home where my imagination could run wild and dreams were always within reach. You have always nurtured my creativity, no matter what the project might have been, and never showed doubts in my abilities. You've never said, no when I've needed help and always have been there to listen and provide with me with wisdom and advice. As parents you started me out with a foundation, but now you are my rocks. I cherish you both and all you are and all you do. Love you so much!

SHANE my brother—you have driven thousands of miles, been electrocuted and worked countless hours of physical labor with no great reward in the end besides helping your sister. You have provided me with opportunities so I could move forward with my dream of writing this book. You opened doors for me in so many areas of my life and done so selflessly and wholeheartedly. In the final stages of this book, you gave me the tools necessary to complete my vision, and I am so appreciative. You're the best!

GRANDPA JACK for always giving me the most sound business advice and supporting me in so many different ways during all my crazy adventures in life. Keep the advice coming it's helped cushion the journey.

GRANDMA ANN you have been my cheerleader from day one and provided me with all the latest news in the vegan world while I was too busy in the kitchen. You are an unrivaled beauty with style and class.

BURKHEIMER CLAN for always being enthusiastic to taste my creations and never-ending support.

YANA my soul sister. Blood, sweat and countless tears—this has been one hell of a ride. You stuck by me through the whole thing. Through good times and bad, you were always there for me as a friend, sous chef and travel partner. Thanks to you I have traveled around the world, learned to say yes more, realized it's okay to sleep more, and you've helped me find the courage to finish this book. You have sacrificed so much in order for me to accomplish my dreams. When I've had meltdowns, you've always been there to help piece me back together and supplied words of wisdom, encouragement, and motivation when I needed it the most. I could not have survived this ride without you. Thank you for being willing to learn; having an open mind, heart, and palate; and giving so much dedication to something that meant the world to me. This book is just as much yours as it is mine.

HANNA for being my friend, confidant, therapist, and taste-tester when I first started developing raw food creations in our kitchen in Vegas.

LAUREN for always being down to dance with me, laugh, and be supportive of my wildest dreams from the start.

MOLLY for helping me build my first website, and always being supportive of my food adventures, and of course, rectifying situations when need be.

ALANA for your integrity, loveliness, and constant faith in me. You have always been willing to help in any way.

DARYL thank you for a beautiful friendship, giving me a home when I needed it the most, and always being behind my raw-food projects 100 percent. You have changed my life in so many ways and inspired me beyond words. I will never forget how much you've done for me.

ANNIE AND JEAN LOUIS for giving me an opportunity, trusting in my abilities, and allowing me a space to develop my skills as a chef. You both hold a very special place in my heart.

ASTRID AND JUDAH I have so much gratitude for your never-ending kindness, generosity, and friendship. Thank you for allowing me the opportunity to share my food and supporting my business when it was just getting off the ground. It means the world to me.

TARAN you gave me a commercial kitchen on wheels and a space to develop my business into what it is today. What started out as a tragic food truck adventure turned into a beautiful friendship and the means to share my food and passion with the world. I couldn't have done any of this without you. Thank you for your generosity, kindness, and positive energy.

JC for inspirational talks and always being a helping hand when I need it the most.

DEBORAH AND STEPHEN you both believed in me and my business 100 percent from the first day we met in the food truck. You have forever made a positive impact on my life, and I can't thank you enough.

ASHA for opening up new chakras, allowing creative energy to flow through me and helping me to learn to be patient with myself.

PAUL you've given me nothing but creative support and guidance from day one. Thank you for a beautiful friendship and always believing in me. I cherish you and the girls.

ERIN you've been so supportive from day one, always offered a helping hand, and believed in me when I needed it the most. You've been a trusted taste-tester, never doubted my skills in the kitchen, and always been ready and willing to try all my culinary creations whether good, or bad. You've supported and helped me as a friend in more ways than I'll ever be able to count. Thank you for being a constant inspiration!

DAEDRA for being a patient, kind, generous, loving and understanding friend. Let the triad of our lives and unforgettable adventures continue. So much to look forward too.

ALL MY OLYMPIA FAMILIES AND FRIENDS Holly Owens, the Gillets, Finnigans, Evans, Drennons, Moores, Wingfields, Klovee-Smiths, Kramers, and all the friends that encouraged me to keep making raw food with your enthusiasm and support.

RAW CHEFS OF THE WORLD for supplying recipes, whether they be by book, Internet, or word of mouth. It allowed me a foundation to experiment and be inspired in the kitchen when I first began this epic adventure.

THANK YOU TO EVERYONE who attended my book fund-raising party in Malibu! (You know who you are.) That was such an inspirational evening, filled with good people, music, laughter, and of course, food. Thank you for your donations and taking part in what for me was an unforgettable evening filled with magic. This book was made with the help of each of you.

KICKSTARTER BACKERS with your support and pledges, I was able to turn my dream of printing this book into a reality. I am so grateful! In no particular order, a huge thanks to:

Amy louderback
Jan Schindler
Stephanie
Karen Anderson
Melissa Faulder
Susan Park
Eleise Moore
Anonymous
Julie Merriman Chickering
Anonymous
Patricia Del Favero
Karen Frascella
LaCinda Jenson
Sachi Horback
George grubb
Marty Hill
Holly Owens
Shane Anderson
Barbara LaForge
Sarah Danielson
Kris Tucker
Michelle
George H. Truman III
Stephanie and Damien Kolb
Amee Kiefer
Scott & Deborah Windus
Richard Cooper
Shannon
Jessie & Kyle Thompson
Betsy Asmus
Sharon Davis
Susie Cowan
Megan Leigh Manke
Tom Anderson
Nick Felt
Phil Ahrens
Angie
Andrea
Jennifer Schreck
Bill and Jan Hillman
Chelsea and Spencer Kelley
Tony Bjerke
Michael & Ann Humes
Signe Feeney
Lily & Matt
Eric
Elysia Lippman
Sarah Rumbaugh
Nate Koenigsknecht
Helen Pitlick
Ann Anderson
Jeffrey Robinson
Adriana Alexander
Karen
Becky Penn
Josee Goldin
Pauli and Jeff Finnigan
Ron & Barb Hinton
Claire Elizabeth
Janet Jansen Knoblach
Liz & Kevin
Lane Lillquist
Gavin Ridling
Anonymous
Barb Murphy
S Dillon
Anonymous
Corey D
Cindy Strong
Audree Frey
Lianna Durney
Julie Reymore
Garrett Nora & Joey Heaton
Megan Lane
Alix Cave
Jenney K. Oh
Patty Wiedenhoeft
Yisroel Bentsion
Cozine
Ryan Lai
Debra Albury
William Polson
Hannah & Brady McDonald
Susan Christian

ACKNOWLEDGEMENTS

Anonymous
anonymous
Tania Palazzo
Kay Uhl and Don Kneeland
Nancy Green
Dean
Anastasia Burke
Richard A McDermott
Carissa
Anonymous
Erin Pattillo
Anonymous
Laura Parma
Rich
Jamie Scibelli-Jones
Giuseppe Lapenna
Laura Reding
Keith and Susan
Christine Sevec-Johnson
Mary Ellen Psaltis
Angie Westling
Brady Johnstone
Rich Simms
Callie
Camille Locy
Anonymous
Renee McKinley
Nick Baldridge
Kristina Boyer
Renee L. Chua
Don Freas
Kelsey Gross
Malaya Mount
Klovee-Smith
Bre Ballard
Marisa vest
Rachel Elizabeth
Tallie Corey Skye Zane Beau and Raven
Kerry and Marianne Burkheimer
Michael Trees
Garrett Barker
Molly Strong

Allison L. Barker
Lily Harrington
Patricia Hamilton
Alex McManus
Jennifer Gerard
Keya "Bug" Bernhardt
Katie Cestnik
Lamson Nguyen
Jeremy Woodruff
Caitlin Robinson
Kristina Linehan
Little Family
Charlie and Erika Gillet
Josie Preston
Anonymous
Julierose Shepherd-Gaw
Katelyn Peil
Tiffany Jolly <3
Nate and Marcia Naismith
Lani Taylor
Christie Mae Wagaman
Anonymous
Jenipher & Patti
Yana Frascella
Tami Mason Lathrop
Cory Graham
Katie O
Barbara and Rob
Shelly R Poole
anonymous
Spencer Gillet
Marilyn Frasca
Anonymous
Jen Hilliard
Sally & Ron Penley
Anonymous
Morgan Beck Mullaney
Roseann Salerno
Jeff!
Annie Johns
Duane Crago
Brandy J Jenkins
Ann Willis

Erika Beck Willie
Mary Skelton & Paul Meury
Carlann
Anonymous
Constantine Papanicolaou
April Gentry
Michelle Devon
Maria Gisela Pacho
Deirdre O'Donoghue
Alana Duran
Maureen Karras
Sharon Shepherd
Gerry Cardinal III
Patti Fisher
Linnie Hodge
For Tricia Caron - Love, your friend, Debi
Jacqueline
Jean Mandeberg & Joel Greene
Alyse
Christina Duchek
Amandun Albert
Lois Beck
Daedra!
Saylor & Finn Gillet
Frances Fisher
John and Jane Wingfield
Lindley LeClerc
Patrick and Shawn Berschauer
Ariel Donnette
Joan and Jordan
Kim Merriman
Jean Louis
Molly Moore
Leo Flowers
Carl Burkheimer Jr.
Holly Wood
JC
Kimberly
Kathy Evans
Duke Drennon
Amy Evans
Mikey
Ada
Joy
Astrid

Mike and Anne Miller
Rachel Prince
Rody
Sam
Pat Cole
Marie and Jacob

INDEX

A

ACAI 5
acai bowl with granola, fresh strawberries, banana, coconut, and honey 264
goji berry, golden peach, and pure acai 64

ALMONDS 29
almond butter, honey, coconut oil, spirulina, and carob 208
coconut crepes, almond butter, vanilla honey, and sliced banana 262
cherry almond granola 266
creamy vanilla almond milk 76
dark chocolate almond milk 77
dark chocolate amaretto truffles 218
golden flax almond bread 146
grated nutmeg, cinnamon, ginger, and almond milk 80
mixed greens, avocado, edible flowers, and herb dressing 114
sweet almond, coconut, and dark chocolate milkshake 84
veggie chili with cashew cream 168

APPETIZERS
aged macadamia nut cheese 138
avocado, garlic, and zesty lemon guacamole 142
avocado, green onion, cucumber, and seaweed guacamole 143
avocado, lime, cilantro, and sweet mango guacamole 144
butter lettuce cups with marinated shitakes and garlic chili sauce 136
cashew basil mozzarella, heirloom tomatoes, basil, and balsamic fig sauce 140
cashew cheese sauce with spicy jalapeño, tomato, and sweet onion 152
coconut lemongrass soup with basil and kaffir lime leaves 156
creamy cashew garlic spinach dip 154
creamy tomato bisque with basil oil and fresh cracked pepper 134
crispy herb kale chips 148
cucumber rolls with basil, mint, cilantro, and spicy coconut sauce 150
golden flax almond bread 146
pineapple, mango, lime, and shredded coconut salsa 158
red onion, lime, garlic, cilantro, and cherry tomato salsa 158

APPLE
apple, carrot, and kiwi juice 35
chai-infused chia seed porridge with apple, raisins, and pecans 260
eggplant bacon with apple and smoked paprika 256
green apple, cucumber, and pineapple mint juice 37
green kale, cucumber, and apple juice 34
parsley, kale, celery, apple, ginger, and lemon juice 36
romaine, apple, celery, carrot, and walnut with lemon poppy seed dressing 112

ASIAN PEAR 5
kale, Asian pear, red onion, candied pecans, and mustard dressing 126

AVOCADO
avocado, garlic, and zesty lemon guacamole 142
avocado, green onion, cucumber, and seaweed guacamole 143
avocado, lime, cilantro, and sweet mango guacamole 144
eggplant bacon, lettuce, avocado, and tomato sandwich 164
herb cashew cream cheese, carrots, tomato, cucumber, avocado, and sprout sandwich 200
mache, avocado, pumpkin seeds, and blood orange with citrus dressing 122
mixed greens, avocado, edible flowers, and herb dressing 114
mixed greens, nori, avocado, and cucumber with creamy sesame ginger dressing 110
spanish rice burrito with cabbage, salsa, avocado and lime cream 172
watermelon radish, avocado, green onion, and sweet sesame 118

B

BANANA
acai bowl with granola, fresh strawberries, banana, coconut, and honey 264
banana cream pie drizzled in caramel rum sauce 220
coconut crepes, almond butter, vanilla honey, and sliced banana 262
fresh spinach, banana, mango, pineapple and spirulina 68

salted caramel chocolate banana milkshake 90
tangy orange, banana, and hot pink beet 65

BASIL

cashew basil mozzarella, heirloom tomatoes, basil, and balsamic fig sauce 140
coconut lemongrass soup with basil and kaffir lime leaves 156
creamy cashew basil mozzarella 96
creamy tomato bisque with basil oil and fresh cracked pepper 134
cucumber rolls with basil, mint, cilantro, and spicy coconut sauce 150
fresh basil oil 94
marinated vegetable herb pizza 176
raviolis, cashew cheese, and truffle-infused pesto 202
water, basil, hydrating cucumber, and mint 60

BEETS

ginger root, pineapple, and beet juice 35
tangy orange, banana, and hot pink beet 65

BLACKBERRIES

coconut yogurt, summer berries, and honey 250
mashed blackberry, whipped cream, and lemon custard 252
vanilla bean pudding, blackberry, and edible orchid 206
vanilla malt milkshake with blackberry swirl 88

BLUEBERRIES

coconut yogurt, summer berries, and honey 250
fragrant lavender blueberry lemonade 50

BREAKFASTS

acai bowl with granola, fresh strawberries, banana, coconut, and honey 264
chai-infused chia seed porridge with apple, raisins and pecans 260
cherry almond granola 266
coconut crepes, almond butter, vanilla honey, and sliced banana 262
coconut yogurt, summer berries, and honey 250
coconut yogurt with sencha green tea swirl and ripe mango 258
eggplant bacon with apple and smoked paprika 256
mashed blackberry, whipped cream, and lemon custard 252

BROCCOLI

coconut curry vegetables with cauliflower-scented rice 190
orange teriyaki noodles, carrot, broccoli, kale, and red pepper 162

pineapple, cucumber, broccoli, and spinach juice 36

C

CABBAGE

mixed cabbage, carrot, and kale slaw with creamy dill dressing 116
spanish rice burrito with cabbage, salsa, avocado, and lime cream 172

CAROB 5

almond butter, honey, coconut oil, spirulina, and carob 208

CARROTS

carrot, apple, and kiwi juice 35
coconut curry vegetables with cauliflower-scented rice 190
cucumber rolls with basil, mint, cilantro, and spicy coconut sauce 150
herb cashew cream cheese, carrots, tomato, cucumber, avocado, and sprout sandwich 200
mixed cabbage, carrot, and kale slaw with creamy dill dressing 116
orange teriyaki noodles, carrot, broccoli, kale, and red pepper 162
romaine, apple, celery, carrot, and walnut with lemon poppy seed dressing 112
veggie chili with cashew cream 168

CASHEWS 29

banana cream pie drizzled in caramel rum sauce 220
butter lettuce cups, marinated shitakes, and garlic chili sauce 136
cashew basil mozzarella, heirloom tomatoes, basil, and balsamic fig sauce 140
cashew cheese sauce with spicy jalapeño, tomato, and sweet onion 152
cashew cream, sour lemon, and sea salt 104
cauliflower rice, grapevine leaves, sun-dried tomato, mint, and creamy dill dressing 128
chocolate cream tartlets with flaky cashew crust and whipped cream 240
classic cheesecake with pecan graham crust and red raspberry sauce 232
coconut curry vegetables with cauliflower-scented rice 190
collard leaf tacos with seasoned nut-meat, cashew cream, guacamole, and fresh salsa 194
creamy cashew basil mozzarella 96
creamy cashew garlic spinach dip 154

INDEX

272

crispy herb kale chips 148
eggplant bacon, lettuce, avocado and tomato sandwich 164
herb cashew cream cheese, carrots, tomato, cucumber, avocado, and sprout sandwich 200
Kona coffee macadamia nut cheesecake with mocha fudge sauce 224
marinated mushroom, caramelized onions, garlic aioli, and arugula sandwich 184
mixed cabbage, carrot, and kale slaw with creamy dill dressing 116
mixed greens, nori, avocado, and cucumber with creamy sesame ginger dressing 110
pasta alfredo, garlic butter shitakes, and fresh parsley 170
raviolis, cashew cheese and truffle-infused pesto 202
romaine, apple, celery, carrot, and walnut with lemon poppy seed dressing 112
smoked portobello, jicama puree, garlic greens, and smoked paprika cream 196
spanish rice burrito with cabbage, salsa, avocado, and lime cream 172
stone-ground mustard, cashew cream, and lemon spread 100
veggie chili with cashew cream 168

CAULIFLOWER
cauliflower, sprouted quinoa, and pomegranate seed salad 120
coconut curry vegetables with cauliflower-scented rice 190

CELERY
parsley, kale, celery, apple, ginger, and lemon juice 36
romaine, apple, celery, carrot, and walnut with lemon poppy seed dressing 112
veggie chili with cashew cream 168

CHEESES
aged macadamia nut cheese 138
cashew basil mozzarella, heirloom tomatoes, basil, and balsamic fig sauce 140
cashew cheese sauce with spicy jalapeño, tomato, and sweet onion 152
creamy cashew basil mozzarella 96
herb cashew cream cheese, carrots, tomato, cucumber, avocado, and sprout sandwich 200
raviolis, cashew cheese, and truffle-infused pesto 202
wild mushroom spinach crepes with macadamia ricotta and lemon cream sauce 180

CHERRIES
cauliflower, sprouted quinoa, and pomegranate seed salad 120
cherry almond granola 266

CHIA SEEDS 5
chai-infused chia seed porridge with apple, raisins, and pecans 260

CHOCOLATE 25
dark chocolate almond milk 77
buttery caramel, celtic salt, and dark chocolate truffles 244
chocolate cream tartlets with flaky cashew crust and whipped cream 240
chocolate molten pyramid cake, liquid fudge, and mint chip ice cream 234
classic chocolate milkshake 86
dark chocolate amaretto truffles 218
dark chocolate hand-dipped strawberries 228
dark chocolate mousse with tangelo créme and zest 210
fresh mint chocolate chip ice cream 230
Kona coffee macadamia nut cheesecake with mocha fudge sauce 224
raw tempered chocolate base 246
salted caramel chocolate banana milkshake 90
sweet almond, coconut, and dark chocolate milkshake 84

CILANTRO
avocado, lime, cilantro, and sweet mango guacamole 144
butter lettuce cups, marinated shitakes, and garlic chili sauce 136
cauliflower, sprouted quinoa, and pomegranate seed salad 120
coconut curry vegetables with cauliflower-scented rice 190
coconut lemongrass soup with basil and kaffir lime leaves 156
cucumber rolls with basil, mint, cilantro, and spicy coconut sauce 150
pineapple, mango, lime, and shredded coconut salsa 158
red onion, lime, garlic, cilantro, and cherry tomato salsa 158
spanish rice burrito with cabbage, salsa, avocado, and lime cream 172

COCONUT 9, 21, 27
acai bowl with granola, fresh strawberries, banana, coconut, and honey 264
coconut crepes, almond butter, vanilla honey, and sliced banana 262
coconut curry vegetables with cauliflower-scented rice 190
coconut lemongrass soup with basil and kaffir lime leaves 156
coconut, pecans, raspberries, and Tahitian vanilla bean 214
coconut yogurt, summer berries, and honey 250
coconut yogurt with sencha green tea swirl and ripe mango 258

creamy coconut, pineapple, and strawberry puree 70
cucumber rolls with basil, mint, cilantro, and spicy coconut sauce 150
fresh coconut cream 74
Kona coffee macadamia nut cheesecake with mocha fudge sauce 224
orange blossom shredded coconut macaroons 238
pineapple, mango, lime, and shredded coconut salsa 158
raviolis, cashew cheese, and truffle-infused pesto 202
spanish rice burrito with cabbage, salsa, avocado, and lime cream 172
sweet almond, coconut, and dark chocolate milkshake 84
sweet and spicy chai coconut milk 78
sweet mango, coconut cream, with pineapple and papaya 64
wild mushroom spinach crepes with macadamia ricotta and lemon cream sauce 180

COFFEE, KONA 7
Kona coffee macadamia nut cheesecake with mocha fudge sauce 224

CONDIMENTS
cashew cream, sour lemon, and sea salt 104
creamy cashew basil mozzarella 96
fresh basil oil 94
garlic chili sauce 98
irish moss sea gel 102
sea-salt candied pecans 106
stone-ground mustard, cashew cream, and lemon spread 100

CRANBERRIES
romaine, apple, celery, carrot, and walnut with lemon poppy seed dressing 112

CUCUMBER
fresh-pressed watermelon juice, mint, and sliced cucumber 40
green apple, cucumber, and pineapple mint juice 37
green kale, cucumber, and apple juice 34
herb cashew cream cheese, carrots, tomato, cucumber, avocado, and sprout sandwich 200
mixed greens, nori, avocado, and cucumber with creamy sesame ginger dressing 110
parsley, kale, celery, apple, ginger, and lemon juice 36
pineapple, cucumber, broccoli, and spinach juice 36
water, basil, hydrating cucumber, and mint 60

D

DATES 22
buttery caramel, celtic salt, and dark chocolate 244
cherry almond granola 266
chocolate molten pyramid cake, liquid fudge, and mint chip ice cream 234
coconut, pecans, raspberries and Tahitian vanilla bean 214
Kona coffee macadamia nut cheesecake with mocha fudge sauce 224
orange teriyaki noodles, carrot, broccoli, kale, and red pepper 162

DEHYDRATION 19

DESSERTS
almond butter, honey, coconut oil, and spirulina 208
banana cream pie drizzled in caramel rum sauce 220
buttery caramel, celtic salt, and dark chocolate 244
chocolate cream tartlets with easy cashew crust and whipped cream 240
chocolate molten pyramid cake, liquid fudge, and mint chip ice cream 234
classic cheesecake with pecan graham crust and red raspberry sauce 232
coconut, pecans, raspberries and Tahitian vanilla bean 214
dark chocolate amaretto truffles 218
dark chocolate hand-dipped strawberries 228
dark chocolate mousse with tangelo créme and zest 210
fresh mint chocolate chip ice cream 230
Kona coffee macadamia nut cheesecake with mocha fudge sauce 224
lavender ice cream, peaches, vanilla bean, and cinnamon 212
orange blossom shredded coconut macaroons 238
raw tempered chocolate base 246
vanilla bean pudding, blackberry, and edible orchid 206

DILL
cauliflower rice, grapevine leaves, sun-dried tomato, mint, and creamy dill dressing 128
crispy herb kale chips 148
mixed cabbage, carrot, and kale slaw with creamy dill dressing 116
mixed greens, avocado, edible flowers, and herb dressing 114

E

EGGPLANT
breakfast burrito with vegetable scramble 268
eggplant bacon, lettuce, avocado, and tomato sandwich 164
eggplant bacon with apple and smoked paprika 256

ENTREES
coconut curry vegetables with cauliflower-scented rice 190
collard leaf tacos with seasoned nut-meat, cashew cream, guacamole, and fresh salsa 194
eggplant bacon, lettuce, avocado, and tomato sandwich 164
herb cashew cream cheese, carrots, tomato, cucumber, avocado, and sprout sandwich 200
marinated mushroom, caramelized onions, garlic aioli, and arugula sandwich 184
marinated vegetable herb pizza 176
orange teriyaki noodles, carrot, broccoli, kale, and red pepper 162
pasta alfredo, garlic butter shitakes, and fresh parsley 170
raviolis, cashew cheese, and truffle-infused pesto 202
smoked portobello, jicama puree, garlic greens, and smoked paprika cream 196
spanish rice burrito with cabbage, salsa, avocado, and lime cream 172
tossed sesame noodles with green onion and crushed red pepper flakes 188
veggie chili with cashew cream 168
wild mushroom spinach crepes with macadamia ricotta and lemon cream sauce 180

F

FIGS 5
cashew basil mozzarella, heirloom tomatoes, basil, and balsamic fig sauce 140

FLAX
golden flax almond bread 146
marinated vegetable herb pizza 176
spanish rice burrito with cabbage, salsa, avocado, and lime cream 172
sweet cream, vanilla, and strawberries 65

FLOURS 29
Almond flour 29
chocolate molten pyramid cake, liquid fudge, and mint chip ice cream 234
golden flax almond bread 146
Kona coffee macadamia nut cheesecake with mocha fudge sauce 224
marinated vegetable herb pizza 176
Cashew flour 29
banana cream pie drizzled in caramel rum sauce 220
chocolate cream tartlets with flaky cashew crust and whipped cream 240
Pecan flour 29
classic cheesecake with pecan graham crust and red raspberry sauce 232

FLOWERS 6
Hibiscus 6
fresh-squeezed lemon, agave, and hibiscus flowers 52
Lavender 6
fragrant lavender blueberry lemonade 50
lavender ice cream, peaches, vanilla bean, and cinnamon 212
Mixed edibles 6
 mixed greens, avocado, edible flowers, and herb dressing 114
Orchid
vanilla bean pudding, blackberry, and edible orchid 206

G

GARLIC
avocado, garlic ,and zesty lemon guacamole 142
avocado, lime, cilantro, and sweet mango guacamole 144
cashew basil mozzarella, heirloom tomatoes, basil, and balsamic fig sauce 140
coconut curry vegetables with cauliflower-scented rice 190
coconut lemongrass soup with basil and kaffir lime leaves 156
creamy cashew garlic spinach dip 154
creamy tomato bisque with basil oil and fresh cracked pepper 134
crispy herb kale chips 148
cucumber rolls with basil, mint, cilantro, and spicy coconut sauce 150
garlic chili sauce 98

marinated mushroom, caramelized onions, garlic aioli, and arugula sandwich 184
marinated vegetable herb pizza 176
mixed greens, avocado, edible flowers, and herb dressing 114
orange teriyaki noodles, carrot, broccoli, kale, and red pepper 162
pasta alfredo, garlic butter shitakes, and fresh parsley 170
raviolis, cashew cheese, and truffle-infused pesto 202
red onion, lime, garlic, cilantro, and cherry tomato salsa 158
romaine, capers, and Meyer lemon caesar dressing 124
smoked portobello, jicama puree, garlic greens, and smoked paprika cream 196
tossed sesame noodles with green onion and crushed red pepper flakes 188
veggie chili with cashew cream 168
wild mushroom spinach crepes with macadamia ricotta and lemon cream sauce 180

GINGER

coconut curry vegetables with cauliflower-scented rice 190
coconut lemongrass soup with basil and kaffir lime leaves 156
ginger root, pineapple, and beet juice 35
grated nutmeg, cinnamon, ginger, and almond milk 80
mixed greens, nori, avocado, and cucumber with creamy sesame ginger dressing 110
orange teriyaki noodles, carrot, broccoli, kale, and red pepper 162
parsley, kale, celery, apple, ginger, and lemon juice 36
tossed sesame noodles with green onion and crushed red pepper flakes 188
watermelon radish, avocado, green onion, and sweet sesame 118

GOJI BERRIES 6

classic chocolate milkshake 86
goji berry, golden peach, and pure acai 64

GRAPEFRUIT

ruby red grapefruit, orange, and refreshing lime juice 42

GREENS + LETTUCES

Arugula
marinated mushroom, caramelized onions, garlic aioli, and arugula sandwich 184
Butter lettuce
butter lettuce cups, marinated shitakes, and garlic chili sauce 136

Collard
collard leaf tacos with seasoned nut-meat, cashew cream, guacamole, and fresh salsa 194
Kale
cauliflower, sprouted quinoa, and pomegranate seed salad 120
crispy herb kale chips 148
green kale, cucumber, and apple juice 34
kale, Asian pear, red onion, candied pecans, and mustard dressing 126
mixed cabbage, carrot, and kale slaw with creamy dill dressing 116
orange teriyaki noodles, carrot, broccoli, kale, and red pepper 162
parsley, kale, celery, apple, ginger, and lemon juice 36
smoked portobello, jicama puree, garlic greens, and smoked paprika cream 196
Mache 7
mache, avocado, pumpkin seeds and blood orange with citrus dressing 122
Mixed
mixed greens, avocado, edible flowers, and herb dressing 114
mixed greens, nori, avocado, and cucumber with creamy sesame ginger dressing 110
Romaine
collard leaf tacos with seasoned nut-meat, cashew cream, guacamole, and fresh salsa 194
cucumber rolls with basil, mint, cilantro, and spicy coconut sauce 150
eggplant bacon, lettuce, avocado, and tomato sandwich 164
romaine, apple, celery, carrot, and walnut with lemon poppy seed dressing 112
romaine, capers, and Meyer lemon caesar dressing 124
Spinach
creamy cashew garlic spinach dip 154
fresh spinach, banana, mango, pineapple, and spirulina 68
pineapple, cucumber, broccoli and spinach juice 36
smoked portobello, jicama puree, garlic greens, and smoked paprika cream 196
wild mushroom spinach crepes with macadamia ricotta and lemon cream sauce 180

H

HIBISCUS 6
fresh-squeezed lemon, agave, and hibiscus flowers 52

HONEY 23
almond butter, honey, coconut oil, spirulina, and carob 208
coconut crepes, almond butter, vanilla honey, and sliced banana 262
coconut yogurt, summer berries, and honey 250
coconut yogurt with sencha green tea swirl and ripe mango 258
granola, fresh strawberries, banana, coconut, and honey 264
passion fruit lemonade sweetened with manuka honey 54
raw pistachios, cantaloupe, honeydew, and wild honey 66

I

INFUSED H2O
coconut-infused fresh-squeezed limeade 56
fragrant lavender blueberry lemonade 50
fresh-squeezed lemon, agave, and hibiscus flowers 52
passion fruit lemonade sweetened with manuka honey 54
sparkling water, lime, blood orange, and fresh mint 58
water, basil, hydrating cucumber, and mint 60

INTRODUCTION 2

IRISH MOSS 6
chocolate cream tartlets with flaky cashew crust and whipped cream 240
creamy cashew basil mozzarella 96
mashed blackberry, whipped cream, and lemon custard 252

J

JICAMA 7
smoked portobello, jicama puree, garlic greens, and smoked paprika cream 196

JUICES
apple, carrot, and kiwi juice 35
fresh-pressed watermelon juice, mint, and sliced cucumber 40
ginger root, pineapple, and beet juice 35
green apple, cucumber, and pineapple mint juice 37
green kale, cucumber, and apple juice 34
orange, Hawaiian papaya, and strawberry juice 44
parsley, kale, celery, apple, ginger, and lemon juice 36
pineapple, cucumber, broccoli, and spinach juice 36
pineapple and summer raspberry juice 46
ruby red grapefruit, orange, and refreshing lime juice 42

K

KAFFIR LIME LEAVES 7
coconut lemongrass soup with basil and kaffir lime leaves 156

KALE
cauliflower, sprouted quinoa, and pomegranate seed salad 120
crispy herb kale chips 148
green kale, cucumber, and apple juice 34
kale, Asian pear, red onion, candied pecans, and mustard dressing 126
mixed cabbage, carrot, and kale slaw with creamy dill dressing 116
orange teriyaki noodles, carrot, broccoli, kale, and red pepper 162
parsley, kale, celery, apple, ginger, and lemon juice 36
smoked portobello, jicama puree, garlic greens, and smoked paprika cream 196

KELP NOODLES 7
orange teriyaki noodles, carrot, broccoli, kale, and red pepper 162
pasta alfredo, garlic butter shitakes, and fresh parsley 170
tossed sesame noodles with green onion and crushed red pepper flakes 188

KIWI
apple, carrot, and kiwi juice 35

L

LAVENDER 6
fragrant lavender blueberry lemonade 50
lavender ice cream, peaches, vanilla bean, and cinnamon 212

LEMON

avocado, garlic, and zesty lemon guacamole 142
butter lettuce cups, marinated shitakes, and garlic chili sauce 136
cashew cream, sour lemon, and sea salt 104
cauliflower rice, grapevine leaves, sun-dried tomato, mint, and creamy dill dressing 128
cauliflower, sprouted quinoa, and pomegranate seed salad 120
classic cheesecake with pecan graham crust and red raspberry sauce 232
coconut curry vegetables with cauliflower-scented rice 190
coconut, pecans raspberries, and Tahitian vanilla bean 214
creamy cashew basil mozzarella 96
creamy cashew garlic spinach dip 154
fragrant lavender blueberry lemonade 50
fresh-squeezed lemon, agave and hibiscus flowers 52
garlic chili sauce 98
golden flax almond bread 146
herb cashew cream cheese, carrots, tomato, cucumber, avocado, and sprout sandwich 200
kale, Asian pear, red onion, candied pecans, and mustard dressing 126
Kona coffee macadamia nut cheesecake with mocha fudge sauce 224
lavender ice cream, peaches, vanilla bean, and cinnamon 212
marinated vegetable herb pizza 176
mashed blackberry, whipped cream, and lemon custard 252
mixed cabbage, carrot, and kale slaw with creamy dill dressing 116
parsley, kale, celery, apple, ginger, and lemon juice 36
passion fruit lemonade sweetened with manuka honey 54
raviolis, cashew cheese, and truffle-infused pesto 202
romaine, apple, celery, carrot, and walnut with lemon poppy seed dressing 112
romaine, capers, and Meyer lemon caesar dressing 124
smoked portobello, jicama puree, garlic greens, and smoked paprika cream 196
stone-ground mustard, cashew cream, and lemon spread 100
wild mushroom spinach crepes with macadamia ricotta and lemon cream sauce 180

LEMONGRASS 7

coconut lemongrass soup with basil and kaffir lime leaves 156

LIME

avocado, lime, cilantro, and sweet mango guacamole 144

ruby red grapefruit, orange, and refreshing lime juice 42
coconut-infused fresh-squeezed limeade 56
cucumber rolls with basil, mint, cilantro and spicy coconut sauce 150
pineapple, mango, lime, and shredded coconut salsa 158
red onion, lime, garlic, cilantro, and cherry tomato salsa 158
spanish rice burrito with cabbage, salsa, avocado, and lime cream 172
sparkling water, lime, blood orange, and fresh mint 58
tossed sesame noodles with green onion and crushed red pepper flakes 188

LIVING CUISINE 3

M

MACA 7

sweet almond, coconut, and dark chocolate milkshake 84
vanilla malt milkshake with blackberry swirl 88

MACADAMIA NUTS

aged macadamia nut cheese 138
classic chocolate milkshake 86
Kona coffee macadamia nut cheesecake with mocha fudge sauce 224
wild mushroom spinach crepes with macadamia ricotta and lemon cream sauce 180

MACHE 7

mache, avocado, pumpkin seeds, and blood orange with citrus dressing 122

MANGO

avocado, lime, cilantro, and sweet mango guacamole 144
coconut yogurt with sencha green tea swirl and ripe mango 258
fresh spinach, banana, mango, pineapple and spirulina 68
sweet mango and coconut cream with pineapple and papaya 64

MELONS

fresh-pressed watermelon juice, mint, and sliced cucumber 40
raw pistachios, cantaloupe, honeydew, and wild honey 66

MILKS AND CREAM

creamy vanilla almond milk 76
dark chocolate almond milk 77

fresh coconut cream 74
grated nutmeg, cinnamon, ginger, and almond milk 80
sweet and spicy chai coconut milk 78

MILKSHAKES
classic chocolate milkshake 86
salted caramel chocolate banana milkshake 90
sweet almond, coconut, and dark chocolate milkshake 84
vanilla malt milkshake with blackberry swirl 88

MINT
cauliflower rice, grapevine leaves, sun-dried tomato, mint, and creamy dill dressing 128
chocolate molten pyramid cake, liquid fudge, and mint chip ice cream 234
cucumber rolls with basil, mint, cilantro, and spicy coconut sauce 150
fresh mint chocolate chip ice cream 230
fresh-pressed watermelon juice, mint, and sliced cucumber 40
green apple, cucumber, and pineapple mint juice 37
mashed blackberry, whipped cream, and lemon custard 252
sparkling water, lime, blood orange, and fresh mint 58
vanilla bean pudding, blackberry, and edible orchid 206
vanilla malt milkshake with blackberry swirl 88
water, basil, hydrating cucumber, and mint 60

MUSHROOMS
butter lettuce cups, marinated shitakes, and garlic chili sauce 136
marinated mushroom, caramelized onions, garlic aioli, and arugula sandwich 184
marinated vegetable herb pizza 176
pasta alfredo, garlic butter shitakes, and fresh parsley 170
smoked portobello, jicama puree, garlic greens, and smoked paprika cream 196
wild mushroom spinach crepes with macadamia ricotta and lemon cream sauce 180

N

NUTRITIONAL YEAST 7
cashew cheese sauce with spicy jalapeño, tomato, and sweet onion 152
pasta alfredo, garlic butter shitakes, and fresh parsley 170

raviolis, cashew cheese, and truffle-infused pesto 202
romaine, capers, and Meyer lemon caesar dressing 124

O

OILS
Basil oil
  cashew basil mozzarella, heirloom tomatoes, basil, and balsamic fig sauce 140
  creamy tomato bisque with basil oil and fresh cracked pepper 134
  fresh basil oil 94

Coconut oil 10
  almond butter, honey, coconut oil, spirulina, and carob 208
  banana cream pie drizzled in caramel rum sauce 220
  cherry almond granola 266
  chocolate cream tartlets with flaky cashew crust and whipped cream 240
  chocolate molten pyramid cake, liquid fudge, and mint chip ice cream 234
  classic cheesecake with pecan graham crust and red raspberry sauce 232
  classic chocolate milkshake 86
  coconut, pecans, raspberries, and Tahitian vanilla bean 214
  creamy cashew basil mozzarella 96
  creamy vanilla almond milk 76
  dark chocolate almond milk 77
  dark chocolate mousse with tangelo créme and zest 210
  fresh mint chocolate chip ice cream 230
  kona coffee macadamia nut cheesecake with mocha fudge sauce 224
  lavender ice cream, peaches, vanilla bean, and cinnamon 212
  mashed blackberry, whipped cream, and lemon custard 252
  sea-salt candied pecans 106
  sweet almond, coconut, and dark chocolate milkshake 84
  vanilla malt milkshake with blackberry swirl 88

Grape-seed oil
  coconut lemongrass soup with basil and kaffir lime leaves 156
  collard leaf tacos with seasoned nut-meat, cashew cream, guacamole and fresh salsa 194
  eggplant bacon with apple and smoked paprika 256
  garlic chili sauce 98
  kale, Asian pear, red onion, candied pecans, and mustard

dressing 126
mixed cabbage, carrot, and kale slaw with creamy dill dressing 116
smoked portobello, jicama puree, garlic greens, and smoked paprika cream 196
stone-ground mustard, cashew cream, and lemon spread 100

Olive oil
cashew basil mozzarella, heirloom tomatoes, basil, and balsamic fig sauce 140
cauliflower rice, grapevine leaves, sun-dried tomato, mint, and creamy dill dressing 128
cauliflower, sprouted quinoa, and pomegranate seed salad 120
creamy tomato bisque with basil oil and fresh cracked pepper 134
crispy herb kale chips 148
fresh basil oil 94
marinated mushroom, caramelized onions, garlic aioli, and arugula sandwich 184
marinated vegetable herb pizza 176
mixed greens, avocado, edible flowers, and herb dressing 114
pasta alfredo, garlic butter shitakes, and fresh parsley 170
raviolis, cashew cheese, and truffle-infused pesto 202
romaine, capers, and Meyer lemon caesar dressing 124
smoked portobello, jicama puree, garlic greens, and smoked paprika cream 196
spanish rice burrito with cabbage, salsa, avocado, and lime cream 172
veggie chili with cashew cream 168
wild mushroom spinach crepes with macadamia ricotta and lemon cream sauce 180

Sesame oil
butter lettuce cups, marinated shitakes, and garlic chili sauce 136
cucumber rolls with basil, mint, cilantro, and spicy coconut sauce 150
mixed greens, nori, avocado, and cucumber with creamy sesame ginger dressing 110
orange teriyaki noodles, carrot, broccoli, kale, and red pepper 162
tossed sesame noodles with green onion and crushed red pepper flakes 188
watermelon radish, avocado, green onion, and sweet sesame 118

Truffle oil
raviolis, cashew cheese, and truffle-infused pesto 202

ONIONS

Chives
cucumber rolls with basil, mint, cilantro, and spicy coconut sauce 150

Green onions
avocado, green onion, cucumber, and seaweed guacamole 143
coconut lemongrass soup with basil and kaffir lime leaves 156
collard leaf tacos with seasoned nut-meat, cashew cream, guacamole, and fresh salsa 194
mixed greens, nori, avocado, and cucumber with creamy sesame ginger dressing 110
orange teriyaki noodles, carrot, broccoli, kale, and red pepper 162
watermelon radish, avocado, green onion, and sweet sesame 118
butter lettuce cups, marinated shitakes, and garlic chili sauce 136
tossed sesame noodles with green onion and crushed red pepper flakes 188

Red onion
avocado, lime, cilantro, and sweet mango guacamole 144
cauliflower, sprouted quinoa, and pomegranate seed salad 120
kale, Asian pear, red onion, candied pecans, and mustard dressing 126
marinated vegetable herb pizza 176
mixed greens, avocado, edible flowers, and herb dressing 114
pineapple, mango, lime, and shredded coconut salsa 158
red onion, lime, garlic, cilantro, and cherry tomato salsa 158
romaine, apple, celery, carrot, and walnut with lemon poppy seed dressing 112
veggie chili with cashew cream 168

Shallots
mache, avocado, pumpkin seeds, and blood orange with citrus dressing 122
pasta alfredo, garlic butter shitakes, and fresh parsley 170

Sweet onion
cashew cheese sauce with spicy jalapeño, tomato, and sweet onion 152
coconut curry vegetables with cauliflower-scented rice 190
coconut lemongrass soup with basil and kaffir lime leaves 156
creamy tomato bisque with basil oil and fresh cracked pepper 134
marinated mushroom, caramelized onions, garlic aioli, and arugula sandwich 184
mixed cabbage, carrot, and kale slaw with creamy dill dressing 116
spanish rice burrito with cabbage, salsa, avocado, and lime cream 172

INDEX

280

Yellow onion
- cauliflower rice, grapevine leaves, sun-dried tomato, mint, and creamy dill dressing 128
- collard leaf tacos with seasoned nut-meat, cashew cream, guacamole, and fresh salsa 194
- creamy cashew garlic spinach dip 154
- marinated vegetable herb pizza 176
- smoked portobello, jicama puree, garlic greens, and smoked paprika cream 196

ORANGES
- mixed greens, avocado, edible flowers, and herb dressing 114
- orange blossom shredded coconut macaroons 238
- orange, Hawaiian papaya, and strawberry juice 44
- orange teriyaki noodles, carrot, broccoli, kale, and red pepper 162
- ruby red grapefruit, orange, and refreshing lime juice 42
- tangy orange, banana, and hot pink beet 65

Blood orange 5
- mache, avocado, pumpkin seeds, and blood orange with citrus dressing 122
- sparkling water, lime, blood orange, and fresh mint 58

Tangelo
- dark chocolate mousse with tangelo créme and zest 210

P

PAPAYA
- orange, Hawaiian papaya, and strawberry juice 44
- sweet mango, and coconut cream with pineapple and papaya 64

PASSION FRUIT 7
- passion fruit lemonade sweetened with manuka honey 54

PEACH
- goji berry, golden peach, and pure acai 64
- lavender ice cream, peaches, vanilla bean, and cinnamon 212

PEAS
- coconut curry vegetables with cauliflower-scented rice 190
- watermelon radish, avocado, green onion, and sweet sesame 118

PECANS 29
- chai-infused chia seed porridge with apple, raisins, and pecans 260
- classic cheesecake with pecan graham crust and red raspberry sauce 232
- coconut, pecans, raspberries, and Tahitian vanilla bean 214
- kale, Asian pear, red onion, candied pecans, and mustard dressing 126
- sea-salt candied pecans 106

PEPPERS
Jalepeño peppers
- cashew cheese sauce with spicy jalapeño, tomato, and sweet onion 152
- pineapple, mango, lime, and shredded coconut salsa 158
- red onion, lime, garlic, cilantro and cherry tomato salsa 158

Red bell peppers
- coconut curry vegetables with cauliflower-scented rice 190
- cucumber rolls with basil, mint, cilantro, and spicy coconut sauce 150
- orange teriyaki noodles, carrot, broccoli, kale, and red pepper 162
- spanish rice burrito with cabbage, salsa, avocado, and lime cream 172
- veggie chili with cashew cream 168

PINEAPPLE
- creamy coconut, pineapple, and strawberry puree 70
- fresh spinach, banana, mango, pineapple, and spirulina 68
- ginger root, pineapple, and beet juice 35
- green apple, cucumber, and pineapple mint juice 37
- pineapple, cucumber, broccoli, and spinach juice 36
- pineapple and summer raspberry juice 46
- sweet mango and coconut cream with pineapple and papaya 64

PISTACHIOS
- raw pistachios, cantaloupe, honeydew, and wild honey 66

POMEGRANATE
- cauliflower, sprouted quinoa, and pomegranate seed salad 120

PUMPKIN SEEDS
- mache, avocado, pumpkin seeds, and blood orange with citrus dressing 122

raviolis, cashew cheese, and truffle-infused pesto 202

Q

QUINOA 8
cauliflower, sprouted quinoa, and pomegranate seed salad 120

R

RADISH
watermelon radish, avocado, green onion, and sweet sesame 118

RASPBERRIES
classic cheesecake with pecan graham crust and red raspberry sauce 232
coconut, pecans, raspberries, and Tahitian vanilla bean 214
coconut yogurt, summer berries, and honey 250
pineapple and summer raspberry juice 46

S

SALADS
cauliflower rice, grapevine leaves, sun-dried tomato, mint, and creamy dill dressing 128
cauliflower, sprouted quinoa, and pomegranate seed salad 120
kale, Asian pear, red onion, candied pecans, and mustard dressing 126
mache, avocado, pumpkin seeds, and blood orange with citrus dressing 122
mixed cabbage, carrot, and kale slaw with creamy dill dressing 116
mixed greens, avocado, edible flowers and herb dressing 114
mixed greens, nori, avocado and cucumber with creamy sesame ginger dressing 110
romaine, apple, celery, carrot, and walnut with lemon poppy seed dressing 112
romaine, capers, and Meyer lemon caesar dressing 124
watermelon radish, avocado, green onion, and sweet sesame 118

SEAWEEDS
Irish moss
chocolate cream tartlets with flaky cashew crust and whipped cream 240
creamy cashew basil mozzarella 96
irish moss sea gel 102
mashed blackberry, whipped cream, and lemon custard 252
raviolis, cashew cheese, and truffle-infused pesto 202

Kelp noodles 7
orange teriyaki noodles, carrot, broccoli, kale and red pepper 162
pasta alfredo, garlic butter shitakes, and fresh parsley 170
tossed sesame noodles with green onion and crushed red pepper flakes 188

Nori 110
mixed greens, nori, avocado, and cucumber with creamy sesame ginger dressing 110

Wakame 8
avocado, green onion, cucumber, and seaweed guacamole 143

SESAME
Sesame oil
butter lettuce cups, marinated shitakes, and garlic chili sauce 136
cucumber rolls with basil, mint, cilantro, and spicy coconut sauce 150
mixed greens, nori, avocado, and cucumber with creamy sesame ginger dressing 110
orange teriyaki noodles, carrot, broccoli, kale and red pepper 162
tossed sesame noodles with green onion and crushed red pepper flakes 188

Sesame seeds
mixed greens, nori, avocado, and cucumber with creamy sesame ginger dressing 110
orange teriyaki noodles, carrot, broccoli, kale and red pepper 162
tossed sesame noodles with green onion and crushed red pepper flakes 188
watermelon radish, avocado, green onion, and sweet sesame 118

Tahini
creamy tomato bisque with basil oil and fresh cracked pepper 134
tossed sesame noodles with green onion and crushed red pepper flakes 188

SHOPPING FOR YOUR PRODUCE 15

...t, pineapple and strawberry puree 70
..., banana, mango, pineapple, and spirulina 68
... golden peach, and pure acai 64
...hios, cantaloupe, honeydew, and wild honey 66
sw... eam, vanilla, and strawberries 65
sweet mango and coconut cream, with pineapple and papaya 64
tangy orange, banana, and hot pink beet 65

SOAKING 17
SPINACH
creamy cashew garlic spinach dip 154
fresh spinach, banana, mango, pineapple, and spirulina 68
pineapple, cucumber, broccoli, and spinach juice 36
smoked portobello, jicama puree, garlic greens, and smoked paprika cream 196
wild mushroom spinach crepes with macadamia ricotta and lemon cream sauce 180

SPIRULINA 8
almond butter, honey, coconut oil, spirulina, and carob 208
fresh mint chocolate chip ice cream 230
fresh spinach, banana, mango, pineapple, and spirulina 68

SPROUTS
Alfalfa
  herb cashew cream cheese, carrots, tomato, cucumber, avocado, and sprout sandwich 200
Mung bean
  cucumber rolls with basil, mint, cilantro, and spicy coconut sauce 150

STRAWBERRIES
acai bowl with granola, fresh strawberries, banana, coconut, and honey 264
creamy coconut pineapple and strawberry puree 70
dark chocolate hand-dipped strawberries 228
orange, Hawaiian papaya, and strawberry juice 44
sweet cream, vanilla, and strawberries 65

SWEETENERS 21

T

TANGELOS 8
dark chocolate mousse with tangelo créme and zest 210

TOMATOES
cashew basil mozzarella, heirloom tomatoes, basil, and balsamic fig sauce 140
cashew cheese sauce with spicy jalapeño, tomato, and sweet onion 152
creamy tomato bisque with basil oil and fresh cracked pepper 134
eggplant bacon, lettuce, avocado, and tomato sandwich 164
herb cashew cream cheese, carrots, tomato, cucumber, avocado, and sprout sandwich 200
marinated vegetable herb pizza 176
Cherry tomatoes
  coconut lemongrass soup with basil and kaffir lime leaves 156
  red onion, lime, garlic, cilantro, and cherry tomato salsa 158
Sun-dried tomatoes
  cauliflower rice, grapevine leaves, sun-dried tomato, mint, and creamy dill dressing 128
  creamy tomato bisque with basil oil and fresh cracked pepper 134
  garlic chili sauce 98
  marinated vegetable herb pizza 176
  spanish rice burrito with cabbage, salsa, avocado, and lime cream 172
  veggie chili with cashew cream 168

TOOLS AND EQUIPMENT 11

V

VANILLA BEAN
banana cream pie drizzled in caramel rum sauce 220
chocolate cream tartlets with flaky cashew crust and whipped cream 240
chocolate molten pyramid cake, liquid fudge, and mint chip ice cream 234
coconut crepes, almond butter, vanilla honey, and sliced banana 262